Windows® XP Professional:
A Beginner's Guide

Windows® XP Professional:
A Beginner's Guide

Martin S. Matthews

McGraw-Hill/Osborne

New York   Chicago   San Francisco
Lisbon   London   Madrid   Mexico City
Milan   New Delhi   San Juan
Seoul   Singapore   Sydney   Toronto

The McGraw·Hill Companies

McGraw-Hill/Osborne
2600 Tenth Street
Berkeley, California 94710
U.S.A.

To arrange bulk purchase discounts for sales promotions, premiums, or fund-raisers, please contact **McGraw-Hill**/Osborne at the above address. For information on translations or book distributors outside the U.S.A., please see the International Contact Information page immediately following the index of this book.

Windows® XP Professional: A Beginner's Guide

1234567890 CUS CUS 0198765432

ISBN 0-07-222608-0

Publisher   Brandon A. Nordin
Vice President & Associate Publisher   Scott Rogers
Executive Editor   Jane K. Brownlow
Project Editor   Laura Stone
Acquisitions Coordinator   Tana Allen
Technical Editor   John Cronan
Copy Editor   Robert Campbell
Proofreaders   Paul Medoff, Linda Medoff
Indexer   Valerie Perry
Computer Designers   Carie Abrew, Tara A. Davis, Lucie Ericksen
Illustrators   Michael Mueller, Lyssa Wald
Series Design   Jean Butterfield
Cover Series Design   Sarah F. Hinks

This book was composed with Corel VENTURA™ Publisher.

Page and Tom Baenen are the kinds of friends
for whom there are never enough ways to say thanks,
so all I can do is once again say "Thanks Page and Tom,
for always being there for us."

About the Author

Over 20 years ago, Martin S. Matthews wrote his first computer book, on how to buy minicomputers. Eighteen years ago, Marty and his wife Carole began writing books as a major occupation. In the intervening years, they have written over 50 books, including ones on desktop publishing, web publishing, Microsoft Office, and Microsoft operating systems from MS-DOS through Windows XP. Recent books published by McGraw-Hill/Osborne include *FrontPage 2002: The Complete Reference, Windows 2000: A Beginner's Guide, Windows 98 Answers! Certified Tech Support,* and *Office 2000 Answers! Certified Tech Support.*

Marty, Carole, and their son live on an island in the Puget Sound where, on the rare moments when they can look up from their computers, they look west across seven miles of water and the main shipping channel to the snow-capped Olympic mountains.

Contents at a Glance

Contents

Acknowledgments

It takes a number of people to create a book like this, especially to make it a really good book. The people at McGraw-Hill/Osborne, especially Jane Brownlow, Tana Allen, Laura Stone, and many others I do not know, have put in untold hours turning my poor attempts at writing into a good book and have made my job manageable. In addition I'd like to acknowledge:

John Cronan, the technical editor for the book, who corrected many errors, added many tips and notes, and generally improved the book. John is also a great friend. Thanks, John!

Carole Matthews, my life partner for over 30 years, my very best friend, and sharer of our parenting adventure, who provided the necessary support that made this book possible. Thanks, my love!

Introduction

Windows XP did for the Windows 9x/Me world what Windows 2000 did for the Windows NT world. It is a new operating system that takes the very best of Windows 9x/Me and upgrades it for the latest operating system technology. The net result is an extremely capable operating system that is more reliable, easier to install, and faster. It also is much more secure, supports most current hardware, is easier to manage, and provides support for many of the advances in digital audio and video.

The purpose of this book is to show you how to use these features and many others and get the attendant benefits.

How This Book Is Organized

Windows XP: A Beginner's Guide is written the way most people learn. It starts by reviewing the basic concepts and then uses a learn-by-doing method to demonstrate the major features of the product. Throughout, the book uses detailed examples and clear explanations with many line drawings and screenshots to give you the insight needed to make the fullest use of Windows XP. *Windows XP: A Beginner's Guide* has four main parts, each providing a discussion of a major aspect of Windows XP.

Part I: The Windows XP Environment

Part I introduces you to the Windows XP environment and what's new about it. This part establishes the foundation for the rest of the book.

● **Module 1, Exploring Windows XP,** provides an overview of Windows XP and serves as a guide to the more in-depth discussions that will take place in the later modules. It compares the Windows XP editions; looks at the basic Windows XP functions; reviews communications and networking features; and discusses the Windows XP management, setup, and maintenance functions.

● **Module 2, Components of Windows XP,** shows you how to begin to use Windows XP: how to start it; how to get around in it; how to perform the basic functions in XP that are required to use it; and how to locate and open the major components that give Windows XP its power.

● **Module 3, Customizing Windows XP,** looks at a number of ways that Windows XP can be tailored to your needs and desires, including changing the screen, Start menu, desktop, taskbar, and file folders. It also discusses how the mouse, keyboard, and sound can be modified, and it looks at ways to compensate for physical disabilities.

Part II: Primary Uses of Windows XP

Part II looks at the primary uses of Windows XP, including filing, printing, communicating, and using the Internet, as well as using multimedia. All of these areas are discussed in depth along with how they can be most efficiently and effectively employed.

● **Module 4, Using Files, Folders, and Disks,** discusses the storage of information, how to manipulate information in storage, and how to manage that storage. This includes how to use and manage files, folders, and disks, and how to handle the information they contain.

● **Module 5, Printing and Faxing,** defines printing and faxing, the installation of printers, the use and management of printing, the handling of fonts, and the setup and use of faxing.

● **Module 6, Using Communications and the Internet,** describes how to set up and configure communications connections, including both dial-up and broadband. It then looks at how to connect to and use the Internet, including browsing with Internet Explorer and sending e-mail with Outlook Express. Finally, it discusses how to use Windows Messenger and HyperTerminal.

● **Module 7, Using Audio and Video Media,** explores how to handle sound and both still and moving visual images by storing them, editing them, playing or displaying them, and writing them to CDs using Windows Media Player, Windows Movie Maker, and CD Writer.

Part III: Advanced Uses of Windows XP

Part III turns to those areas that are more business related and require a higher degree of dedication to use. These include networking, computer and networking security, implementing and maintaining user profiles, the Control Panel and other tools for managing the computer environment, and remote access and terminal services facilities.

● **Module 8, Setting Up and Using a Network,** provides a comprehensive foundation on networking by describing the schemes, hardware, and protocols or standards that are used to make it function, and then describes how networking is set up and managed in Windows XP.

● **Module 9, Controlling Security,** describes the many aspects of computer and networking security, along with how to set up and maintain a reasonable level of security. This includes authenticating the user, controlling access, securing stored data, and implementing secure data transmission.

● **Module 10, Managing a Windows XP System,** discusses the general-purpose tools in Windows XP, those that are not part of setting up, networking, file management, printing, communications, security, or multimedia. The discussion is broken into system management tools, disk management tools, and user management tools.

● **Module 11, Using Remote Desktop, Remote Access, and VPN,** looks at how to transfer information between computers and utilize resources on one computer from another at a distance, not necessarily using a local area network (LAN) connection. The Windows XP components for this are Remote Desktop, a tool for remotely controlling a computer, and RAS and VPN, both ways to access remote computers.

Part IV: Setting Up and Maintaining Windows XP

Part IV covers planning for and carrying out the installation of Windows XP, as well as how to maintain a Windows XP system, including installing new hardware and software.

● **Module 12, Preparing for a Windows XP Installation,** looks at all the steps that must be carried out prior to installing Windows XP, including the possible pitfalls to stay clear of. This includes looking at the system requirements for Windows XP, discussing what you can do to prepare for the installation, and then planning a Windows XP migration.

● **Module 13, Installing Windows XP,** takes you through the various steps necessary to install the server from different starting points, as well as if you are upgrading or doing a clean install. It then looks at installing a number of optional components.

● **Module 14, Maintaining Windows XP,** describes how to add and remove software and hardware, use Remote Assistance, get system information, update Windows XP, and restore Windows XP.

● **Appendix A, Mastery Check Answers,** provides the answers to the Mastery Check questions at the end of each module.

● **Appendix B, Shortcut Keys,** lists the shortcut keys that are used on the desktop, in windows and dialog boxes, and to start the accessibility options.

Conventions Used in This Book

Windows XP: A Beginner's Guide uses several conventions designed to make the book easier for you to follow:

- **Bold type** is used for text that you are to type from the keyboard.

- *Italic type* is used for a word or phrase that is being defined or otherwise deserves special emphasis.

- SMALL CAPITAL LETTERS are used for keys on the keyboard such as ENTER and SHIFT.

- When you are expected to enter a command, you are told to press the key(s). If you are to enter text or numbers, you are told to type them.

- Window and dialog box titles, as well as option labels appearing on the screen, are shown here with all words using leading capital letters to distinguish them, even though on the screen many of the words do not have leading capitals.

The intent of this book is to start you down a path that will not only get you using Windows XP, but also make it an efficient and effective tool to help you accomplish what you need to do on your computer. I wish you success in this endeavor.

Part I

The Windows XP Environment

Module 1

Exploring Windows XP

Windows XP is the first recent Microsoft operating system that is meant for use in both homes and businesses. It combines all of the ruggedness and security of Windows NT and Windows 2000 with the ease of use of Windows 9x/Me. Windows XP is an extension of the Windows NT/2000 line of operating systems and includes the first home user operating system in that line. The Windows 9x/Me line, which grew out of MS-DOS and early versions of Windows, was ended with Windows Me, and was replaced by Windows XP.

As an operating system, Windows XP performs *the* central role in managing what a computer does and how it is done. It provides the interface between you and the computer hardware, facilitating your storing a file, printing a document, connecting to the Internet, and transferring information over a local area network without your knowing anything about how the hardware does that. Windows actually performs a large number of functions, and in this module you will look briefly at a number of them and see the area or component of Windows that does that job. In the process, I'll describe how the areas relate to one another and what is new in each area. This is a functional look at Windows XP, covering such functions as filing, printing, networking, communications, system management, and security. At the end of the module, an exercise will lead you through a brief tour of Windows XP that will let you see on your screen how Windows XP performs these functions. In Module 2, you will look in more detail at the components of Windows that perform these functions and are briefly mentioned here.

CRITICAL SKILL
1.1 Compare Windows XP Editions

Windows XP comes in two editions: Windows XP Home Edition and Windows XP Professional. Both editions are based on the same Windows NT/2000 technology, and both editions perform the vast majority of the functions we'll discuss here and throughout this book with the same components in the same way. There are, however, several features that should be considered in making the choice between the two editions; some features are available only in Windows XP Professional. Among these are

- **Domains**, which are used in structuring networks in larger organizations, are supported only by Windows XP Professional. If your company, school, or agency uses domains and you want to connect to the organization's network within the domain, you will need to use Professional.

- **Remote Desktop**, which allows a person on a remote Windows computer (Windows 95 or later) to take over the desktop and perform functions as if they sitting in front of the other computer, is available only on Windows XP Professional. If you are at home and want to get a document on your Windows XP Professional computer at work, you can do so using Remote Desktop. A Windows XP Home Edition computer can be used as the remote computer.

- **Encrypting File System** and **Restricted File Access**, which enable you to encrypt individual files and folders and restrict access to files, folders, and other resources, are available only on Windows XP Professional. If you are in an environment where others may be using your computer or where someone might steal it, with Windows XP Professional you can protect the contents by encrypting files or folders, or restrict, with permissions, who can access the file. Both of these capabilities depend on using the NTFS file system.

- **Upgrading** is more limited for Windows XP Home Edition than for Windows XP Professional. You can upgrade to Windows XP Home Edition only from Windows 98 and Windows Me. Windows XP Professional is an upgrade from those two products, as well as Windows NT 4.0 Workstation and Windows 2000 Professional. In addition, you can upgrade from Windows XP Home Edition to Windows XP Professional.

- **Other** features that are available only in Windows XP Professional are

  - Enhanced Backup and System Restore

  - Enhanced automatic updating

  - Ability to use multiple languages

  - Built-in support for wireless networks

  - Support for computers with multiple processors

For typical home use—such as Internet browsing; e-mail exchange; budgeting; working with digital photos, videos, and music; and home (peer-to-peer) networking—Windows XP Home Edition is an excellent choice. For most business use—such as connecting to large client/server networks; working with sensitive information; using major business applications such as accounting, manufacturing, and drawing—Windows XP Professional is the best choice.

In this book, when I talk about "Windows XP" I am talking equally about both Windows XP Professional and Windows XP Home Edition. If something I'm discussing applies to just one edition, I will identify which one.

Ask the Expert

Q: I have a small business with 12 people in one office. We use productivity applications (Word, Excel, and Access), a small accounting package, and a custom order entry and inventory system. We are also on the Internet quit a bit. We currently are using Windows 98 and Me and, except for the frequent system failures, are pretty happy with them. We are ordering several new computers and can choose between Home and Professional for about $100 difference in price. Is Professional worth it?

(continued)

A: The easy answer is that because Windows 98/Me has been doing the job for you, there is no reason that Windows XP Home Edition won't as well. Two things make me question that answer. First, most businesses expect to grow, and Home could be limiting to your growth because Windows XP Home Edition cannot use domains, Remote Desktop, or improved security. Second, while you are probably currently using a peer-to-peer network, it is likely that both your accounting system and the order entry/inventory system would work well, possibly better, in a client/server environment, which leads to needing Windows XP Professional. Unless you are a very small business and don't expect to grow, the quick answer is "go Pro."

CRITICAL SKILL
1.2 Use Basic Windows XP Functions

Windows XP can perform a large number of functions, only the most important of which will be discussed in an introductory form in this module. These same functions will be briefly discussed again in Module 2 from the vantage point of the Windows components that perform them, and many of these functions have their own modules later in the book. Here we'll look at the basic functions of file handling, printing, and working with multimedia. The following table shows these functions, the primary components they use, and the modules that are dedicated to them.

Function	Components	Modules
Handle files	Windows Explorer, My Computer	Module 4
Print and fax	Printers and Faxes	Module 5
Use multimedia	Windows Media Player, Sound Recorder, Movie Maker	Module 7

The next several sections will discuss each of these functions, describing what it entails and how Windows performs it, as well as showing one or more examples of it.

Handle Files

By *file handling,* I mean creating, storing, retrieving, naming, renaming, moving, copying, organizing, and deleting computer files. (There are other file functions, such as securing, printing, and transmitting that could be discussed here, but they are discussed as separate topics.) A computer *file* is a collection of information that you want to handle as a distinct entity. For example, a letter, an e-mail message, a web page, a drawing, a piece of music, a photograph, and a video clip are all files.

In Windows XP, as in the last several versions of Windows (back to Windows 95), the primary component that performs file handling is Windows Explorer. In a good attempt to confuse us, Microsoft also calls Windows Explorer "My Computer." In Windows XP, they are really one and the same component, and you can accomplish the same tasks in exactly the same way in either. My Computer opens up with one particular view, shown in Figure 1-1, that you can also achieve in Windows Explorer. In Module 3, you'll see how this is done and why they are one and the same.

NOTE

Prior to Windows 95, file handling was performed with the File Manager.

Although Windows Explorer is used for most file handling tasks, original files are created by other programs. A word processing program such as Microsoft Word is used to create a letter, a drawing program such as Paint is used to create a drawing, and an audio recording

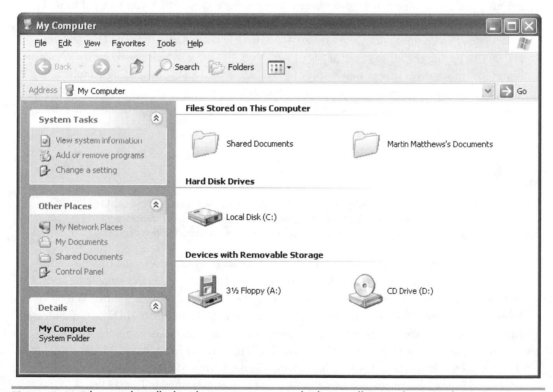

Figure 1-1 Files are handled with My Computer, which is really Windows Explorer.

program such as Sound Recorder is used to create a sound file. Once a file is created, it is stored on your computer with a name. Everything on your computer is stored as a file. Besides the files you create, all the programs that you run, including Windows itself, have a set of files, and every time you browse the Internet, files are left on your computer. After a very short time, a large number of files are stored on your computer. These files must be organized so that they can be easily found, and a means must be available to manage the files.

Organize Files

To organize files, containers are created to hold them. For obvious reasons, file containers are called and pictured as *folders,* as you can see at the top of Figure 1-1. At the highest level, folders are contained in disk drives. *Disk drives* are mechanical devices ("hardware") on which information is recorded. In Figure 1-1, you can see three disk drives: Local Disk (C:), which is also called a "hard drive"; 3½ Floppy (A:), a "floppy drive"; and CD Drive (D:), a "CD-ROM" drive. A hard drive uses a spinning hard metal platter on which to write or record information. A floppy drive used a spinning flexible plastic platter for the same purpose, and a CD-ROM uses a spinning hard plastic platter from which information can be read (*ROM* stands for read-only memory). You may have other disk drives, including a CD-R, which can be used to write information on a CD that cannot be erased and written over, or a CD-RW, on which you can write, erase, and write again. Your primary hard drive is always called "drive C:," and your primary floppy drive is always called "drive A:." Your CD drive, which can be set by Windows Setup to various drive letters, may or may not be called "drive D:," depending on whether you have additional hard drives, which would be called "drive D:" for the second hard drive, and so on. With multiple hard drives, your CD drive would have the next drive letter after the last hard drive.

 NOTE

Back in the dark ages of computing (several years ago) folders were called "directories." Every once in a while someone, including me, will slip and call a folder a directory. They are one and the same thing, and you should not be confused by the two names.

On a disk drive, files are contained either in a folder or in the *root* of the drive; in other words, the files are on the drive without being in a folder and so are at the same level, the root, as the highest-level folders. Figure 1-2 shows on the right or *details* pane of Windows Explorer that three files and four folders are contained in the root of Local Disk (C:). Folders can be stored in other folders to create a hierarchical organization. For example, Figure 1-2 shows on the left or *folders* pane of Windows Explorer that the My Music folder is contained in the My Documents folder, which is contained in the Martin Matthews folder, which is contained in the Documents and Settings folder, which is contained in Local Disk (C:).

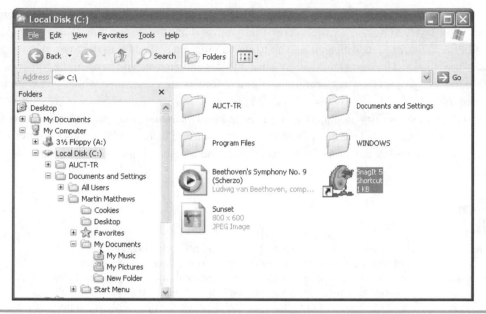

Figure 1-2 Files and folders in the root of drive C: and folders within folders

Manage Files

With any collection of files and folders, it is obvious that you will need to do more than create and look at them. Windows provides a number of functions, such as moving, copying, deleting, and renaming, that you can perform on files and folders. The number of functions that you can perform depends on whether something is a file or a folder and, if a file, the type of file, such as music files, word processing documents, or drawings. There are also several ways that these functions can be implemented. One is to right-click the file or folder, which opens a *context menu* such as the three menus you see next.

The context menu on the left is for a music file, so it has the added functions of Play and Add To Playlist. The middle menu is for a program and has the unique functions of Run As and Pin To Start Menu, which allow you to start a program and add it to the Start menu so that it is easy to use. The menu on the right is for a folder and enables you to open the folder in Windows Explorer (Explore), search for files and folders, and determine whom you want to share the folder with.

Other ways to carry out functions on files and folders include dragging them to move or copy them, double-clicking them to open or start them, and using the Windows Explorer's menus. A detailed description of these techniques and a description of all the file handling functions are presented in Module 4.

NOTE

The program icon SnagIt 5 shown in Figure 1-2 is called a *shortcut* because it is not the program itself, but rather a means to start the program from a location other than where the program is stored. A program can have as many shortcuts as you want. They can be on the desktop, so that you immediately see them when you start your computer, or on the taskbar at the bottom of the screen, so that they are always visible when you running other programs. Module 4 will show you how to create shortcuts and place them where you want them. (SnagIt is the program I use to capture the images on the screen that you see in this book.)

Progress Check

1. What is the primary tool that Windows XP provides for working with files?

2. What are the containers currently called that hold files?

3. What does a shortcut do?

Print and Fax

Once you create a file, it is likely that you will want to do something with it besides look at it. If the file contains text, a drawing, or a photograph, you probably will want to print it. Faxing a document that is in a file on your computer is very similar to printing the document, so

---

1. Windows Explorer
2. Folders
3. Start a program from a location other than where the program is stored

Windows XP handles them both in the same component, called Printers and Faxes, which is shown in Figure 1-3.

 NOTE

The notion that computers would lead to a paperless society is pure myth; the exact opposite is true. It is so easy to print things out that it is done much more frequently than would otherwise be the case, and much of it gets thrown away.

Printers and Faxes doesn't actually do the printing or faxing; rather, it sets up the printers and faxes that are then used by other programs to do it. For example, if you choose to print a web page in Internet Explorer, the Print dialog box shown in Figure 1-4 will open and allow you to choose which device to use (I can choose among the devices that appear in Figure 1-3). Different applications have different Print dialog boxes, but most of them have the features shown in Figure 1-4.

Printers that are available to you can be attached to the computer that you are using, attached to another computer on the same local area network (LAN) as your computer, or attached directly to the LAN. They can also be on the Internet if you are attached to the

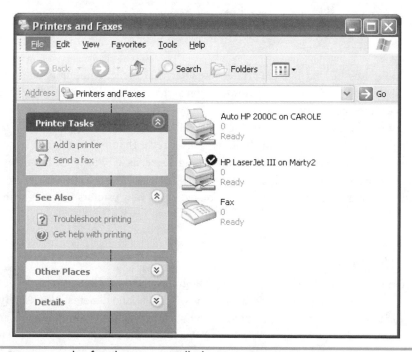

Figure 1-3 Printers and a fax that are installed on my computer

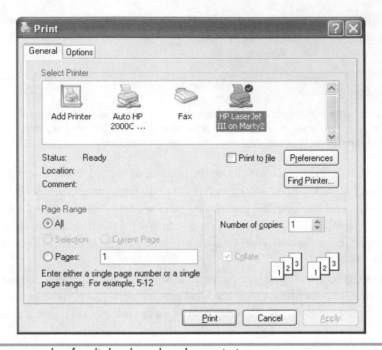

Figure 1-4 An example of a dialog box that does printing

Internet. In Figures 1-3 and 1-4, the printers are attached to other computers on my LAN. You can tell this by the "pipe" beneath the printer icon and because they say they are on a particular computer (Carole and Marty2 respectively).

 When you print a document, a small icon like the one shown here appears in the notification area on the right of the taskbar at the bottom of the screen. If you click this icon, the printer management window opens showing the current print queue, as in Figure 1-5. From this window, you pause and cancel print jobs and change their priority.

Module 5 contains a detailed discussion of setting up new printers and then using and managing them, as well as faxes.

Use Multimedia

Multimedia includes audio, video, and still photographs. As I've already said, all of these mediums are stored as files in Windows XP, but as with text documents, you usually want to do more than have a file on your computer—you want to listen to the audio, listen and look at the video, and look at the pictures. Windows XP includes the capability to both create and play back audio and video files and to display photographs. The primary component for playing

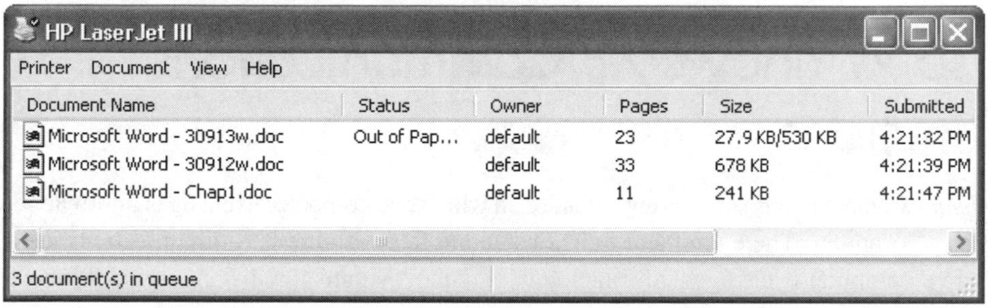

HP LaserJet III					
Printer Document View Help					
Document Name	Status	Owner	Pages	Size	Submitted
Microsoft Word - 30913w.doc	Out of Pap...	default	23	27.9 KB/530 KB	4:21:32 PM
Microsoft Word - 30912w.doc		default	33	678 KB	4:21:39 PM
Microsoft Word - Chap1.doc		default	11	241 KB	4:21:47 PM
3 document(s) in queue					

Figure 1-5 A typical printer management window

back audio and video is the Windows Media Player, which can play back digital audio, video, music CDs, DVD movies, and Internet radio. You must, of course, have a sound card in the computer, and it must be connected to speakers.

If you were to play the Beethoven music file shown in Figure 1-2 earlier in the module, the Windows Media Player would open, and the music would begin to play through your computer's speakers. In the same fashion, if you play a video file the Windows Media Player will open, the video image will appear in the Media Player window, and you will hear the sound from your computer's speakers.

If you put an audio CD in your CD drive or a DVD movie in a DVD drive, they will cause the Media Player to open and play the CD or DVD. When you are playing either a DVD or a video file, you can play it within the Media Player window or you can expand it to the full screen. Internet radio stations can also be played through the Media Player.

If you want to create audio or video files, Windows XP has a separate component for each of these, the Sound Recorder for audio recording and the Windows Movie Maker, which can record both audio and video. Module 7 describes in detail how to work with audio and video media.

Progress Check

1. Do you print from Windows XP or from an application?

2. How do you cancel a print job?

3. What is the multimedia playback component in Windows XP?

---

1. Application
2. Using the printer icon in the notification area of the taskbar
3. Windows Media Player

CRITICAL SKILL

1.3 Use Windows XP Communications Functions

Communications in this sense is any situation in which one computer exchanges information with another computer. There are three functions within this definition: communications itself, where a computer exchanges information with others that are at a distance from it; networking, where the exchange takes place locally; and remote services, where one computer takes control of another computer either locally or at a distance. The next table lists these functions, the components they use, and the modules that are dedicated to them.

Function	Components	Modules
Communications	Internet Explorer, Outlook Express, HyperTerminal	Module 6
Networking	Network Connections	Module 8
Remote services	Remote Desktop Connection	Module 11

Use Communications

Historically, computer communications involves connecting with other computers over phone lines, but today you have to include connecting wirelessly with cell phones, as well as satellites, TV cable, and phone lines. Most communications takes place via the Internet, and for the majority of computer users, an Internet connection is the only form of computer communications that they use.

Like networking, communications, and especially connecting to the Internet, has become much easier to set up and in many cases totally automatic. Depending on how you are connected to your Internet provider, Windows XP Setup may be able to automatically set up your connection. If not, the New Connection Wizard, which you can open by clicking Start and choosing All Programs | Accessories | Communications | New Communications Wizard, will lead you through the process of connecting to the Internet.

Within Internet communications, most people use only two major functions: e-mail and Internet browsing.

Use E-Mail

Internet e-mail, which is the exchanging of messages over the Internet, is probably the single most popular use of a computer. At the same time, it has greatly improved how well people communicate because it is so easy and almost instantaneous. Within Windows XP, e-mail is handled by Outlook Express, shown in Figure 1-6, which performs all of the related functions including

- Downloading your incoming e-mail
- Storing and printing incoming mail in the Inbox
- Replying to and forwarding incoming mail
- Maintaining an address book
- Creating new e-mail messages
- Sending and storing outgoing messages

Besides handling e-mail, Outlook Express allows you to participate in newsgroups. *Newsgroups* are a form of sponsored e-mail on a particular topic. For example, Microsoft sponsors newsgroups on its products. Someone *posts* a message on a particular subject, such as the color of the taskbar in Windows XP. A second person responds to the original message with further thoughts, and a third person responds to the second message, creating a *thread* on the original subject.

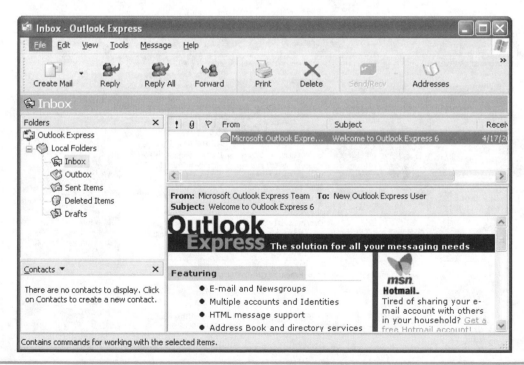

Figure 1-6 Outlook Express is Windows XP's e-mail component.

Use Internet Browsing

Internet browsing is viewing and interacting with images or *web pages* that people have made available on the World Wide Web (or just Web) of the Internet. Web pages are attached to an address, called a *Universal Resource Locator (URL),* that can be used to locate and view the page; http://www.microsoft.com is an example. In Windows XP, this is done with Internet Explorer. A web page can contain text, pictures, and forms, as you can see in Figure 1-7, and can cause both sound and video to be sent down *(downloaded)* to your computer.

Internet Explorer provides a number of ways to find the web page you are looking for. Among these are

● Storing the URL for a page you have found in the Favorites folder so that you can easily find the page again

● Keeping the page's URL on the Links bar so you just have to click to open the page

Figure 1-7 The MSN web page displayed in Internet Explorer

- Keeping a history of the pages you have visited so that you can return to a page you have previously viewed

- Providing a built-in search engine, although not a very good one

Use Communications Other Than the Internet

Although few people use it, Windows XP still retains the capability to directly connect two computers using phone lines. This is done with the HyperTerminal component. It allows one computer to connect to a phone line, dial a number, and transfer information to another computer that uses HyperTerminal or another program to answer the call.

Module 6 describes communications in general and using the Internet in particular.

Use Networking

Networking in its basic form is the connecting of computers within the confines of a single building of a business or an organization. This is called a *local area network,* or a LAN. LANs are not new, but current-day hardware, principally network interface cards (NICs) in the computers attached to a network, and Windows XP make networking very easy and not the nightmare that is was only a few years ago.

There are two forms of networking, *peer-to-peer* networks, where all computers are both clients and servers and thus equal, and *client/server* networks, where there are one to a few servers and many clients. Windows XP can operate in a peer-to-peer network and can be a client or workstation in a client/server environment. Peer-to-peer networks are limited in size, generally less than ten computers, and are normally used in homes and small businesses. A peer-to-peer network is also called a *workgroup.* In peer-to-peer networks, all computers share

Ask the Expert

Q: If there is so much garbage on the Internet, as I have heard, is it really worthwhile using it?

A: In my opinion, the good on the Internet far outweighs the garbage that is also there. On the Web, you can find most of the world's newspapers and magazines, numerous encyclopedias, most major stores and a great many more that are available only on the Internet, support for most products that you buy, many radio stations, travel services with deals that are available only on the Internet, schools of all types, and unique information that some industrious person has compiled and put on the Web. There is so much information on the Web that there are a number of *search engines* to help you find it.

their resources, such as printers and hard disks. In client/server networks, this is still true, and the majority of shared resources are on the server.

The primary networking component in Windows XP is Network Connections, shown in Figure 1-8. Here you can see the existing connections, troubleshoot them, and set up new connections. In many cases your primary network connection (the Local Area Connection in Figure 1-8) is automatically set up for you when you install Windows XP. If your network connection was added after installing Windows XP or for some other reason your connection was not automatically set up, you can do it by clicking Set Up A Home Or Small Office Network, which will open the Network Setup Wizard, which is new to Windows XP, to lead you through the process.

There are several other kinds of network connections, such as remote access, where you connect to your computer at work from your computer at home, that are set up by clicking Create A New Connection in the Network Connections window.

Through the Local Area Connection icon, you can determine if and how you are connected to the network and control how your network connection will function. In many situations, though, you will never need to open these dialog boxes. Your network will be automatically set up with the appropriate setting when Windows XP is installed, and you will never need to do more than use the network. This is a huge step from the early days of networking.

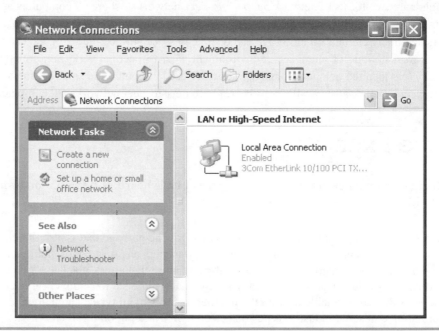

Figure 1-8 Access to your network connections is through the Network Connections window.

Module 8 describes how networking works and how to set up and use a network.

Progress Check

1. What is the Internet web browsing tool in Windows XP?

2. What is the Internet e-mail component in Windows XP?

3. Is there a stand-alone server in a peer-to-peer network?

Remote Services

Remote services cover several different functions, including

- **Remote Desktop**, where one computer takes over another's desktop, such that a person in front of the first computer can operate as if she were sitting in front of the second.

- **Terminal Services**, where a Windows XP computer can connect to a Windows 2000 or .NET server and run programs on the server as if the programs were running on the XP computer.

- **Remote Access Service (RAS)**, where a computer can come in over phone lines to a server and attach to the local network.

- **Virtual Private Networking (VPN)**, where a computer can come in over the Internet to a server and attach to the local network.

Windows XP can serve as a client for any of these remote services, and Windows XP Professional can be the computer whose desktop is taken over in Remote Desktop. Both Remote Desktop and Terminal Services use the Remote Desktop Connection component of Windows XP, shown in Figure 1-9. RAS and VPN are a combination of communications and networking and are set up with the New Connection Wizard mentioned above under Networking.

Remote Desktop, Terminal Services, RAS, and VPN are described in Module 11.

---

1. Internet Explorer
2. Outlook Express
3. No. All computers are both clients and servers.

Figure 1-9 A Remote Desktop Connection to a server

Use Windows XP Management Functions

Windows XP management functions are in two major categories: security functions and all other management functions. Here are the categories, the components they use, and the modules that are dedicated to them.

Function	Components	Modules
Security	Local Security Settings	Module 9
Managing Windows XP	Control Panel, Computer Management, Policies	Modules 3, 10, and 14

Control Security

Computer security has a number of meanings. It is

- Protecting a computer from unauthorized access

- Protecting your files and settings from someone who is also using the same computer
- Protecting your files from someone who is looking through your computer
- Protecting your files when you transmit them over the Internet or other communications links
- Protecting a computer from being entered from the Internet

Each of these levels of defense is addressed in Windows XP using different components, several of which are new to Windows XP. This provides multiple layers of protection.

Unauthorized Access

Unauthorized access is handled with a password entered when you first turn on the computer and whenever you bring it out of hibernation mode. If you have the needed hardware, you can use a smart card (like a credit card with an electronic circuit on it) or physical recognition technology, such as fingerprint recognition, in place of or in addition to the password. If this is important to you, you might also want to use file encryption (see "File Encryption" below).

Separating Multiple Users

A new feature of Windows XP enables you to create completely separate users on a single computer. Each user can have his own files, programs, desktop, and computer settings. Each user can be password-protected from the other users' areas and be prevented from seeing those users' files or be impacted by anything they have done on the computer. Each user can customize the computer any way that she wants without affecting other users. The users can quickly switch from one user account to another without having to close any programs they are running.

Multiple users are handled with the User Accounts feature of Windows XP. When the computer is started, one of the users *logs on* by selecting his or her account and entering a password. If the other person needs to jump on and quickly do something, the first person can log off without closing any programs or files, the second person logs on, does his task, and logs off; the first person can log back on and be exactly where she was before the interruption.

File Encryption

File encryption is the systematic scrambling of information in a file using a cryptographic key. Without the key, the information is not readable, but with the key it is. You can encrypt information in two different areas of Windows XP, individual files on the disk and e-mail messages you are about to send.

NOTE

File encryption is not available in Windows XP Home Edition and requires that the NTFS file system be used.

At any time, you can go into Windows Explorer, select one or more files or folders, and choose to encrypt them. When you are logged on to the computer, you will be able read the file as you always have and will not know that it is encrypted. If someone steals your computer, say a laptop, and somehow gets onto your hard drive, he will not be able to read the file. To him it will be gibberish.

When you create an e-mail message in Outlook Express 6, which is a component of Windows XP, you can choose to encrypt the message. For you to do this, both you and the person to whom you are sending the message must both have a *digital ID* or a *certificate* and you must exchange these IDs. This allows you and the recipient to verify who you are, encrypt your messages very securely, and safely send messages over the Internet.

Hacker Protection

You have probably read about how someone surreptitiously got into a computer and did some damage. Such a person is called a *hacker.* The protection against such a person is called a *firewall.* Windows XP includes the Internet Connection Firewall (ICF) component to provide hacker protection. ICF is enabled in the Network Connections windows you saw earlier in this module. ICF cannot be used if you want to use VPN or certain other type of connections.

Controlling security is discussed in Module 9.

Manage Windows XP

As you can probably tell, Windows XP is a complex operating system with many components and many options in those components. As a result, managing Windows XP is complex with a number of components used to that end. Among these are

- The Control Panel to handle many of the components within Windows XP

- Computer Management to handle storage and disk management, system users, and some of the services that are available

- Local Security Policies, Group Policies, and Permissions to set up the rules used to control many features in Windows XP

Control Panel

The Control Panel, shown in Figure 1-10, is the most common management component in Windows XP. Similar components have been included in most of the later versions of Windows. As you can see, it handles most of the hardware on a computer and a number of other components. This enables you to customize much of Windows and to locate and cure problems. The Control Panel is discussed in Modules 3, 10, and 13.

Figure 1-10 The Control Panel allows for customization and problem resolution.

Computer Management

There is one significant omission in the Control Panel: storage and disk management. For whatever reason, Microsoft put this in Computer Management, which is one of the Administrative Tools that is opened from the Control Panel. Besides Disk Management, which is shown in Figure 1-11, the other Computer Management features are generally advanced topics that are discussed briefly in Modules 10 and 14.

Policies and Permissions

Much of the advanced management of Windows XP is done through policies and permissions. The policies establish the rules that control many functions within Windows and allow you to promulgate the same rules over many computers. Permissions then are used to apply different rules to different groups or individual users. Policies and permissions are looked at further in Modules 9 and 10.

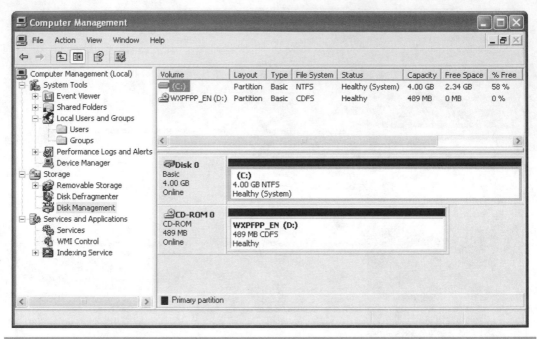

Figure 1-11 Computer Management hides the Disk Management function, among others.

CRITICAL SKILL
1.5 # Install and Maintain Windows XP

The following table shows Windows XP's installation and maintenance functions, the components they use, and the modules that are dedicated to them.

Function	Components	Modules
Install Windows XP	Windows XP Setup	Modules 12 and 13
Install other software and hardware	Add/Remove Programs, Add Hardware	Module 14
Maintain Windows XP	Remote Assistance, Windows Update, and Windows Restore	Module 14

Install Windows XP

Like many parts of Windows XP, installation is very easy and almost automatic if you use the default settings and if you have common, relatively recent hardware. With new computers,

Windows XP comes already installed, and you can't get more automatic than that. If you are upgrading from an earlier version of Windows (see the discussion on upgrading under "Compare Windows XP Editions" early in this module) you simply insert the Windows XP CD in its drive and follow the instructions on the screen.

One of the most important aspects of installing an operating system, especially if you are doing it on several computers, is to plan it out so that the resulting system is the way you want it. It is also an excellent opportunity to clean up the hard disk. If you get really serious about cleaning up your hard disk, the very best way is to back up all the important information on it, reformat it, do a clean install of Windows XP instead of an upgrade, and then reinstall only the programs and data that you want. This definitely takes more effort than an upgrade, but you can cure a great many ills this way and it is as close as you can get to a new system without buying one. Module 12 provides a roadmap on how to go about planning the installation of Windows XP; the procedure it outlines is advisable for a single-computer installation and mandatory for a multiple-computer installation. Module 13 provides detailed information and guidance in the installation of Windows XP.

Install Other Software and Hardware

A part of maintaining a computer system is handling the installation and removal of hardware and other software. Historically this was an area of many problems, most of which have been substantially cured in Windows XP. When you install a new program, it is registered with XP and listed in Add Or Remove Programs. If you want to update or remove the program, you can easily do so through this Control Panel component. Most programs use links to the operating system called *dynamic link libraries (DLLs)*. Sometimes two programs use a DLL with the same name. When the second program is installed, its DLL replaces the first program's file, which historically caused the first program not to run properly. In Windows XP, this has been fixed so that each program's files are used just for that program.

When hardware is installed, if it is Plug and Play compatible (and most recent hardware is), it will be detected by Windows XP and either its driver will be automatically installed (if it is in the Windows driver database) or you will be requested to insert a disk containing the driver. If you don't have the disk, it is possible that Windows Update, discussed next, will have the driver and that by opening Windows Update you can download and install it. If all else fails, you can often bring up the hardware manufacturer's web site and find a driver there.

Module 14 goes into the many aspects of adding hardware, application software, and utility software.

Maintaining Windows XP

Once Windows XP is installed, you need to periodically look at the installation and make adjustments to keep it in top condition. This includes keeping your hard disk clean, backed up, and defragmented; making sure the settings in Windows XP are still the way you want them;

reviewing your security procedures; and finally making sure that the latest Windows XP updates have been installed.

A major new feature in Windows XP is Windows Update, which provides either automatic or manual updates of XP. When you complete installing Windows XP, you are asked if you want automatic updates (they are currently free). If you say "yes," you will periodically be told that "New Updates Are Ready To Install." You can then choose to install them or not. If you do not select automatic updates, you can use the Start menu command to go to Windows Update on the Microsoft web site and have it determine what updates you need. Module 14 looks at the many aspects of maintaining Windows XP.

Progress Check

1. What does Remote Desktop do?

2. What do you use to handle multiple users on a computer?

3. What is the most common management component in Windows XP?

4. What does Windows Update do?

Ask the Expert

Q: I get real tired entering a password every time I start the computer and every time I come back to it after the screen saver has come up. Do I really need to do that?

A: The quick answer is no. Only you can determine if you need to password-protect your computer when you are not in front of it. If it is in a secure location where no one will bother it, than you don't. Module 9 describes how to add or remove the password protection from your system.

---

1. Remote Desktop allows one computer to take over another's desktop.
2. User Accounts enables you to set up and switch between multiple users.
3. The Control Panel provides access to many of the hardware and software settings needed for maintenance.
4. Windows Update provides either automatic or manual updates of Windows XP.

Project 1 The Functions You Need

In this module, I have laid out a number of functions that can be performed with an operating system and have briefly discussed what the function is, how it is performed in Windows XP, and what components of the operating system will do that task. Not everybody uses all these functions. Most people have ones that are critical to what they do and other functions they hardly ever use. The purpose of this project is to identify what functions are most important to you and then prioritize how you will learn about them in the following modules.

Step by Step

1. Review the functions that have been discussed in this module. Possibly go back and scan what was said in earlier sections to recollect what the function does.

2. Determine which functions are most important to you and assign a priority order for each.

3. Lay out a schedule based on your priority and read the related modules in the order given by that schedule.

Function	Modules	Priority (Dates)
File handling	Module 4	
Printing and faxing	Module 5	
Communications	Module 6	
Handling multimedia	Module 7	
Networking	Module 8	
Security	Module 9	
Managing Windows XP	Modules 3, 10, and 13	
Remote services	Module 11	
Installing Windows XP and other software and hardware	Modules 12, 13, and 14	

Project Summary

After you have completed the prioritization project, you will have a schedule for reading the rest of the book. There are two exceptions to this. First, if you have not already installed Windows, go immediately to Module 12 and do the installation as described there. The remaining modules assume that Windows XP is installed and running in front of you as you read. There are many instances where you will want try for yourself what you are reading

(continued)

about. Second, after you have installed Windows XP and before diving into your priority modules, quickly go through Modules 2 and 3. Module 2 will give you a good foundation in how to start, use, and navigate through Windows XP, as well as where to find the many components that you will be needing in future modules. Module 3 will help you customize Windows XP, so that it looks and operates the way that is most pleasing to you.

Module 1 Mastery Check

1. What does an operating system, such as Windows XP, do?

2. What are three features that are in Windows XP Professional and not in Windows XP Home Edition?

3. What is the difference between My Computer and Windows Explorer?

4. Match up the function on the left with the component on the right.

Primary tool for working with files	Outlook Express
Containers that hold files	Windows Update
Starts a program from a remote location	Remote Desktop Connection
Multimedia playback component	User Accounts
Internet web browsing tool	Shortcuts
Internet e-mail component	Windows Explorer
Provides for multiple users on a computer	Folders
Allows one computer to take over another	Internet Explorer
Provides automatic and manual updates	Windows Media Player

5. What is your primary hard drive normally called, and what is your primary floppy drive always called?

6. Where is printing done in Windows XP?

7. What is the difference between client/server and peer-to-peer networks?

8. How are policies and permissions used in Windows XP?

9. What does the Control Panel do?

10. What does "Plug and Play hardware" mean?

Module 2

Components of Windows XP

This module will show you how to begin to use Windows XP: how to start it; how to get around in it; how to perform the basic functions in XP that are required to use it; and how to locate and open the major components that give Windows its power. This module is meant to be read while you are following along by executing the steps in the book on your computer. The module assumes that you have Windows XP, either Home Edition or Professional, installed on your computer. If that is not the case, go to Module 12 and complete the installation first.

CRITICAL SKILL
2.1
Start and Shut Down Windows

The procedure for starting Windows XP depends on how many people use the computer you are using, whether you are connected to a network and the kind of network, and whether you are using password protection. The assumption here is that there are multiple users; they are connected to a workgroup network, not a domain; and they are using passwords. I'll also look at alternative assumptions as we go along. With my primary assumptions, there are four functions we are concerned about here: starting Windows, logging on, logging off and switching users, and shutting down.

Starting Windows XP begins with starting your computer. There are different ways of doing this, from a switch on the back, a switch on the side, a button on the front, or a button on the keyboard. It could also be some combination of these. If it is not obvious to you, you will need to look at the manufacturer's information that came with the computer. When you first apply power to the computer, it will go through and check itself. Often there will be a sound or beep. This is called the Power-on Self Test, or POST. The memory is checked, and you are given a list of the hardware that is found. This process may be masked by a manufacturer's screen with their name on it. You are then told that Windows is starting, and a Welcome message appears. When Windows completes loading (under our multiuser assumption), a list of users will appear as shown in Figure 2-1. Otherwise, Windows XP itself will open.

NOTE

If this is the first time your computer has been started after installing Windows XP, you will be asked to activate Windows and optionally register with Microsoft. If this happens, which it might if you have purchased a new computer with Windows XP already installed, turn to Module 13 and go to the section "Activate Windows XP." When you are done activating Windows XP, return here.

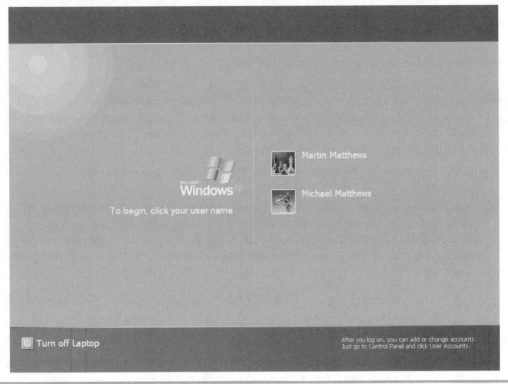

To begin, click your user name

Martin Matthews

Michael Matthews

Turn off Laptop

After you log on, you can add or change accounts. Just go to Control Panel and click User Accounts.

Figure 2-1 Logon window with the possible users

Log On

In the Logon screen shown in Figure 2-1, click (move the mouse point to and press the left mouse button—see "The Mouse" later in this module) your name and, if requested, enter your password and Windows will open. If a systems administrator installed your system, he or she should have given you your username and password. If you installed the system, then you may not have set up users yet. Setting up users is discussed in Modules 9 and 10.

NOTE

If you are logging on to a domain, you will be asked to press and hold CTRL-ALT-DELETE until all three keys are pressed, then enter your username and password, and press ENTER or click OK.

Ask the Expert

Q: Why do domains require CTRL-ALT-DELETE?

A: This is an extra layer of security. CTRL-ALT-DELETE temporarily stops every program running in the computer while you enter your username and password. This prevents a program (called a "Trojan horse") from surreptitiously capturing your logon information.

Q: Can't two users use the same computer without creating separate user accounts?

A: Yes, and that was the way it was done for many years. The problem is that multiple users tend to get in each other's way. They may want to install their own programs, have different screen settings, and most important, have information they want to be private and inaccessible to the other users. The easiest way to do this is to have separate user accounts.

Log Off and Shut Down

Logging off and shutting down are two ways to stop using the computer. Logging off is different from shutting down and even different from switching users. Here are the three meanings:

- **Logging off** means to close your programs, close your connection to the network, and close your user account, but leave the computer running.

- **Switching users** means to leave your programs running, remain connected to the network, and keep your user account active while you switch to let another user use the computer.

- **Shutting down** means to log off all users and shut down the computer.

  The steps to carry out these procedures are very similar.

To Log Off   Click the Start button to open the Start menu and click Log Off. In the Log Off Windows dialog box, click Log Off, as shown next.

To Switch Users   Click the Start button to open the Start menu and click Log Off. In the Log Off Windows dialog box, click Switch User.

To Shut Down   Click the Start button to open the Start menu and click Turn Off Computer. In the Turn Off Computer dialog box, click Turn Off, like this:

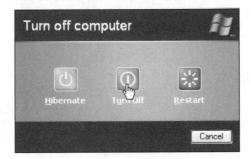

These are the options in the Turn Off Computer dialog box :

- **Turn Off** means to gracefully shut down Windows so that no information is lost and then to turn off the computer (if it can be done automatically) or tell you that it is now safe for you to do that.

- **Restart** means to gracefully shut down Windows so that no information is lost and then restart the computer. This is usually done when there is some problem that restarting Windows will fix or to complete setting up some programs.

- **Hibernate** means to save the current state of the computer, including the programs and files that are open and the network connections that are active, and then shut down the computer. This allows you to start up the computer at a later date and resume with exactly the same programs, files, and network connections that you had open when you shut down.

Ask the Expert

Q: **Why not use hibernate all the time?**

A: There is no major reason you can't, but if you are not going to use the same program(s) the next time you start, there is no real benefit because your network connections are restarted in any case. When you hibernate, shutting down is somewhat slower and takes up a fair amount of disk space. In addition, starting up is slower.

NOTE

On laptop, notebook, and some desktop computers, the Hibernate option may be replaced with Stand By, which does everything Hibernate does but puts the computer into a special low-power state that conserves power and preserves the battery but allows you to quickly restart. On these computers, if you want to go into true hibernation, hold down SHIFT while clicking Stand By.

Progress Check

1. What is the simple and primary step to start Windows XP?

2. Do you always have to log on when you start up?

3. What is the difference between logging off and switching users?

CRITICAL SKILL
2.2 Navigate Within Windows XP

When Windows XP starts for the first time, you see a very simple screen with a pastoral scene, a bar at the bottom, the Start button on the left, the time on the right, and the Recycle Bin above the

---

1. Turn on your computer.

2. No, unless you are part of a domain. If you choose not to have more than one user account and are outside a domain, Windows will assume you are the single user and log you on automatically.

3. Switching users keeps all of your programs and network connections active so that you can quickly resume using them. Logging off shuts them down.

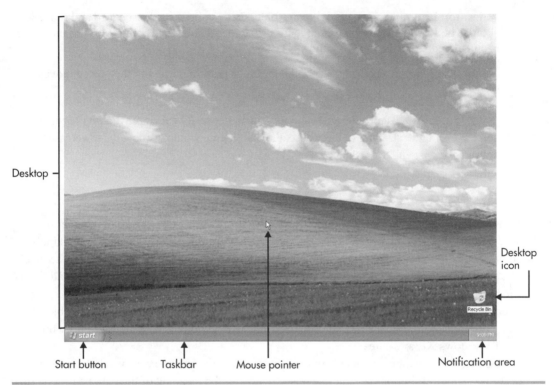

Desktop

Desktop icon

Start button   Taskbar   Mouse pointer   Notification area

Figure 2-2 Initial Windows startup screen

time, as you can see in Figure 2-2. The items you see on the screen have names that are generally used and are used throughout this book. These are shown in Figure 2-2 and are as follows:

● The **desktop** is the entire screen except for the bar at the bottom. Your programs are displayed on the desktop, and it can contain icons such as the Recycle Bin.

● **Start** on the lower left is a "button" that when "clicked" with the mouse opens the Start menu, the primary entry to the programs, utilities, and settings that are available on the computer.

● The **taskbar** at the bottom of the screen contains the icons and titles of the programs that are running on the computer or folders that are open, as well as the Start button and the notification area.

● The **notification area** on the right of the taskbar contains the icons of only certain programs, as well as the time of day.

- A **desktop icon** represents a program or folder that can be started or opened and moved about. The Recycle Bin is a desktop icon for a folder that contains all of the files that have been deleted since the Recycle Bin was last emptied.

- The **mouse pointer** represents where the mouse is pointing. Moving the mouse moves the pointer.

Using Windows XP and getting around its screen, generally called *navigating,* requires that you have an understanding of the mouse, the Start menu, windows (note the lowercase "w"), dialog boxes, icons, and the taskbar.

The Mouse

Although most people use a mouse intuitively, it is worthwhile making sure that the terms used here are clearly understood. A *mouse* means any pointing device—including trackballs; pointing sticks; and graphic tablets with one, two, three, or more buttons and possibly a wheel. The most common, though, is a two-button mouse that you roll across a flat surface, and that is what is assumed in this book. Moving the mouse moves the mouse pointer on the screen. You select an object on the screen by moving the mouse pointer so that it is on top of the object and then pressing a button on the mouse. You need at least two buttons on a mouse to fully utilize all of Windows XP's features.

You can use the mouse with either your left or right hand, and you can switch the meanings of the left and right buttons to facilitate this. (Switching the meaning of the buttons is done in the Mouse control panel, which you reach by choosing Control Panel from the Start menu— see Module 3.) In normal usage, the right hand controls the mouse and the left mouse button is the primary one. The left mouse button is therefore called "the mouse button." The right button is always called the "right mouse button." If you switch the meaning of the buttons, you will have to mentally change how you interpret these phrases.

The standard terminology for using the mouse that is used this book and in most other sources is as follows:

- **Point** means to move the mouse until the tip of the pointer is on top of the object you want to select.

- **Click** means to point at an object you want to select and quickly press and release the left mouse button.

- **Right-click** means to point at an object you want to select and quickly press and release the right mouse button. This normally opens a *context* menu, also called a shortcut menu, which allows you to do things to the object that you clicked.

- **Double-click** means to point at an object you want to select and quickly press and release the left mouse button twice in rapid succession.

- **Drag** means to point at an object you want to move and press and hold the left mouse button while moving the mouse and dragging the object with you. When you get the object where you want it, release the mouse button.

In most instances, you select an object on the screen by clicking it and open or start an object by double-clicking it. In addition, you can temporarily select an object by just pointing at it. When you do that, the object becomes *highlighted* to indicate its selection, as you will see with the Start button in a minute.

The Start Menu

Open your Start menu now so that you can look at it as it is discussed. Do that now in this way:

1. Point at the Start button by moving the mouse pointer so that it is over the Start button. You will see that the button changes color and is said to be *selected*.

2. Press and release the left mouse button (given that your mouse buttons have not been switched) while the mouse pointer is on the Start button. The Start menu will open.

These two steps can be replaced with the two words "click Start." You can also open the Start menu by pressing the WINDOWS key on your keyboard, if you have that key, or by pressing both the CTRL and ESC keys at the same time (written CTRL-ESC). In the rest of this book, you will see the phrase "open Start." This means open the Start menu using any technique you wish.

Ask the Expert

Q: Why would you want to open the Start menu from the keyboard?

A: There are several reasons. If for some reason your mouse dies and you need to get to the Start menu, for example to shut down, you can use the keyboard. Second, if a handicap prevents use of a mouse, the keyboard is available. Finally, some people just don't like the mouse.

The Contents of the Start Menu

The Start menu provides access to all of what you can do on your computer; it is the door to your computer and to Windows XP. The Start menu contains icons for programs and folders, plus three buttons, as shown in Figure 2-3. The three buttons are All Programs, which opens a subsidiary menu, and Log Off and Turn Off Computer, which were discussed earlier in this module. All other objects on the menu are icons for folders and programs. The five or six lower icons on the left change to reflect the programs you used most recently, and your five or six will most probably be different from the five shown in Figure 2-3.

The remaining icons in the Start menu fall into three categories: Internet programs, file-related folders and programs, and system management programs.

Internet Programs   The two icons above the five or six variable ones start programs that let you use the Internet. The top one, Internet Explorer, lets you browse the World Wide Web; the second icon, Outlook Express, opens an e-mail program that lets you send e-mail over either your local network or the Internet. Both of these programs are described in Module 6.

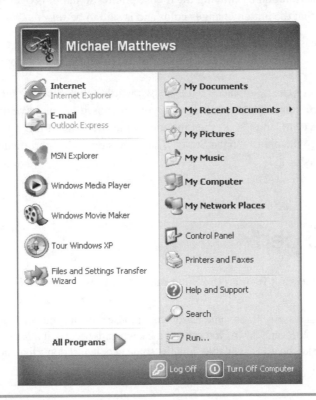

Figure 2-3 The Start menu

If you do not see these programs or something similar, such as Outlook in place of Outlook Express, it means that you do not have an Internet connection, in which case, go to Module 13 and see how to set one up.

File-Related Folders and Programs

The top six icons (My Documents, My Recent Documents, My Pictures, My Music, My Computer, and My Network Places) on the right in Figure 2-3 (you may have only five icons if you are not connected to a network) relate to the handling and storage of files. All of these icons start the Windows Explorer program and then display within that program the item identified by the icon. Windows Explorer gives you access to all the files, folders, disk drives, and other file-related devices on your computer. Windows Explorer enables you to locate files or folders; open them or run them if they are programs; and copy, move, rename, and delete them. Windows Explorer is the primary file-handling tool in Windows XP. It will be discussed more later in this module and again in Modules 3 and 4.

The three file folders (the top, third, and fourth icons from the top on the right) represent areas on your hard disk that are meant to hold files related to their name (documents, pictures, and music), but these are only suggestions and you can use them as you wish. Clicking one of the file folders opens that folder in Windows Explorer. The second icon from the top, My Recent Documents, opens a list of the most recent files of any type that you have used.

The My Computer icon displays the disk drives and highest-level folders on your computer, while My Network Places displays the shared disk drives and folders on other computers on the network to which your computer is connected. If you are not connected to a network or just started your computer for the first time, even if it is connected to a network, you will not see My Network Places until the computer has had a chance to look around the network and identify the shared resources. My Network Places is discussed further in Module 8.

System Management Programs

The bottom five icons on the right in the Start menu help you manage your computer and use its resources. The function of each is as follows:

- **Control Panel**, which you saw in Module 1, provides access to many of the settings that govern how most of the hardware and other components on the computer operate. This allows you to customize much of Windows and to locate and cure problems. The Control Panel is discussed in Modules 3, 10, and 14.

- **Printers And Faxes**, which is also in the Control Panel, allows you to set up and control how these devices operate and are shared with others. Printers are discussed further in Module 5. (If you are using Windows XP Home Edition, you will not see Printers And Faxes, but you can add it as discussed in Module 3.)

- **Help And Support** opens a window from which you can search for information on how to use a part of Windows XP, including a tutorial and a troubleshooting guide. From this window, you can also find information on the Microsoft Knowledge Base and how to get additional support. Help is discussed in more detail later in this module and in Module 10.

● **Search** allows you to search for files, folders, computers, people, and information on your computer, on your local area network (LAN), and on the Internet. You will read more about Search later in this module.

● **Run** allows you to type a command that opens a folder or a file, or starts a program or an Internet resource. Run is principally used to diagnose and cure problems. It is a throwback to the days of MS/PC-DOS when all commands were typed instead of selected from menus.

Using the Start Menu

Once the Start menu is open, you can initiate one of its options by moving the mouse pointer to it and clicking (pressing the left mouse button). As with the Start button, when you move the mouse pointer to an option it changes color and becomes selected, and if you don't immediately click, a little message box will appear that gives you information about the option you selected, like this:

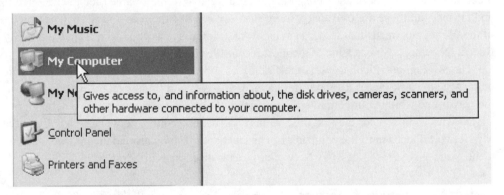

The Start menu can also be used with the keyboard. After opening the menu with either the WINDOWS key or CTRL-ESC, make sure NUM LOCK is turned off and then use the arrow keys (UP, DOWN, LEFT, RIGHT, HOME, END, PGUP, PGDN) to move the selection around the Start menu. When you reach the option, you want press ENTER.

Use either the mouse or the keyboard to open My Computer now.

Windows

Windows got its name because when you start a program or open a folder, the program or folder appears in a "window" on your screen, as does the My Computer window in Figure 2-4. You can have a number of windows open at one time, on top of one another or *tiled* so that you can see a small part of all open windows. A window can be quite small or completely fill the screen, and if it doesn't fill the screen it can be dragged around the screen.

A window has a number of features, each of which has a name and a specific function. In the balance of this book, we will refer to window features by name, so it is important to know what they are.

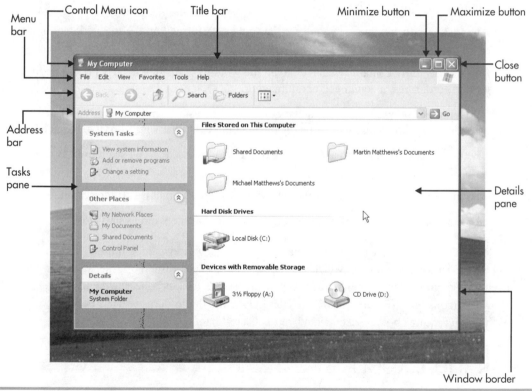

Figure 2-4 My Computer window on the Windows desktop

The following features are shown in Figure 2-4:

- The **title bar** contains the name of the program folder in the window and is used to drag the window around the screen.

- The **Control Menu icon** opens the Control menu, also called the System menu, for the window, which allows you to move, size, and close the window.

- The **menu bar** contains the menus that are available in the window.

- The **toolbar** contain tools related to the contents of the window. The toolbar is optional and might not be displayed.

- The **address bar** contains the path to reach the window's contents. The address bar is optional and might not be displayed.

- The **tasks pane** contains a list of tasks that can be performed on the selected item in the details pane. The tasks pane is optional and might not be displayed.

- The **details pane** contains whatever detail the window is displaying. This could be files, folders, programs, a document, or an image.

- The **window border** separates the window from the desktop and can be used to size the window either horizontally or vertically by dragging either the vertical or horizontal border.

- The **minimize button** decreases the size of the window so that you see it only as a task on the taskbar.

- The **maximize button** increases the size of the window so that it fills the screen.

- The **close button** shuts down any program contained in the window and closes it.

Not all windows have all of these features, and some windows look quite different. Figure 2-5 shows a window in which the address bar has been turned off, the status bar has been turned on, the tasks pane has been replaced with the folders pane, the details pane is shown in Icons view (Figure 2-4 was in Tiles view), and the folders pane has been sized such that it requires both horizontal and vertical scroll bars.

Ask the Expert

Q: **Why have a Control or System menu when you can do everything in it using the mouse?**

A: The Control menu is principally for use when you can't or don't want to use the mouse. You can open it by pressing ALT-SPACEBAR and then use the arrow keys and ENTER to select an option, all with the keyboard.

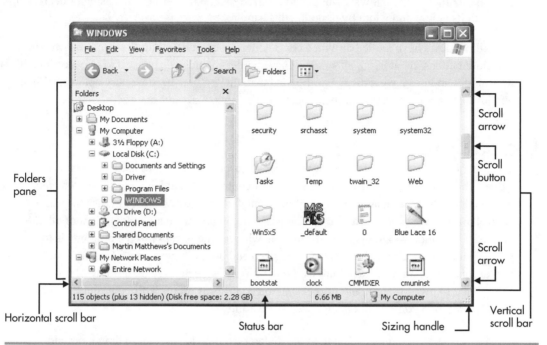

Figure 2-5 A folder window with different features displayed

The purposes of these additional features are as follows:

- The **folders pane** replaces the tasks pane and provides a hierarchical view of the disk drives and folders on the computer.

- The **horizontal scroll bar** allows moving the contents of the pane horizontally so that you can see information that isn't otherwise displayed.

- The **status bar** provides messages and information about what is displayed or selected in the window.

- The **vertical scroll bar** allows moving the contents of the pane vertically so that you can see information that isn't otherwise displayed. All scroll bars have three elements: *scroll arrows,* which when clicked move the window contents in small increments in the direction of the arrow; the *scroll bar* itself, which when clicked moves the contents in large increments; and a *scroll button,* which can be dragged in either direction to move the contents in that direction. The size of the scroll button is inversely proportional to the distance the contents can be moved.

- The **sizing handle** allows a window to be sized diagonally, either increasing or decreasing both its height and width by dragging this handle.

  All windows have a title bar with a control menu icon; a title; and the minimize, maximize, and close buttons. In addition, all windows have borders, which can be used to size the window. *Almost* all windows have a menu bar. Beyond that, the features become very optional. When windows are made smaller than their contents, they almost always have scroll bars.

Dialog Boxes

To gather detailed information for any number of purposes, Windows uses an object called a dialog box. A *dialog box* uses a common set of controls to enable you to select and enter information. There are a large number of different dialog boxes, but they all use the same controls. You have several ways to distinguish a dialog box from a window. First of all, the purpose of a window is to display information, whereas the purpose of a dialog box is to gather information. Dialog boxes cannot be sized and do not have a control menu icon, a menu bar, or minimize and maximize buttons. Figure 2-6 shows a dialog box used by Microsoft Word 2002 to print. It has many of the common controls as identified in the figure.

The common controls in dialog boxes are as follows:

- The **title bar** contains the name of the dialog box and is also used to drag it around the desktop.

- **Tabs** (not shown) enable you to select from among several pages in a dialog box.

- A **drop-down list box** opens a list of items from which you can choose one that is displayed when the list is closed.

- A **list box** (not shown) enables you to select one or more items from a list; it may include a scroll bar to move the list.

- **Option buttons**, also called *radio buttons,* enable you to select one among mutually exclusive options.

- A **text box** enables you to enter and edit text.

- **Command buttons** perform immediate functions such as closing the dialog box and accepting the changes (the OK button), or closing the dialog box and ignoring the changes (the Cancel button).

- A **spinner** enables you to continuously vary a number up or down.

- A **slider** (not shown) enables you to select from several values.

- **Check boxes** enable you to turn features on or off.

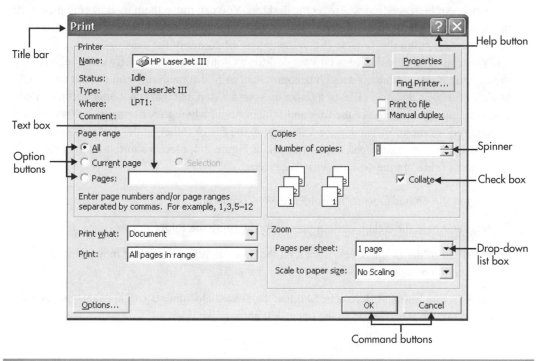

Figure 2-6 Sample dialog box with many of the standard controls

● The **Help button** changes the pointer to a question mark, which can be clicked on a feature to learn more about it.

You will have a great many opportunities to use dialog boxes, and for the most part, you can try out dialog boxes and see what happens; if you don't like it, you can come back and reverse the setting.

Icons and Shortcuts

The Recycle Bin on your screen is an icon. An *icon* is a small graphic representation of some Windows component: a program, a folder, or a file. The actual Recycle Bin is a folder on your hard disk. What you see on the screen is just a representation of that folder called a *shortcut*. Every time you delete something in Windows, it goes into this folder as a precaution, so if you change your mind, you can "undelete" it. When you are really sure you want to delete the items in the Recycle Bin, you can empty it by right-clicking it and choosing Empty Recycle Bin from the context menu that opens.

Icons can be placed anywhere on the desktop. You can move them by dragging them with the mouse (point at the icon and press and hold the mouse button while moving the mouse). Try this by dragging the Recycle Bin to the upper-left corner of the desktop.

You can have as many icons on your desktop as you want, although if you have too many, the desktop becomes cluttered and it becomes hard to find something. You can put an actual program file, or a document file, or a folder on your desktop, but that is not often recommended. The best approach is to leave the files and folders stored where they normally are (which may be required for programs) and place a shortcut to the file or folder on the desktop. Assuming that My Computer is still open as shown back in Figure 2-4, place a shortcut of the Shared Documents folder on the desktop with these steps:

1. Point at the Shared Documents folder in My Computer.

2. Press and hold the right mouse button while dragging the folder.

3. When the folder is where you want it on the desktop, release the right mouse button. A context menu will open.

4. Click Create Shortcut Here. The Shortcut To Shared Documents will appear. I moved mine up next to the Recycle Bin in the upper-left corner, like this:

In Module 3, you'll see other ways of getting some standard icons and other shortcuts on the desktop.

The Taskbar

The taskbar, which is by default at the bottom of the window, tells you which folders are currently open and what programs are currently running. You should see My Computer in the taskbar at this moment, telling you that My Computer is currently open. This is pretty obvious to you because it is the only thing open on your desktop. Double-click both the Recycle Bin and Shared Documents icons to open them and have three windows on your desktop. It is now not so easy to locate a particular window. On the taskbar, though, all three windows are very obvious, and you only need to click a task to have the corresponding window brought to the top of the stack and made available to you. The window that is on top of the stack and available to work in is called the *active* window. Its task on the taskbar is highlighted, as are the window's title bar and border, as you can see in Figure 2-7.

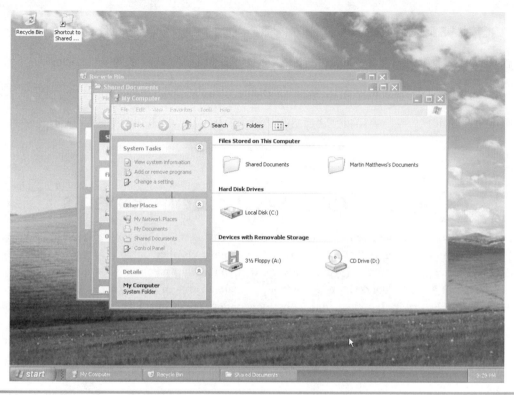

Figure 2-7 Several windows on the desktop and in the taskbar

In Module 3, you will see how you can move the taskbar around the screen and learn how you can use the notification area on the right of the taskbar and a currently closed area next to the Start menu called the Quick Launch toolbar.

Close the three open windows in three different ways with these steps:

1. In the top window, click the Control menu icon to open the menu and then click Close.

2. In the second window, click the File menu to open it and then click Close.

3. In the third window, click the Close button on the far right of the title bar.

It is not hard to see which of the three techniques is the easiest. You can also close an open window by pressing ALT-F4. When you close a window with a program running in that window, that program is terminated.

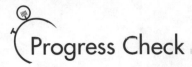

Progress Check

1. What does "right-click" mean?

2. How can you open the Start menu from the keyboard?

3. How can you see information in a window when the window is not large enough?

CRITICAL SKILL

2.3 Use Major Windows XP Components

You saw earlier in the discussion of the Start menu that it is the doorway to Windows XP and all its components, as well as all the programs you have installed on your computer. To start any programs, you must, at least initially, go though the Start menu. In Module 3, you'll see how to put icons on the desktop and in the quick launch area of the taskbar so that you can also start programs from those locations without opening the Start menu. In this module, though, we'll stick to the Start menu.

In the earlier Start menu discussion, you started My Computer by clicking My Computer in the Start menu. You can start any program or open any folder on the Start menu by simply clicking the associated icon.

Often opening a folder or starting a program on the Start menu is only the first step to get where you eventually want to go. See how that works with three examples that look at the Control Panel, the Programs menus, and Windows Explorer in more depth. The purpose in all three cases is to learn how to find your way around Windows and accomplish what you want to do. The actual exploration and explanation of these Windows components is left to future modules.

CRITICAL SKILL

2.4 Use the Control Panel

You'll remember that the Control Panel provides access to many of the system management functions in Windows XP. This enables you to customize much of Windows and to locate

---

1. Point at an object and press and release the right mouse button. This will usually open a context menu that allows you to do things to an object.

2. Press either the WINDOWS key or CTRL-ESC.

3. In two ways: by enlarging the window through dragging either the borders or the sizing handle or by using the scroll bars to move the contents in the window.

and cure problems. Here, let's look at how you get to two of these management functions: to change the appearance and change the time.

Changing the Appearance

Using the Control Panel, locate and explore the dialog boxes to change the appearance of Windows XP with these steps:

1. Open the Start menu and click Control Panel. The Control Panel will open in Category view, as you can see here.

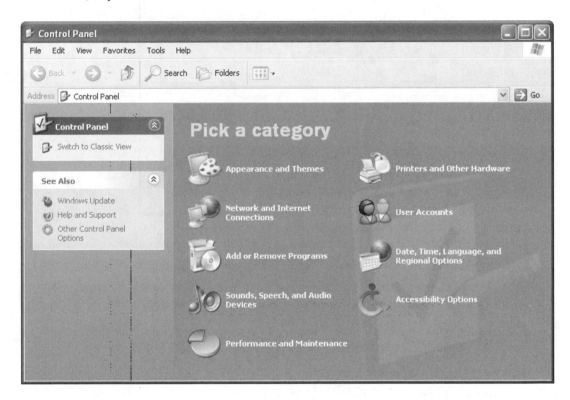

2. Click Appearance And Themes. The Appearance And Themes window will open.

3. Click the Display Control Panel icon near the bottom of the window. The Display Properties dialog box will open like this:

4. Click the Desktop tab at the top of the dialog box. In the Background list, use the scroll bar and click several of the backgrounds to see them in the preview screen above the list.

5. Click the Settings tab. The Screen Resolution control is a slider that was not displayed earlier in the module when we were talking about dialog box controls.

6. Click Cancel to close the Display Properties dialog box without making any changes. In Module 3, you'll see how to change your display characteristics.

Changing Time

Again with the Control Panel, see how to set the time in Windows XP:

1. Back in the Appearance And Themes window, click Back on the left of the toolbar. This returns to the original Category display of the Control Panel.

2. Click Date, Time, Language, And Regional Options. The Date, Time, Language, And Regional Options window will open.

3. Click the Date And Time icon near the bottom of the window. The Date And Time Properties dialog box will open, as you can see next. This allows you to manually change the date and time.

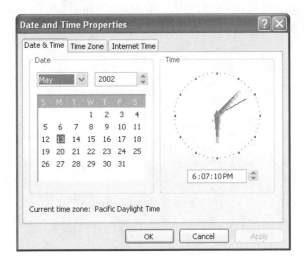

4. Click the Internet Time tab. This allows you to synchronize the clock on your computer with an Internet time source. If you know you are currently connected to the Internet, click Update Now.

5. Click OK to close the Date And Time Properties dialog box and keep the time synchronization. Click the Close button on the Date, Time, Language, And Regional Options window.

Here you have seen how to go in through the Control Panel, locate the area you want to work in, and find and adjust the settings you want to change.

CRITICAL SKILL
2.5 Use the Programs Menu

Several programs are on the Start menu, and as you use others, they will go onto the list of your six most frequently used programs. If a program is not on the Start menu, you must find it some other way. This is the function of the Programs menu opened with the All Programs button. Use this to see how to open the Character Map accessory and how to start the FreeCell Game.

Opening the Character Map

The Character Map allows you to identify a special character not on the normal keyboard and copy it to a document you are preparing. It is particularly useful if you are writing in a language other than English. Here are the steps to open the Character Map, locate the bullet character, and copy it to the clipboard:

1. Open the Start menu and point to the All Programs button. The Programs menu will open, like this:

2. Move the mouse pointer up to Accessories in the Programs menu. The Accessories menu will open.

3. Move the mouse pointer down to System Tools in the Accessories menu. The System Tools menu will open.

NOTE

The series of menus All Programs, Accessories, and System Tools is called a *cascading menu;* Figure 2-8 shows an example. In future sets of instructions, I will abbreviate the preceding set of steps as: Open Start and choose Programs | Accessories | System Tools.

4. Move the mouse pointer down to Character Map in the System Tools menu and finally click. The Character Map will open.

Figure 2-8 Cascading menu

5. Make sure the Arial font is selected. If it isn't, click the arrow in the drop-down list box to open the list, scroll to the top, and click Arial.

6. Scroll down the set of characters about two-thirds of the way until you can see the bullet character between the double-dagger and the ellipsis (when you move the mouse pointer to it, you will see "U+2022: Bullet" in the status bar, as shown in Figure 2-9.

7. Select the bullet character and then click Copy. The character will copied to the clipboard. In most Windows programs, you can identify the location in which you want the character,

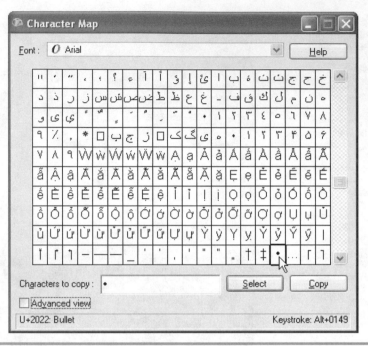

Figure 2-9 The Character Map with the bullet

open the Edit menu, and choose Paste; the special character will then be placed in the spot you identified.

8. Click Close to close the Character Map.

Starting a FreeCell Game

FreeCell is a totally addictive solitaire card game that you play on the computer. The first time your boss catches you playing it at work, you can tell him that I said that it is a wonderful way to practice using the mouse. I'll privately tell you that it is also a wonderful way to blow a lot of time! Here are the steps to open FreeCell and start playing:

1. Open Start and choose Programs | Games | FreeCell (before clicking FreeCell, note the many other games that are available to you, as shown next). The game board will open.

2. Click the Game menu and then click New Game. A deck of cards will be spread out. The objective is to get the complete set of cards in each of the four suites (clubs, diamonds, hearts, and spades) in order from ace to king in the *home cells* in the upper right. To do this, you may temporarily place up to four cards in the *free cells* in the upper left. You may also temporarily place a card on the next highest card of the opposite color in the stacks at the bottom.

3. To move a card, click it and then click where you want it to go. If it is not a legal move, you will be told that. If you get an empty column at the bottom, it is valuable because you can build your own sequence in it.

The secret is to think several moves in the future and never fill up the free cells without having a way to empty them. The game is lost if you have no moves left and haven't gotten all the cards to the home cells. Figure 2-10 shows a game that I have played for a few minutes and is all but won. I have only to move the cards to the home cells. When all your cards are in order, they will be moved to the home cells automatically and you will be told you won.

4. When you are done playing, click Close and then Yes to "resign" from the game if you did not win!

CRITICAL SKILL
2.6 Use Windows Explorer

The Start and Programs menus give you access to most of the programs on your computer, but if you are looking for a data file (a text file, a photographic image, or a piece of music), they

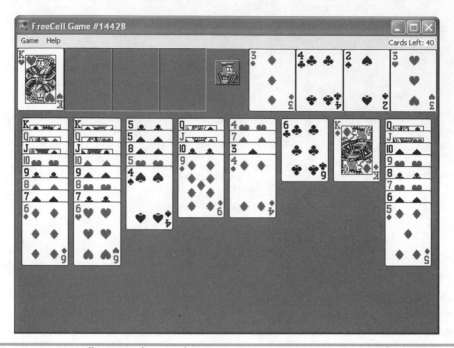

Figure 2-10 A FreeCell game about to be won

won't be in these two menus unless they are in My Recent Documents. To find a document like this, you need to use Windows Explorer. Windows XP gives you five ways (My Documents, My Pictures, My Music, My Computer, and My Network Places) to open Windows Explorer in the upper right of the Start menu (only four ways if you are not connected to a network). Three of the ways, My Documents, My Pictures, and My Music, open specific folders, while My Network Places lets you look for a file on other computers on your network. My Computer opens looking at all the storage devices on your computer, as you saw earlier in this module. As a matter of fact, you can get to any file on your computer or network (given that you have been access privileges) from any of the four or five Start menu options. The only difference is where you start out.

   Use the following set of steps to look at how information is stored on your computer and how Windows Explorer is used to locate and access that information:

1. Open the Start menu and choose My Computer. Windows Explorer will open and display the My Computer window that you saw in Figure 2-4 earlier in this module.

2. Click Folders in the toolbar. The tasks pane on the left of the window will be replaced with the folders pane.

The folders pane shows the hierarchy of storage on your computer and enables you to "drill down" to find a particular file. At the top level, you have the computer's desktop. Beneath that you have My Documents, My Computer, and My Network Places. To the left of My Documents and My Network Places there should be a plus sign in a square. Next to My Computer you should see a minus sign in a square, and beneath My Computer should be the disk drives on your computer, as well as the top-level folders, like this:

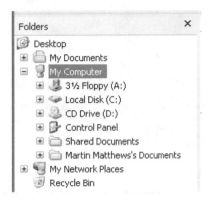

3. Click the plus sign next to My Documents. The plus sign becomes a minus sign, and three folders appear beneath My Documents.

4. Click the plus sign next to Local Disk (C:). Again, several folders will open beneath Local Disk (C:). In sequence, click the plus signs next to Documents And Settings, your username, and My Documents that is under the username. You will see the same folders that were in the My Documents under the Desktop. In fact, the two are the same. The My Documents under the desktop is just a shortcut to the My Documents under your username, as shown in Figure 2-11.

5. Scroll down the folders pane until you see your username Documents. Click the plus sign and you will see the three subsidiary folders to My Documents. Once more, these are shortcuts to the folder under Documents and Settings.

6. Click Close on Windows Explorer.

NOTE

Clicking the plus sign next to a folder is called "opening the folder" because it shows the folders beneath it. Similarly, clicking the minus sign is called "closing the folder."

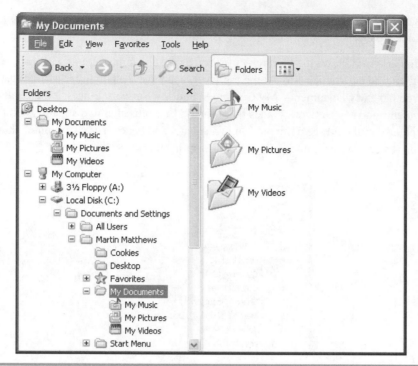

Figure 2-11 My Documents under the Desktop is a shortcut to My Documents on the Local Disk.

In Module 4, you'll see how to work with your storage system in much more detail, including how to make shortcuts and decide where you want information stored.

Ask the Expert

Q: Why have so many "copies" of My Documents and its subsidiary folders?

A: First of all, there is only one copy of My Documents; it is on your hard disk under Documents and Settings. The other "copies" are just shortcuts to the original. The shortcuts make it easier and faster to get to the files stored on these folders.

Progress Check

1. How would you change the appearance of the desktop?

2. How do you open the Character Map?

3. What do you use in Windows Explorer to get the hierarchical view of your computer in the left pane?

Project 2 Using Help

Windows XP has built within it a substantial amount of documentation that you can use to determine how to accomplish a particular task. This is called Help or Windows Help. In this project, you will open Help and become familiar with how to use it.

Step by Step

1. Open the Start menu and click Help And Support. The Help And Support Center window will open like the one in Figure 2-12. This lets you read information on a particular topic, search for information based on keywords you enter, get online assistance, or perform a remedial task.

2. Click Windows Basics under Help Topics, click Core Windows Tasks, and then click Working With Programs. A list of tasks for working with programs will be displayed.

3. Click Start A Program. Steps and notes related to starting a program will be displayed, as shown in the next illustration.

---

1. Open Start, click Control Panel, choose Appearance And Themes, click Display, and then click the Desktop tab. You'll see a faster way in Module 3.

2. Open Start and choose Programs | Accessories | System Tools | Character Map.

3. The Folders button in the toolbar will do this.

To start a program

- Click **Start**, and then click the program you want to open. To open a program you do not see on the **Start** menu, point to **All Programs**, and then navigate through the menus to the program you want and click it. When you open the program, Windows automatically displays it on the **Start** menu.

✏ **Notes**

- After you start a program, a button representing the program appears on the taskbar. To switch from one running program to another, click its taskbar button.

- If a program does not appear on the **Start** menu or one of its submenus, you can perform a search for it. For more information, click **Related Topics**.

4. Click Back in the toolbar until you get back to the Help And Support Center home page. In the Search text box, type **find files** and click the Search arrow. After a moment, the search results will appear with 15 topics, 15 full-text matches, and 15 matches from the Microsoft Knowledge Base.

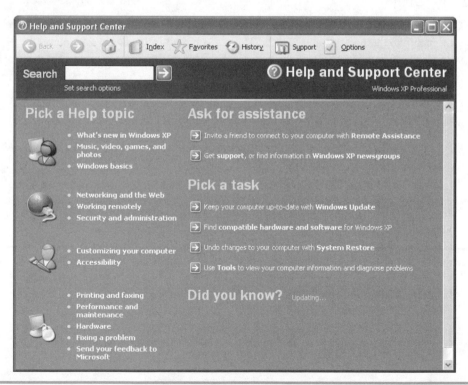

Figure 2-12 Windows XP Help And Support Center window

5. Using the scroll bar, look through the Suggested Topics; then click Full-Text Search Matches, look at its listings, and finally click Microsoft Knowledge Base and review the entries there.

6. Return to Suggested Topics and under Overviews, Articles, And Tutorials, click Using My Computer. After looking at those results, click Using Windows Explorer. Note this gives you considerably more information.

7. Click Full Text Search Matches and click Searching For Files And Folders. This provides the best information yet on our topic.

8. Click Index on the toolbar and in the text box that opens, type **Searching for files and folders**, click Overview, and click Display. The same information that was displayed in the preceding step is again displayed, as you can see in Figure 2-13.

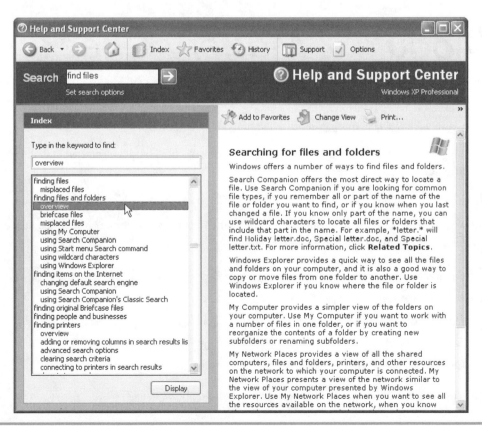

Figure 2-13 Detailed information on a particular topic

9. Click Close to close the Help And Support Center. If you are done with your computer for a while, shut it down by opening the Start menu, clicking Turn Off Computer, and then clicking Turn Off.

Project Summary

Windows Help provides a substantial amount of information and a number of ways to locate it. It is often helpful when you finally find exactly what you want, but just as often it is frustrating locating it. Persistence is the key.

The tools that Windows XP gives you to start, navigate to, and use its many components, as well as your programs and files, are very powerful and generally easy to use. Don't be discouraged if it seems like you are trying to take a drink from a fire hose. Keep using Windows XP, referring back here as often as needed. In time, it will become familiar. Again, persistence is the key.

✓ Module 2 Mastery Check

1. When you first turn on the computer, the computer goes through an initial startup procedure and there may be a beep. What is this sequence called and what does it do?

2. If your network is using a domain, what do you have to do to log on?

3. What are two different ways to temporarily stop using the computer, and what is the difference between them?

4. What does "hibernate" mean?

5. What mouse action would you use in each of the following situations? Match the task on the left to the correct mouse action on the right.

Open a folder or start a program.	Drag
Move the mouse to an object.	Click
Move an object around the desktop.	Double-click
Select an object.	Right-click
Open a context or shortcut menu.	Point

6. Is the illustration in question 7 a window or a dialog box? Why?

7. In the illustration, to what does each of the numbers point (match the numbers and the objects)?

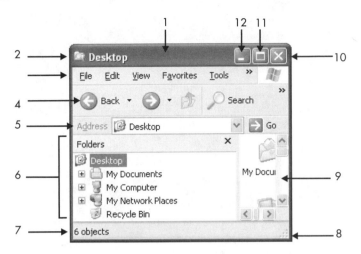

1	Close button
2	Status bar
3	Minimize button
4	Scroll bar
5	Maximize button
6	Sizing handle
7	Control menu icon
8	Folders pane
9	Toolbar
10	Title bar
11	Address bar
12	Menu bar

8. What is meant by the term "cascading menus" and what is an example of one?

9. What are three or four ways you can open Windows Explorer?

10. In Windows Explorer, what do you accomplish when you click the plus or minus sign in the folders pane?

Module 3

Customizing Windows XP

Windows XP is extremely flexible. It can take on many different personas and operate in many different ways. Windows comes with a default setup that many people are happy enough with that they never try anything else. If you take the time, though, you can explore, and utilize if you wish, numerous alternative settings for most of the components in Windows. In this module, you'll look at a number those alternatives and learn how they can be utilized. We'll start with the screen, looking at the Start menu, the desktop, the taskbar, and file folders. Then we'll discuss the different ways Windows can operate with the mouse, keyboard, and sound. Finally, we'll look at the ways Windows XP can compensate for physical disabilities with its accessibility options.

CRITICAL SKILL
3.1 # Customize the Screen and the Start Menu

You spend a lot of your time in front of your computer looking at the basic Windows screen and utilizing its components. It is therefore important that this be as pleasant an experience as possible. We all have different tastes, so Microsoft has built in a number of options for how features look and operate. It is up to you to choose what you like. Do that now in four different screen components, the Start menu, the desktop, the taskbar, and file folders.

As was said in Module 2, the Start menu is the principal way that you access most of the capabilities in Windows XP. You should be able to do that in ways that are easy for you. You can change how the Start menu looks and what it contains.

Change How the Start Menu Looks

You can do two things to change how the Start menu looks. You can change it back to look like a classic Start menu, as was used by Windows 98 (shown in Figure 3-1), and you can switch between large (the default) and small icons. To see how to do both of these, use the following steps:

1. If necessary, start your computer and log on. When ready, right-click the Start button and choose Properties in the context menu. The Taskbar And Start Menu Properties dialog box will open.

2. If the Start Menu page is not selected, click its tab. Here you can choose between the Windows XP–style Start menu and the Classic Start menu.

 NOTE

When you turn on the Classic Start menu, you also turn on some desktop icons, some of which are shown in Figure 3-1. You can also turn these icons on without the Classic Start menu, as you'll see in the discussion of the desktop later in this module.

3. Even if you are pretty sure you don't want the Classic Start menu, select that option just to look at it in the dialog box. If you don't want it (which is what I assume here), click Start Menu to return to the original menu.

4. Click Customize. The Customize Start Menu dialog box opens, as you can see in Figure 3-2. The General tab should be open (if not, click it). At the top you should see the choice between Large Icons (the default) and Small Icons. The small icons allow you to show more in a smaller area.

NOTE

Changing to small icons affects only the left side of the Start menu.

5. If you wish, choose Small Icons. If you want to see what your changes look like, click OK in both the Customize Start Menu and Taskbar And Start Menu Properties dialog boxes and then open the Start menu.

6. If you opened the Start menu, close it by clicking the desktop and reopen the Taskbar And Start Menu Properties dialog box, if necessary click the Start Menu tab, and click Customize.

Figure 3-1 The Classic Start menu

Figure 3-2 Customizing the Start menu

Change What Start Contains

Windows XP gives you a lot of choices on what is included in the Start menu. First of all, as you can see in the Customize Start Menu General tab, which should still be open on your screen, you can determine the number (between 0 and 30) of recent programs that are displayed on the Start menu. You can also select both whether to show Internet programs and what they are, so that they start when clicked as your browser and mail handler, as shown in Figure 3-2.

NOTE

In the General tab of the Customize Start Menu dialog box, you can clear the list of recent programs, allowing you to start over with the current programs you are using.

In the Advanced tab, you can select what programs are shown on the right side of the Start menu (see Figure 3-3) as described in the next set of steps (this assumes that you have Customize Start Menu still open on the screen):

1. Click the Advanced tab. In the middle of the dialog box, you'll see a list box headed Start Menu Items.

2. Scroll this list; you'll see everything on the right side of the menu except Recent Documents, which is handled immediately below the list box.

3. As you look down, ask yourself how often you use each item. If you are not connected to a network, you are not going to use My Network Places. Also consider that My Computer, My Documents, My Pictures, My Music, and My Network Places all open Windows Explorer, just with different contents in the details pane. You may want to remove one or more of these to reduce clutter.

4. As an example, scroll down to My Documents and choose Display As A Menu. Scroll further down to My Music and choose Don't Display This Item. Scroll down once more to My Pictures and again choose Don't Display This Item.

5. When you have made the changes to the list, click OK twice to close the two dialog boxes. Then open the Start menu to see how it looks. If you don't like the results, reopen the properties and Customize dialog boxes and return the items you changed to their original settings.

If you made the changes suggested in Step 4, you can see the difference between Display As A Link and Display As A Menu. When you select an item to be displayed as a link, it opens the item in a new Windows Explorer window. When you select an item to be displayed

Figure 3-3 Selecting items to display on the Start menu

as a menu, the items that would have been displayed in the window are now displayed as menu options on a subsidiary menu to the Start menu. So if you make the changes in Step 4, open the Start menu, and click My Documents, instead of opening Windows Explorer, this little menu opens off to the right of the Start menu:

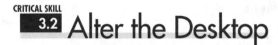

CRITICAL SKILL
3.2 Alter the Desktop

The desktop occupies most of the screen, and depending on your likes and dislikes, this can be a very plain, clean area, or it can have one or more pictures and be cluttered with icons. It can have a solid color background, or you can apply one of a number of themes. In addition, you can determine if you want a screen saver and what it will look like, and the style, color, and font used to create windows, dialog boxes, and buttons. Most of the time for most people, the desktop is hidden by windows and dialog boxes that are open. You need to determine how important the look of the desktop is to you.

In the following sections, you'll learn what you can do to change the theme and background of the desktop, how to add icons to it, how to change and set up a screen saver, how to change the look of Window's components, and finally how to change the screen resolution and color quality. All of these changes are handled through the Display Properties dialog box shown in Figure 3-4. You can open the Display Properties dialog box in two ways:

● Open the Start menu and click Control Panel. In Category view, click Appearance And Themes, and then click Display. In Classic view, double-click Display.

● Right-click the desktop and choose Properties.

The second method is easier but less intuitive.

Change the Theme

A theme is a collection of specifications for all the other characteristics that you can set for the desktop and the screen. It includes the background, the screen saver, and the look of Windows's components. When you choose a theme, you choose all of the characteristics that go with it. After you choose a theme, you can still change any of details and have a modified theme, which can be saved as a new one. Windows XP comes with two themes, Windows XP and Windows Classic. The Windows XP theme is the one you have been looking at since installing Windows XP. Windows Classic is the look of Windows 98/Me. Microsoft sells

Figure 3-4 Changing your Windows visual experience

additional themes in Microsoft Plus! for Windows XP, which you can learn about by selecting More Themes Online. See how to change themes, look at Plus!, and change backgrounds with these steps:

1. Use one of the above methods, such as right-clicking the desktop and choosing Properties, to open the Display Properties dialog box. The Themes tab should be open; if not, click it.

2. Click the arrow to open the drop-down list under Theme. You'll see the list of available themes. My Current Theme is the combination of settings that have produced whatever you are currently looking at on your desktop.

3. Click Windows Classic, and you will see what that looks like in the preview window. Reopen the drop-down list and click More Themes Online. If can connect or are connected to the Internet, your browser will open and display the Microsoft Windows Plus! site. Click Themes and scroll down the page to see the four themes that are available with that add-on package.

4. Close your browser and reselect Windows XP in the drop-down list to keep that theme for the balance of the exercises here. If you want, you can change this later.

NOTE

After you make changes in the areas that follow, you can come back to the Themes tab and save the sum of your changes as a new theme by clicking Save As, giving the theme a name, and clicking Save.

Change the Background

The background occupies most of the desktop. It can be any color you wish it to be, it can be any of several background images that come with Windows XP, or it can be any image that you have. The theme includes a background, but after selecting a theme, you can pick a different background and create a modified theme. If you then go back and reselect the original theme, the background will be changed back to what is in the theme. See how to change the background by itself next:

1. If the Display Properties dialog box is not still open, open it by right-clicking the desktop and choosing Properties.

2. Click the Desktop tab to open that page of the dialog box. On the left is a list of background images that come with Windows XP. When you click one of the images, it appears in the little monitor (called a preview window) at the top of the dialog box.

3. Click several or even all of the images in the list box to see how they look in the preview window. (Be patient—depending on the speed of your computer, it can take several seconds before they appear.) If you see one you particularly like, click OK to see it on your full screen and then reopen the Display Properties dialog box to the Desktop page.

4. If you have your own digital pictures (either from a digital camera or scanned in from prints) that you would like to use, click Browse, click the arrow in the Look In drop-down list and select the drive and folder path leading to the folder containing the image you want, and then double-click the image. (This process in a Browse dialog box is called "navigate to and select....")

5. Open the Position drop-down list. You'll see three choices: Center, Tile, and Stretch. Stretch, which is on by default, takes an image and stretches it to fit the screen. Center places an image in the center of the screen in its natural size. Tile takes a small image and places enough copies of it to fill the screen. If you have a pattern that you want to use as a background, tiling it works well. Generally for photographic images, you use either center or stretch, depending on whether stretching distorts the picture.

6. Select the position you want to use and open the Color pallet. This is the color of the background if you don't have any other image on the screen. If you have another image, this color is still present but covered up except for the background of the icon captions, which should go well with the image.

7. Select the background color you want to use, click Customize Desktop, and then click the Web tab. This lets you use an active (changing daily) web page as your desktop image. You can manually update this page at any time by choosing Synchronize, and in the Properties dialog box, you can set the schedule for automatic updating and how much of the page and its links and related programs to use.

8. If you want to use your current home page (which is determined in your Internet browser, which is discussed in Module 6), click the check box under Web Pages. You can select other pages by clicking New and entering a URL in the Location text box (for example: http://www.cnn.com) or by clicking Visit Gallery and selecting one of several Active Desktop items, including a stock ticker, live information from CBS SportsLine, and live weather information. You can also browse for static web pages that are stored on your computer.

9. If you want to use a web page for your desktop, select it. If you opened your web browser to do this, close it and close any open dialog boxes. This should display the desktop image(s) you have chosen. If this isn't what you want, reopen the Display Properties dialog box and repeat this set of steps.

Probably whatever you choose for your desktop image, you will want to change it sooner or later, and you can do so easily with these steps. I personally like to use my photographs, and I change them regularly.

Add Icons

There are two distinct beliefs about desktop icons. One (Microsoft's) is that desktop icons are just clutter and anything you can do with desktop icons you can do better with the Start menu. The other (mine) is that they are very handy for quickly starting programs you use often; I have 36 of them on my desktop (Microsofties would snicker). There are two types of icons you can place on the desktop: standard icons like My Computer and Internet Explorer, and other icons for your applications and files or folders. You can put anything on the desktop that you think you want to get to quickly.

Standard Icons

Windows XP, following Microsoft's philosophy, comes with only one standard icon, the Recycle Bin, on the desktop. Gone are the standard icons that in earlier versions were by default on the desktop, such as My Computer, My Documents, Internet Explorer, and My Network Places. If you believe as I do that these icons are worth placing on your desktop, you can do so with the next set of steps:

1. Reopen the Display Properties dialog box as you have done earlier, click the Desktop tab, and click Customize Desktop. The Desktop Items dialog box will open, as you can see in Figure 3-5. Here you can add the four standard desktop icons, as well as change their appearance.

2. For the sake of example, click My Documents, My Computer, and Internet Explorer to turn them on and place the icons on the desktop.

3. Again for an example, click the My Computer icon and click Change Icon. You see a set of alternative icons you can choose. If you want to, click an alternative icon and click OK.

Figure 3-5 Selecting standard icons to place on the desktop

4. Back in the Desktop Items dialog box click OK and then click it again in the Display Properties dialog box. The icons should appear on your desktop like this:

Other Desktop Icons

Besides the standard desktop icons, you can also have other icons on your desktop for any program, file, or folder that you want to load quickly. The key to doing this is to find the programs. For example, place icons for Outlook Express and Microsoft Word (or any programs you have) on the desktop. See how next:

1. Double-click My Computer on your desktop (see how easy that is?). Click Folders in the toolbar and open, by clicking the plus sign: Local Disk (C:) | Program Files. Then click Outlook Express.

2. Drag the Msimn.exe (you may not see the .exe) file to the desktop. When you have completed this, an icon will appear on the desktop with a curved arrow in it and the caption "Shortcut to msimn," as you can see next. This *shortcut* is not the program itself, but rather a pointer to the program that allows to start the program remotely. You can have a number of shortcuts to a single program so that you can start the program in many different places. The icons on the Start menu are shortcuts.

3. Right-click the caption for the shortcut you just placed on the desktop and choose Rename. Type **Outlook Express** and press ENTER. The shortcut will be renamed.

4. In the Windows Explorer window, locate the Microsoft Word program (Winword.exe) in C:\Program Files\Microsoft Office\Office10\ for Word 2002. Drag this file to the desktop, and another shortcut will be created.

5. Click slowly twice on the caption for the Microsoft Word icon (don't double-click), type **Word**, and press ENTER. (Note this second way to change a caption.)

6. If you want to delete one of the standard icons, repeat the steps in the preceding section and uncheck the top check boxes.

7. If you want to delete an icon you have dragged to the dektop, click the icon to select it and press DELETE. Alternatively, you can drag the icon to the Recycle Bin. In either case, the icon will end up in the Recycle Bin; you can permanently delete it by right-clicking the Recycle Bin and clicking Empty Recycle Bin. For example, delete the Shortcut to Shared Documents that you put on the desktop in an earlier module by dragging it to the Recycle Bin and then emptying it.

When you are done, you should have these icons on your desktop:

Change the Screen Saver

A *screen saver* is an image that comes on the screen when the computer is turned on but unused for a period of time. The screen saver image moves around the screen, so that no one area has the same image on it for a long period of time, which can permanently burn a ghost of the image onto the screen. Windows XP comes with a number of screen savers, and you can buy additional ones from several sources, including Windows XP Plus! from Microsoft. By default, the standard Windows XP screen saver is turned on. In the same area as the screen saver, you can also control whether the computer automatically shuts down when it is not being used. Here's how to change the screen saver and control the power features:

1. Open the Display Properties dialog box and click the Screen Saver tab. The page will open as shown in Figure 3-6.

2. Open the drop-down list and look at the alternatives in the preview windows. If one looks interesting to you, click Preview to see it full screen. One of my favorites is My Pictures

Slideshow. This displays the pictures you have in the My Pictures folder (C:\Documents and Settings*username*\My Documents\My Pictures).

3. Once you have chosen a screen saver, there may be several settings that you can change, depending on the screen saver. For example, if you choose the My Pictures screen saver, you can determine how long each picture is on the screen, how big the pictures are, where the pictures are located, and so forth. Click Settings and see for yourself. When you are done, click OK.

4. One setting that is in the main Display Properties dialog box is the time to wait before turning on the screen saver and whether to require a password to start using the computer after the screen saver has come on. You want the time to be long enough that you are not constantly going out to your screen saver and short enough not to damage your screen. This time will differ depending on your needs.

5. Click the Power button. The Power Options Properties dialog box will open showing the power settings that are available. These are particularly important if you are using a laptop with battery settings, as shown in Figure 3-7. With a laptop there are two extra tabs, Alarms and Power Meter. Look through the power settings that you have available, make the changes that are correct for you, and then click OK to close the Power Options Properties dialog box.

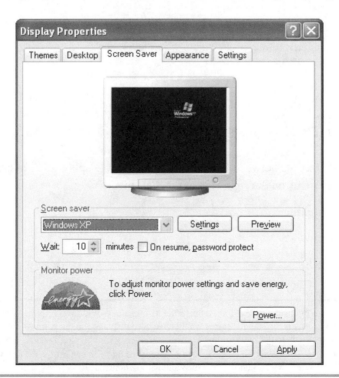

Figure 3-6 Changing the screen saver and power settings

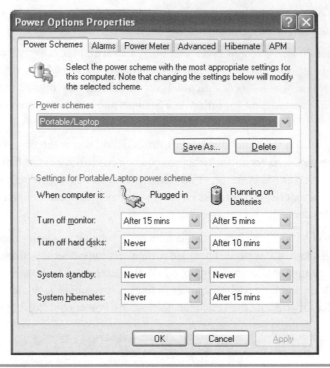

Figure 3-7 Power settings for a laptop

Progress Check

1. What is the difference between Display As A Link and Display As A Menu in determining how to display items on the right side of the Start menu?

2. What is a desktop theme?

3. What is a shortcut?

1. When you select an item to be displayed as a link, it opens the item in a new Windows Explorer window. When you select an item to be displayed as a menu, the items that would have been displayed in the window are now displayed as menu options on a subsidiary menu to the Start menu.

2. A theme is a collection of specifications for all the other characteristics that you can set for the desktop and the screen. It includes the background, the screen saver, and the look of Windows components.

3. A shortcut is not the program itself, but rather a pointer to the program that allows you to start the program remotely.

Change the Look of Windows Components

Buttons, dialog boxes, and windows have a shape or style and a color, and they display text in a certain font. You can change these settings in the Appearance tab of the Display Properties dialog box. Do that next:

1. Click the Appearance tab in the Display Properties dialog box. The default is of course the Windows XP style, but open the Windows And Buttons drop-down list and select Windows Classic Style to see what it looks like in the preview window.

2. Leaving Windows Classic style for a minute, open the Color Scheme drop-down list. You can see a number of options. Try several of the options to see the different colors.

3. Open the Font Size drop-down list and note the three sizes. Large and Extra Large are helpful if you are having difficulty reading the screen.

4. Reopen the Windows And Buttons drop-down list and return to Windows XP style. Look at the Color Scheme drop-down list and see only three choices. Look also at the Font Size and see the same three choices, although here they are called "Large Fonts" and "Extra Large Fonts," whereas in Windows Classic style they are called just "Large" and "Extra Large." (You think maybe Microsoft made a mistake—nah, couldn't be!)

5. Click Effects to open the dialog box of that name. Here you will see a list of special effects that are or can be used with default settings for Windows XP in place. Make any changes that you want and click OK.

6. Click Advanced to open the Advanced Appearance dialog box. You can click objects in the preview window or select them from the Item drop-down list and then change their size, color, font, font size, and font color, as well as whether the font is bold and or italic. Open the Item drop-down list to see the many items that make up components on a Windows screen. Make the changes you desire and click OK.

NOTE

In older versions of Windows, you could make changes to the Windows elements and save them under a new name; in XP you create and save a theme.

Change the Screen Resolution and Color Quality

The final bit of customization that you can do to the desktop actually changes the entire screen by changing the screen resolution (the number of pixels displayed on the screen) and the color quality (the size of the color field, which determines the number of colors available). What you can do here depends on your hardware. The size and quality of your monitor and the capability of your video adapter (the board in your computer that drives the monitor) determine the resolutions and color qualities that are available to you.

Generally speaking, the larger the monitor, the higher the resolution. If you have a 15-inch cathode ray tube (CRT, as used in televisions) monitor most people feel that the 800×600 resolution is the maximum acceptable. If you have a 17-inch CRT or a 15-inch flat panel, you can normally go to 1024×768. I also use 1024×768 on a 14.1-inch flat panel in my laptop, where text is a little small, but readable.

The color quality can be 8-bit, 16-bit, or 32-bit (newer cards may be only 16- and 32-bit), representing the size of the field that specifies the color to be displayed. Obviously, the larger the color field, the more data that has to be pushed around, taking memory space and time. Therefore, even if your hardware can handle 32-bit color, you may not want to use it unless precise color is important to you.

The Troubleshoot button opens the Help window and leads you through a troubleshooting session for your display. This is useful if you have display problems. The Advanced button opens a dialog box with settings specific to your monitor and video adapter. Most often, the settings in this dialog box are not something you want to change. They are set during installation, and if they are not correct, you need to uninstall the hardware drivers and reinstall them, not make changes here.

Make any changes you want in the Settings tab and then click OK to close the Display Properties dialog box.

CRITICAL SKILL
3.3 Tailor the Taskbar

The taskbar, which is normally at the bottom of the screen, is really quite flexible. You can drag it to any side (left, right, top, or bottom) of the screen, you can change its size, you can add toolbars to it, you can change several characteristics of the taskbar, and you can change some things about the notification area on the right. Experiment with the taskbar using these steps:

1. Point at the middle of the taskbar and drag it to the right side of the screen. Point at the left edge of the taskbar and drag it to the left a bit so that you can see the full day and date. This works quite well with Internet Explorer at 1024×768 resolution, as you can see in Figure 3-8. It may not work so well with a word-processing application.

2. Drag the taskbar back to the bottom of the screen. Right-click the taskbar and select Properties. The Taskbar And Start Menu Properties dialog box opens, showing the settings you can make on the taskbar (see Figure 3-8). The meaning of the Taskbar Appearance items is as follows:

   ● **Lock The Taskbar** prevents it from being dragged and prevents the Quick Launch toolbar, if present, from being sized.

- **Auto-Hide The Taskbar** causes the taskbar to disappear, popping up only when you move the mouse pointer to the bottom of the screen.

- **Keep The Taskbar On Top Of Other Windows** causes the taskbar to always be visible. It cannot be covered up by other windows.

- **Group Similar Toolbar Buttons** causes several buttons from one program to be shown on the taskbar as a single button with the number of buttons it represents. When you move the mouse over it, the individual buttons pop up.

- **Show Quick Launch** causes the Quick Launch toolbar to be displayed in the taskbar. The Quick Launch toolbar should contain the programs you use most often. By default, this includes Internet Explorer, a Show Desktop program that minimizes all of the open windows on the desktop so that you can see the icons that are there, and Windows Media Player. You can add your own programs, as you'll see in a bit.

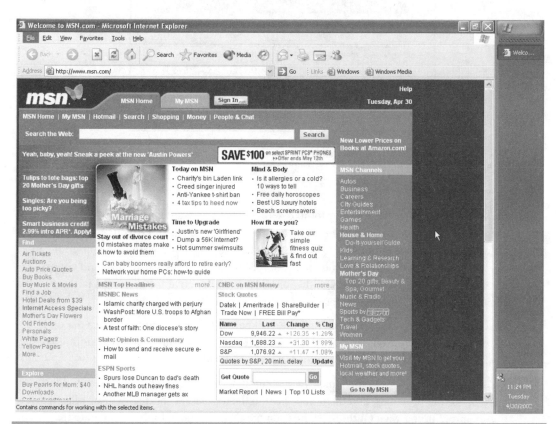

Figure 3-8 The taskbar fits nicely on the right with Internet Explorer.

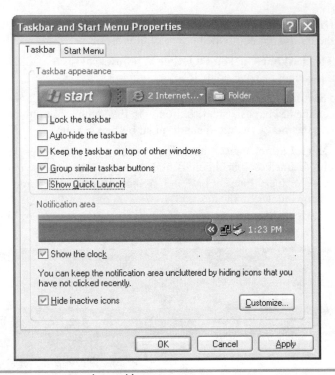

Figure 3-9 Settings to customize the taskbar

3. Make the changes to the first four toolbar settings that you want and click Show Quick Launch to turn it on. Also decide if you want to show the clock and if you want to hide notification area icons if they have not been recently used. If you want some programs to always be displayed and others hidden if not recently used, click Customize and choose whether to Always Hide, Always Show, or Hide When Inactive for each icon in the notification area. Click OK to close the Customize Notifications dialog box.

4. When you are ready, click OK to close the Taskbar And Start Menu Properties dialog box. If you want to remove one or more of the icons in the Quick Launch toolbar, right-click the icon, choose Delete, and click Yes you are sure you want to it.

5. To add additional icons to the Quick Launch toolbar, open My Computer, click Folders, navigate to the programs, and then drag them to the toolbar. A shortcut will be placed there. For example if you want Outlook Express on the Quick Launch toolbar, navigate to C:\Program Files\Outlook Express and drag msimn.exe to the toolbar.

6. If you have more icons on the Quick Launch toolbar than can be shown, you can drag the right border of the toolbar to the size you need. If you do not enlarge it, you will get a little chevron symbol that when clicked shows the extra icons above the toolbar, like this:

CRITICAL SKILL

3.4 Customize Windows Explorer and File Folders

Windows Explorer (called just "Explorer" from here on) is probably the most used of the programs included with Windows. It is therefore important that it be set up the way that is most useful to you. In Module 4, you'll see how to make the best use of Explorer, but here you'll see how you can customize it to your needs and tastes.

Explorer provides a way to navigate to a particular folder and open and display the contents of that folder. With the folder open, you can perform a number of activities on the files in the folder, which is the subject of Module 4. Folders, though, have a number of settings that determine how you look at them, and these folder settings are important part of setting up Explorer.

Ask the Expert

Q: **Why have both the folders and the tasks panes available in Explorer?**

A: Prior to Windows XP, Explorer had only a folders pane, which is used to navigate to a particular folder. It is possible, though, to navigate by double-clicking a drive or folder in the details pane on the right to open it and go on to open the next folder in the details pane until you get where you want to go. In this case, you don't need the folders pane. In my mind, this is both slower than using the folders pane and lacking a visual representation of where you have navigated, something I find very useful. The tasks pane, on the other hand, does provide a handy place to perform a number of file and folder tasks.

3

Customizing Windows XP

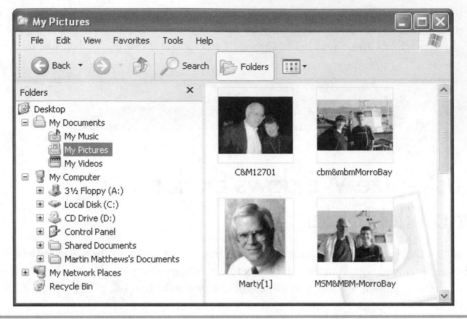

Figure 3-10 Default Windows Explorer window

Customize Windows Explorer

Explorer's window, shown in Figure 3-10, has all of the features of a standard window, many of which you can customize. See how here:

1. Double-click the My Computer icon on your desktop and then click Folders in the toolbar. Click the plus sign next to My Documents and then click My Pictures to open it. Your result should look something like Figure 3-10, except of course, you will have different pictures.

2. Click View in the menu bar to open the View menu shown next. Then move the mouse down to Toolbars to open its subsidiary or flyout menu. By default, only the Standard Buttons toolbar is turned on. The Links bar allows you to put in toolbar links to particular folders that you go to often, thus allowing you to quickly go to a folder by clicking a link. The Links toolbar is shared with Internet Explorer, and so it could get confusing.

3. In the Toolbars flyout menu, click Customize. Here you can determine what icons or *buttons* are on the Standard Buttons toolbar. The current buttons on the toolbar are shown on the right, and the available buttons that can be placed on the toolbar are on the left. By selecting a button, you can use the Add or Remove buttons to change the buttons you have displayed to those that are most useful to you.

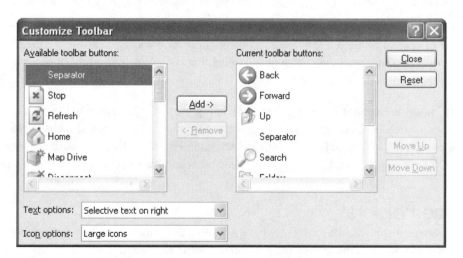

4. At the bottom of the Customize Toolbar dialog box, click the down arrow to open the Text Options drop-down list. You can choose that the text associated with the toolbar buttons appear on labels on the bottom of the button, on the right of the icon, or not at all. Choose Show Text Labels.

5. Click the down arrow to open the Icon Options drop-down list. Select Small Icons. Click Close. Look at how this looks to you. I personally like this better than the default look.

6. Reopen the View menu and click Status Bar. I also find this very useful and have it normally turned on.

7. Again in the View menu, open the Explorer Bar flyout menu. The Explorer Bar is what I call the "left pane." By default, it contains the tasks pane, but it can also contain a file search capability, a list of favorite sites or folders, a small media (audio or video) player, a history of the sites you have visited, and a hierarchical list of folders. Most of these choices are Internet related and not applicable to file folders. In most cases, the left pane is used by either the tasks pane or the folders pane.

8. Open the View menu again and look at the six options below the Explorer Bar. These are six different ways of viewing the contents of a folder in the right pane of Explorer. Click each of these and look at the results. I like either Thumbnails, which shows a bit of the file contents, as you can see in Figure 3-10, or Details, which shows the file size, type, and date last modified.

9. Below the six views in the View menu there are options to sort the folder's contents by one of several fields and arrange the contents in several ways, to choose the details that are displayed in Detail view, change the folder that is viewed, and refresh the current view. Try these yourself to see how they work.

If I take the Explorer window shown back in Figure 13-3, change the toolbar to small icons with labels beneath, turn on the Address toolbar and the status bar, and change the view from thumbnails to details, I get the window shown in Figure 3-11. Only you can determine which is better for you, and it may well be some other combination of the available options.

Change Folders

The contents displayed in a folder also have a number of options that allow you to choose what is shown and how it is displayed. See for yourself with these steps:

1. Open the Tools menu and choose Folder Options to open the dialog box of that name. On the General tab, you have three choices:

- Whether to show the tasks pane when the folders pane is not shown or to show nothing, as was done classically. It does no harm to have the tasks pane shown and can be beneficial, so I would leave the default to show tasks.

- Whether to have every folder open in its own window or to have all folders open in the same window, each replacing the last. Having each folder open a new window creates a lot of clutter, and it is often hard to find a previous window in the unlikely event you want it. I think that it is clearly the best practice is to use the same window, which is the default. You can always use the Back and Forward buttons to get to other folders.

- Whether to use a single- or double-click to open a folder, program, or file. This is really a matter of preference, and to some degree experience. If you have been double-clicking for 15 years, it is hard to single-click. On the other hand, if you're just starting out, single-clicking may be simpler. If you choose to single-click, I would underline the title only when you point on it, first to confirm you have pointed at the correct object and second to reduce the screen clutter.

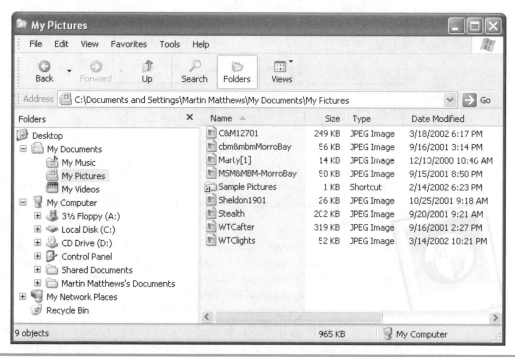

Figure 3-11 Windows Explorer window with changes

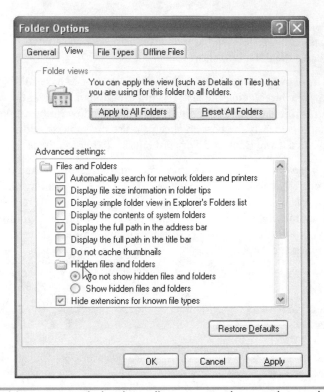

Figure 3-12 The Folder Options dialog box allows you to choose what to display.

2. Make the changes in the General tab you want and then click the View tab to open that page. The View tab, which is shown in Figure 3-12, gives you a large number of options on what to display in a folder and how to display it. Only you can decide what is right for you, but here are some thoughts:

● I don't like to have files and folders hidden from me on the off chance that I might do some harm to them. I therefore turn on (check) Display The Contents Of System Folders, I select Show Hidden Files And Folders, and I turn off (uncheck) Hide Extensions For Known File Types and Hide Protected Operating System Files (answering Yes when asked if I really want to do that).

● I turn on Display The Full Path In The Title Bar; with that I don't really need to have the Address toolbar displayed, again reducing clutter. I leave the remaining defaults simply because I don't have a good reason to change them.

3. Decide the options that you want and then close the Folder Options dialog box.

Progress Check

1. What resolution would you use with a 17-inch CRT?

2. How do you use the Quick Launch toolbar and where is it?

3. What are two additional bars that can be added to the Windows Explorer window?

CRITICAL SKILL
3.5 # Tailor the Mouse, Keyboard, and Sound

In the preceding major section, you saw how to customize the way Windows looks on the screen. In this section, you see how to change the way Windows interrupts information coming from the mouse and keyboard and how Windows uses sound.

Change the Mouse

The mouse is a primary way to communicate with Windows. Although it is possible to use Windows without a mouse, it is not easy, and I do not recommend it. The mouse provides an easy way to select an object on the screen, indicate a choice, move an object on the screen, and start and stop programs. The primary change that you might want to make is to switch the left and right mouse buttons in order to use the mouse with your left hand. Other changes include adjusting the speed of what is considered double-clicking, changing how the mouse pointer appears on the screen, and setting several special effects for the mouse pointer. The following steps will show you how to make these changes:

1. Open the Start menu and click the Control Panel. In Category view, click Printers And Other Hardware and then click Mouse. In the Classic view, double-click Mouse. The Mouse Properties dialog box will open, as shown in Figure 3-13.

2. Click Switch Primary And Secondary Buttons. Close the Mouse Properties dialog box and try using the mouse with your other hand. If you are not left-handed (or even if you are), it may be difficult (I'm left-handed and use the mouse with my right hand).

---

1. A resolution of 1024×768 is normally used with a 17-inch CRT or 15-inch flat-screen monitor.

2. The Quick Launch toolbar is on the taskbar; it contains shortcuts to frequently used programs so that they can be quickly started.

3. You can add Address and Links toolbars, and you can add a status bar.

Figure 3-13 Changing how Windows responds to the mouse

3. Reopen the Mouse Properties dialog box as you did in Step 1. If you don't like the mouse buttons switched, uncheck the top check box.

4. Double-click the folder on the middle right. If the folder opens, the double-click speed is correct for you. If not, drag the Speed slider one way, try double-clicking, and if it still doesn't work drag the slider the other way and try it. Through this trial-and-error approach, you will find a speed that is correct for you.

5. If you have trouble holding down the mouse button while dragging an object, click Turn On ClickLock. This is pretty handy for dragging and doesn't seem to get in the way of other mouse actions. Remember, you still have to hold the mouse button down for a time longer than you would for normal clicking. If you click Settings, you can adjust how long you have to hold down the button before ClickLock takes effect.

6. Click the Pointers tab. Here you have two ways to change how the mouse pointer looks on the screen under various conditions. First, you can select a different scheme using the Scheme drop-down list. Click that drop-down list now to see the many options and choose

one to try if you wish. Second, with any scheme you can replace any individual pointer with any other by selecting the pointer you want to change, clicking Browse, and choosing the new pointer you want to use. At any time, you can return to the default by reselecting the pointer and clicking Use Default.

7. Click the Pointer Options tab. This page allows you to change several characteristics of the mouse pointer.

- **Motion** determines how fast the mouse pointer moves for a given hand movement. Dragging the slider toward Fast means the pointer will mover proportionally faster than the hand movement. The Enhance Pointer Precision option, which is on by default (and I believe you want to leave it there), allows the pointer to follow very small movements of the mouse.

- **Snap To** automatically moves the pointer to the default button when you open a dialog box. It is my experience that you seldom want to use the default button when you first open a dialog box, and so this does me little good. If you question this, try it for a while. You can always come back and change the setting.

- **Visibility** enhances your ability to see the mouse on the screen. These settings are particularly important on laptops where seeing the mouse can be difficult. If you are having any difficulty seeing the mouse or finding it, turn on both Display Pointer Trails and Show Location Of Pointer When I Press The CTRL Key. I find the pointer trails annoying, but the use of CTRL is handy. Hiding the pointer while typing keeps the pointer out of your way, but you sometimes lose it with this turned on.

8. Make the changes to the mouse settings that are correct for you and then click OK to close the Mouse Properties dialog box.

The Hardware page of the Mouse Properties dialog box is useful only if you are having problems with your mouse. Troubleshoot opens an interactive Help window where you can try to determine what is wrong by answering questions. Depending on the type of mouse you have, you may have other tabs in the Mouse Properties dialog box. For example, if you a mouse with a wheel, you will have a Wheel tab that lets you choose the number of lines on the screen to scroll per increment of the wheel.

Ask the Expert

Q: I have three buttons on my mouse and a wheel. How are these used?

A: The wheel has been programmed into Windows XP, Microsoft Office XP, and other programs to scroll the active window. For example, if you have Windows Explorer active on your screen, the wheel will scroll the right or details pane. The third or middle button does not have a standard meaning and is set by a program that comes with the mouse. Sometimes single-clicking it is used in place of double-clicking the primary mouse button.

Change the Keyboard

The keyboard is necessary for any textual communications with Windows and is required. You cannot operate Windows without a keyboard. Windows can use different keyboards depending on the primary language you are using. When you install Windows, one of the determinations is the language and keyboard you are going to use. Once Windows has accepted the language specification, there are very few settings that you can change for the keyboard, as you can see in Figure 3-14. If you do want to customize the settings, follow these steps:

1. Open the Keyboard Properties dialog box in the same way you opened the Mouse Properties dialog box, except you click Keyboard at the end. The top two sliders determine how long to wait when a key is held down before repeating the character, and once the system has started repeating a character, how fast to do it.

2. Click in the text box that says Click Here, and then hold down a key to see how the repetition works. If you are a slow typist, leaving your fingers on the keys too long, you might want to increase the Repeat Delay.

3. The Cursor Blink Rate is purely a personal choice. It does not affect anything but your eye. Increase or decrease it as you choose. When you are done, close the Keyboard Properties dialog box.

Figure 3-14 Minimal changes available for the keyboard

As with the mouse, the Hardware page of the Keyboard Properties dialog box is for troubleshooting and has the same type of call to Help.

Change How Sound Is Used

Most computers today have sound capability, and Windows XP makes good use of it. First, Windows uses it to alert you of various events, such as stopping for an error, receipt of mail, or a low battery. Second, you can use it to play sound from CDs, Internet radio, or Internet and other communications. Finally, the Windows sound system can digitally record or play through the speakers sound fed into the computer via a microphone or other device such as a tape recorder, and it can work with other programs to convert text to speech and vice versa.

Control Windows XP Sound

All of Windows XP's sound capabilities, except text-to-speech and speech recognition, are controlled through the Sounds And Audio Devices Properties dialog box. See how that is done with these steps:

1. Open the Start menu and click Control Panel. In Category view, click Sounds, Speech, And Audio Devices and then click Sounds And Audio Devices. In Classic view, double-click Sounds And Audio Devices. In either case, the Sounds And Audio Devices Properties dialog box will open, as shown in Figure 3-15.

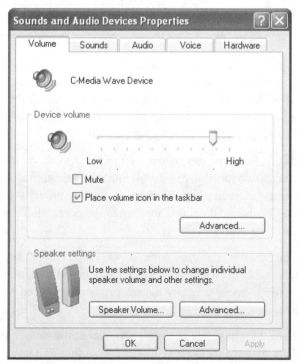

Figure 3-15 Controlling sound and audio devices

The Volume tab should be open. Here you can adjust the overall volume produced by your sound device (sound card or built-in chip set). You can also mute the device so that it produces no sound and determine whether to place the volume control icon in the notification area of the taskbar. The taskbar icon, shown on the left, is on by default. If you click this icon once, you get a small master slider control and the ability to mute all sound. If you double-click the volume control icon, you get a large mixing panel, which you can see next. You get the same mixing panel when you click the Device Volume Advanced button.

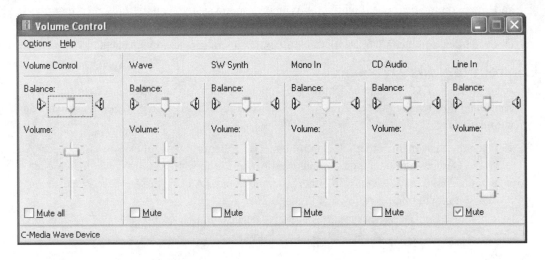

2. Click Advanced in the Speaker Settings area. This opens the Advanced Audio Properties dialog box. Open the Speaker Setup drop-down list. Here you can select the type of speaker setup that you have and set the hardware performance that you desire. Click OK when you have selected the setup you want. Back in the Volume tab, you individually set the volumes of your left and right speakers by clicking Speaker Volume.

3. Click the Sounds tab. Here you can choose a set of sounds that Windows will use for the various events that can occur. You can do this either by selecting a sound scheme or by picking a program event, seeing and listening (by clicking the right-pointing arrow) to the sound. If you want to change the sound attached to the event, click Browse, and double-click a different sound.

4. Click the Audio tab. On this page, you can select the sound device used for various purposes, as well as set the volume. In all cases, the Volume button opens the audio mixer Volume Control. The Sound Playback Advanced button opens the Advanced Audio Properties dialog box that you saw earlier.

5. Click the Voice tab. This page has two more sets of controls similar to what you saw on the Audio tab, but here they are for the playback and recording of human voices. Also on this page there is a Test Hardware button, which starts the Sound Hardware Test Wizard. If you

have any question whether your sound system is working properly, use this wizard to go through your hardware and test it out.

As with the mouse and the keyboard, the Hardware page of the Sounds And Audio Devices Properties dialog box is for troubleshooting and has the familiar interactive Help window. Close the Sounds And Audio Devices Properties dialog box when you are ready.

Text and Speech

Text-to-speech (TTS) and speech recognition (SR) are two technologies that are slowly getting off the ground, and Windows XP provides some support for them. To actually use them, though, you need another program, such as Microsoft Word 2002, that provides the actual interface to the text. Windows XP just supplies the hardware interface. You can try out TTS by clicking Speech in the Sounds, Speech, And Audio Devices Control Panel context window or double-clicking Speech in the Control Panel classic window. In the Speech Properties dialog box that opens, click Preview Voice and you will hear the synthesized voice read the sample sentence. It is interesting that it works at all, but in my opinion, it is not ready for prime time. Close the Speech Properties dialog box when you are ready.

Progress Check

1. What is the primary purpose of switching mouse buttons?

2. If you get two or more of the same letter when you meant to type just one, what can you do about it?

3. What can you do with the little speaker icon in the notification area of the taskbar?

Use Accessibility Options

Accessibility Options allows a user with physical challenges to more easily use Windows XP, as well as any program that is being run. The Accessibility Options dialog box, shown in Figure 3-16, is opened by clicking Accessibility Options in the Category view of the Control Panel and then clicking Accessibility Options again, or by double-clicking Accessibility Options in the Classic view of the Control Panel. The Accessibility Options dialog box provides four areas (keyboard, sound, display, and mouse) where there are options that can be used to improve accessibility. A description of each of the options in each area is provided in Table 3-1 along with how that option is turned on or off outside the dialog box.

1. To enable using the mouse with the opposite hand.
2. In the Keyboard Properties dialog box opened from the Control Panel, you can increase the wait time before producing repetitive letters.
3. Single-clicking the speaker icon opens a simple volume control, while double-clicking open a full audio mixer.

Figure 3-16 Accessibility Options provides ways to make the use of Windows XP easier.

Area	Option	Description	Turn On or Off
Keyboard	StickyKeys	Enables a user to simulate pressing a pair of keys, such as CTRL-A, by pressing one key at a time. The keys SHIFT, CTRL, and ALT "stick" down until a second key is pressed, and Windows XP interprets this as the two keys pressed together.	Press either SHIFT key five times in succession.
Keyboard	FilterKeys	Enables a user to press a key twice in rapid succession and have it interpreted as a single keystroke, and also slows down the rate at which the key is repeated if it is held down.	Hold down the right SHIFT key for eight seconds.

Table 3-1 Accessibility Options

Area	Option	Description	Turn On or Off
Keyboard	ToggleKeys	Plays a tone when CAPS LOCK, NUM LOCK, or SCROLL LOCK is pressed.	Hold down NUM LOCK for five seconds.
Sound	SoundSentry	Displays a visual indicator when the computer makes a sound. The indicator can be a flashing active caption bar, a flashing active window, or a flashing desktop.	Open Accessibility Options and click Use SoundSentry in the Sound tab.
Sound	ShowSounds	Tells compatible programs to display captions when sound and speech are used.	Open Accessibility Options and click Use ShowSounds in Sound tab.
Display	High Contrast	Uses high-contrast colors and special fonts to make the screen easy to use.	Press together: left SHIFT, left ALT, and PRINT SCREEN.
Display	Cursor Options	Enables the user to change the cursor blink rate and the width of the cursor to make it easier to see.	Open Accessibility Options and set the Blink Rate and Width in the Display tab.
Mouse	MouseKeys	Enables the user to use the numeric keypad instead of the mouse to move the pointer on the screen.	Press together: left SHIFT, left ALT, and NUM LOCK.

Table 3-1 Accessibility Options *(continued)*

The use of each option can be turned on by clicking the respective check box in the Accessibility Options dialog box, or in many cases, you can use the shortcut keys shown in Table 3-1. Many of the accessibility options have a related Settings dialog box where you can turn off the shortcut key and make other adjustments in the behavior of the option. The General tab of the Accessibility Options dialog box provides settings for managing the options, including when to automatically turn off the options and whether to give a warning when turning on an option.

Ask the Expert

Q: I don't really need to use the accessibility options, but a couple of them, especially MouseKeys, look like they would be handy. Is there any reason not to use them?

A: No, not really. I have used MouseKeys on several occasions and found it useful. If you don't use the numeric keypad for numeric data entry, then having MouseKeys turned on when NUM LOCK is on makes a lot of sense. MouseKeys is particularly

(continued)

useful for doing very detailed mouse work. Here is a layout of the MouseKeys on a numeric keypad.

Progress Check

1. Explain how StickyKeys is used?

2. Explain how ToggleKeys is used?

3. Explain how MouseKeys is used?

1. StickyKeys allows you to press SHIFT, CTRL, ALT, or the Windows logo key plus one other key and have the computer interpret it as a single keystroke.

2. ToggleKeys plays a tone when CAPS LOCK, NUM LOCK, and SCROLL LOCK are pressed.

3. MouseKeys allows you to use the numeric keypad instead of the mouse to move the pointer on the screen.

| **Project 3** | Customizing a New Computer | | **3** |

Windows XP provides a number of ways that you can tailor it to your needs and desires. This module has looked at most of them, but most customization involves only a few of these methods. For this project, say that you have just gotten a new computer and you want to

- Change the screen resolution to 1024×768 and Medium (16 bit) color

- Change the desktop background to an image or picture you have on your computer

- Add several of the standard icons to the desktop

- Change the Start menu options to remove My Music and My Pictures

- Add the Quick Launch toolbar to the taskbar

- Change several of the folder options to show the hidden files

- Switch the mouse buttons so that it can be used with the left hand

Step by Step

1. Start up and log on to Windows XP. Right-click the desktop and choose Properties.

2. Click the Settings tab. Drag the Screen Resolution slider to 1024×768. Open the Color Quality drop-down list and click Medium (16 bit).

3. Click the Desktop tab. Click Browse, open the Look In drop-down list, and select the folder with the image you want to use for your background, double-click that image, and click it in the Background list back in the Display Properties dialog box. Open the Color pallet and choose the background color to go with your image.

4. Click Customize Desktop. In the Desktop Icons area, click My Documents, My Computer, and Internet Explorer to add these icons to the desktop. Click OK to close the Desktop Items dialog box and then click OK again to close the Display Properties dialog box.

5. Right-click the Start button and choose Properties. In the Taskbar And Start Menu Properties dialog box, click Customize. In the Customize Start Menu dialog box Advanced tab, click Don't Display This Item under My Music and My Pictures. Click OK to close the Customize Start Menu dialog box.

6. Click the Taskbar tab in the Taskbar And Start Menu Properties dialog box. Click Show Quick Launch to turn it on. Click OK to close the Taskbar And Start Menu Properties dialog box.

(continued)

Customizing Windows XP

Project 3

Customizing a New Computer

7. Open the Start menu and click My Computer. Click the Tools menu and choose Folder Options. Click the View tab and click Display The Contents Of System Folders and Show Hidden Files And Folders to turn on those options. Click OK to close the Folder Options dialog box and click the close button to close the My Computer window.

8. Open the Start menu and click Control Panel. In Category view click Printers And Other Hardware and then click Mouse or in Classic view double-click Mouse. Click Switch Primary And Secondary Buttons, click OK to close the Mouse Properties dialog box and click the close button to close the Printers And Other Hardware window.

Project Summary

You can see that with only a few steps you can make some major changes in the way that Windows XP operates. Although you may be happy with the default settings resulting from a standard installation, it is so easy to change from these defaults that it is worth trying alternative settings to see if you like them even better. It is just as easy to change back should you wish. Windows XP gives you a large number of alternatives; try them out.

Module 3 Mastery Check

1. What are three changes you can make to the Start menu?

2. What is an icon on the desktop called and what does it do?

3. What are two ways to get standard icons on the desktop, such as My Computer and Internet Explorer?

4. What is the area on the left of the taskbar that you can create and how is it used?

5. What are three changes that you can make to the Windows Explorer window?

6. If you are having trouble double-clicking, what can you do?

7. What are a couple of the options you have in displaying the mouse pointer?

8. If you get two or more of the same letter when you meant to type just one, what can you do about it?

9. How do you open the volume control?

10. What are three accessibility options and what do they do?

Part II

Primary Uses of Windows XP

Module 4

Using Files, Folders, and Disks

A computer is basically a device for handling information. The information can be a text document, a photograph, a business presentation, a piece of music, a page of numbers, or a video clip. Whatever the information, it is brought into the computer, it is stored, it is brought out of storage to be worked on, it gets restored, and it is brought out of storage once more and possibly passed on to others or removed from the computer. Independent of the type of information, all of it is stored on the computer, if only for a short while. The purpose of this module is to understand the storage of information, how to manipulate information in storage, and how to manage that storage.

CRITICAL SKILL
4.1 Use Files and Folders

All information is stored on a computer in *files*. Files may be grouped in *folders,* and folders in turn may be grouped in other folders, as many times as you wish. Both files and folders are physically held on the computer in a disk. As you work with information on your computer, you are in one way or another working with files, folders, and disks.

Use Files

A file is the smallest amount of information that you can independently manipulate outside of a specialized program created to work on a particular type of file. A file is named; can be identified on your screen; and can be copied, moved, and deleted. The information in a file, for example the words, characters, and symbols in a word processing file, or the lines, shapes, and colors in a drawing file, can be handled only inside a program designed to work with that kind of file. As you work with files, you are primarily concerned with their size and their type.

The Size of Files

All information in a file is stored as *bits,* which is a binary digit, a zero or a one, or a switch that is either on or off. Eight bits make up a *byte,* which is what most programs work with. When you talk about the size of files, you talk about the number of bytes they contain, normally, in terms of thousands, millions, or even billions of bytes. With computers, though, you don't want to make it too easy and say "thousands," "millions," and "billions"; instead you say "kilo," "mega," and "giga," which you abbreviate K, M, and G. So when you see a file size of 80.5KB, it is approximately 80.5 thousand bytes. I say "approximately" because, once again not wanting to make things too simple, a kilobyte is not one thousand bytes, but rather it is 1,024 bytes because it is the binary number 2^{10}. Table 4-1 provides a quick translation between the real world and that of the computer.

Computer Term	Approximation	Actual Number
1 bit (b)	A binary digit	A zero or a one
1 byte (B)	A character	8 bits
1 kilobit (Kb)	1 thousand bits	1,024 bits or 128 bytes
1 kilobyte (KB)	1 thousand bytes	1,024 bytes or 8,192 bits
1 megabit (Mb)	1 million bits	1,048,576 bits or 131,072 bytes
1 megabyte (MB)	1 million bytes	1,048,576 bytes or 8,388,608 bits
1 gigabit (Gb)	1 billion bits	1,073,741,824 bits or 134,217,728 bytes
1 gigabyte (GB)	1 billion bytes	1,073,741,824 bytes or 8,589,934,592 bits

Table 4-1 Bits and Bytes Table

TIP

A rough, but handy rule of thumb is that a byte is equal to a character. So if you
see that a file contains 5KB, or a little over five thousand bytes, you can think of it
as approximately five thousand characters.

Types of Files

There are a large number of file types. One resource on the Internet lists over 500 of them
(http://www.computeruser.com/resources/dictionary/filetypes.html). Most programs have their
own file types, and there are a number of system file types. In addition, the Macintosh and
UNIX operating systems have different file types than does Windows or DOS. Each type of
file has a *file extension* at the end of its filename that becomes the easiest way to distinguish
the file type. For example, Mod4.doc is the file named Mod4 (for this module) that uses the
.DOC file extension telling you and Windows that it needs Microsoft Word, WordPad, or
another program that uses the .DOC file extension or has Word conversion capability to open
the file. Windows uses the file type to associate programs with a file so that when you double-
click a file, Windows can start the program that has been associated with that file and have
the program load the file. Some of the more common types of files and their extensions are
shown in Table 4-2.

Extension	Type	Description, Often with a Program That Will Open It
.ASP	Application	Internet Explorer Active Server Pages
.AVI	Application	Media Player movie format
.BAK	Application	Backup files in many applications
.BAT	System	Batch script files popular in DOS
.BIN	System	Binary files common with device drivers
.BMP	Application	Bitmap image files used by several programs
.CAB	System	Microsoft compressed "cabinet" files
.CDR	Application	CorelDraw files
.DLL	System	Dynamic Link Library files
.DOC	Application	Microsoft Word files
.EXE	Application	Executable program files
.HTM & .HTML	Application	Internet Explorer Web pages
.JPG & .JPEG	Application	Photographic image files used by many programs
.MDB	Application	Microsoft Access database files
.MOV	Application	QuickTime movie files
.MP3	Application	Compressed audio files used by many programs
.MPG & .MPEG	Application	Compressed movie files used by several programs
.PMx	Application	PageMaker publication files (x = 3, 4, 5, 6, or d for version)
.PPT	Application	Microsoft PowerPoint files
.PUB	Application	Microsoft Publisher files
.TIF & .TIFF	Application	Bitmap image files used by many programs
.TXT	Application	Simple text files used by many applications
.TTF	System	TrueType font files
.VBS	Application	Visual Basic files
.WAV	Application	Audio files used by many programs
.WKx	Application	Lotus 1-2-3 files (x = 1, 3, or 4 for the version)

Table 4-2 Common File Extensions

Extension	Type	Description, Often with a Program That Will Open It
.WP	Application	WordPerfect files
.XLS	Application	Microsoft Excel files
.XML	Application	Internet Explorer files
.ZIP	Application	Compressed files used by several programs

Table 4-2 Common File Extensions *(continued)*

Use Folders

Folders are containers. They provide a means to organize the other folders and files they contain. The easiest way to organize a set of files is to create a hierarchical structure that you can easily follow down to the files you want. For example, if you have a number of photographs of your vacations, you might want to use a structure similar to the one shown in Figure 4-1, where all the photos for a particular trip are in a folder (Yellowstone), which is

Figure 4-1 A hierarchical structure of folders

contained in a folder for the year I took the trip (2002), which is contained in a folder for vacations within My Pictures. There are of course many ways to organize information, and you should use the system that is the easiest for you. Windows XP assumes that you will start with the My Documents, My Music, My Pictures, and My Videos set of folders. There is nothing that says you have to use these folders, but their availability on the Start menu and separated out in the list of folders makes their use convenient.

Create Folders

To create the folder structure just described, you must create the subsidiary folders. Microsoft gives you the My Documents and the My Pictures folders. You must go on from there. You can do that in two ways, depending on the view you are using in the Explorer. Look at both of these.

Use Tasks View   Creating folders may be the one of the reasons Microsoft came up with the Tasks view, where it is trivial compared to what you have to go through in Folders view. See for yourself with these steps:

1. If necessary, start your computer and log on to Windows XP.

2. Open the Start menu and either click My Pictures, if it is directly available, or if you did the customization in Module 3, point your mouse to My Documents to open its menu and then select My Pictures. (If you use My Pictures very often, you might want to undo the customization steps in Module 3.)

3. If Folders view is open, click the close button or click the Folders button on the toolbar to close Folders view and open Tasks view.

4. With My Pictures open in the Explorer in Tasks view, click Make A New Folder under File And Folder Tasks. A new folder appears with its name highlighted and ready to change, as you can see in Figure 4-2.

5. Type **Vacations** and press ENTER. You now have a new folder named Vacations.

6. Double-click the Vacations folder to open it. Click Make A New Folder, type **2002**, and press ENTER. Double-click the 2002 folder to open it.

   You can see how you can repeat Step 6 as many time as you want to continue creating folders.

Figure 4-2 Creating a new folder

Use Folders View   Folders view lets you see the structure you are creating, which you can't do in Tasks view, but getting at the New Folder command is not as easy. The following steps assume you have done the immediately preceding ones and that you have the Explorer with ...\My Pictures\Vacations\2002\ open in it:

1. Click Folders in the toolbar to switch from Tasks to Folders view.

2. Right-click in the right pane of the Explorer window and choose New | Folder. Type **Yellowstone** and press ENTER.

3. Double-click the Yellowstone folder to open it. Right-click in the right pane, choose New | Folder, type **Animals**, and press ENTER.

Compare Step 6 in the preceding set of steps with Step 3 here. The Tasks view is marginally easier. Decide what that is worth compared to having the visual representation of the structure you are building, like this:

Use Disks

Disks are the physical devices inside your computer that hold the files and folders that you are creating. There are several types of disks, including hard disks (also called hard disk drives, hard drives, and fixed disks or fixed drives), floppy disks, compact disks (CDs, CD-ROMs, CD-Rs, CD-RWs), digital video disks (DVDs, DVD-ROMs, DVD-RAMs, DVD-Rs, DVD-RWs), and removable disks. In this part of the module, I'll talk about hard disks, floppy disks, and CDs. Later in the module, I'll talk about removable disks, and in Module 7, I'll talk about the various forms of CDs and DVDs.

NOTE

In this book I call all round rotating objects on which data is stored a "disk," spelled with a "k." Some people and organizations have felt the need to differentiate CDs, DVDs, and other optical devices by calling then a "disc" with a "c." I believe that this is more confusing than helpful.

Use Hard Disks

Hard disks are the primary storage medium in all but the smallest handheld computers, and even for those, IBM has built a 1GB drive that is smaller than a paper matchbook. All of the file and folder structure discussed earlier is contained on a hard disk. Physically, a hard disk most commonly used today consists of a metal case that is roughly 4 inches by 5 inches by 1 inch. Inside the case there is one or more 3.5-inch spinning metal platters (the "disk") on which information is magnetically written and read. Hard disks are truly a marvel of technology. They first appeared about 35 years ago, when they were a 3-foot-diameter platter in a box 6 feet tall by 4 feet square and held relatively little information. Around 25 years ago, hard disks had come down to the size of a large suitcase and held more information. By 15 years ago, they were the size of a large book and held still more information. Roughly seven years ago, they came down to their current size and commonly held 300MB. Today a common hard disk is around 20GB, 40GB is quite often used, and 80GB is available.

On your computer and on all PCs, the primary hard disk is labeled Local Disk (C:). You may have another hard disk, which would be labeled Local Disk (D:), but most people have only one. If you open the Explorer, switch to Folders view, and click the plus sign opposite your My Computer | C drive, you will see the top level of the folder structure that is built into Windows XP. Here are these folders and their purposes:

- **Documents And Settings** contains all of the data files plus the settings that identify how the desktop, Start menu, and so on are set up for all of the users on the computer. See the following "Ask the Expert" section.

- **Program Files** contains all of the program files for the programs that use the Microsoft installation standards.

- **Recycler** contains the Recycle Bins for all of the users on the computer.

- **System Volume Information** contains information you can't see that identifies the computer and the disk.

- **Windows** contains all of the files used by Windows XP.

You may have other folders on your C: drive, but at a minimum with Windows XP, you will have the ones just identified. You can add new folders anywhere on your hard disk using the steps you saw earlier, but it is recommended that you keep your new folders within the My Documents folder.

Use Floppies and CDs

At the beginning of the personal computer era, floppy disks were the only form of disk storage. Today, floppy disks are quickly going out of existence, and you may actually have a computer that no longer has a floppy disk drive. A floppy disk consists of a removable disk with a hard plastic case a little over 3.5 inches square and a flexible plastic disk inside, on which information is recorded, all of which fits into a special disk drive installed in your

Ask the Expert

Q: You said that all my data files should be in the My Documents folder, and you also said that all users' (I assume that I'm a user) files are in the Documents And Settings folder. My Folders view shows the My Documents folder outside of Drive C. I don't understand, what is going on?

A: Unfortunately, the Folders view that Windows XP gives you is more than a little confusing. The Desktop and My Documents folder at the top of the folders pane are shortcuts to the actual current user's folders within Documents And Settings. If you open (click the plus sign next to) Documents And Settings, then open the current user, open My Documents within the current user, and finally open My Pictures within that, you'll see the same folder contents that we were working on earlier in the module, as shown here.

computer (if it has one). Most current 3.5-inch floppy disks hold 1.44MB of information. Your first floppy disk is always labeled drive A:, and you may have a second drive labeled B:. The primary use of a floppy disk is to transfer information from one computer to another or to provide storage of information outside the computer. The transfer of information today, especially this small amount of information, is better handled by networks and the Internet (see Module 6). The *offline* (outside the computer) storage of information is better handled by recordable CDs, which hold more information and are a much more permanent storage medium. Floppies have a relatively short life and can be easily corrupted with a magnet.

Compact disks or CDs originally came to computers as a means of playing music and very quickly as a way to install programs. Today all programs come via CD or are downloaded over the Internet. In the last several years, recordable CDs (CD-Rs) and rewritable CDs (CD-RWs) have become inexpensive and relatively common. With either of these devices, you can write information onto a CD, which can hold either 650MB or 700MB. Once written on, a CD will hold the information for a long time if not subject to high heat or physical abuse.

Progress Check

1. How many bits are there in a byte, and how many bytes are in a kilobyte?

2. What are .EXE, .JPG, and .TXT files used for?

3. What are hard disks used for?

CRITICAL SKILL
4.3 Handle Information

It doesn't take long after setting up a set of folders and putting a few files in them that you find yourself needing to move one or more files, copy them, rename them, or any one of a number of different tasks that are a normal part of handling information. Windows XP provides several ways you can perform each of these tasks and a group of tasks that you may not have thought you needed to do. In this section, you'll first look at a basic set of tasks that include selecting, copying, moving, renaming, deleting, and creating a shortcut. Then you'll

---

1. There are eight bits in a byte, and there are 1,024 bytes in a kilobyte.
2. .EXE files are used for programs, .JPG files are used for photographs, and .TXT files are used for simple text files.
3. Hard disks are used for the storage of information within a computer.

see how to do a more advanced set that includes recovering a deleted item, compressing files, searching for a file or folder, and sending files and folders.

Perform Basic Tasks

Most of the basic tasks can be performed by dragging with a mouse, through the keyboard, and with the tasks pane. In addition, all of the basic tasks can be performed using menu options. In the following sections, we'll look at all four of these methods individually to see how they work. In practice, most people use a combination of the methods based on what is easiest for them at the moment.

Select and Drag Objects

One of the great benefits of the graphical user interface (GUI and pronounced "gooey") around which Windows is built, is that you can use the mouse to select and drag an object on the screen that represents a file or a folder and have that action accomplish something useful, such as copying or moving a file. This has a very intuitive nature to it because it is so much like reaching out with your hand and moving an object from one place to another. Unlike when working by hand, though, you can do more that just move an object; you can also copy it, delete it, create a shortcut to it, and rename it, depending on how you do it.

Select Files and Folders   Before you can perform an operation on one or more files, you must first select it or them. It is intuitive that to select an object, you simply need to click it. When you do that, it becomes the *active* object (an icon, a file, a folder, a window, or a dialog box) and becomes in some way highlighted, as Folder Two is here:

Folder One   Folder Two

You can select multiple objects by encircling them either with the mouse or with the keyboard. Look at mouse technique here and keyboard technique later under the Keyboard topic. (These steps assume you have done the steps earlier in this module and you have a Vacations folder within My Pictures. If you didn't do that and you want to do these steps, go back and create such a folder now.)

1. Open the Explorer with the folders pane open; then open the My Documents and My Pictures folders. Finally, double-click the Sample Pictures folder to open it.

2. Click the Blue Hills.jpg file to select it. It will become selected and show the fact by becoming highlighted, in a way that will vary depending on the Explorer view you are using.

3. Point in the upper-left corner (move the mouse pointer to the upper-left corner) of the Explorer's details pane. Press and hold the left mouse button while moving the mouse to the lower-right corner. A dotted line will appear around all of files and they will become selected, as you can see in Figure 4-3.

4. Release the left mouse button, and all the files will remain selected. This is sometimes called "rubber banding." In this book, I'll just say to select the objects.

Move, Copy, and Create Shortcuts   Moving, copying, and creating shortcuts using the mouse are almost the same operation with only minor differences. You have seen in earlier modules how you can move an icon on the desktop by dragging it. Similarly, you can move a file or folder in the Explorer from one folder to another by dragging it, but if you drag a file or folder from one disk drive to another, you will automatically copy it instead of moving it. In addition, if you drag a program file (one with an .EXE extension) from one folder to another (consider both the desktop and the Start menu as folders), you will automatically create a shortcut to the original program file. Holding down CTRL while dragging a file will copy the file. Finally, if you right-drag a file (drag it by holding down the right mouse button) a menu

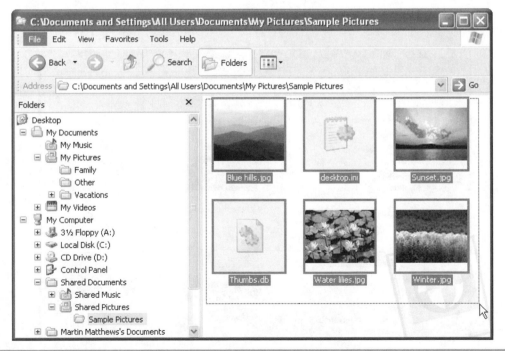

Figure 4-3 Selecting several objects

will open when you get to your destination and release the mouse button that allows you to choose whether you want to copy, move, or create a shortcut for the file. In all these operations, you can drag between one part of a window to another part of the same window, you can drag from one window to another, or you can drag from a window to the desktop. See how dragging works with this set of steps, which assume you have done the immediately preceding steps:

1. Point at the Sunset.jpg file, press and hold the left mouse button, move the mouse until it is over the Vacations folder in the folders pane, as you can see in Figure 4-4, and then release the mouse button. You have just dragged the Sunset.jpg file from the Sample Pictures folder to the Vacations folder, and in the process moved it from one folder to another. Note that the Sunset.jpg file is no longer in Sample Pictures.

2. Open Vacations and you will find Sunset.jpg there. In the folders pane, scroll down toward the bottom until you see My Computer\Shared Documents\Shared Pictures\Sample Pictures, which should have all of the subfolders visible as a result of the last step.

3. Press and hold CTRL while dragging Sunset.jpg back to Sample Pictures. When you reach Sample Pictures, release the mouse button *before* releasing CTRL. Sunset.jpg remains in Vacations, but it also is now back in Sample Pictures. You have copied the picture instead of moving it.

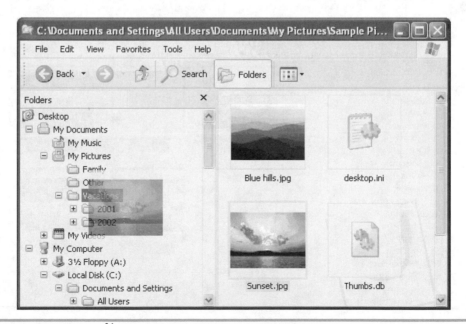

Figure 4-4 Dragging a file to move it

NOTE

When you are copying a folder or a file, there is a plus sign next to the mouse pointer to indicate copying.

4. Move the mouse pointer to the Vacations folder in My Pictures. Press and hold both CTRL and SHIFT while dragging Vacations to the desktop. A folder icon will appear on the desktop with a curved arrow on the icon and the caption Shortcut To Vacations. Release the mouse button *before* releasing CTRL-SHIFT. By dragging with CTRL-SHIFT, you have created a shortcut.

NOTE

When you are making a shortcut of a program file, there is a curved arrow next to the mouse pointer to indicate what you are doing.

5. In the folders pane, open your C: disk drive, the Program Files folder, and finally the Movie Maker folder. Drag the Moviemk.exe file to the desktop. The Movie Maker icon will appear with the caption Shortcut To Moviemk.exe. You have made a shortcut of the program file instead of moving or copying it.

Shortcut to   Shortcut to
Vacations   moviemk.exe

6. In the Movie Maker folder, move the mouse pointer to the Sample.asf file, press and hold the right mouse button while dragging the file to the desktop, and then release the right mouse button. A small menu will open asking if you want to copy, move (which is bold, showing that is the default action), create a shortcut, or cancel the action. Click Cancel.

Rename and Delete a File   Two operations that are still mainly mouse operations but are a little more than dragging are renaming a file and deleting a file by moving it to the Recycle Bin.

1. If Shortcut To Moviemk.exe is not selected (it shouldn't be if you did the last step in the preceding sequence), click it once to select it, wait a moment, and then click it again. Don't double-click or it will start the Movie Maker program. If it is already selected, you only need to click it again. This will open the caption field so that you can rename the file (or shortcut in this case, which is actually a small file) by simply typing a new name.

2. Type the name **Movie Maker** and press ENTER. The new name appears in the caption. Because the curved arrow appears in the icon, you will know that it is a shortcut, and you don't need that word to take up room in the caption.

3. Drag the shortcut to Movie Maker on the desktop to the Recycle Bin icon. A message will pop up saying that deleting the shortcut does not delete the program. Click Delete Shortcut.

4. Drag the shortcut to Vacations on the desktop to the Recycle Bin icon.

TIP

Rules of dragging:
  Dragging all but program files (those with an .EXE extension) within the same disk will move the file.
  Dragging all files between disk drives will copy the files.
  Dragging any file anywhere while holding down CTRL will copy the file.
  Dragging any file anywhere while holding down CTRL-SHIFT will make a shortcut of the file.
  Dragging a program file will create a shortcut.
  Right-dragging any file opens a menu allowing you to choose to move, copy, or create a shortcut.
  You can drag within a window, between windows, and between a window and the desktop.
  Dragging an object to the Recycle Bin deletes that object.

Use Menus

Right-clicking an object opens a menu called either the context menu or the shortcut menu. I like the term *context menu* and will use it throughout this book because it refers to an object on which you clicked and its context, and it does not get confused with a shortcut to a program file. This menu provides a list of options indicating all the actions you can perform on the object you clicked. This list of actions is of course different depending on the type of file or folder. Next are shown four context menus for (from left to right) a folder, a program, a text file, and an image file. As you can see, the bottom seven options are the same. Here we'll discuss that middle five: Cut, Copy, Create Shortcut, Delete, and Rename. The remaining options will be discussed later in this module under Advanced tasks.

Copy and Move Files and Folders   Copying and moving using the menu are done in two steps. To copy a file or folder, you use the Copy option on the menu to create a copy on the *Clipboard,* a temporary holding area. Then you select or right-click in the folder where you want the copy to go and choose Paste. To move, you use the Cut option to place the original on the Clipboard, and then use Paste as you did in copying. See how this works next:

1. Open the Vacations folder where you should have a copy of Sunset.jpg. Right-click Sunset.jpg and choose Copy.

2. Open the My Pictures folder. Right-click in any open area and choose Paste. Open any other folder, right-click in any open area, and choose Paste. The original picture stayed in Vacations, and you have created two copies in two different folders. The ability to create multiple copies with a single Copy operation can be useful.

3. In the folder in which you placed the second copy, right-click the Sunset.jpg and choose Cut. The image will become dim but remain until you Paste (or until you Cut or Copy another file because the Windows Clipboard holds only one file at a time). If you were to shut the computer down at this point, the image would remain in the original folder.

4. Right-click the desktop and choose Paste. The image appears on the desktop. If you go back and look at the original folder, the image is gone.

5. Go to any other folder and right-click. You will see that Paste is dim, so you cannot use it.

NOTE

When you choose Copy to copy an object to the Clipboard, you may choose Paste Shortcut and create a shortcut as a result.

Ask the Expert

Q: Why would you use a menu to do copying and moving when dragging is so easy?

A: Dragging is not always so easy if you cannot easily see the destination of the copy or move. Second, there are times when the mouse is not available and so having another method to handle this is critical. Finally, some people just find the menu method better for them.

Delete, Rename, and Create a Shortcut   Deleting, renaming, and creating a shortcut are straightforward:

1. Right-click the Sunset.jpg image file on the desktop and choose Delete. A Confirm File Delete message opens asking if you are sure you want to send the file to the Recycle Bin. Click Yes.

2. Open the other folder in which you made a copy of Sunset.jpg. Right-click the image file, press and hold SHIFT, and click Delete. The Confirm File Delete message opens and now asks if you are sure you want to *delete* the file. It does not say anything about going to the Recycle Bin.

TIP

When you press SHIFT in any delete operation, the deleted information does not go to the Recycle Bin, but rather is immediately removed from your computer.

3. Answer No. Right-click the same Sunset.jpg image file and choose Rename. The caption under the picture is highlighted, and you can type a new name. Type **Apicture.jpg** and press ENTER.

CAUTION

When you rename a file, be sure to leave the extension the same, so that the association that Windows has created between the file and the program that is used to open it remains intact.

4. Open the My Pictures folder, right-click the Vacations folder that you created, and choose Create Shortcut. Another Folder labeled Shortcut To Vacations appears in the My Pictures folder.

5. Drag the new folder shortcut to the desktop. Double-click the new icon. A second instance of Explorer will open and display the contents of Vacations.

   Later in this module, you will see how the Send To option can be use to create a shortcut on the desktop to a file or folder elsewhere on the disk.

Use the Tasks Pane

The tasks pane, which can be on the left of the Explorer window, can perform all of the same actions that you have seen using dragging and with menus, except creating shortcuts. Try this method with the steps that follow. (The Vacations folder should be open in the Explorer window with the tasks pane shown, and at least one folder [2002] should be in the details pane. If this is not correct, use the procedures you have already learned to set up such a window.)

1. Click the 2002 folder to select it and display the File And Folder Tasks list shown next.

2. Click Copy This Folder in the tasks pane. The Copy Items dialog box will open. Here you can navigate to any folder in which you want to place the copy. For this example, click Desktop and click Copy. The folder will appear on the desktop.

3. The 2002 folder should still be selected in the Explorer. Click Move This Folder in the tasks pane. The Move Items dialog will open, looking very much like the Copy Items dialog box. Click My Documents to select it, and click Move. The folder will disappear from the Vacations folder.

4. Open the Edit menu in the menu bar and click Undo Move; the 2002 folder will return.

TIP

Undo can also be used with any of the methods used to copy, move, rename, and delete.

5. Use the Up button in the toolbar to navigate up to the desktop. Select the Shortcut To Vacations folder that should be on your desktop, and click Rename This File in the tasks pane. (The term "file" is used to refer to this object because it is a shortcut, not an actual folder.) The caption becomes selected. Type **Vacations** and press ENTER.

6. Select the 2002 folder that you copied to the desktop and click Delete This Folder. The "Are you sure" message appears wanting to move the folder to the Recycle Bin. Click No.

7. With the 2002 folder on the desktop within the Explorer still selected, press and hold SHIFT and then click Delete This Folder. You now get the message "Are you sure you want to remove the folder…" Click Yes. You may then be asked if you want to remove all the folder's contents. Click Yes To All.

Use the Keyboard

Using the keyboard and keyboard shortcuts with a little help from the mouse and menus, you can do all of the basic operations being discussed. The keys and keyboard shortcuts used with these operations and the Explorer are shown in Table 4-3.

Select with the Keyboard   Earlier you saw how to select one and multiple objects with the mouse, and truthfully, that is the easiest way to do it. However, it can be done with the keyboard, as shown with the following instructions (be patient!). This assumes that the Explorer is open, is the active object, and displays the desktop within it, as it did at the end of the last set of steps:

1. Press TAB one or more times until My Documents is selected, either in Other Places in the tasks pane or in the details pane. A border will appear around the selection caption. In the details pane, press SPACEBAR to complete the selection and then, in either case, press ENTER to open My Documents. My Music should have a border around its caption.

2. Press DOWN ARROW or RIGHT ARROW (whichever is needed in your layout) to select My Picture and then press ENTER to open My Pictures.

3. If necessary, use the arrow keys to initially select Sample Pictures and then press ENTER to open Sample Pictures. Blue Hills.jpg should be initially selected.

4. Press SPACEBAR to complete the selection and then press and hold SHIFT while pressing first RIGHT ARROW or DOWN ARROW to continue selecting files. Notice how all files you pass over become selected. That is the purpose of SHIFT: to extend the selection over all objects crossed.

5. Using the arrow keys, reselect just Blue Hills.jpg. Press and hold CTRL while pressing RIGHT ARROW or DOWN ARROW twice to initially select the third image, press SPACEBAR to complete the selection, and continue pressing CTRL while pressing RIGHT ARROW or DOWN ARROW to initially select the fourth image. Finally press SPACEBAR to complete the selection. Using CTRL, you have selected three noncontiguous files.

You see the reason the mouse was invented! It is much easier to use than the keyboard. Nevertheless, you may be in situations where using the keyboard is your only alternative, for example, with a dead mouse.

Operation	Shortcut Keys
Activate menu bar in the active program	F10
Cancel current operation	ESC
Completing object selection	SPACEBAR
Copy selected item to the Clipboard	CTRL-C
Cut selected item to the Clipboard	CTRL-X
Delete selected item	DEL
Extend the selection inclusively	SHIFT
Extend the selection item by item	CTRL
Move the selection within a pane	ARROW keys
Move the selection within a windows	TAB
Open the address bar in Explorer	F4
Open the System menu for the active window	ALT-SPACEBAR
Open the context menu for the selected item	SHIFT-F10
Open the Help window	F1
Open the Start menu	CTRL-ESC
Paste the most recently copied or cut item	CTRL-V
Rename the selected item	F2
Refresh the active window	F5
Search for a folder or file	F3
Select all items in a folder	CTRL-A
Undo the last action	CTRL-Z

Table 4-3 Keyboard Shortcuts for Use with File and Folder Operations

Perform Basic Tasks Using Both the Keyboard and the Mouse   Looking at Table 4-3, it is pretty obvious how the basic tasks are performed with the keyboard. See for yourself with this set of steps:

1. Click the Vacations folder shortcut on the desktop to select it and press CTRL-C to copy it to the Clipboard.

2. Press CTRL-V to paste a copy of the Vacations shortcut on the desktop. Press CTRL-V to paste a second copy on the desktop. Your desktop should include these three icons:

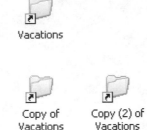

Vacations

Copy of   Copy (2) of
Vacations   Vacations

NOTE

In Step 2, you just pressed CTRL-V without indicating where you wanted the copy because you wanted it on the desktop, which was already active due to selecting the icon in Step 1. What is *active* depends on what you last did or where you last clicked. If you are unsure what is active, simply click on what you want to be active, on what you want the next operation to use.

3. Click the first Copy Of Vacations and press CTRL-X to cut this shortcut. In the Explorer, open the folders pane and then the My Documents folder, click in the right or details pane, and press CTRL-V. A folder shortcut will appear in My Documents, and the same folder will have disappeared from the desktop.

4. Click the new Copy Of Vacations Shortcut in My Documents to select it, and press F2 to highlight just the name so that a new name can be entered. Type **Vacations** and press ENTER.

NOTE

In My Documents, unlike the desktop, the word "Shortcut" gets permanently attached to the name.

5. Click the second copy of the Vacations shortcut (Copy (2) Of Vacations) on the desktop to select it and press DEL. You are asked are you sure you want to send this file to the Recycle Bin. Click Yes.

6. Click the copy of the Vacations shortcut in My Documents to select it; then press and hold SHIFT while pressing DEL. You are asked if you are sure you want to delete this file. Click Yes.

7. Press CTRL-Z to undo "the last operation." Note that the Copy (2) Of Vacations that was on the desktop and deleted in Step 5 reappears on the desktop, *not* the Vacations Shortcut that was in My Documents and deleted in Step 6. In other words, Undo uses the Recycle Bin and does not literally undo the last operation if the last operation was a literal deletion.

TIP

To create a shortcut on the desktop with the keyboard, use the arrow keys to select the object for which you will make a shortcut, press SHIFT-F10 to open the context menu, and press N twice to select Send To. Then press RIGHT ARROW to open the flyout menu, press DOWN ARROW to select Desktop (Create Shortcut), and press ENTER. A shortcut to the file or folder will appear on the desktop.

Perform Advanced Tasks

The vast majority of tasks that you will perform are the basic tasks that you have just read about. Occasionally, though, you will want to do other operations that, for the lack of a better name, I call Advanced Tasks. These include recovering a deleted item, compressing or "zipping" files, opening or editing files, searching for files and folders, sending files, and working with file and folder properties. In the following sections, we'll look at each of these tasks and the ways they can be performed.

Recover Deleted Items

The reason for the Recycle Bin is that everybody changes their mind sometimes. Something that we thought we could delete we now don't want to. The Recycle Bin serves as a temporary depository for the things you think you want to delete. If you change your mind, you can go rummage in the Recycle Bin and hopefully find what you deleted. You saw in the previous exercises how you can use Undo either through a menu or pressing CTRL-Z from the keyboard. You can also add an Undo toolbar button in the Explorer using the Customize dialog box you read about in Module 3 to undo with the mouse. The problem is that Undo at the Windows level undoes only the last retrievable event (in Microsoft Office and other programs, you can undo several times to undo several recent events). To undo at a deeper level, you must go to the Recycle Bin. Do that next:

1. Double-click the Recycle Bin to open it in an Explorer window. It should open and look something like Figure 4-5, although your contents may be different. You can see in the tasks pane that you can Empty The Recycle Bin, meaning permanently delete all of the contents, or Restore All Items.

2. Click the shortcut to Movie Maker. The tasks pane Restore option changes to Restore This Item. Click that and the shortcut to Movie Maker moves from the Recycle Bin to the desktop.

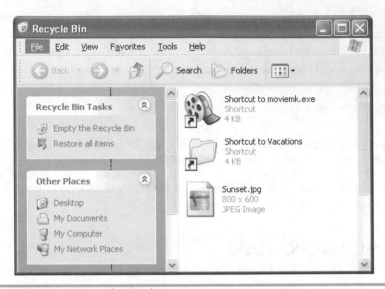

Figure 4-5 Recycle Bin open in the Explorer

3. Drag one of the other objects in the Recycle Bin to the desktop. It makes the transition smoothly.

4. Right-click an object in the Recycle Bin and the following menu appears. Restore places the object back in its original location. Cut places the object on the Clipboard so that it can be pasted where you wish. Delete permanently removes the object from the computer. Properties applies to the file and is not a Recycle Bin–specific option.

5. Open the File menu in the toolbar of the Recycle Bin. You see the Restore and Delete options. Open the Edit menu. If Undo is active, it is not related to your two Restore actions. You will see both Cut to place the active object on the Clipboard and Move To Folder, which opens the Move Items dialog box, where you can select the folder to which you want to move the selected item.

6. Select both items you restored to the desktop and drag them back to the Recycle Bin. Click Empty The Recycle Bin to permanently delete all contents, click Yes, you are sure, and then close the Recycle Bin.

Ask the Expert

Q: I've been using my computer for about a year and my Recycle Bin has an awful lot of files in it. What is the best procedure for cleaning it out?

A: The first tip is to not let it go so long. Depending on how fast you delete files, you should not wait longer than it takes you to have about 25 files in the Recycle Bin. You can pretty easily go through that number. If you have a large number of files, say over 50, the best technique is to sort the Recycle Bin to group the files. Do this by opening the Recycle Bin in the Explorer, opening the View menu, and choosing Details view. In this view, the columns of information on each file are Name, Original Location, Date Deleted, Size, Type, and Date Modified (the date last changed). You can sort on any one of these columns by clicking in the column heading in that field. The first time you click, you sort the files on that field in ascending order, from lowest to highest; the second time you click, you sort the files on that field in descending order, from highest to lowest. Try sorting the Recycle Bin on several fields and see if this doesn't provide some suggestions on what to get rid of. One obvious technique is to sort on date deleted and get rid of the oldest files.

Compress or Zip Files and Folders

Many files, especially drawings and photographic images, are quite large, over 1MB, but contain large amounts or repetitive information. Such files can be compressed or "zipped" without losing any information. For example, if you have a file in which 1,000 contiguous bytes are all the same, and in ten bytes you can describe that the next 1,000 bytes are a certain way, then you can replace the 1,000 bytes with the 10 bytes and achieve a 100-to-1 compression. Some formats are by their nature already compressed, such as the .JPG photographic image format, and so you can't save much by compression. Zipping can also be a handy way to group files that you are going to e-mail and make them as small as possible. Here is how to use a new feature in Windows XP to zip or compress some files:

TIP

When sending zipped files to other users on other computers, it's helpful to limit the file name to eight characters and use a .ZIP extension to make it easier for the other person to open the files.

1. Open Windows Explorer and navigate to the Sample Pictures folder as you have done earlier in this module.

2. Select the four sample pictures—Blue Hills, Winter, Water Lilies, and Sunset—using any of the techniques you have learned.

3. Right-click one of the pictures and choose Send To | Compressed (Zipped) Folder. A new folder will appear with a zipper on it and the name of the file that you last clicked, like this:

Sunset.zip

NOTE

If you already have WinZip or another file compression program installed, you will get a message box that asks if you want compressed (zipped) folders to be associated with zipped files. If you say "Yes," you will get a WinZip or other program icon instead of the "zipper" folder.

4. Double-click the zipped folder to look at its contents. You will see the four sample pictures. If you go back to the original Sample Pictures folder, open the View menu, and choose Details, you will see that the files sizes total 284KB for the original files and 277KB for the zipped folder. The .JPG files are already compressed, so there is not much more to be removed.

You can treat zipped files like any others, dragging, moving, and copying them like any other files in a folder. When you right-click a zipper folder and choose Extract All, the Extraction Wizard opens and lets you choose where to extract the files.

TIP

There is an excellent product called WinZip that allows you to do a lot more to create and use zipped files. You can download an evaluation version and then buy it if you like it. Go to http://www.winzip.com.

Open and Edit Files

The purpose, of course, of files on your computer is to store information that you want to use. To use them, you must be able to open them and then do something with them. For the most part, you are going to use applications outside of Windows XP such as Microsoft Office (Word, Excel, and so on). There are some minimal applications in Windows, and for the sake of our work here, they are adequate to show how to open and edit files. Do that with these steps:

1. Open the Start menu and choose All Programs | Accessories | WordPad. Type some text, it can be anything, but if you can't think of anything else type **Now is the time for all good women and men to come to the aid of their country**.

2. Click the Save icon in the toolbar. The Save As dialog box opens, suggesting that you save the file in My Documents as Document.rtf. Accept that and click Save. Close WordPad.

3. Open Start | All Programs | Accessories | Paint. In Paint, draw anything, it doesn't matter. (If you saw what I drew, you would know why I'm a writer and not an artist!) Open the File menu, choose Save, click Up One Level in the toolbar to go up to My Documents, type **Drawing** for the File Name, and click Save. Close Paint.

4. Open the Explorer showing My Documents. Click one of your new files, make sure the tasks pane is showing, and you should see a window similar to what is shown in Figure 4-6. As you can see, there are no commands in the tasks pane to open or edit these files.

5. First right-click the drawing to display the context menu, the top part of which is shown on the left here, then right-click the document, the top part of whose context menu is shown on the right.

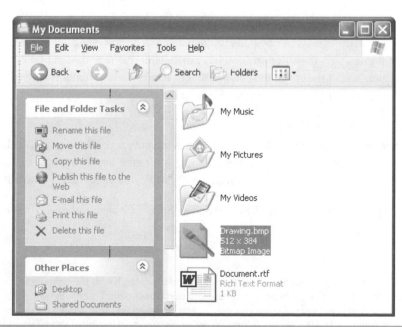

Figure 4-6   Created files in My Documents

6. Click the drawing to select it and then open the Explorer's File menu, the top of which looks just like the context menu. Choose Preview. Your drawing will be displayed in the Windows Picture And Fax Viewer. Close the Viewer. Open the File menu and choose Edit. Paint will open and display your drawing, which you can change as you wish. Close Paint. Once more open the File menu and choose Print. The Photo Printing Wizard will open. This, as the name implies, is for printing photos and offers several options for that purpose. Go through it if you wish or close it.

7. Select the text document you created, open either the context menu or the File menu, and select one after the other the Open, Edit, New, and Print options, closing WordPad after each time it opens (if you have Microsoft Word, it will open in place of WordPad). You can see that Open and Edit do exactly the same thing; New allows you to save the same file, with or without changes, but with a new filename, and Print once more opens WordPad but immediately prints the file.

8. Right-click first the document file and choose Open With, then do the same thing with the drawing. You can see that Open With gives you a choice of the programs on your computer that are registered to open this type of file, plus Choose Program. Take that last choice now. The Open With dialog box opens, as shown in Figure 4-7. Here you can choose among all the possible programs on your computer. Close Open With.

9. Double-click the drawing file. The Windows Picture And Fax Viewer will open as it did with the Preview menu option. Close the Viewer and double-click the document file. WordPad opens as it did with the Open and Edit menu options. Close WordPad.

Most common files on your computer are registered to be automatically opened, previewed, edited, and printed with the programs you have installed. This registration process is done at the time you install the programs. This is a very handy feature that allows you, in a file management sense, to work just with the files and not worry about the programs.

Search for Files and Folders

After you use a computer for a while (if you have a memory like mine), you will find you have forgotten where (in which folder) you placed a file. Microsoft has recognized that some of us have this problem and has added a search capability to Windows XP. Here's how it works:

1. In the Explorer, click Search in the toolbar. The Search Companion opens in the left pane.

TIP

If you are like many people, after about the third time you use Search with the animated dog at the bottom, you will want to get rid of him. The dog does nothing useful, except maybe look cute the first couple of times you use Search, so when you start Search, you can click Turn Off Animated Character to put the dog out of his misery in the initial search pane.

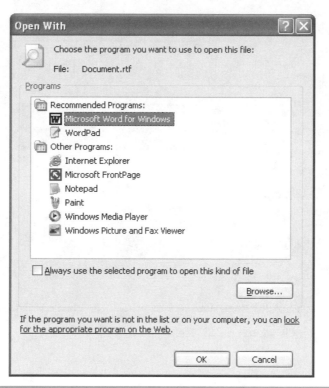

Figure 4-7 Choosing which program to use to open a file

2. Select the type of files to search—for now click Pictures, Music, Or Video. If possible, continue to narrow it down. Here, choose just Pictures And Photos. Then enter as much of the filename as you can. Type **Sunset** and click Search. The results will appear. Mine are shown in Figure 4-8. You should have at least one Sunset image from the Sample Pictures.

TIP

You want to pick the smallest set of files to search so that the search is as small and fast as possible.

3. If you want to refine your search, you can do so. For now, click Yes, Finished Searching.

The Search capability in Windows XP is very powerful and something you should explore more on your own.

Figure 4-8 Results of a file search on "Sunset"

Send Files

As you have seen earlier, both the context and File menus have a Send To option. This is used to do something with a file in addition to leaving it where it is. In other words, the Send To options send a copy of the file(s) to one of several destinations. One option you have already seen is to send one or more files to a Compressed (Zipped) Folder. See how some of the other options work:

1. In the Explorer, return to My Documents (your tasks pane should be open and have that option).

2. Right-click one of your new files (Drawing or Document) and select Send To. This flyout or submenu will open:

3. Choose Desktop. A shortcut immediately appears on the desktop.

4. Reopen the Send To submenu and choose My Documents. Because you are already in My Documents, a copy of the file is placed there with the title Copy Of....

5. If you have a floppy disk drive, place a formatted disk in the drive, reopen Send To, and choose (in my case) 3½ Floppy (A:). A copy of the file will be written to the floppy. You should see a message box telling you that it is happening.

  The Send To option is handy when dragging is cumbersome.

Progress Check

1. How do you create a shortcut when dragging a file or folder?

2. How do you open a context menu?

3. What are the keystrokes for cutting, copying, and pasting?

4. What is zipping used for?

CRITICAL SKILL
4.4 # Manage Files and Folders

Two management functions will be discussed here. First, at the file and folder level the properties of each are discussed along with how they can influence how the file or folder behaves. Second, at the disk level you will read about the disk management functions of disk cleanup, error checking, defragmentation, and backup. Other file and folder management functions will be discussed in other modules. Sharing files will be discussed in Module 9, and disk management will be discussed in Module 10.

Use File and Folder Properties

File and folder properties are almost exactly alike, as you can see in Figure 4-9 for NTFS. In both cases, they determine if a file or folder is

- Hidden or read-only

- Ready for archiving (to be backed up for safekeeping)

---

1. A shortcut is created when you press and hold SHIFT-CTRL while dragging the file.
2. The context menu is opened when you right-click a file or folder, or most other Windows objects.
3. The keystrokes are CTRL-X to cut, CTRL-C to copy, and CTRL-V to paste.
4. Zipping is used to compress large files with a lot of empty space, like some graphics files.

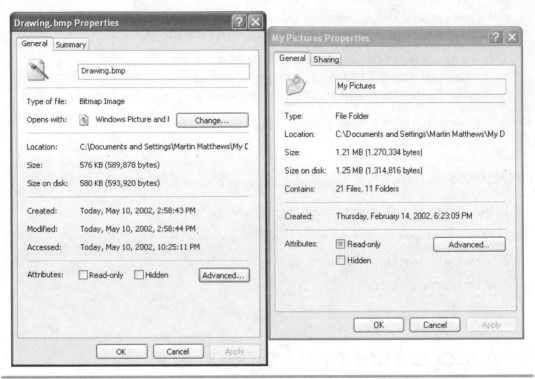

Figure 4-9 File and Folder Properties dialog boxes

- Indexed
- Compressed
- Encrypted

NOTE

Depending on whether you have NTFS or FAT/FAT32, you have different options in the
file and folder Properties dialog boxes. For example, the Properties dialog box in NTFS
has the Advanced button and no Archive check box; with FAT/FAT32 there is no
Advanced button (and therefore no encryption option), but there is an Archive check box.
There may also be other differences, depending on the programs you have installed.

In addition, for files you can set the program with which it will open, and in both cases,
you can change the name. In both cases, the archiving, indexing, compressing, and encrypting

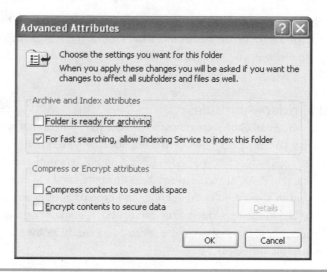

Figure 4-10 Advanced attributes for folders

are done on a similar Advanced Attributes dialog box, which is shown for folders in Figure 4-10. The only difference between this and the one for files is the note about affecting subfolders and files (see the following Note).

NOTE

When you make a change to a folder's properties, you can choose whether to change all of the files and folders it contains or not.

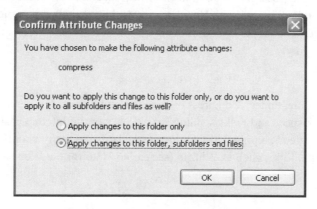

In all cases, you can change these attributes by right-clicking a file or folder and choosing Properties. If the attribute is one of the advanced ones, click the Advanced button. When you are done making the changes you want, click OK (twice, if you are in the Advanced Attributes dialog box).

Read-Only and Hidden Attributes

The *read-only* and *hidden* attributes are meant to protect files you do not want changed. Read-only means that someone can read the file but not change it. Hidden means that the file or folder is hidden *if* the Do Not Show Hidden Files And Folders option is selected in the Folder Options View tab. A lot of the need for these attributes and the encryption attribute that will be discussed in a moment is the number and type of people around your computer. Although read-only and hidden provide a little protection, it is mainly protection from very unsophisticated users; these attributes can be reversed as easily as they are set. As a default, read-only and hidden are turned off.

Archive

Archiving and the remaining attributes are in the Advanced Attributes dialog box, opened by clicking Advanced in the Properties dialog. The archiving attribute tells the Backup program that the file or folder has changed and is ready to be backed up. Windows XP automatically turns on the attribute when the file or folder is created and whenever the file or folder is changed. The Backup program automatically turns off the attribute when the file or folder is backed up. You can force or prevent backup by manually changing the attribute.

Index

Windows XP has a background Indexing Service that periodically goes through your hard disk and indexes the files and folders it finds. This greatly speeds up searches, although it does take some processing resources. By default, this is turned on, and I can't think of a good reason a file or folder should not be indexed. Here, you are deciding whether a particular file or folder should be indexed. You might wonder if being off might help hide a file, but a search will still find it, just more slowly.

Compress

Earlier in this module, under "Compress or Zip Files and Folders," you read how compressing can help save disk space and make sending large files over the Internet easier. This form of compression, called "zipping," is an industry standard, and many people have the means to unzip such a file. Firms such as WinZip (see earlier Note for the Web site) and PKZip

Ask the Expert

Q: **Do you recommend that file and folder compression be used?**

A: With today's inexpensive large disk drives, I don't. The zipping of files, as discussed earlier in the module, is handy for e-mailing larger files over the Internet. However, the form of file and folder compression discussed here is really a carryover from the days when disks were much smaller and much more expensive, and running out of disk space was a common occurrence.

(http://www.pkware.com) provide third-party products that can be downloaded over the Internet to do that. In addition to zipping, Windows XP has another technology for compressing files and folders that has been in Windows products for some time. This is the compression that is applied through the advanced attributes. It works well, saving a reasonable amount of space, and you can work with the compressed files and folders in the same way as if they were not compressed. The only difference is that it takes a very small added amount of time every time you open a compressed file or folder or save it back to disk.

Encrypt

Encrypting a file or a folder makes it very difficult or nearly impossible to read if you don't have permission to open it. The permission, though, is not set on a file-by-file or folder-by-folder basis, but at the computer user level. If you have permission to log on as a user who can access the file or folder, you will have access to it in the same way as you would if it weren't encrypted. In that case, the encryption is transparent. Anyone without the user-level permission who tries to access the file will not be able to do so.

Setting permissions and passwords to enforce them is discussed in detail in Module 9.

NOTE

If you once encrypt anything and then lose the password that gives you access to it, plan on the file or folder being gone forever. To break the encryption requires supercomputers, super-smart mathematicians, and a lot of time (like years).

You can encrypt either files or folders, or both, but if you just encrypt a file, you will get a message shown next that recommends you also encrypt the parent folder so that every time you open and edit the file it will automatically be re-encrypted. If the file alone is encrypted, you will have to manually re-encrypt it each time it is opened and resaved.

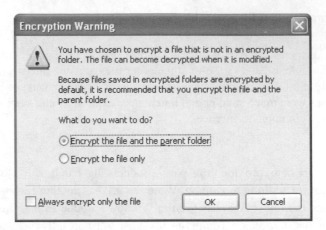

CRITICAL SKILL

4.5 Manage Disks

There are several basic management tasks that need to be performed periodically on any hard disk to keep it running smoothly and to keep your data for getting lost. These are

- Disk cleanup
- Error checking
- Defragmentation
- Backup

All of these tasks are accessed via the disk Properties dialog box; all but Error Checking are also available through the Start menu | All Programs | Accessories | System Tools. Open My Computer now in the Explorer, right-click your C: hard disk, and choose Properties. On the General tab, you will see Disk Cleanup, and in the Tools tab, you will see Error Checking, Defragmentation, and Backup.

Disk Cleanup

One of the hardest jobs in using a computer is getting rid of old files on your hard disk. Disk Cleanup helps you do that. When you click Disk Cleanup, Windows goes through your hard disk, looks for certain types of files that you can possibly delete, and then lists these types of files, as you can see in Figure 4-11. You can then go through and decide by checking or unchecking the file types those that you want to delete. If you want, you can look at the files

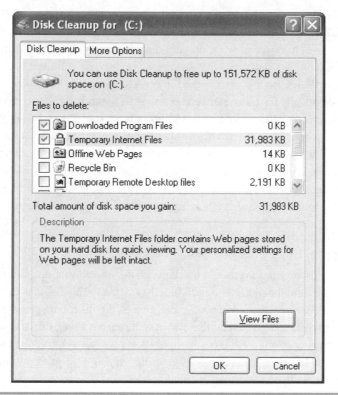

Figure 4-11 Disk Cleanup lists types of files that you can delete.

in each type by selecting a type and clicking View Files. One option that generally saves a lot of space is to compress old files. If you badly need space, this is a good alternative, but it is the same compression discussed with file and folder properties and will add time every time you open and close the file.

The More Options tab gives you three advanced options:

● **Windows Components** opens the Windows Components Wizard, where you can add or remove components like Fax Services or Networking Services that you may not be using.

● **Installed Programs** opens Add Or Remove Programs, where you can remove programs that you have installed but no longer use.

● **System Restore** removes the information on your computer that allows you to restore it to the settings used at a given point in time. Each restore point takes a fair amount of information, so you probably don't want to keep more than one or two. The System Restore option removes all but the most recent restore point. If you have only one restore point, you will be asked if you want to remove it. You probably do not.

Error Checking

Error Checking tries to read and write on your disk, without losing any information there, to determine if there are any bad areas that should not be used. If it finds a bad area, it will flag it and the system will not use that area in the future. After selecting to do Error Checking, you can have it automatically fix file system errors and scan for and attempt recovery of bad sectors, which I recommend. If you are on a network and/or have started any Windows components, which most likely have been automatically started for you, you will get a message that Error Checking cannot proceed. You are asked if you want to schedule this to happen the next time you start Windows. If you want to do error checking, click Yes. The next time you start Windows, a five-stage process will be undertaken to thoroughly test your disk and determine if it is in good shape. Depending on the size and speed of your disk, this can take some time.

Defragment

Files are not stored on your hard disk in one large chunk of information. Rather, a file is broken into smaller pieces and the pieces are individually written to the disk. As the disk gets full, the pieces may not be written all to one contiguous area of the disk, but spread around as needed. This means that when you go to read that file, it will require a lot of disk activity, slowing down access considerably. To fix this situation, Windows has a defragmentation process that will go through and rewrite the contents of your disk, trying as best as possible to collect all of the pieces of a file in one contiguous area.

When you choose Defragment Now, the Disk Defragmenter will open. Click Analyze and you will be told if your disk needs to be defragmented and graphically shown the fragmentation. To go ahead, choose Defragment. Depending on the size of your disk and the speed of your computer, this can take a while. You will be shown the process graphically as it proceeds. When it is done, you will see how well it did, as you can see in Figure 4-12. It may be that some fragments may be left at the end.

Backup

Backing up takes important files on your disk and writes copies of them on another device such as a recordable CD, a Zip drive, a removable hard drive, a tape drive, or another hard drive, possibly on another computer.

When you select Back Now, the Backup Or Restore Wizard opens. Click Next, choose Back Up Files And Settings, and click Next again. You are given a choice of backing up just your documents and settings, everybody's documents and settings, all information on the computer, or data of your choice. I prefer choosing what to back up because to me some things are very important and others are not. If you select to choose what to back up, the dialog box shown in Figure 4-13 opens; it lets you select the folders and files to include. Clicking Next

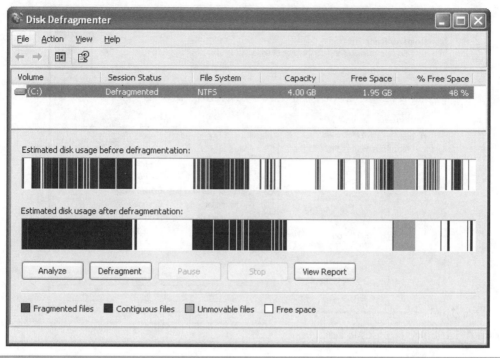

Figure 4-12 Defragmenting brings pieces of a file together in one contiguous area.

Ask the Expert

Q: How often should I back up my disk?

A: That is a very difficult question, and there is a different answer for every person and business. The quick answer is, how long can you go before you can no longer afford to lose the information on your disk? Some firms have systems that back up continuously. Their computers write all of their data twice on two disks, called a mirrored system. Many businesses write all of their data to tape every night. I write the module files I am currently working on to a floppy disk at least once and sometimes twice a day, and then I back up all of my data files on my hard disk to a CD about once every two months. People who use their computer only for e-mail and Web surfing may never back it up, although they might miss their address book and list of favorite Web sites if something happened to their hard disk.

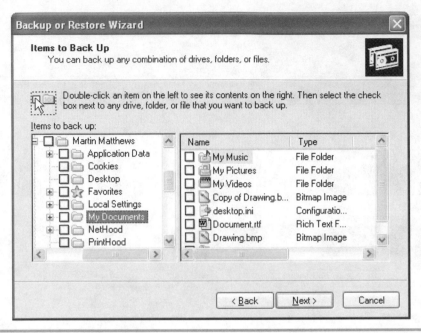

Figure 4-13 Selecting files to back up

allows you to choose the backup type and the media to use. Depending on the media you are using, you may be asked additional questions as you complete the backup.

Progress Check

1. What are three file or folder attributes that you can set?

2. What is the difference between zipping and compressing files?

3. What does defragmentation do?

---

1. The six file or folder attributes that you can set are read-only, hidden, archive, index, compress, and encrypt.

2. On the surface, there is no difference; zipping is a form of file compression. In Windows XP, though, "zipping" is using the industry standard form of file compression that most people can open and is frequently used to send files on the Internet. "Compression," on the other hand, uses an older form of file compression that meant to simply save space on a hard drive.

3. Defragmentation gathers all the pieces (fragments) of a file and places them in one contiguous area of the hard disk.

Project 4 Setting Up a File System

In this project, we'll continue the same scenario we began in Module 3 of setting up a new computer. Here we'll

- Create a folder structure for a small business
- Create some shortcuts on the desktop
- Create and copy files
- Rename a file
- Delete and undelete some files
- Zip some files
- Search for a file
- Do a disk cleanup

This looks like a lot of work, but with the Windows GUI, it is very simple.

Step by Step

1. Start up and log on to Windows XP. Open My Documents (if it is on the desktop, double-click it; otherwise, open the Start menu and click My Documents).

2. Create a new folder in My Documents named "Company" by either clicking Make A New Folder in Tasks view or right-clicking in the right pane of My Documents and choosing New | Folder. In either case, type the name **Company**.

3. Double-click your new folder to open it. Make three folders here named "Accounting," "Marketing," and "Production." Double-click Accounting to open it and make two folders named "2002" and "2003."

4. Select both the 2002 and 2003 folders by clicking one, holding down SHIFT and clicking the other, and then press CTRL-C to copy them. Click Up in the toolbar, double-click Marketing to open it, and press CTRL-V to paste the two folders there. Once more click Up, double-click Production, and press CTRL-V.

(continued)

5. Open the folders pane if it isn't already. In the folders pane, click the plus sign to open My Documents, Company, Accounting, Marketing, and Production. Your folder structure should look like this:

6. Open the Company folder, select all three subfolders (Accounting, Marketing, and Production) by clicking while holding down SHIFT, and then hold down CTRL-SHIFT while dragging the folders to the desktop to create three shortcuts.

7. Open the Start menu and choose All Programs | Accessories | WordPad. Type **These are instructions for the budget process.** Open the File menu, choose Save As, open the Save In drop-down list and select \My Documents\Company\Accounting\2002, name the file **2002 Instructions**, and click Save. Close WordPad.

8. Open the Accounting\2002 folder; make sure the folders pane is open; and press and hold CTRL while dragging a copy of the text file to Marketing\2002, to Production\2002, and to Accounting\2003.

9. Open the Accounting\2003 folder and slowly click the filename twice (don't double-click it) to open it for revision. Change "2002" to "2003" and press ENTER. Then copy (CTRL-drag) that file to Marketing\2003 and Production\2003.

10. You are told that the company has decided to subcontract the production work, so you no longer need that department. Click Company in the folders pane to open that folder. Right-click Production, choose Delete, and click Yes to confirm you want to send that folder and all of its contents to the Recycle Bin.

11. Next you are told that the subcontractor is not working out and production is being brought back in house, so you need the Production department again (sound realistic?). Open the

Recycle Bin, select (click) the Production folder, and click Restore This Item in the tasks pane. Production will return to the Company folder.̇ Close the Recycle Bin.

12. Open My Documents, right-click Company, and choose Send To | Compressed (Zipped) Folder. This will create a zipped folder containing the Company folder, all the subfolders, and the files you created. It would be very easy to e-mail this zipped folder to whoever needed it. The recipient would just double-click the zipped folder and then drag the company folder with all its contents to where she wanted it on her computer.

13. Click Search in the Explorer toolbar. Click Documents to search for that. Enter the document name **2002 Instructions**, and click Search. You should get the three copies you made, plus the zipped copies.

14. Drag all of the Company folders, zipped and otherwise, plus the three shortcuts from the desktop and the Search window to the Recycle Bin. Open My Computer, right-click your C: hard disk, and choose Properties. Click Disk Cleanup. Click Recycle Bin to empty it and any other files you want to delete, such as Temporary Internet Files and Temporary Files. If you are not sure about a category, click View Files. When you are ready to get rid of the files, click OK and click Yes, you are sure.

Project Summary

Isn't it amazing how much you just did and how fast and easy it was? Did you also notice how there was a mixture of dragging, tasks pane commands, keyboard shortcuts, and menus used? Although I did make a point of that, it also reflected how I, and I believe most people, operate. Windows XP provides a lot of tools for handling information on your computer, with the result that it is very fast and easy to do.

✔

Module 4 Mastery Check

1. Can you store a 2,340KB file on a 1.44MB floppy disk?

2. A program you just installed has several .DLL files, an .EXE file, and a .TXT file. Which one do you double-click to start the program?

3. What is the difference between Tasks view and Folders view in Windows Explorer?

4. How does Windows' graphical user interface (GUI) help manipulate files and folders?

5. Match up the action on the left with the command on the right. There may be more than one command for one action, and some actions may not have a command.

Action	Command
Copy a file or folder	Drag
Back up a file or folder	Drag it to the Recycle Bin
Create a shortcut	Click-F2
Open a context menu	Click-DEL
Create a folder	CTRL-C
Move a file or folder	CTRL-drag
Rename a file or folder	CTRL-SHIFT-drag
Create a zipped file	CTRL-X then CTRL-V
Delete a file	Right-click
Search for a File	Slowly click twice

6. What are two ways you can recover deleted items?

7. What is WinZip and how does it affect Windows zipping?

8. How do file attributes differ between FAT and NTFS files?

9. What is the difference between hidden files and read-only files, and what are these properties called?

10. What is Backup used for?

Module 5

Printing and Faxing

Although talk of a paperless society continues, it does not look like it will occur any time soon. As a result, the ability to transfer computer information to paper or other media is very important and a major function of Windows XP.

Define Printing and Faxing

It may seem obvious what printing is, but does your obvious definition include "printing" to a file or "printing" to a fax? In addition, although "printing" to a network printer does end up using a physical printing device, to the local computer, this form of "printing" is just a network address. So what does "printer" mean to Windows?

- **Printer**   A name that refers to a set of specifications used for printing, primary among which is a hardware port, such as LPT1 or USB1, a software port, such as FILE or FAX, or a network address.

- **Printer driver**   Software that tells the computer how to accomplish the printing task desired; part of the printer specifications that defines a "printer."

- **Printing device**   The actual piece of hardware that does the printing. *Local printing devices* are connected to a hardware port on the computer requesting the printing; *network printing devices* are connected either to another computer or directly to the network.

- **Print server**   The computer controlling the printing, and to which the printing device is connected.

There are three types of printers:

- **Local devices** connected to your computer

- **Network devices** somewhere else on your local area network (LAN)

- **Software devices** that create files and facilitate sending faxes

Ask the Expert

Q: I still don't see why printing and faxing are discussed together. Can you explain that?

A: Think of faxing as printing over a phone line. You generally take a file on your computer, maybe something you scanned, a document you wrote, or a digital photograph you downloaded to your computer, and you send it over phone lines to be printed on a fax machine on the other end. It is very similar technology to sending the same item to a local printer. Receiving a fax is similar. You receive a file over phone lines that can be viewed and printed.

All three types of printers are set up, used, and managed in a very similar way. All of them use the Printers And Faxes window to set up and to manage, and all of them can be used from almost all programs independent of whether they are local, network, or software devices.

CRITICAL SKILL
5.2 Install Printers

All types of printers are installed in the same way using the Printers And Faxes window. However, because there are differences as you work through the installation, look first at installing a local printer, then a networked one, and finally look at how to set up printing to a file. Later in the module, you'll see how to set up faxing.

Install a Local Printer

A local printer is one that is physically attached to your computer using cable made for that purpose. Prior to starting to install a local printer, make sure it

- Is plugged into the correct connector (port) on your computer (see the instructions that came with the printer)

- Is plugged into an electrical outlet

- Has fresh ink or toner cartridges and they and the print heads are properly installed

- Has adequate paper

- Is turned on

With these points assured, use the following steps to install a printer:

1. If necessary, start up your computer, log on, open the Start menu, and click Printers And Faxes (see following Note if you are using Windows XP Home). You might be surprised to see some network printers, and even a local printer, already in the Printers And Faxes window. After you install and start up Windows XP, it looks around the network for folders, disks, and printers that have been shared and are available for your use. Figure 5-1 shows the printers on my network that were found and automatically installed within an hour of installing Windows XP. If you see the printer you are trying to install in this window, it has already been installed and you need to do nothing further except test it out, so you can jump to Step 6.
   If you have a Plug and Play printer (one that talks to Windows XP and automatically sets itself up) and you just plugged it in and turned it on, as just suggested, it might already be installed or be in the process of being installed. In this case, when you first started up Windows, you should have gotten a message Found New Hardware. If Windows has all the information it needs, it will go ahead and complete the installation without further input

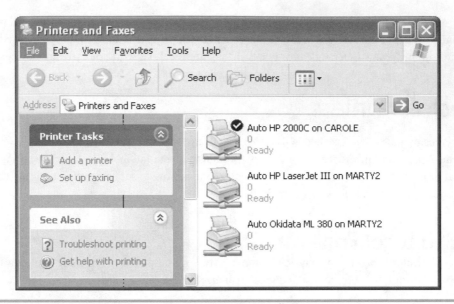

Figure 5-1 Network printers that are automatically installed

from you, in which case you can skip to Step 6. If Windows found the printer but doesn't have all the needed information, the Found New Hardware Wizard will open and lead you through the steps to complete the installation. Jump to Step 5. In all other cases, continue with Step 2.

NOTE

In Windows XP Professional there is by default a Printers And Faxes option on the Start menu. In Windows XP Home, it doesn't appear by default, but it can be added through the Taskbar And Start Menu Properties dialog box as discussed in Module 3. If Printers And Faxes is not on the Start menu, you can open it from the Control Panel, which you must open first.

2. Click Add A Printer in the tasks pane. The Add Printer Wizard will open. In the Welcome message, you are told that if you have a Plug and Play printer that is "hot-pluggable" (one you can plug in while the computer is turned on) and you haven't plugged it in, do so now and turn it on. Close the Add Printer Wizard and Windows will install the printer for you if possible or start the Found New Hardware Wizard, as described in Step 1. To continue in the Add Printer Wizard, click Next.

3. You are asked if you want to install a local or a network printer. Local is the default, so click Next. Windows will search for a Plug and Play printer (which if you had one it should have already found) and then tell you it can't find one. Click Next.

4. Select the port you printer will use. The default of LPT1 (parallel communications port 1, originally "line printer terminal 1," but nobody ever uses the words) handles the majority of printers. The very newest may use USB (universal serial bus) and are probably Plug and Play, so you shouldn't have to worry about them, and the very oldest may use COM1–COM4 (serial communications ports 1–4), but these are almost extinct. See the following Tip or refer to the printer manufacturer's information if you have questions. Click Next.

TIP

Both parallel printer cables and serial printer cables may use a 25-pin connector called a DB-25. The parallel cable has a male DB-25 in the end that plugs into the computer and a totally different connector called a Centronics 36-pin connector on the end that plugs into the printer. The serial cable may have one of several combinations, with a DB-25 male on one end and a DB-25 female on the other being most common.

5. Select your printer's manufacturer and model. For example, in Figure 5-2 I'm selecting an HP Color LaserJet 4500 (in my dreams). If you go through the lists—and you need to do

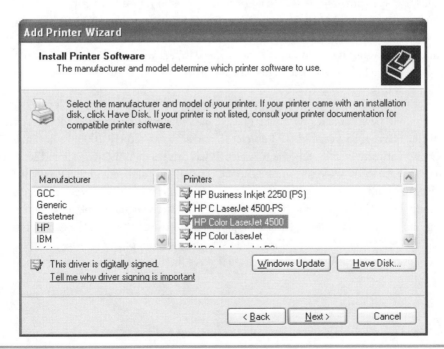

Figure 5-2 Selecting a printer manufacturer and model

this carefully because there are thousands of printers listed—and if you can't find your printer, you have two options, Have Disk and Windows Update.

If a CD came with your printer *and* it has a Windows XP driver (the disk or box must say "For Windows XP"), it most likely has its own installation program on the disk. In this case, click Cancel in the Add Printer Wizard, place the disk in the CD-ROM drive, and follow the instructions that appear on the screen. If nothing happens when you put the CD in the drive, restart the Add Printer Wizard, follow the first four steps, and in the fifth step click Have Disk. If you don't have a CD or the CD is not for Windows XP (most often drivers for older versions of Windows do not work), then click Windows Update at this point. If that still does not help you, then you need to go to the manufacturer's web site and download a recent driver. You use it the way a CD is described as being used here, but instead of being a CD, it will be a file on your hard drive, which you will have to point to. When you have installed the correct driver, click Next.

6. You are asked to enter a name for the printer (the manufacturer's name is shown as a default), and you are asked if you want to use this printer as a default. Select Yes if this will be your primary printer. Click Next.

7. Click Yes to print a test page and then click Next. The choices you have made are shown. If they are not correct, click Back as many times as necessary to make the correction, and then when you are ready, click Finish. The printer will be installed and a test page will be printed. If the test page came out okay, click OK to that question; you have correctly installed the printer and can click Finish again to close the Add Printer Wizard. Otherwise, click Back to change any of the settings. Also make sure the obvious things are correct, like paper in the printer, and having it turned on. If none of these things work, click Troubleshoot in the message box asking if the test page came out okay.

Under most circumstances, with recent equipment and Windows XP, the local printer installation will be automatic. With widely used, but older printers, the preceding steps should work well. (I have a 15-year-old HP LaserJet III and a 3-year-old HP 2000C color inkjet. The 2000C automatically installs, and the LaserJet III has drivers in Windows XP and so is easy to install with these steps.) If your printer is not automatically installed and you do not have a disk that will work with XP, try first Windows Update (which is a Microsoft web site) and see if there is anything there. If not, go to the printer manufacturer's web site and look for either an install program or drivers for Windows XP. Also, at the manufacturer's web site, make sure to get the instructions for downloading, installing, and using the program or driver. Most manufacturers have very good and helpful web sites because it saves them money in customer support.

TIP

If your printer was automatically installed, but a CD came with your printer and you wonder if you should install using the CD, the general answer is no. Most printer drivers in Windows XP originally came from the manufacturers and have been tested by Microsoft, so they should work well. Unless the printer came out after the release of Windows XP (October 2001), the driver in XP should be newer.

Install a Networked Printer

Network printers are not directly connected to your computer but are available to you as a result of your computer's connection to a network and the fact that the printers have been shared. There are three types of network printers:

- Printers connected to someone else's computer, which they have shared

- Printers connected to a dedicated printer server, which have been shared

- Printers directly connected to a network (they in effect have a built-in computer)

The first two types of network printers are installed with the Network Printer option in the Add Printer Wizard, whereas the third option is installed (generally automatically) with the Local Printer option.

Before installing a networked printer, make sure you have the full network address (called a UNC, for uniform naming convention) in the form *servername**printername*. For example, \\Carole\HP2000C is a printer on my network. Carole is the name of the computer acting as a print server (and of my wife who uses that computer), and HP2000C is the printer name. It also may be necessary to have a user name and password if the printer has not been shared with everyone on the network. With this information, here are the steps to install a network printer:

1. If necessary, start up your computer, log on, open the Start menu, and click Printers And Faxes (see the earlier Note if you are using Windows XP Home). Click Add A Printer in the tasks pane and click Next at the Welcome message.

2. Given you are connecting to a printer connected to another computer, be it a server or a workstation, click A Network Printer… and click Next. If you are connecting to a stand-alone network printer directly connected to the network, follow the steps earlier in the module for installing a local printer.

3. You are asked to specify the printer you are going to connect to. This is where you can use the UNC you hopefully got in preparing for these steps. If so, click Connect To This

Printer, type the UNC, click Next, and skip to Step 5. Otherwise, click Browse For A Printer (if you are connected to a domain, this will read Find A Printer In The Directory) and click Next.

4. A list of shared printers on your network will be displayed. Figure 5-3 shows the list for my network. Select the printer you want to use and click Next.

5. Choose whether you want this printer to be the default printer and click Next. You are shown a summary of the choices you have made. If they are not correct, click Back as needed, make the changes, and click Next as needed to return to the ending dialog box. When you are ready, click Finish. The printer will be installed.

6. Unlike when installing a local printer, you may not be automatically asked if you want to print a test page. It is still a good idea to do that. Here's how: right-click the new printer and choose Properties. At the bottom right of the General tab of the Properties dialog box, click Print Test Page. You will be told that a page is being printed. Go and get the test page. If it is fine, click OK; otherwise, click Troubleshoot. When you are ready, close the Properties dialog box.

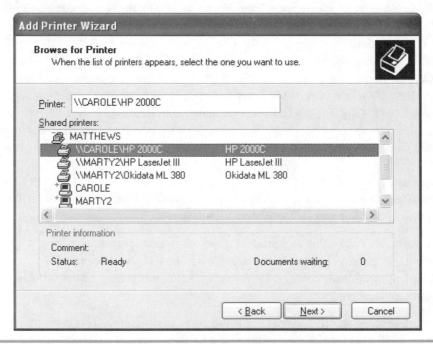

Figure 5-3 List of available network printers

Ask the Expert

Q: I know there are network printers on our network, but none are automatically installed on my computer, when I go and look for them none appear, and when I enter the UNC I get an error message to the effect that I don't have permission to use the printer. I know I have the permission to use several of the network printers.

A: You have been bitten by the great Windows XP Permissions dragon. It is one of the most difficult problems to solve. In summary, the permissions on your computer are different than those required to use the printers. There are many possible reasons for this, and of course, I cannot know all the variables in your network and on your computer. The easy answer is to get someone to help you, like a network administrator or consultant in your company or available to you. The second best answer is to read Module 9 and see if the answer is there. Although I try in that module to give you a complete picture of how security is implemented, I cannot anticipate all the possible combinations of settings that could be affecting you. The final answer, which may or may not be possible for you, is to reinstall Windows XP from scratch on a clean hard disk. I have seen reinstallation solve more permissions problems than any other solution.

Set Up Printing to a File

There are two primary reasons to print to a file, and each takes a different setup. The first is to print to a file that you can take to a remote location to print on a particular printer. This requires formatting the information for a printer, but then sending it to a file instead of the printer. The second is to get information out of one program and into another when there is no data export command in the first program. In this case, you want the "printer" to produce unformatted generic text. In the first case, you install, as a normal printer, the ultimate printer you want to use and then at the time of printing tell Windows that you want the output to go to a file. In the second case, you must actually create a "printer" to produce the unformatted generic text. Here look at creating a generic text file device. Later in the module, when I talk about actually doing printing, I'll explain how to switch to printing to a file:

1. Open the Printers And Faxes window if it isn't already open. Click Add A Printer and click Next at the Welcome message.

2. Select Local Printer, but uncheck Automatically Detect And Install My Plug And Play Printer, and click Next.

3. In the Select A Printer Port dialog box, open the drop-down list opposite Use The Following Port and choose File (Print To File). Click Next.

4. In the Install Printer Software dialog box, scroll down and choose Generic as the manufacturer, and Generic / Text Only printer. Click Next.

5. You are asked what you want to name the printer and whether or not you want to use it as your default. Name it "Print to File" and do not use it as your default. Click Next. Select No to printing a test page, click Next, and Finish. A new icon will appear in your Printers And Faxes window, like this:

Print to File

Progress Check

- What is a printer?
- What are the three types of printers?
- What does the UNC look like for a printer?

Use and Manage Printing

If your primary printing concern is with a fully functioning printer attached to your computer and you are the only user, you do not have much of a printer management problem. On the other hand, if you have several printers and more users, the challenge can be significant. In this section, we'll look at printer configuration, printing, managing a print queue, handling fonts, and handling multiple printers.

1. A printer is a name with a set of software specifications and a driver so that Windows can use it.

2. The three types of printers are local devices, network devices, and software devices.

3. The UNC for a printer on your network should look like *servername**printername*.

Printer Configuration

As a general rule, the default configuration for a printer works well, so unless you have a unique situation, it is recommended that you keep the default settings. It is also worthwhile knowing what your alternatives are, so look at the settings you can use to control your printer (these settings vary depending on the printer that you are configuring, so look at your printer during this discussion).

A printer's settings are contained in its Properties dialog box. This is accessed by opening the Printers And Faxes window (Start menu | Printers And Faxes), right-clicking the icon of the printer you want to configure, and choosing Properties. For purposes of this discussion, the tabs in the printer Properties dialog box can be grouped into categories of printer configuration, printing configuration, and user configuration.

Configure a Printer

Configuring a printer has to do with controlling the printer itself. On the General tab of your printer's Properties dialog box, you can change the name of the printer, identify its location, and enter a comment about it. In the Ports tab, you can change the port used by the printer; add, delete, and configure ports; turn on and off bidirectional communication with the printer; and set up printer pooling. In the Device Settings tab, you can set what is loaded in each paper tray, how to handle font substitution, and what printer options are available. Your particular printer may have different or additional options, so review these tabs for your printer. Most of the printer configuration settings are self-explanatory, such as the name and location, and others are rarely changed from their initial setup, such as the port and bidirectional communication (which speeds using the printer if it is available). Several items, though, are worthy of further discussion: printer pooling, printer priority, and assigning paper trays.

Printer Pooling   Printer pooling allows you to have two or more physical printing devices assigned to one printer. The printing devices can be local or directly connected to the network, but they must share the same print driver. When print jobs are sent to the printer, Windows determines which of the physical devices is available and routes the job to that device. This eliminates the need for the user to determine which printing device is available, provides for better load sharing among printing devices, and allows the management of several devices through one printer definition.

You can set up printer pooling with these steps:

1. Install all printers as described previously in "Install Printers."

2. In the Printers And Faxes window, right-click the printer to which all work will be directed and choose Properties. The printer's Properties dialog box will open.

3. Click the Ports tab and click Enable Printer Pooling.

4. Click each of the ports with a printing device that is to be in the pool.

5. When all the ports are selected, click OK to close the Properties dialog box.

6. If the printer that contains the pool isn't already selected as the default printer, right-click the printer and choose Set As Default Printer.

Printer Priority   You can do the opposite of printer pooling by assigning several printer names to one printing device. The primary reason that you would want to do this is to have two or more settings used with one device. For example, if you want to have two or more priorities automatically assigned to jobs going to a printing device, you could create two or more printers, all pointing to the same printer port and physical device, but with different priorities. Then, have high-priority print jobs printed to a printer with a priority of 99, and low-priority jobs printed to a printer with a priority of 1.

Create several printers with one print device using the following steps:

1. Install all printers as previously described in "Install Printers." Name each of the printers to indicate its priority. For example, "High Priority Printer" and "Low Priority Printer."

2. In the Printers And Faxes window, right-click the high-priority printer and choose Properties. The printer's Properties dialog box will open.

3. Select the Advanced tab, enter a Priority of **99**, and click OK.

4. Similarly, right-click the other printers, open their Properties dialog box, select the Advanced tab, and set the priority from 1 for the lowest priority to 98 for the second-highest priority.

Jobs that are printed with the highest priority will print before jobs with a lower priority if they are in the queue at the same time. If you have a program that automatically prints, such as incoming orders, you might want to assign it a lower priority than a word processing task, such as a new proposal.

Assign Paper Trays   Depending on your printer, it may have more than one paper tray, and as a result, you may want to put different types or sizes of paper in each tray. If you assign types and sizes of paper to trays in the printer's Properties dialog box, and a user requests a type and size of paper when printing, Windows XP automatically designates the correct paper tray for the print job. Here's how to assign types and sizes of paper to trays:

1. In the Printers And Faxes window, right-click the printer whose trays you want to assign and choose Properties. The printer's Properties dialog box opens.

2. Select the Device Settings tab. Open each tray and select the type and size of paper in that tray, similar to what you see in Figure 5-4.

3. When you have set the paper type and size in each tray, click OK.

Print Configuration

Printing configuration has to do with controlling the process of printing, not the printer itself or particular print jobs. Printing configuration is handled in the Advanced tab of a printer's Properties dialog box. As I said earlier, in most cases, the default settings are appropriate and should be changed only in unique situations. Two exceptions to this are the spooling settings and using separator pages, discussed next.

Spool Settings   In most instances, the time it takes to print a document is considerably longer than the time it takes to transfer the information from an application to the printer. The information is therefore stored on disk in a special preprint format, and then Windows, as a

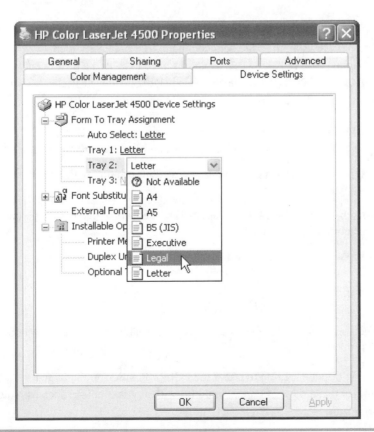

Figure 5-4 Setting the paper type and size in each paper tray

background task, feeds the printer as much information as it can handle. This temporary storage on disk is called *printer spooling*. Under the majority of cases, you want to use printer spooling and not tie up the application waiting for the printer. However, an alternative pair of settings is available.

- **Start Printing After Last Page Is Spooled** By waiting to print until the last page is spooled, the application finishes faster and the user gets back to the application faster, but it takes longer to finish printing.

- **Start Printing Immediately** The printing will be done sooner, but the application will be tied up a little longer.

There is no one correct choice for this. Normally, the default Start Printing Immediately provides a happy medium between getting the printing and getting back to the application. However, if you want to get back to the application in the shortest possible time, then choose to wait until the last page is spooled.

Use Separator Pages If you have a number of different jobs on a printer, it might be worthwhile to have a separator page between them, to more easily identify where one job ends and another begins. You can also use a separator page to switch a printer between PostScript (a printer language) and PCL (Printer Control Language) on Hewlett-Packard (HP) and compatible printers. Four sample SEP separation files come with Windows XP:

- **Pcl.sep** Prints a separation page before the start of each print job on PCL-compatible printers. If the printer handles both PostScript and PCL, it will be switched to PCL.

- **Pscript.sep** Does *not* print a separation page, but printers with both PostScript and PCL will be switched to PostScript.

- **Sysprint.sep** Prints a separation page before the start of each print job on PostScript-compatible printers.

- **Sysprtj.sep** The same as Sysprint.sep, but in the Japanese language.

NOTE

The separation files work with HP and PostScript or compatible printers. They will not work with all printers.

If you know or have a guide to either the PCL or PostScript language (or both), you can open and modify these files (or copies of them) with any text editor, such as Notepad, to suite your particular purpose.

User Configuration

rolling the users of a printer. This is the one area where
hich is not to share the printer and not to allow anyone
iguration is controlled in the Sharing tab of the printer's
ing on and off.

liscussed in Module 9. Here we want to just discuss the
some the detail issues of security with these steps:

ight-click the printer that you want to share and choose
ialog box opens.

ou Understand The Security Risks But Want To Share
d, Click Here. A warning message appears, click Just
. (If doing this concerns you, skip it here because we'll
dule 9.) The Sharing tab changes.

hare Name. Click OK. Back in the Printers And Faxes
w the printer showing it is shared, like this:

or LaserJet 4500

of Windows on the computers using the printer you
drivers for those other versions of Windows and
t. Click Additional Drivers, choose the drivers you

l supplies the drivers to do the printing, the actual
programs or applications that create the material to
PhotoShop, and CorelDraw. All of these programs,
lo the printing.

l want to print, you commonly open the File menu
xplorer and locate a file you want to print, you
you do this in Explorer, it will load the application
process. In the case of printing from within the
own in Figure 5-5. Here you can control several

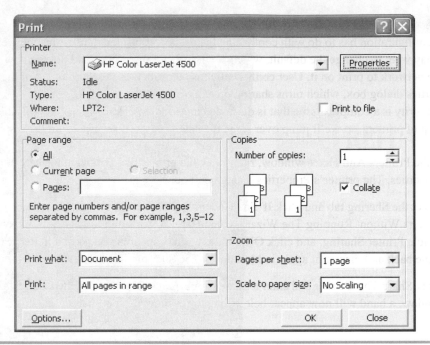

Figure 5-5 Options that are available when you print from an application

options we'll discuss in a moment. When you print from Explorer, it uses all the default settings and you have no choices, except that if it is a long enough print job, you can cancel it, as you'll see later in the module under "Manage Print Jobs."

Print Options

The Print dialog box shown in Figure 5-5, which opens when you choose to print from within an application, can vary from application to application (the one here is from Microsoft Word 2002) and depends on the printer. These are key choices that are available in just about all Print dialog boxes:

● **Printer** allows you to choose which printer to use (by opening the drop-down list), change the Properties of that printer, and choose to print to a file.

● **Page Range** allows you to choose the pages to print. In the text box, you can enter a page number, several separated pages, or a range of pages. For example, if I wanted to print the first, fourth, and sixth through ninth pages, I would enter it as **1,4,6-9**.

● **Copies** allows you to enter the number of copies you want and lets you specify if you want them collated. If you say you do not want the job collated and you want three copies, three copies of page one will print followed by three copies of page two, and so on.

● **Print What** allows you to print either the document or ancillary material attached to the document, as shown here:

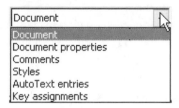

● **Print** allows you to print all pages or just the odd or even pages.

● **Zoom** allows you to change the page size and to fit the document to a different size paper.

Your Print dialog box may have more or less options, but many of the preceding options should be available.

Print to a File

Earlier in this module, under the section "Set Up Printing to a File," I talked about how there are two ways of printing to a file, one so that the file can be used to remotely print a document, and the other so that the file can be used to transfer information from one application to another. In the first case, you install the final destination printer as if it were attached to your computer. Then you select that printer when you go to print, but in the Print dialog box you choose Print To File, which you can see in Figure 5-5.

In the case where you want to transfer information between applications, you must install a special generic text printer as described earlier in the module. When you go to print, you select this special printer and you choose Print To File.

When you choose Print To File and click OK, the Print To File dialog box opens and asks you where you want the file and what you want it named. When you enter that information and click OK, the file is written where you selected. If you are writing a file to print on a remote printer, you want to, and will by default, create a .PRN file. If you are writing a file to transfer to another application, save it with a .TXT extension. You can print a .PRN file by opening the Command Prompt (Start | All Programs | Accessories | Command Prompt), typing **print** ***path**filename*.prn**, pressing ENTER, closing the Command Prompt by typing **exit**, and pressing ENTER.

Manage Print Jobs

As jobs are printed by applications, they are spooled onto a disk and then fed out to the printer at whatever rate the printer can handle. If several print jobs are spooled at close to the same time, they form a queue, waiting for earlier jobs to finish. Controlling this queue is an important administrative function and covers pausing and resuming printing, canceling printing, redirecting documents, and changing a document's properties. These tasks are handled in the printer's window, which is similar to Figure 5-6 and is opened by double-clicking the appropriate printer in the Printers And Faxes window or by clicking the printer icon in the notification area of the taskbar.

Pause, Resume, and Restart Printing

As printing is taking place, a situation may occur in which you want to pause the printing. This may be caused by the printer—the need to change paper, for example—in which case you would want to pause all printing. The situation may also be caused by a document, in which case you would want to pause only the printing of that document—for example, for some problem in the document, such as characters that cause the printer to behave erratically. In Windows XP, you can pause and resume printing of all documents, and pause and resume or restart printing of a single document.

Pause and Resume Printing for All Documents   Pausing and resuming printing of all documents is in essence pausing and resuming the printer. See how that is done with these steps:

1. In the printer's window, such as the one shown in Figure 5-6, open the Printer menu and choose Pause Printing. "Paused" will appear in the title bar, and if you look in the Printer menu, you will see a checkmark in front of Pause Printing.

2. To resume printing, again open the Printer menu and choose the checked Pause Printing. "Paused" disappears from the title bar and the checkmark disappears in the Pause Printing option in the Printer menu.

Document Name	Status	Owner	Pages	Size	Submitted
Remote Downlevel Document	Error - Print...	Guest	N/A	117 KB	9:17:58 AM
Microsoft Word - PackList.doc		Guest	1	62.9 KB	9:18:02 AM
Microsoft Word - Chap2.doc	Spooling	Martin Matt...	4	99.5 KB	9:18:08 AM

Figure 5-6   Documents waiting to be printed

Pause, Resume, and Restart Printing for a Single Document   When you want to interrupt the printing of one or more, but not all, the documents in the queue, you can do so and then either resume printing where it left off or restart from the beginning of the document. Here are the steps to do that:

1. In the printer's window, select the documents or document that you want to pause, open the Document menu, and choose Pause. "Paused" will appear in the Status column of the document(s) you selected.

2. To resume printing where the document was paused, select the document and choose Resume. "Printing" will appear in the Status column of the document selected.

3. To restart printing at the beginning of the document, select the document and choose Restart. "Restarting" and then "Printing" will appear in the Status column.

NOTE

If you want to change the order in which documents are being printed, you cannot pause the current document that is printing and have that happen. You must either complete the document that is printing or cancel it. You can use Pause to get around intermediate documents that are not currently printing. For example, suppose you want to immediately print the third document in the queue, but the first document is currently printing. You must either let the first document finish printing or cancel it. You can then pause the second document before it starts printing, and the third document will begin printing when the first document is out of the way.

Cancel Printing

Canceling printing can be done either at the printer level, which cancels all the jobs in the printer queue, or at the document level, which cancels selected documents. A canceled job is deleted from the print queue and must be restarted by the original application if that is desired. Here's how to cancel first one job and then all the jobs in the queue:

1. In the printer's window, select the job or jobs that you want to cancel. Open the Document menu and choose Cancel. The job or jobs will disappear from the window and no longer be in the queue.

2. To cancel all the jobs in the queue, open the Printer menu and choose Cancel All Documents. You are asked whether you are sure you want to cancel all documents. Click Yes. All jobs will disappear from the queue and the printer window.

Redirect Documents

If you have two printers with the same print driver, you can redirect the print jobs that are in the queue for one printer to the other printer, where they will be printed without the user's having to resubmit them. You do this by changing the port to which the printer is directed:

1. In the printer's window, open the Printer menu, choose Properties, and select the Ports tab.

2. If the second printer is in the list of ports, select it. Otherwise, click Add Port, which opens the Printer Ports dialog box. Choose Local Port, and click New Port, which opens the Port Name dialog box.

3. Enter the UNC name for the printer (for example, \\Carole\HP2000C) and click OK.

4. Click Close and then click OK. The print queue will be redirected to the other printer.

Change a Document's Properties

A document in the print queue has a Properties dialog box, shown in Figure 5-7, which is opened by right-clicking the document and selecting Properties. This allows you to set the

Figure 5-7 Setting the properties of a document in the print queue

relative priority to use in printing the document from 1, the lowest, to 99, the highest; who to notify when the document is printed; and the time of day to print the document.

Set Priority   A document printed to a printer with a default priority setting (see "Printer Priority," earlier in the module) is given a priority of 1, the lowest priority. If you want another document to be printed before the first one, and the "first one" hasn't started printing yet, then set the second document priority to anything higher than 1 by dragging the Priority slider to the right.

Who to Notify   Normally, the printer notifies the owner of a document of any special situations with the printing and when the document is finished printing. The owner is the user who sent the document to the printer. Sometimes it is beneficial to notify another user. You can do that by putting the name of the other user (their username on a shared computer or network, not their proper name) in the Notify text box of the document's Properties dialog box.

To notify the owner or other person specified when a document has competed printing, open the Printers And Faxes window | File menu | Server Properties | Advanced tab and click Notify When Remote Documents Are Printed; this is off by default.

Set Print Time   Normally, a job is printed as soon as it reaches the top of the print queue. You can change this to a particular time frame in the document's Properties dialog box General tab (see Figure 5-7), by selecting Only From at the bottom under Schedule and then entering the time range within which you want the job printed.

This allows you to take large jobs that might clog the print queue and print them at a time when there is little or no load.

Handle Multiple Printers

If you have several printers in your Printers And Faxes window, you will need to handle some minor management functions. These include selecting one printer as your default, storing printing for a printer that is disconnected, renaming a printer, and possibly deleting one. All of these functions can be handled in a printer's context menu, opened by right-clicking a printer icon in the Printers And Faxes window. Some of these functions can also by handled by selecting the printer and then using the tasks pane to select the function.

Open
Set as Default Printer
Printing Preferences...
Pause Printing
Sharing...
Use Printer Offline
Create Shortcut
Delete
Rename
Properties

Set the Default Printer   If you have only one printer, it is obviously your default. When you install more than one, you are asked with the second and so on if you want each to be your default. After you have completed installation, you can change the default by opening the context menu and choosing Set As Default Printer. Your default printer should be the one you use most often. It is automatically chosen when you print anything in any application. In some cases, such as choosing to print a file in Explorer, you do not have a chance to change the default. In other cases, such as printing from Microsoft Word 2002, you can change from the default if you wish. Use these thoughts to select a default.

Use a Printer Offline   Using a printer that is *offline* means that anything you print is stored while you are disconnected from the printer and then printed in the future when you reconnect with it. If you simply let the printing sit in the spooler, you are liable to lose some of the printing as you reconnect to the printer. If you use the context menu's Use Printer Offline option, the printing information is securely held until you come back at a later date and choose Use Printer Online.

Rename a Printer   When you first install a printer, you have a chance to name it. After installation, you can then rename it the way you would a file, by clicking twice slowly on the name in the Printers And Faxes window and typing the new name or changing the name in the printer's Properties dialog box. You can also select Rename from the context menu. That highlights the name in the Printers And Faxes window, allowing you to type a new name.

Delete a Printer   If you no longer have a need for a printer in your Printers And Faxes window, you can remove it by selecting it and pressing DELETE or by opening the context menu and choosing Delete. In both cases, a dialog box appears asking if you are sure you want to delete the printer. Clicking Yes removes the printer.

CRITICAL SKILL
5.4 Handle Fonts

A *font* is a set of characters with the same design, size, weight, and style. A font is a member of a *typeface* family, all members of which have the same design. The font 12-point Arial bold italic is a member of the Arial typeface with a 12-point size, bold weight, and italic style. Systems running Windows XP have numerous fonts that you can choose from, including

- **Resident fonts**   Built into printers

- **Cartridge fonts**   Stored in cartridges plugged into printers

- **Soft fonts**   Stored on disks in the computer to which the printer is attached and downloaded to the printer when they are needed. Some large printers also have hard disks with soft fonts on them.

A number of soft fonts come with Windows XP, and there are many, many more that you can add from other sources, including the Internet, or that are automatically added when you install an application. The font management job is to minimize the time taken downloading fonts, while still having the fonts you want available. Minimizing download time means that resident and cartridge fonts are used when possible, which is automatically done by the print driver whenever a font that is both resident and available for download is requested. Font availability means that the fonts you want are on the print server's disk and fonts you don't want are not on the disk wasting space and handling time. In this section, you'll look at the fonts in Windows XP, how to add and remove fonts, and how to use fonts.

Fonts in Windows XP

There are three types of soft fonts in Windows XP:

- **Outline fonts**   Stored as a set of commands that is used to draw a particular character. As a result, the fonts can be scaled to any size (and are therefore called *scalable* fonts) and can be rotated. Outline fonts are the primary fonts both used onscreen and downloaded to printers. Windows XP supports three types of outline fonts: TrueType fonts developed by Microsoft for Windows 95; OpenType fonts, also developed by Microsoft and an extension of TrueType; and Type 1 fonts, developed by Adobe Systems, Inc. All the outline fonts in Windows XP are OpenType fonts.

- **Bitmapped fonts** Also called *raster fonts,* these are stored as a bitmapped image for a specific size and weight, and a specific printer. They cannot be scaled and rotated. They are included for legacy purposes and are not used in most cases.

- **Vector fonts** Created with line segments and can be scaled and rotated. Primarily used with plotters and not onscreen or with printers.

You can view and work with the fonts in Windows XP by opening the Fonts folder to display the Fonts window, shown in Figure 5-8. The Fonts folder is opened by opening the Start menu, choosing Control Panel, and then double-clicking Fonts if the Control Pane is in Classic view.

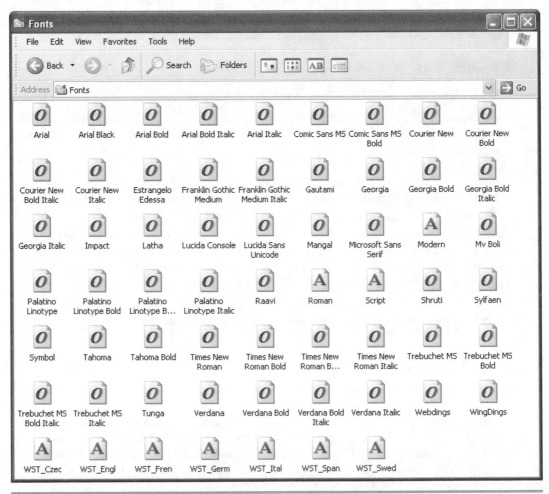

Figure 5-8 Fonts installed with Windows XP

If the Control Panel is in Category view, click Appearance And Themes and then click Fonts in the tasks pane. The Fonts windows will open.

If you haven't installed any other fonts or had them automatically installed by an application, you will see the 61 fonts that are installed by Windows XP Professional (Windows XP Home Edition installs 66 fonts, with the additional five fonts being older fixed-size fonts to provide compatibility with older systems). Fonts with the *O* in the icon are OpenType fonts, and those with an *A* are either bitmapped or vector fonts. If you have fonts with a *TT,* in the icon they are TrueType fonts.

In the Fonts folder, you can look at a font by double-clicking its icon. This opens a window for the font, showing it in various sizes and giving some information about it, as shown in Figure 5-9. From this window, you can print the font by clicking Print. It is sometimes handy to keep a notebook with printed samples of all the fonts on a print server.

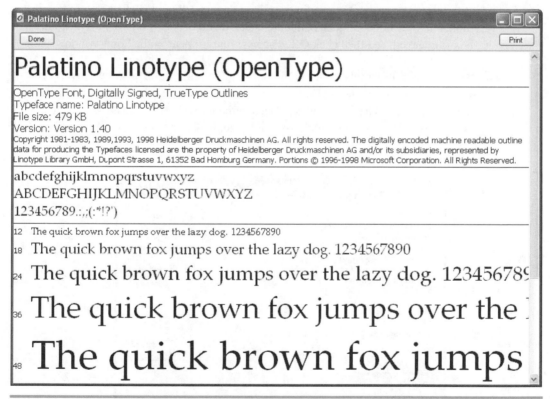

Figure 5-9 Detailed font description opened by double-clicking a font

Add and Remove Fonts

You can add fonts to those that are installed by Windows XP with the following steps:

1. Open the Start menu, click Control Panel, and in Classic view, double-click Fonts; or in Category view, click Appearance And Themes and then click Fonts in the tasks pane. The Fonts window opens, similar to the one previously shown in Figure 5-8.

2. Open the File menu and choose Install New Font. The Add Fonts dialog box opens, like the one in Figure 5-10.

3. Open a drive and folder that contains the fonts you want to install (this can be a floppy disk, a CD/DVD, or another hard drive on the network, which is what is shown in Figure 5-10).

4. Select the fonts you want to install from the list (hold down SHIFT and click the first and last font to select several contiguous fonts, or hold down CTRL and click each font to select several fonts that are not contiguous), double-check that the Copy Fonts To Fonts Folder check box is checked, and then click OK. The new fonts appear in the Fonts window.

You can remove fonts simply by selecting them and pressing DELETE. Alternatively, you can right-click the font(s) and choose Delete. In either case, you are asked whether you are sure. Click Yes if you are. The fonts will be placed in the Recycle Bin, in case you made a mistake and want to retrieve one. If you haven't mistakenly deleted any, you can empty the Recycle Bin.

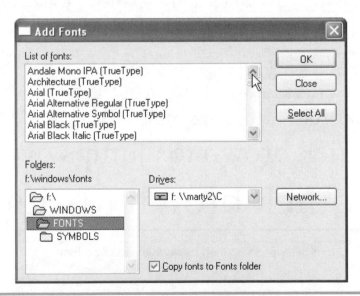

Figure 5-10 Adding fonts from another computer on the network

Use Fonts

Fonts are normally used or specified from within an application. For example, in Microsoft Word, you can select a line of text and then open the font drop-down list, as shown in Figure 5-11. Every application is a little different, but they all have a similar function. One nice feature of Microsoft Word 2000, Word 2002, and several other recent applications is that they show what the font looks like in the list, as you can see in Figure 5-11.

Fonts used correctly can be a major asset in getting a message across, but they also can detract from a message if improperly used. Two primary rules are not to use too many fonts, and to use complementary fonts together. In a one-page document, two typefaces should be enough (you can use bold and italic to have as many as eight fonts), and in a longer document, three—or at most four—typefaces are appropriate. Complementary fonts are more subjective. Arial and Times Roman are generally considered complementary, as are Futura and Garamond, and Palatino and Optima. In each of these pairs, one typeface (for example, Arial) is *sans serif* (without the little tails on the ends of a character) and is used for titles and headings, while the

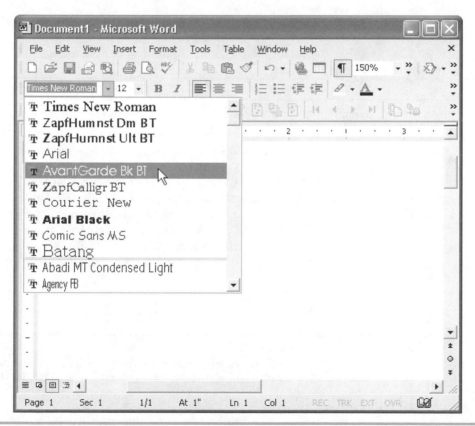

Figure 5-11 Selecting a font to use in Microsoft Word 2002

other typeface (for example, Times Roman) is *serif* (it has the tails) and is used for the body text. There are of course many other options and considerations in the sophisticated use of fonts.

The Fonts window View menu has two options that help you look at similar fonts. The List Fonts By Similarity option re-sorts your fonts according to similarity to a selected font, and the Hide Variations option hides the bold and italic variations of a font, making it easier for you to look at just the typefaces.

Progress Check

- What do you use to configure a printer?

- What is printer pooling and what is its opposite?

- Can you pause and restart a print job to insert a higher-priority job?

- What types of fonts come with Windows XP?

Ask the Expert

Q: **Why are there so many fonts and why shouldn't I delete all but the couple I need?**

A: There are a large number of fonts for two reasons. First, they are to accommodate the wide variety of tastes of the millions of people that use Windows. Second, some of the fonts have special purposes. For example Courier, Lucida Console, MS Sans Serif, MS Serif, Symbol, and Tahoma are all used by Windows on the screen. Times New Roman and Arial are the standby defaults for most printing, and Modern, Roman, and Script are vector fonts to use with a plotter. When you add bold, italic, and bold italic for many of these, you have accounted for many of the fonts in Windows. If you have a real need for disk space, you can delete many of the others. Look at each and ask yourself if you will ever use it.

---

1. The printer's Properties dialog box is used to configure it.

2. Printer pooling is having two or more physical printers with the same printer driver share one printer definition in the Printers And Faxes window. The opposite is to have one physical printer have several printer definitions. The different definitions would have different configurations, such as different priorities.

3. No, you would have to cancel and restart the current job or wait until it is finished.

4. The majority of Windows XP fonts are OpenType outline fonts, but a few are Adobe bitmapped or vector fonts.

CRITICAL SKILL

5.5 Set Up and Use Faxing

A capability to send and receive faxes has been included in Windows XP as part of its printing functionality. This allows an application such as Microsoft Word to "print" to a remote fax by specifying a "fax" as a printer and having the software for that printer ask for a phone number, interface with a modem in the computer to dial the phone number, and then work with the fax on the receiving end to transfer the information and print it out. In addition, there is a Fax Console that lets you directly send and receive faxes as you would an e-mail message. This service requires that you have a fax/modem in your computer and a phone line connected to it (see Module 6 for information on setting up and working with modems). This Fax Service is not fully installed by default when you install Windows XP, but you can easily install it from the Printers And Faxes window. In this section, you'll see how to set up and use the service to send faxes from an application and then how to set up and use the Fax Console to receive faxes.

Set Up and Use Faxing from Applications

Setting up faxing is done from the Printers And Faxes window using Setting Up Faxing in the tasks pane. You can then use faxing by starting an application and "printing" to the fax printer. Here's how:

1. Open the Start menu and click Printers And Faxes. In the Printers And Faxes window that opens, click Set Up Faxing in the tasks pane. When requested, insert your Windows XP CD and click Exit to close the introductory Windows XP Installation window. When Setup is done copying files, you are returned to the Printer And Faxes window, which has a new Send A Fax option added. A fax "printer" icon appears in the Printers And Faxes window, like this:

Fax

NOTE

In Windows XP Home Edition, you have to go through an extra step by clicking Install A Local Fax Printer.

2. Open a document in an application such as Microsoft Word (or WordPad). Open the File menu and choose Print. Open the Printer name drop-down list, choose Fax, and click OK. (If you do not have a modem installed, you will be told you need to install a modem. See Module 6.) The Fax Configuration Wizard will open.

3. Click Next. Fill in the sender information; click Next; and select the modem to use, whether send and receive are enabled, and if receive, whether you want manual or automatic answer. Click Next again.

4. Enter your Transmitting Subscriber Identification (TSID—normally your fax number and company name, displayed at the top of the fax when you send it), and click Next.

5. Enter your Called Subscriber Identification (CSID—normally your fax number and company name, sent back to the caller when you receive a fax), and click Next.

6. Choose whether to print an incoming fax or store it in a folder, or to do both. If you want to print a fax, specify on which printer, and if you want to store it in a folder, specify the path to the folder (the fax is automatically stored in the Inbox folder, so the folder you specify would be storing a second copy). Click Next.

7. Your configuration settings are displayed and you are asked if these are correct. If not, click Back and make the necessary corrections. When you have the correct settings, click Finish. The Send Fax Wizard will open. Click Next.

8. Enter the recipient's name and phone number and click Next. If you want to send a cover page, click Select A Cover Page Template…, fill in the information you want on the cover page, and click Next.

9. Enter when you want to send the fax and the priority and click Next. You are shown the settings you have made. Use Back to make any corrections and then click Finish. The Fax Monitor will open, and if you click More, you will see the progress of faxing: Dialing, Sending, Completed, as shown in Figure 5-12.

Use the Fax Console to Receive Faxes

Given that you installed faxing in Step 1 of the preceding sequence or elsewhere and went through the Fax Configuration Wizard in Steps 3 through 8, you are ready to receive faxes using the Fax Console. You can open the Fax Console from the Start menu (Start | All Programs | Accessories | Communications | Fax | Fax Console) or by double-clicking the Fax "printer" in the Printers And Faxes window.

1. Open the Fax Console by one of the methods just mentioned.

2. If you choose Manual Answer Mode in the Fax Configuration Wizard (preceding Step 3), you must wait until you hear the phone ring with the fax message and then click the

Figure 5-12 History of a fax transmission

Receive Now button on the toolbar or open the File menu and choose Receive A Fax Now. A third method of manually answering a fax call is, prior to the call, to open the Tools menu and choose Fax Monitor. The Fax Monitor will appear and wait on the desktop. When a call comes in, click Answer Now.

3. If you chose Automatic Answer Mode in the Fax Configuration Wizard, any calls on that line will be automatically answered.

4. In all cases of receiving a fax, the Fax Monitor will handle the call. Given that there is a fax machine (or a computer impersonating one) on the other end, a fax will be received and the Fax Monitor will display the progress. When the call is complete, the Fax Monitor will hang up and the received message will appear in the Inbox of the Fax Console, as you can see in Figure 5-13. Also, a message saying you received a fax will pop out of the notification area, like this:

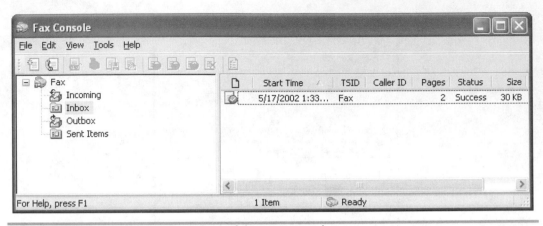

Figure 5-13 Received fax in the Inbox of the Fax Console

5. Double-click the fax in the Inbox to view it. Right-click the fax and choose to View, Delete, Save As (it is already saved in the Inbox), Mail To (attaches the fax to an e-mail message that you can then address), or Print.

In the Fax Console's Tools menu, you can change the Sender information you originally entered in the Fax Configuration Wizard. You can also create and edit fax cover pages, reopen the Fax Configuration Wizard, and by choosing Fax Printer Configuration | Devices tab | Properties, change the detailed sending and receiving parameters, most importantly whether to answer a call manually or automatically.

Ask the Expert

Q: Why would you need a regular fax machine if you have a computer fax capability?

A: It depends on the amount of faxing you do and the type of faxing. If are only occasionally faxing and it is usually a document that is created on your computer, then "printing" that document to a fax is easier than printing it to paper and reading that paper back in to a stand-alone fax machine. On the other hand, if you frequently have a lot of paper documents that don't exist in the computer, then the stand-alone fax machine, especially with a paper feeder, is preferable.

Progress Check

- Is the Fax Service a part of the default Windows XP installation?

- What do TSID and CSID stand for and how are they used?

- How can you answer a fax call?

Project 5   Install Printers, Fonts, and Faxing

Continuing the scenario begun in Module 3 of setting up a new computer, we'll install printers, fonts, and faxing service on this computer with these tasks:

- Installing a local printer

- Installing a network printer

- Configuring printers including priority, spooling, and sharing

- Printing a document

- Adding fonts

- Setting up and using faxing

Step by Step

1. Start up and log on to your computer. Open the Start menu and click Printers And Faxes in Windows XP Professional or open the Start menu, click Control Panel, click Printers And Other Hardware, and click Printers And Faxes in Windows XP Home Edition. The Printers And Faxes window will open.

---

1. No, it is normally not installed when you install Windows XP, but a command is placed on the tasks pane of the Printers And Faxes window to do the installation.

2. TSID stands for Transmitting Subscriber Identification and identifies the sender of a fax to the person receiving it. CSID stands for Called Subscriber Identification and identifies the recipient of a fax to the sender.

3. A fax call can be answered either manually at the moment of the call or automatically when the call occurs. To answer a call manually, you can use the Fax Console with the Receive Now button on the toolbar, with the File menu Receive A Fax Now option, or by putting the Fax Monitor on the desktop with the Tools menu Fax Monitor option.

(continued)

2. Click Add A Printer in the tasks pane to open the Add Printer Wizard. Click Next. Click Local Printer and click Next. If the Printer is found and is correct, click Next and skip to Step 4. If the printer is not correct, click Select A Printer and click Next. If no printer was found, click Next.

3. If you are selecting the printer, choose the port your printer is using and click Next. Select the manufacturer and printer model and click Next.

4. Enter a name for the printer or accept the default name, determine if the printer will be your default, and click Next. Decide if you want to print a test page and click Next. Click Finish, click OK if the page printed correctly, or click Troubleshoot and answer the questions to determine why it did not print.

5. To install a network printer with the Printers And Faxes window open, click Add A Printer, click Next, click A Network Printer, and click Next. Click Browse For A Printer, select the printer you want to use, and click Next.

6. Determine if the printer will be your default and click Next. If asked, decide if you want to print a test page and click Next. Click Finish and handle the results of the printer test, if it appears, as you did in Step 4.

7. Right-click one of your new printers and choose Properties. Click the Advanced tab. Choose the priority you want you want assigned and how you want to handle spooling. Click the Sharing tab. If you know you want to share the printer, click If You Understand…, click Just Enable Printer Sharing, click OK, click Share This Printer, enter a share name, and click OK.

8. To print, start the application from which you want to print, for example Microsoft Word, open the File menu, choose Print, select the printer you want to use and any other settings, and click Print or OK.

9. To add fonts, open the Start menu, click Control Panel, click Appearance And Themes, and click Fonts in the tasks pane. In the Fonts window that opens, open the File menu and choose Install New Font. Select the drive and folder from which you want to copy the fonts. A list of fonts will appear. Select the ones you want and click OK. Close the Fonts window.

10. To install faxing services, click Set Up Faxing in the tasks pane of the Printers And Faxes window. If and when asked, insert the Windows XP CD and close the initial installation window. If Install A Fax Printer appears, click it, so that a fax printer appears in the Printers And Faxes window.

11. To use the faxing service, start an application from which you want to fax, open the document to send, open the File menu, choose Print, select the Fax printer, and click Print or OK. If this is the first time you have used the faxing service, the Fax Configuration Wizard will open. Answer the questions and click Next as needed and Finish at the end.

12. In the Send Fax Wizard that opens, enter the name and phone number of the person to whom you are sending the fax and other necessary information. Click Next and then Finish. The Fax Monitor will open and send the fax.

Project Summary

Windows XP has a very comprehensive printing capability with many ways to tailor it to your needs. You may never need to do anything but print from the applications you use, but when you do, the features and capabilities are there, including a good faxing capability.

Module 5 Mastery Check

1. As a general rule, should you use the CD that came with your printer or Windows XP to install your printer?

2. What are some of the things you should do before installing a printer?

3. What are three kinds of network printers?

4. What are the two situations where you would want to print to a file and how do they work?

5. What are the tasks that are part of controlling a printer queue?

6. What is a good method of handling several printing priorities?

7. What is the one thing you have to do if you have multiple printers?

8. What is a font, what is a typeface, and how do they differ?

9. What are the three kinds of fonts?

10. What are two of the three ways of loading the Fax Console?

Module 6

Using Communications and the Internet

*C*ommunications means connecting your computer to other computers over primarily nondedicated forms of transmission, such as phone lines, satellite links, cable Internet, and cellular wireless. In Module 8, I'll talk about forms of networking that connect computers over primarily dedicated forms of transmission, such as dedicated cabling and wireless systems. There is a lot of similarity between communications and networking, and it is easy to cross over from the discussion of one to the other. For the sake of this discussion, think of communications as connecting to computers outside your home or business using phone lines, and think of networking as connecting to computers inside your home or business using network cabling or wireless connections. This is very simplistically shown in Figure 6-1.

In this module, we'll discuss how to set up and configure communications connections, including both dial-up modem connections and broadband connections. Then we'll look at how to connect to and use the Internet, including browsing the World Wide Web (or just Web) with

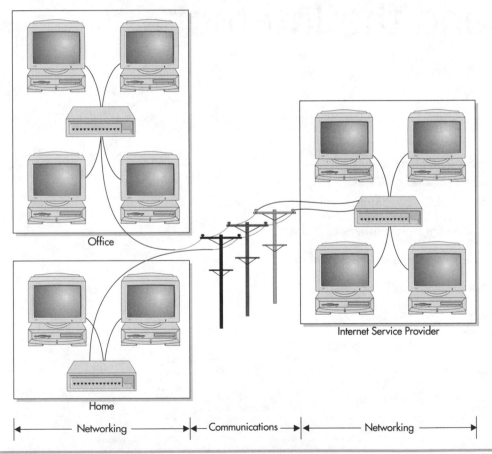

Figure 6-1 Networking versus communications

Internet Explorer and sending e-mail with Outlook Express. Finally, we'll describe how to use other Windows XP communications tools, including Windows Messenger and HyperTerminal.

NOTE

Another form of communications that you will see on the Communications menu, Remote Desktop Connection, is discussed in Module 11.

CRITICAL SKILL
6.1 Set Up Communications Connections

There are two primary types of communications: *dial-up* communications and *broadband* communications. The primary distinction between these two types is the speed. The upper limit of dial-up is less than 56 Kbps (kilobits per second or thousands of bits per second), whereas broadband begins at 128 Kbps and goes past 1.5 Mbps (megabits per second or millions of bits per second). Another distinction is that dial-up uses analog technology, where the current is varied to generate a signal, and broadband uses digital technology, where the current is fixed but quickly turned on and off to the create a signal. Digital technology is inherently more reliable and much faster. In this section, we'll look first at dial-up service and then at broadband.

Ask the Expert

Q: How do I know if I have dial-up or broadband service?

A: If you are at home or have your own small business, you would have had to specifically buy broadband services. There are several types: ISDN (Integrated Services Digital Network), DSL (digital subscriber line), ADSL (asymmetric DSL), cable Internet, satellite Internet, or a T1 line (these will be discussed further under the discussion of broadband). If you or someone representing you or your business didn't specifically buy one of these services, then it is pretty a good bet you don't have broadband (some office suites now come with DSL, but I think you would know that). If you are in a medium to large company, it is likely that you have broadband service over your local area network (LAN). Ask an associate if you connect to the Internet over the company's network. If so, you have broadband. It is important that you find out the answer to this question. One quick test is to jump to the "Set Up an Internet Connection" section later in this module and use the instructions to try to connect. If you quickly connect without going through a dial-up sequence, then you have broadband. If you connect and go through the dial-up sequence, you have a dial-up service, your modem is installed and working, and you can skip the next section. If you don't connect, then you probably need to install one or the other. If you are in a medium to large company, ask around. If you are on your own, start by assuming you will use a dial-up service.

Dial-Up Service

Dial-up service uses *telephony*—telephone lines, their switches, and their terminations—to connect computers. The most common approach to dial-up service is to use a *modem* (short for "modulator-demodulator") to convert a digital signal (patterns of ones and zeros) in a computer to an analog signal (current fluctuations) in a phone line and then use a second modem on the other end to convert the analog signal back to digital for use in the connecting computer. Modems can be inside a computer (called an "internal" modem), in which case the phone line connects to the computer, or external, where the phone line plugs into the modem and the modem plugs into a serial port in the computer. The fastest modems today receive data at up to 56 Kbps and send data at up to 33.6 Kbps.

Install a Modem

It is likely, with a newer computer or a computer that came with Windows XP already installed, that your modem was automatically installed as a part of the installation of Windows XP. If so, you should have seen a message to that effect at the conclusion of installation (see Module 13). If you do not know if your modem is installed, jump to the "Set Up an Internet Connection" section later in this module and use the instructions to try to connect. If you can connect, you don't need to install a modem and can stay in that later section. Otherwise, return here.

There are several ways to install modem support within Windows XP. During installation of the operating system or the first time you attempt to connect to the Internet, support for a modem will be installed for you if you have a Plug and Play modem. If you set up an Internet connection and you don't have modem support installed, it will be installed for you, again with a Plug and Play modem. Here, though, we'll look at installing a modem by itself, which you will need to do if it has not been automatically installed. Later, we'll also look at installing it with an Internet connection.

To install a modem, of course, you must have one plugged in or attached to your computer. There are two types of modems, internal and external. An *internal* modem is a card that plugs in to an expansion slot on the main or "mother" board inside your computer. An *external* modem is a small box that plugs into a serial communications (COM) port on the outside of your computer. In addition, both external and internal modems may have switches or jumpers that need to be set, or they may be *Plug and Play,* which means that the modem does not have switches or jumpers—software sets it up. Whichever kind of modem you have, the instructions that came with it tell you whether it is internal or external, how to plug it in, and how to set it up.

With a modem physically attached to your computer (and if external, turned on), use the following instructions to install it in Windows XP:

1. Open the Start menu, choose Control Panel, and if in Classic view, double-click Phone And Modem Options. In Category view, click Printers And Other Hardware and then click Phone And Modem Options. The Phone And Modem Options dialog box will open.

2. Open the Modems tab. If it shows Unknown Modem, select that and click Remove. If it shows a likely modem, such as what is shown next, you already have a modem installed and you can skip to the next section.

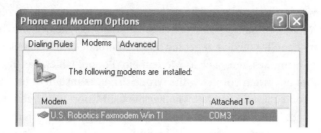

3. Click Add. You are told that Windows will try to detect your modem, and you are reminded to turn on the modem and to quit any programs that may be using it. Click Next. A list of possible modems may be shown to you. If only the correct modem is displayed, skip the next step. If several modems are shown and one is correct and the rest are not, uncheck the incorrect ones and skip the next step. If an incorrect modem or Unknown Modem is shown, select it and click Change. If no modem is found, click Next.

4. Select the correct manufacturer from the list on the left and the correct model from the list on the right and click Next. If your modem is not on the list, but you have a disk that is correct for Windows XP (disks for earlier versions probably will not work), click Have Disk, insert the disk, select the drive, click OK, select the manufacturer and model, and click OK. If your modem is not on the list of drivers and you do not have a disk, there are three other possible ways to get your modem running. The easiest way is to try one of the standard modem drivers included with Windows XP. Select Standard Modem Types as the manufacturer and then the speed of your modem for the model (if you are not sure of the speed of your modem, if it is less than five years old, try 56,000 bps; if it is five to seven years old, try 33,600 bps; if it is older than seven years, try 28,000 bps). If you have selected a standard modem type, click Next and continue with the remaining steps to see if it will work. If it doesn't, try changing the speed choice, or try changing the COM port, as the next step suggests. If none of those attempts work, you can try both the manufacturer's web site and Microsoft's web site to see if you can find a driver for your modem. The final answer is to buy a new modem. They cost from $20 to $80, with $40 buying a good modem.

5. Select the COM port to which the modem is connected and click Next. If you don't know your port number, is one suggested in the list? If so, select it. If several ports are suggested, try COM2 first, then COM3, and finally COM1. Windows starts to install your modem. If you are using an older modem, you may be told that the driver does not have a digital signature. If you are told that, click Yes to continue and use the driver anyway. Finally, you are told that your modem has been installed successfully. Click Finish.

6. Back in the Phone And Modem Options dialog box, select your newly installed modem, and click Properties. In the Properties dialog box, click the Diagnostics tab, and then click Query Modem. You will be told that the query process will take a few minutes.

If your modem is properly installed, you'll see a set of commands and responses, as shown in Figure 6-2. Not all of the responses have to be positive. The point is that Windows XP is talking to the modem. If you do not get the set of commands and responses, you will probably get some sort of error message, such as Modem Not Found, which has three possible causes: the modem is not operating correctly, the wrong driver is installed, or the wrong COM port is being used. You generally can tell whether the COM port is correct by looking at what Windows detected. It may not detect the type of modem correctly, but it generally detects the port that has a modem attached to it. To find the correct manufacturer and model for the driver, you may need to look at the actual modem by physically opening the computer. To get a driver that is not in the Windows driver database, use another computer to connect to the Internet, browse the modem manufacturer's web site, and download the correct driver. Put that driver on a floppy disk and take it to the computer you are installing. If you are certain that both the port and the driver are correct, then the modem may be malfunctioning.

7. Click OK to close the Properties dialog box and then click OK to close the Phone And Modem Options dialog box. Leave the Control Panel (which may be called Printers And Other Hardware) open for the next exercise.

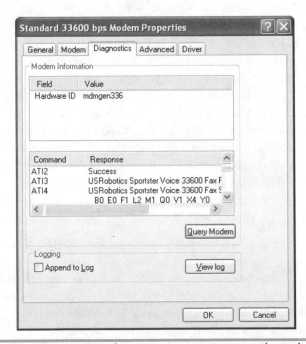

Figure 6-2 Commands and responses showing communication with modem

Establish a Dial-up Connection

Establishing a dial-up connection identifies a particular destination to which you want to dial—a phone number that is dialed and a connection that is made to your modem. The following steps, which assume that a modem has already been set up (as done in the preceding section, but with the Control Panel left open), show how to establish a dial-up Internet connection. For this, you will need to know the phone number of your Internet service provider (ISP), an e-mail address, a user name or ID, and a password:

1. In the Control Panel in Classic view, double-click Network Connections. In Category view, click Back, click Network And Internet Connections, and click Network Connections. In either case, click Create A New Connection. The New Connection Wizard will open. Click Next.

2. Select Connect To The Internet and click Next. Choose Set Up My Connection Manually, click Next, select Connect Using A Dial-Up Modem, and once more click Next. If you have more than one modem, choose the one you want to use and again click Next.

3. Enter the name for the connection you are creating and click Next. Enter the phone number that will be the destination of the connection. If you want to use area/city/country codes, enter them with a 1- at the beginning. Click Next when the phone number has been entered.

4. Enter the user name and password (twice to confirm it) that your ISP gave you to connect to the Internet. Choose whether anyone using this computer can use this user name and password, whether this is the default Internet connection, and whether you want the Internet firewall turned on. There is no right or wrong answer on the first two questions. They are what is correct for you. The firewall is a good idea for security, but you want to remember it is on when you go through Module 11 and attempt to use Remote Access Services (RAS). A firewall can be a problem for RAS. When you are ready, click Next.

5. You are told you have successfully completed the steps necessary for a dial-up connection. If you would like a shortcut on the desktop so that you can quickly open this connection, click the check box and then click Finish to create the connection. An icon will appear in the Network Connections window, and the Connect dialog box opens with your user name and the phone number you need to dial to get on the Internet.

Using Communications and the Internet **6**

6. To dial the connection, click Dial in the Connect dialog box, or when it is closed, double-click its icon. If your sound is activated, you should hear the modem dialing, the ring at the other end, and the answering tone. When a connection is established, a balloon will appear out of the notification area, like this:

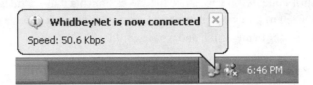

7. Click the Connection icon in the notification area to open the Status dialog box for your connection. It should look similar to Figure 6-3. If you are going immediately to the section on setting up an Internet connection, then leave the connection established and click Close in the Status dialog box; otherwise, click Disconnect.

If you did not connect, there could be a number of reasons, but if your modem returned some command responses as shown in Figure 6-2, then it is working properly and you can narrow down the problem to the dial-up connection. If so, your problem is probably in one of three areas:

● The physical connection to the phone line. Is there a cable between the modem and a telephone outlet and is the outlet turned on (does a normal phone work in the outlet)?

● The user name and password. Did you correctly enter the user name and password that the ISP gave you? Check with them and then reenter it.

● The ISP's phone number for the modem speed you are using. Did you enter the phone number correctly and is the service on that phone number fast enough to handle your modem? Generally, if your modem is slower than the service, there is not a problem, but if you are using a 56 Kbps modem and the service on phone number you are using is rated at 33.6 Kbps, you most likely will not be able to connect. Once more, talk to your ISP.

If all three of these conditions are satisfactory and your modem worked as described at the end of the last section, then you should be able to connect.

Set Up a Broadband Connection

In recent years, telephone companies have started to offer several forms of digital signals over phone lines so that a modem isn't necessary—all you need is a connection between the digital line and the computer. Two common forms of digital telephone service are ISDN and DSL. ISDN was the first digital service and is both expensive and relatively slow (a maximum speed of 128 Kbps) when compared to DSL. Most often, an ISDN or DSL line is terminated in a router

Figure 6-3 The connection Status dialog box shows you how much information has been transferred.

that directly connects to your LAN and not to a computer. Each computer on the network then has access to the Internet through the LAN.

NOTE

Sometimes an ISDN or DSL adapter is called a "modem," but it is not an analog-to-digital converter, which is the major point of a **mo**dulator-**dem**odulator. Therefore, in this book they are called "adapters."

In addition to the standard pair of copper wires used in normal phone service, which supports dial-up, ISDN, and DSL, there are four other means of transmission: cable Internet, satellite Internet, high-speed dedicated connections, and wireless. ISDN has become almost extinct due to its high price and slow speed. There are several different forms of both high-speed dedicated connections and wireless connections, all of which are expensive (beginning around $1,000 per month), require a custom installation, and in the case of wireless, are just coming on the market. So for the sake of this broadband discussion, we'll focus on DSL, cable Internet, and satellite Internet.

DSL/ADSL   DSL, although it uses standard telephone wiring, uses a unique form of digital transmission over those wires. This requires that you buy DSL *telephone* service, as well as an

Internet service. There are several ways that DSL is implemented in hardware. In one, a DSL router is used to plug into a telephone outlet and then connect either to a network interface card (NIC) in your computer or to a LAN hub (see Module 8) directly on your network so that multiple people can use the connection. In another hardware form, a DSL adapter card in your computer uses a phone cable to plug into a telephone outlet just as an internal modem would. You may have another DSL hardware setup. There are several different types of DSL, and they can run at a variety of speeds. The most common form of DSL is ADSL (asymmetric digital subscriber line), where the speed of downloading to your computer is much greater than the upload speed. Most purveyors of ADSL have several speed offerings, but a very common combination is 768 Kbps downloading and 128 Kbps uploading. Pricing for this service, including the extra telephone charge as well as the Internet charge to replace a dial-up Internet connection charge, runs from $40 to $80. Faster ADSL service, which can go up to 1.5 Mbps down and 512 Kbps up, can cost as much as $180 a month. Some of the pricing variability has to do with what other services are included in the price, such as web site hosting and number of e-mail addresses.

NOTE

Pricing stated here and elsewhere in this book is my best effort to give you representative pricing. I have looked at what is available in the Pacific Northwest, and then, using the Internet, at what is available in the rest of the country in spring 2002. There is no implication that these prices are available in your area or for that matter anywhere at any other time.

There are several other characteristics of DSL. With some services, if you get a new DSL line, you can also have a full-time telephone or fax on the line without affecting the Internet service, which is on 24 hours a day, seven days a week. DSL is quite reliable and has become very common in most major cities, but the service degrades in speed the further you are from the telephone company switch. The standard is a limit of 18,000 feet, or under 3.5 miles from a switch. The way around this is for the telephone company to put remote switches on fiber-optic lines closer to a group of customers in order to service them. Normally, an ISP will work with a phone company to provide DSL service at a combined rate within the range stated earlier.

Cable Internet   Cable Internet uses the standard TV cable outside most homes and many businesses in America to provide one-way or two-way Internet connections to computers though *cable modems,* which connect your computer(s) to a TV cable outlet. One-way cable uses the cable for downloading information to your computer, which normally handles most of the traffic, and a standard dial-up connection for uploading information from your computer. In two-way cable, both legs are handled by the cable. Many cable companies are upgrading their systems to allow two-way transmission, including newer and higher-speed cable modems, which they can supply. Two-way cable systems have download speeds of up to 1.5 Mbps and upload speeds of up to 500 Kbps. Cable Internet services cost around $40 to $60 per month and may or may not include the cost of the cable modem, which typically adds about $10 per month or can be purchased outright from $150 to $250. Cable modems, which generally include routing capabilities, normally plug into a NIC in a computer or a LAN hub. NICs cost from $20 to $80, with $40 buying a good one. Installation fees range from $20 to $100 if you have TV cable service already at your site. If you don't have TV cable, there will be an additional charge to bring it to your site. Cable Internet systems are generally quite reliable.

Satellite Internet   Satellite Internet systems provide one-way and two-way Internet connections to computers though a transceiver and a satellite antenna two to three feet in diameter. One-way satellite Internet uses the satellite for downloading information to your computer, which normally handles most of the traffic, and a standard dial-up connection for uploading information from your computer. In two-way satellite Internet, both legs are handled by the satellite. Two-way satellite Internet systems have download speeds of up to 1.5 Mbps and upload speeds of up to 150 Kbps. Satellite Internet services cost between $60 and $100 per month, not including the cost of the transceiver and antenna, which cost around $500. Satellite Internet transceivers plug into a NIC in a computer or a LAN hub. Installation fees range from $150 to $500, and you must have good clear exposure to the southern sky. Besides being expensive, satellite systems have two other drawbacks. First, your signal must travel from your antenna about 25,000 miles to the satellite and another 25,000 miles back to the ISP's ground station and then the same distance back to you. Even at the speed of light, approximately 186,000 miles per second, it is over half a second for one round trip. Heavy precipitation, either rain or snow, can increase the error rate, causing the signal to be retransmitted, increasing the time and decreasing the speed. The big benefit of satellite Internet is that it is available anywhere in the United States, including Alaska and Hawaii. Two satellite services are currently available: Hughes DirecPC or DirecWay (http://www.direcpc.com) and Starband (http://www.starband.com).

Ask the Expert

Q: **What is the best choice among dial-up, ISDN, DSL/ADSL, cable modem, satellite, and high-speed phone lines services?**

A: There are two major criteria: cost and availability. How much are you or your business going to use the service, and what is that worth to you in dollars? What services are available to you in your area? If being on the Internet is important to you or your business, and you expect to use it for more than an hour a day, then it is probably worth the added cost for a broadband service. See the following table for some representative speeds, costs, and reliability of four types of internet connections.

Service	Download Speed	Upload Speed	Monthly Cost	Reliability
Dial-Up	48 Kbps	33.6 Kbps	$20	Fair
ADSL	768 Kbps	128 Kbps	$50	Good
Cable Internet	1 Mbps	500 Kbps	$50	Good
Satellite Internet	1 Mbps	150 Kbps	$70	Fair

NOTE

This table is meant to give you some basic comparative information. Speeds vary greatly by vendor, time of day, and your particular service and distance from the vendor. Costs vary by vendor and service. When you talk to vendors, they are going to give you minimum cost and maximum speed, neither of which is likely be what you experience.

If you live or work in an urban area, it is highly likely that you have DSL or ADSL available to you. Fewer areas currently have cable Internet, but it is growing rapidly. Satellite Internet is available almost everywhere, providing you can see the southern sky. If you have DSL/ADSL or cable Internet available to you, you don't want to consider satellite Internet. If you have any choices other than one-way cable or one-way satellite, use it. One-way is a real hassle. If you have both DSL/ADSL and cable Internet, you have a very tough decision. It all depends on how well the vendors have implemented their service. It looks in the table as if cable Internet would win hands down with a faster service at the same price. The actual cable Internet speed, though, is a factor of the number of people on the cable link you are using because it is shared. It is possible to get faster DSL, but not at the same price as cable Internet. The best answer is for you to get the actual prices in your area and ask for several references who can tell you the actual speed they have experienced.

Progress Check

1. What is the simple difference between networking and communications?

2. What is the difference between dial-up and broadband communications?

3. What are two forms of broadband communications and what are some of the differences among them?

CRITICAL SKILL

6.2 Set Up an Internet Connection

An Internet connection is one of the major reasons (and sometimes the only reason) to own a computer. In businesses, more and more work is being done through business-to-business transactions over the Internet. Making the most of the Internet connection is therefore of significant importance.

If a computer can connect to the Internet over the LAN, Windows XP Setup will automatically connect that computer to the Internet and no further work needs to be done to accomplish it. The problem is that it is not obvious whether you are connected or not. The only way to tell is to try to use the Internet and see what happens. Try that now with the next set of steps. These steps assume that neither a modem and a dial-up connection nor a broadband connection has been previously set up, although they do assume that one of these services is connected to the computer, possibly over a LAN, and that Internet service is available.

NOTE

To connect to the Internet, you need to have an existing account with an Internet service provider (ISP), you need to know the phone number for your modem to dial (the ISP's modem phone number), and you need to know the username and password for your account. If you want to use Internet mail, you need to know your e-mail address, the type of mail server (POP3, IMAP, or HTTP), the names of the incoming and outgoing mail servers, and the name and password for the mail account.

---

1. Networking uses dedicated connections within an establishment (home or business), whereas communications use shared connections outside of any one establishment.

2. Dial-up uses normal phone lines and equipment in analog mode with a modem at speeds not exceeding 56 Kbps. Broadband uses digital phone lines and other forms of transmission at speeds greater than 128 Kbps.

3. Broadband services in common use with individuals and smaller firms are DSL, cable Internet, and satellite Internet. DSL uses regular phone lines with digital service, cable Internet uses TV cable systems, and satellite Internet uses TV satellite. Satellite Internet costs the most, whereas DSL and cable Internet are about the same price. Cable Internet and satellite Internet are potentially faster than DSL at the same price point, but actually they are pretty close in speed due to limitations in cable and satellite Internet.

1. Open the Start menu and click Internet. If Internet Explorer opens with the MSN initial page, as shown in Figure 6-4, you know you already have an Internet connection and you can skip the remainder of these steps. If the New Connection Wizard opens, you know you need to create an Internet connection. In that case, if XP detects a modem present, the Location Information dialog box will open where you will need to enter your country or region, area or city code, and other information. Do that, and click OK twice to return to the New Connection Wizard.

TIP

If Internet Explorer did not connect to the Internet and the New Connection Wizard did not open, you can start the New Connection Wizard by opening the Start menu and choosing All Programs | Accessories | Communications | New Connection Wizard.

2. Click Next, accept the default Connect To The Internet, and click Next again. If you have an ISP you want to use and they have given you a CD, click that option. If you have an ISP

Figure 6-4 Initial connection to the Internet

without a CD, click Set Up My Connection Manually. If you don't have an ISP, click Choose From A List of Internet Service Providers (ISPs). Whether using the CD choice or choosing from a list, follow the instructions on the screen. If you are using the manual choice, follow on with these steps.

3. Choose how you want to connect to the Internet. If you are going to use a modem, leave the default choice of the first option. If you are using a broadband connection such as DSL or a cable modem, determine if you have to sign on. If so, select the second choice; otherwise, select the third choice. In any case, once you have made the choice you want, click Next. If you made the third choice (Always On), click Finish and skip to Step 6.

4. Enter the name of your Internet service provider, which will be the name of this connection, and click Next. Enter the phone number of the data connection to your ISP and click Next.

5. Enter the user name and password (twice) given to you by your ISP, choose the options that are correct for you and the computer you are using, and click Next. You are shown a summary of the connection that you want to make. If it is not correct, click Back and make the necessary corrections. When it is correct, click Finish.

6. Once more, open the Start menu and click Internet. If asked, click Connect and then Dial. If you still do not connect to the Internet, you may need to install your modem, in which case you should go to "Install a Modem" earlier in this module and then return here. Otherwise, go to the next step.

TIP

If you think you have your modem set up and you are not getting connected when you open Internet Explorer, look at the Internet Options in Internet Explorer by opening the Tools menu, choosing Internet Options, and clicking the Connections tab. See if you have a dial-up connection specified and that it dials the connection. If not, make the necessary corrections.

7. If you are using a modem, when you have successfully installed your Internet connection and attempt to open Internet Explorer, the Dial-up Connection dialog box will appear. Click Connect and then Dial. Your modem dials the number, you will be connected, and a connection icon will appear in the tray on the right of the taskbar, as you saw earlier in the module. By default, you will be connected to MSN's Home page, similar to the one shown earlier in Figure 6-4. The next section shows you how to change this default.

If you want to set up an Internet mail account, go to Step 8; otherwise, go to Step 10.

8. Open the Start menu and click E-Mail. The Internet Connection Wizard will open and ask you to enter the name you want to be displayed when your account is referenced. Do that and click Next. Enter your e-mail address, and click Next. Select the type of mail service that you have (POP3 is the most common), enter the names of the incoming and outgoing mail servers, and click Next.

9. Enter the mail account's name and password, choose whether you want Windows to remember the password, choose whether you need to use Secure Password Authentication, click Next, and then click Finish. Outlook Express will open, as you can see in Figure 6-5, and connect you to your mail account. In the future, when you open Outlook Express and are not yet connected to the Internet, you will be. Close Outlook Express, but leave Internet Explorer and the Internet connection active.

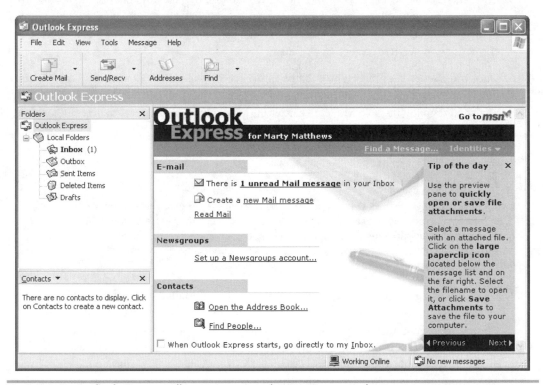

Figure 6-5 Outlook Express allows you to send messages over the Internet.

CRITICAL SKILL
6.3 Browse the Internet

The World Wide Web component of the Internet stores information on pages that you can download and view using a *browser* such as Internet Explorer. Looking at these pages—and there are many millions of them—is called *browsing*. Once you are connected to the Internet with Internet Explorer open, you most probably will want to go to pages other than the MSN Home page. There are a number of ways to do that, including the following:

- Navigating within a web site

- Going directly to a web site

- Searching for a web site

- Setting up a different default home page

Navigate Within a Web Site

A good web site gives you many ways to navigate within it. As you move the mouse around your current view of the MSN Home page (shown in Figure 6-4), you see a number of terms or phrases that become underlined as the mouse moves over them. These are *links* that, when clicked, take you to another part of the web site. The Home page is almost all links of several kinds. It has horizontal menus (MSN Home, My MSN, Hotmail, and so forth), vertical menus (Autos, Business, Careers, and so on), block menus (Air Tickets, Auctions, and so forth), headings, terms by themselves (Help), and article lists. In addition, there is normally a text search capability, similar to the one at the top of the MSN Home page. Here, you can enter a term or a phrase and click Search.

TIP

Often, if you enter a phrase in a text search, the search will be done on each word, not on the complete phrase. To fix that, in many text searches, you can enclose the phrase in quotation marks and the search will be done only on the entire phrase.

Internet Explorer also provides tools to navigate within a site: the Back and Forward arrows on the toolbar take you to the preceding and next pages, respectively. Also, the down arrows on the right of the Back and Forward arrows will list the last several pages you have viewed in each direction.

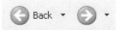

Go Directly to a Web Site

To go directly to a site, you must know the address, or URL (Uniform Resource Locator), for that site. With increasing frequency in publications, letterheads, and advertising, you will find an organization's URL. When you have a site's URL, you can enter it into the Address box under the toolbar in Internet Explorer, as shown next, and then press ENTER, click the right-pointing arrow, or click Go, which takes you directly to the site. URLs that you frequently use can be stored in the Favorites folder, on the desktop, and in the Links toolbar on the same line as the Address toolbar of Internet Explorer. If you select one of these addresses and you are not already connected to the Internet, you will be connected automatically (or you might have to click Dial in a connection dialog box), Internet Explorer will open, and the addressed site will be displayed.

Place a URL in Favorites   You can store a URL in the Favorites folder by entering it or otherwise displaying it in the Address box of Internet Explorer, opening the Favorites menu, and choosing Add To Favorites. The Add Favorite dialog box will open, show you the name the site will have in the Favorites folder, and allow you to place the URL in a subfolder with the Create In option.

NOTE

The Favorites folder is in each user's area of the hard disk. By default, this is C:\Documents and Settings*user*\Favorites.

Place a URL on the Desktop   You can place a URL on the desktop or in the Quick Launch toolbar by dragging the icon in the Address box of Internet Explorer to the desktop or Quick Launch toolbar. This creates a shortcut that, when double-clicked, connects to the Internet, opens Internet Explorer, and displays the site.

Place a URL in the Links Toolbar   The Links toolbar, which displays a subfolder of Favorites, appears on the right of the Address bar in the upper part of Internet Explorer windows. Unlock the toolbars by opening the View menu and choosing Toolbars | Lock The Toolbars. Then drag the Links bar to the left to display more of it or below the Address bar to display it full width. You can add a URL to the Links bar by dragging the icon in the Address box to the Links bar on the right. You can place it within the Links bar in the location you want. You can remove any unwanted links by right-clicking them and choosing Delete.

Search for a Web Site

If you don't know a web site's URL, you can search for it in either of two ways. If it is a web site that you have been to recently, you likely can find it in your web site history. If you have not been to the site recently, you can do a full search of the Internet to find it.

Check History

To check the history of your web site visits, click History in the Internet Explorer toolbar. A History pane will open and show you the sites you have visited by day for the current week, and then by week for the last several weeks. By opening a day or week, you can see and select a URL that you have previously visited and have it quickly displayed.

You can determine how many days to keep History and clear History by opening the Tools menu and choosing Internet Options. In the General tab of the dialog box that opens, in the bottom panel, you can set the Days To Keep Pages In History and Clear History.

Search the Internet

You can search for a web site on the Internet at three levels:

- Type in the Address box what you believe is part of the URL, and Internet Explorer will search for a site that has in its URL the text you entered. If what you enter has been indexed to a site, for example "3com" or "united" (for United Airlines), you will be taken directly to the site, even though the actual URL may not contain what you typed (United's URL is http://www.ual.com). In other cases, such as "Osborne," a Search site appears displaying a list of possible URLs, as you can see in Figure 6-6, even though a site exists with what you typed in it (McGraw-Hill/Osborne's URL is http://www.osborne.com). In still other cases, for example "martymatthews," you get "Sorry, no results were found" even though a site exists with that name (my URL is http://www.martymatthews.com). It all depends on how well the site has been indexed.

TIP

You can change how Internet Explorer responds to Address box search (typing less than a full URL) by opening the Tools menu, choosing Internet Options, clicking the Advanced tab, and scrolling down to Search From The Address Bar.

- Click Search in the toolbar, and the Search pane will open on the left of Internet Explorer. Here, you can enter a word or phrase and click Search. A list of web sites containing that word or phrase will be displayed. You can then click a site in the list and it will be displayed

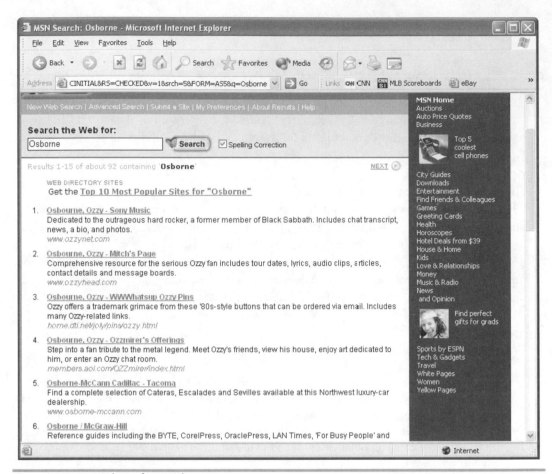

Figure 6-6 Searching for "Osborne"

on the right. As described earlier in the tip under "Navigate Within a Web Site," if you want to search for a complete phrase, you need to place the phrase within quotation marks.

● Use another search site such as Google, Yahoo, Excite, Go, Lycos, or AltaVista by typing the name in the Address bar (see Figure 6-7 for Go.com). Internet Explorer 6.0 (IE) in Windows XP depends entirely on the MSN search engine and does not give you direct links to other search engines that were available in IE 5.0. These other search sites provide different results for the same searches, and so it is often worthwhile to check several sites. You can do this not only when searching for web pages, but also when searching for a person's mailing address or e-mail address, finding a business, locating a map, looking

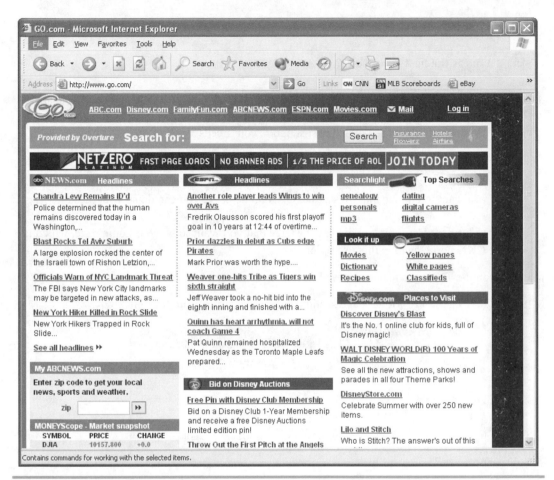

Figure 6-7 The Go.com search site

up a word, finding a picture, finding a reference in a newsgroup, and searching your previous searches.

Set Up a Different Default Home Page

The page that opens when you first start Internet Explorer or click the house icon in Internet Explorer's toolbar is called Home, your home page. By default, when you first install Windows XP with Internet Explorer, this page is the MSN (Microsoft Network) Home page.

Ask the Expert

Q: What is the best search site?

A: In many people's opinion Google (http://www.google.com) is the best pure search site, but it doesn't have all the category links that are on the other sites. I recommend that you try them all and see which best supports your needs.

If you want to change that to, say, the CNN home page, you can do so with these steps:

1. Open Internet Explorer and display the page that you want to be your home page, which is the CNN home page in this example.

2. Open the Tools menu and choose Internet Options.

3. In the General tab, Home Page section, click Use Current, and then click OK.

If you ever want to return to using MSN as your home page, reopen Internet Options and click Use Default.

TIP

If you don't have a particular site you want to go to every time you open Internet Explorer and don't want to wait while one displays, click Use Blank.

CRITICAL SKILL

6.4 Send and Receive Internet Mail

It is arguable which is the more important aspect of the Internet, the World Wide Web or Internet e-mail. E-mail provides one-on-one communications, which is vital to carrying out business functions, as well as building and maintaining relationships. With Windows XP, e-mail is handled with Outlook Express, which enables you to do the following:

- Send, receive, and store e-mail
- Participate in newsgroups
- Maintain and use an address book

Opening the Start menu and clicking E-Mail starts Outlook Express (unless you or someone else has changed your default e-mail program), which you saw in Figure 6-5.

Send, Receive, and Store E-Mail

When you first open Outlook Express, it automatically connects, if possible, to the Internet and retrieves any mail that your ISP is holding for you. Then as long as Outlook Express is loaded, it will periodically try to get your e-mail, by reconnecting to the Internet as necessary. You can change if and how often your mail is checked by opening the Tools menu, choosing Options, and looking under Send/Receive Messages in the General tab. You can also manually retrieve your mail by clicking Send/Recv in the toolbar, or by clicking the down arrow on the right of Send/Recv to choose to either send or receive, and select the account to send to or receive from. By opening Local Folders and clicking Inbox in the left pane of the Outlook Express window, you will see in the upper-right pane a list of the messages you have received. If you click a message, some of the content of the message appears in the bottom-right pane. If you double-click a message, the message opens in its own window. If you do not delete the message, it stays in the Inbox for as long as you want.

You can create a new message to send by clicking Create Mail in the toolbar. This opens a New Message window in which you enter the e-mail address(es) of the recipients (separated by semicolons), a subject, which is helpful for identifying and locating messages, and the body of the message. When you are done with the message, click Send, and it will go into the Outbox.

Ask the Expert

Q: **I have Microsoft Office XP, which has Outlook; how does this compare with Outlook Express and which should I use?**

A: Outlook Express is a subset of Outlook. The mail features in Outlook are very similar to Outlook Express. Outlook also provides a comprehensive scheduling package, the ability to track tasks and keep notes, and a more comprehensive address book. In addition, you can share schedules, tasks, notes, and contacts within a workgroup to successfully coordinate activities. If you need the added functionality of Outlook, then that is what you should use. If you don't use the added features, then I believe that Outlook Express is the better tool.

(continued)

If you use Outlook Express often, you can make it easier to start by placing its icon on the desktop and in the Quick Launch toolbar. Do that with the following steps:

1. Open My Computer or Windows Explorer and navigate to the C:\Program Files\Outlook Express folder, as shown in the following illustration.

2. Drag the Msimn.exe file in the Outlook Express folder (pointed at in the illustration) to the desktop to create a shortcut to that program.

3. Drag the Msimn.exe file to the Quick Launch toolbar to create a shortcut there. (If your Quick Launch toolbar is not open, you may open it by right-clicking the taskbar and choosing Toolbars | Quick Launch. If the Quick Launch toolbar is constricted, unlock the taskbar on its context menu and drag the Quick Launch toolbar border to size it.)

NOTE

If you upgraded from Windows 2000 to Windows XP, there may already be Outlook Express shortcuts on the desktop and in the Quick Launch toolbar.

If you are connected to the Internet, it will be sent. If you are not connected, it will try to connect you; if that fails, the message will remain in the Outbox until you are next connected. You can also get a New Message window with the recipient(s) and subject already filled in by clicking Reply or Reply All in the toolbar of a message you have received. Reply will fill in only the address of the sender of the original message, whereas Reply All fills in the addresses of all the people, sender and recipients, in the original message. If you click Forward on a message you receive, the original message is copied to a New Message window, but the address fields are left blank for you to fill in.

You can attach one or more computer files to an e-mail message either by dragging the file from Windows Explorer or the desktop to the New Message window or by clicking Attach in the toolbar of a New Message window and entering the file path and name or browsing for the attachment.

Participate in Newsgroups

Newsgroups are an organized chain of messages on a particular subject. Newsgroups are sponsored by some organization, such as a company, university, or club, and allow people to enter new messages and respond to previous ones. To access a newsgroup, you need to set up a new account for the newsgroup, similar to the account you set up for your e-mail. To set up and use a newsgroup account, you need the name of the news server and possibly an account name and password. Use the following steps:

1. In the Outlook Express window, open the Tools menu and choose Accounts. The Internet Accounts dialog box will open.

2. Click Add | News. Enter the name you want displayed and click Next. Enter your e-mail address if not already displayed so that people can directly reply to you and click Next.

3. Enter the name of your news server. Your ISP or another sponsoring organization will give this to you. If you do not need to enter an account name and password, your ISP or sponsoring organization will tell you this, in which case you can skip to Step 5.

4. If you need to enter an account name and password, click My News Server Requires Me To Log On and click Next. Enter your account name and password, click Remember Password (if desired), and then, if necessary (your ISP or sponsor will tell you), click Log On Using Secure Password Authentication (SPA).

5. Click Next, click Finish, and you are returned to the Internet Accounts dialog box where the new account is now listed. Click Close. A new folder will appear in the Folders pane of Outlook Express.

6. You will see a message asking whether you want to download the newsgroups from the news account you just set up. Click Yes. If necessary, click Connect to connect to the Internet. If all of your entries are okay, you will be connected. If your account name and password are in error, you are told so and given a chance to fix them.

7. A list of newsgroups will be displayed. Double-click the ones to which you want to subscribe (meaning read and reply to messages they contain). After you have selected the newsgroups, click OK. You are returned to Outlook Express.

8. In the Folders pane on the left, click a newsgroup you want to open. A list of messages will be displayed. Click one to have it shown in the bottom pane, or double-click to have a message opened in its own window.

You can treat a newsgroup message like an e-mail message, but with two differences. You can choose to reply to the newsgroup or to the individual, and a new message is called a New Post. In newsgroups, a new message is "posted" as one would be on a bulletin board. If someone replies to this message, it gets added to the end of the original message, thereby creating a chain, or *thread,* of messages on a given subject. For example, Figure 6-8 shows a thread on the topic of creating a boot CD for Windows XP, in a newsgroup on the operating system.

Maintain and Use an Address Book

Outlook Express maintains an address book to help you keep track of your e-mail and snail-mail addresses and phone numbers. When you reply to a message that you have received, the addresses automatically go into the address book. When you create a new message, as you start typing a name, it will be looked up in the address book and completed for you if it's already in the address book. You can also manually add a name to the address book, manually look up an address, and create a group of addresses that can be referred to by the group name and added to a message all at once.

Add a Name to the Address Book

The following are a few ways to add names to the address book:

- From the Outlook Express window, click Addresses in the toolbar to open the Address Book window, click New in its toolbar, select New Contact, and fill in the dialog box that opens.

- From a New Message window, click the address book icon next to the "To" and "Cc" blocks to open the Select Recipients dialog box, click New Contact, and fill in the dialog box that opens.

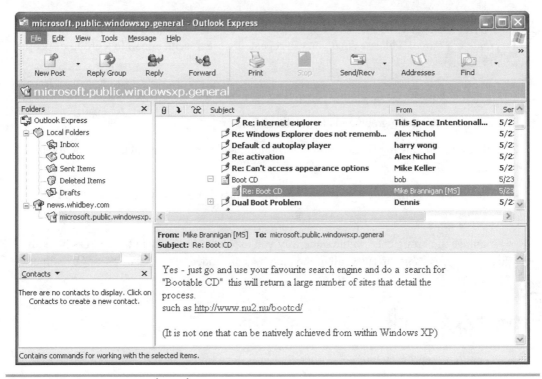

Figure 6-8 A newsgroup thread

- From an existing message, right-click an address anywhere in the message and choose Add (Sender) To Address Book.

Look Up an Address

You look up addresses in much the same way as you add them to the address book:

- From the Outlook Express window, click Addresses in the toolbar to open the Address Book window. Use the scroll bar or begin typing a name to locate it. When it is found, the e-mail address is shown in the Address Book window. If you want the postal address or other information not shown in the window, double-click the name to open the Properties dialog box, which shows all of the information on that individual.

- From a New Message window, click the address book icon next to the "To" and "Cc" blocks to open the Select Recipients dialog box. Double-click all the entries you want to receive the message and click OK.

Create and Use a Group

To create a group of addresses that you can repeatedly use to send e-mail to a group of people, use these steps:

1. Open the Address Book window, open the File menu, and choose New Group.

2. Enter a name for the group and click Select Members.

3. Either type a name or use the scroll bar to find it, and then double-click the name to add it to the list of members.

4. When you are done, click OK twice. An entry with a distinctive icon will appear in the address book.

You use the group entry in the same way you use any other entry in the address book, but when you choose a group entry, all of the members are added to the list of message recipients.

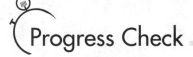

Progress Check

1. What are two primary Internet services?

2. What are two ways to go to a web site in Internet Explorer?

3. What are the two primary services provided in Outlook Express?

CRITICAL SKILL
6.5 Use Windows Messenger

Windows Messenger started out as MSN Messenger and has now been included in Windows XP. It allows you to instantly send and receive messages (or *chat*) with others who are online at the same time as you. Windows Messenger also has replaced NetMeeting in handling teleconferencing, the live, remote interaction of several people. Additionally, Windows Messenger allows two or more people to play a game together, to handle both audio and video transmission, to track stock and e-mail, and to send messages to pagers. The heart of Windows

---

1. World Wide Web browsing and Internet e-mail.

2. The primary ways to go to a web site are to use links within a web site to go to another site, directly enter the URL for a web site in the address bar, use searching programs or "engines" to locate the web site, use the Links bar, or select the entry in the list of Favorite sites.

3. Sending and receiving e-mail and participating in newsgroups.

Messenger, though, is the communicating between two people when they are both online; like speech, it does not normally create a permanent record, unless you specifically save the exchange.

Windows Messenger is installed automatically when you install Windows XP and it automatically starts whenever you log on. Windows Messenger requires that you have a Microsoft Passport or an MSN or Hotmail account, so that is your first step. Next you must set up your contacts and make other changes to personalize Messenger to your tastes. You can then use it to chat. Finally, if you want to go beyond chatting, you can look into audio and video conferencing, playing games, and sharing control of programs, whiteboards, and files.

Establish a Passport

Soon after you complete the installation of Windows XP, you will be asked if you want to set up a .NET Passport account. Do that now:

1. If you have already installed XP and canceled out of the .NET Passport question, you can start the wizard after the fact by clicking the Windows Messenger icon in the notification area on the right of the taskbar or by opening the Start menu and clicking All Programs | Windows Messenger.

2. Click Next. You are asked if you already have an e-mail account or if you would like to open an MSN e-mail account. If you haven't already established an e-mail account as discussed earlier in this module under "Set Up an Internet Connection," it is recommended that you go back and do that first.

3. Assuming you have an e-mail account, accept the default of Yes and click Next. Enter your e-mail address and click Next. If you have never had a Passport account, or an MSN, Hotmail, or MSN Passport account, you will be asked to create and confirm a password of at least six characters. Passwords should be easy to remember and hard to guess. If you are serious about having a secure password, you should mix upper- and lowercase letters and numbers of at least eight characters. If possible, the letters and numbers should not make sense on their own. In other words, no names or dates. If you already have a Hotmail/Passport/MSN account, after entering your username and password you skip to Step 5.

4. When you have entered and confirmed your password, click Next. Select the secret question you want to supply an answer for, and then enter the answer. Click Next. Enter your country, state, and ZIP code. If you forget your password, you can enter the answer to your secret question, as well as your country, state, and ZIP code to get a new password. Click Next.

5. Click I Accept The Agreement (is there really someone somewhere that reads this stuff, what choice do you have if you were to disagree?) and click Next. Decide if you want to share your e-mail address or not and click Next.

6. You are told that your user account is now set up to use the .NET Passport associated with your e-mail address. Click Finish to complete the process and close the wizard. Windows Messenger will open, as you can see in Figure 6-9.

NOTE

There may be a newer version of Windows Messenger available through Windows Update, depending on how old the copy of Windows XP is that you are installing. If you are told this, go ahead and download the update.

Adding Contacts

Once you have a Passport, you can use Windows Messenger, but to do so you must have contacts whom you can talk to, so add contacts next:

1. If Windows Messenger is not already open on your screen, double-click the little humanoid icon in the notification area of the taskbar. If the icon isn't there, open the Start menu and click All Programs | Windows Messenger.

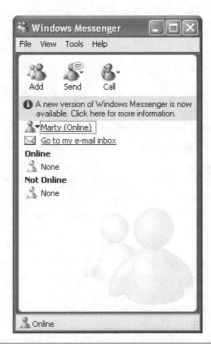

Figure 6-9 Windows Messenger ready for use

2. Click Add in the Windows Messenger toolbar. If you know your contact's e-mail address, click By E-mail Address Or Sign-in Name, click Next, enter the e-mail address, and click Next. Depending on the person's status, several things can occur:

- If the person has a Passport account, you will be told you were successful in establishing the contact.

- If the person is logged on to Windows Messenger, you will be told you can chat with them.

- If the person isn't logged on, you will be told you can send them an e-mail message asking them to sign on.

- If the person doesn't have a Passport account, you will be told you can send them an e-mail message telling them about Passport and how to install it.

NOTE

In sending the e-mail message to the person who you want for a contact, the prewritten body of the message can be sent in any one of 26 languages.

3. In any of the preceding cases, click Next, enter your own message to add to the canned message, and click Finish to close the Add A Contact wizard.

4. If you want to Search For A Contact, click that and click Next. Enter as much of the information as you can of the name, country, and so on, and click Next. If there is more than one person that fits your criteria, select the correct one and click Next. You are told the person was found, but you cannot immediately add him or her to your contact list due to the privacy policy. You can send the person an e-mail message by clicking Next, entering your message, and clicking Finish to close the Add A Contact Wizard.

5. Add as many contacts as you wish.

As you are successful in adding contacts, these people will be notified with a message similar to this (the first line will contain your name and e-mail address):

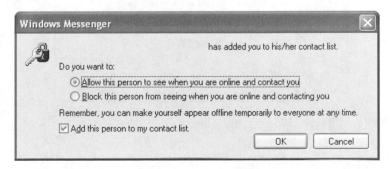

Personalize Messenger

There are a number of ways you personalize Windows Messenger. Here's how:

1. In the Windows Messenger window, open the Tools menu and choose Options. The Options dialog box will open. In the Personal tab, enter the name you want to use and click Change Font to determine the font to use for instant messaging.

2. In the Phone tab, if you want people to know one or more of your phone numbers, enter them. In the Preferences tab, shown in Figure 6-10, look carefully at each of the options and decide what it best for you. There are no real right and wrong answers for any of these. Note this and come back here after you have used Windows Messenger for a while.

3. In the Privacy tab, you can manage your allow and block lists. To move a person from one column to the other, select that person and click Allow or Block. The Connection tab is only needed if you have a firewall or proxy server.

4. When you have personalized Windows Messenger the way you want, click OK.

Figure 6-10 Setting Windows Messenger preferences

Send and Receive Messages

Using Windows Messenger is very simple: simply double-click the person who is online, and a conversation window will open. Type your message in the bottom pane and click Send. If you want to attach a file to the message, open the File menu, select Send File or Photo, select the document to send, and click Open. Figure 6-11 shows a conversation including the transfer of a file. Files you receive through Windows Messenger are stored in My Documents\My Received Files. You can quickly open them by opening the Conversation File menu and choosing Open Received File.

While sending a message, you can change the font including the typeface, style (bold, italic), and size; you can also add one of the smiley faces or objects, shown next, to express emotions. If you want to stop receiving comments from the other person, for example if they are getting offensive, click Block.

There are many other things you can do with Windows Messenger:

- If you have a sound board with speakers and a microphone, you can hold an audio conversation, literally talking over the Internet as you would over a phone. (If you don't have a broadband connection, this will not be very satisfactory.)

- If you have a video camera set up, you can send real-time pictures over Windows Messenger. Here broadband is mandatory.

- You can share an application among two or more people. For example, say you and several associates are working on the budget. You could load the budget into Excel and then share the application. All of you could have a conversation while sharing and working together on the budget.

6

Using Communications and the Internet

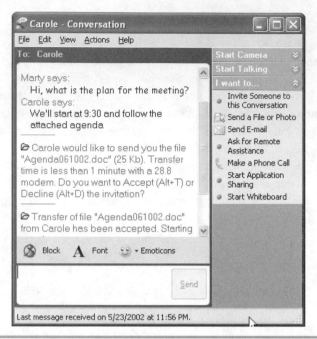

Figure 6-11 Online conversation and transfer of a file

● An offshoot of sharing an application is sharing a whiteboard. Here all the parties to a conversation can use a drawing application as they are holding a conversation, as you can see in Figure 6-12.

All of these additional functions start by initiating a conversation and then starting the additional function. For example, if after starting a normal Windows Messenger conversation you want to use a whiteboard, simply click Start Whiteboard. The other parties will have to agree, but that is all there is to it.

CRITICAL SKILL
6.6 # Use HyperTerminal

In the days before we all became enamored with the Web, data transfer between computers was handled quite effectively (as it still can be) with data communication software, such as HyperTerminal. However, the ease with which the average computer user can use the Internet

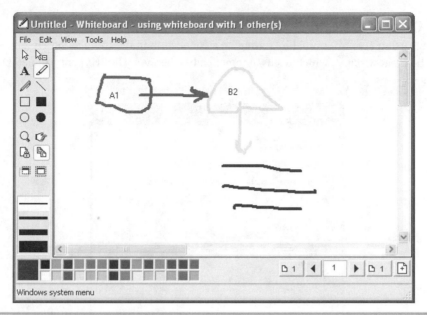

Figure 6-12 Sharing a whiteboard

to access information and transfer files has relegated data communication software to mostly specialized tasks, such as the following:

- Manually sending dialing instructions to your modem
- Configuring devices such as routers either remotely using a modem or locally using a cable
- Transferring files between computers using serial ports and a cable
- Sending and receiving files using modems and a direct phone connection

Among the things you can do with HyperTerminal are three basic functions: making a connection and placing a call, receiving a call, and sending a file.

NOTE

I have purposefully made this similar to what we did with Windows Messenger so you can compare the two services.

Make a Connection and Place a Call

You start using HyperTerminal by setting up a connection in the Connection Description dialog box, shown next, which opens automatically when you start HyperTerminal. Do that with these steps:

1. Open the Start menu and choose All Programs | Accessories | Communications | HyperTerminal. You are asked if you want HyperTerminal to be your default Telnet program. Click Yes.

2. Enter a name for the connection, select an icon, and click OK. A set of dialog boxes asks you for the phone number, how to connect, and other necessary information to make the connection.

3. When you are ready, click Dial. You should hear and see in the dialog box your computer dialing and the other end answering. When a connection is established, you will be presented with a window in which you can type a message and see the responses from the other party, as shown in Figure 6-13.

   After you create a connection, it appears as a new HyperTerminal folder icon in the All Programs | Accessories | Communications | HyperTerminal menu shown next. Here in one click you can both open the HyperTerminal window and establish the connection.

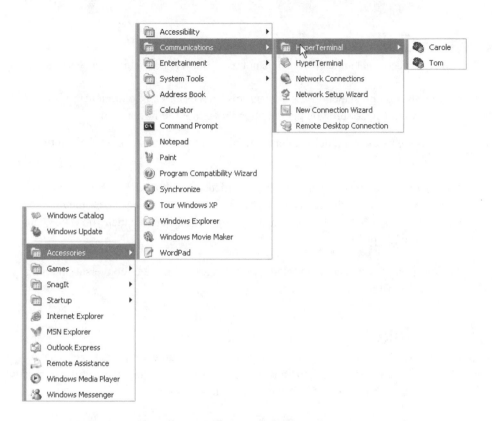

Figure 6-13 An open HyperTerminal session

Receive a Call

To set up HyperTerminal to receive a call is not hard, but it is not intuitive, as you can see next:

1. Open the Start menu and choose All Programs | Accessories | Communications | HyperTerminal (make sure you get the phone icon, not the folder icon).

2. Enter **Receive** as the name for the connection, select an icon, and click OK. In the next dialog box click Cancel.

3. In the HyperTerminal window, open the Call menu and choose Wait For A Call. Waiting For Calls will appear in the status bar. When a call comes in, you'll hear the phone ring, the computer will answer, you'll see Connecting in the status bar, and then you'll be Connected. It is an automatic process.

   When you see that you are connected, you can start typing your conversation and, if you want, transferring files.

Transfer a File

Before widespread use of the Internet and networks, communications packages such as HyperTerminal were widely used to transfer files. It is still occasionally useful when network and Internet connections are not available. Here's how it is done:

1. Establish a connection as you did earlier under "Make a Connection and Place a Call." In the HyperTerminal window, open the Transfer menu and click Send File.

2. Enter the path and Filename or click Browse and select a file. Leave the default Protocol, as shown next, and click Send.

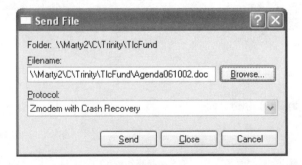

A sending message box will open as you can see in Figure 6-14 and display the progress of the transmission.

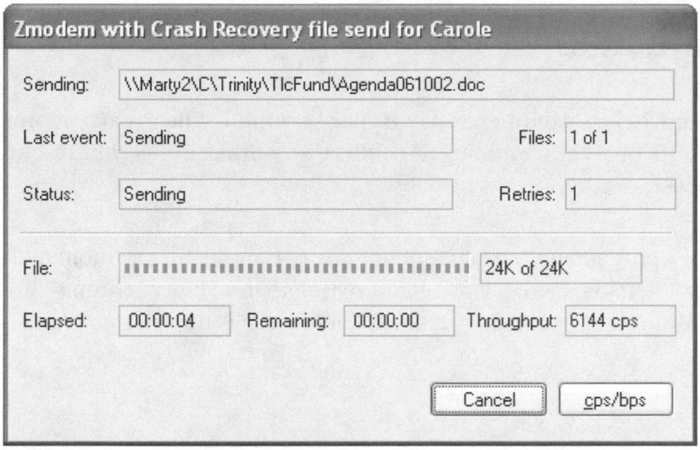

Figure 6-14 Transferring a file in HyperTerminal

As you can see, HyperTerminal works quite well, but it is crude in comparison to Windows Messenger, as it should be in the computer arena; it is roughly ten-year-old technology.

Progress Check

1. What is the first requirement for using Windows Messenger?

2. What are two things you can do to personalize Windows Messenger?

3. What devices are used to make HyperTerminal calls?

---

1. To use Windows Messenger, you must first set up a Passport.

2. To personalize Windows Messenger, you can specify the name you want people to see, you can change the font that is used, you can use one or more of the emotions characters, and you can determine if you want people to have one or more of your phone numbers.

3. HyperTerminal calls are made using either modems and phone lines or a direct cable connection.

Ask the Expert

Q: I don't see where I would ever use HyperTerminal. The areas you mentioned earlier don't fit what I'm doing. Are there any other areas that might be possibilities?

A: If you don't program routers or want to directly transfer files without an Internet or network connection, there is not a lot of reason to use HyperTerminal. It is a product that had a lot of use five to ten years ago, but its use is now marginal at best.

Project 6 Set Up Communications and Internet Services

Continuing the scenario begun in Module 3 of setting up a new computer, we'll install communications and Internet services on this computer with these tasks:

- Setting up a modem
- Establishing dial-up communications
- Attaching an Internet connection
- Setting up an e-mail account
- Establishing a passport
- Adding contacts to Windows Messenger

Step by Step

1. Open the Start menu, click Control Panel, if in Category view, click Printers And Other Hardware, and then click Phone And Modem Options. If in Classic view, double-click Phone And Modem Options.

2. Click the Modems tab and click Add. Make sure the modem is attached to both a communications outlet and the computer, check that it is turned on, and then click Next. If you have a Plug And Play modem, the computer should find and display it. Click Next and skip the next step.

3. If the computer did not find your modem, click Next, select the manufacturer and model, and click Next. Select the port to which it is connected and click Next.

4. Click Finish. In the Phone And Modem Options dialog box, select the modem you just installed and click Properties. Click the Diagnostics tab and click Query Modem. After a moment, you should see a list of Commands and Responses from the modem if it is working properly. Click OK twice to close the various dialog boxes.

5. In the Control Panel, double-click Network Connections if in Classic view, or if in Category view, click Network And Internet Connections and then click Network Connections. Click Create A New Connection. The New Connection Wizard will open. Click Next.

6. Accept the default Connect To The Internet and click Next. With your own ISP, click Set Up My Connection Manually and click Next. With a dial-up modem, click Connect Using A Dial-Up Modem and click Next.

7. Enter the ISP's name, click Next, enter the phone number, click Next, enter your user name and password, confirm the password, choose the options you want, and click Next. If the settings are correct, click Finish; otherwise, click Back and make the necessary corrections.

8. In the Connect dialog box that opens, click Dial. You should see a balloon over the notification area of the toolbar telling you that you are connected. Open the Start menu and click Internet. Internet Explorer should open, asking if you want to make MSN your home page and keep the current settings. Make the choices that are correct for you and browse the Internet as you wish. When you are done, close Internet Explorer.

9. Open the Start menu and click E-Mail to open the Internet Connection Wizard. Enter the name you want others to see, click Next, enter your e-mail address, click Next, select your type of mail server (probably POP3), enter the addresses of your incoming and then outgoing mail servers, click Next, enter your account name and password, click Next, and then click Finish. Outlook Express will open.

10. Click Create Mail to write an e-mail message, click Send when you are ready to do that, click Send/Recv in the toolbar when you want to download you incoming mail (which by default also happens automatically), and click Addresses in the toolbar to open, add, and maintain your address book. When you are done, close Outlook Express.

11. To use Windows Messenger, you must first create a Passport account by opening the Start menu and choosing Windows Messenger. In the .NET Passport Wizard, click Next, accept Yes you have an e-mail account, click Next, enter your e-mail address, click Next, enter your password twice, click Next twice, if asked, select your secret question and enter its answer, click Next, select a country and state, enter your ZIP code, click Next, click I Accept and Next, decide if you want to share your e-mail address and other information, click Next, and click Finish.

(continued)

12. To add contacts to Windows Messenger, you need to click Add, accept the default By E-Mail Address, click Next, enter the e-mail address, click Next, and click Finish. If the person is online, an icon will appear with that person's name under the Online status. To start a conversation, double-click an online icon, type a brief message, and click Send. You'll see the other person respond.

13. When you are done, click Close in both the Conversation window and in the Windows Messenger window. You are told that Windows Messenger will continue to run in the background. Click OK.

Project Summary

Through the first five modules, we've been focused on what Windows XP can do internally with the computer on which it is running. The subject of this module, communications, focuses on how Windows XP helps you interact with other computers and people that are remote not only from you but from your immediate location, everywhere from across the street to around the world. (Module 8, on networking, will look at interacting with computers near you.) With the phenomenal growth in the Internet, communications has taken on a very major importance, one that to some people is the major reason for having a computer. As you have seen, Windows XP provides a great deal of capability in this area and is an excellent tool for very effective use of the Internet.

✓ Module 6 Mastery Check

1. What is a modem and what does it do?

2. What are three types of communication services that can be used for an Internet connection, and how do they differ in terms of their speed and cost?

3. If you use your own ISP, what information do you need from them to connect to the Internet?

4. If you know your modem is working properly and you still did not connect to the Internet, what are some of the possible reasons?

5. What is the most common form of DSL and what are some of its characteristics?

6. What are some of the characteristics of cable Internet?

7. What can you do with Internet Explorer?

8. What can you do with Outlook Express?

9. What are newsgroups and how are they used?

10. What can you do with Windows Messenger?

Module 7

Using Audio and Video Media

Multimedia is the marriage of audio and video with a computer. It is handling sound and both still and moving visual images by storing them, editing them, and playing or displaying them. Windows XP, as an operating system, has to be able to handle the files and accept the input from a number of different devices, which it does. In addition, it has two major programs that enable you to work with these files: Windows Media Player and Windows Movie Maker, along with a new capability to write files onto CDs. The purpose of this module is to explore all three of these areas.

CRITICAL SKILL
7.1 Use Windows Media Player

Windows Media Player enables you to play music CDs, play DVDs, and listen to radio stations that are available over the Internet. It also enables you to copy music tracks off CDs, create a library on your hard disk, and then write it to a recordable CD. Finally, Windows Media Player enables you to select how it looks with a number of different designs called *skins*.

Play Music CDs and DVDs

Playing CDs and DVDs is as easy as inserting a disk in the drive. When you do that, you will be asked if you want Windows Media Player to play the disk. If you click OK, Media Player will open and begin playing the disk, as shown in Figure 7-1. The Media Player window that is shown in Figure 7-1 has five sets of controls that enable you to determine how Media Player functions and looks:

● The **Features taskbar** allows you to select one of the seven following features that can be handled in Media Player:

　● **Now Playing**, the default view, enables you to see visualizations of audio that is playing or the display of a video.

　● **Media Guide** connects to WindowsMedia.com's media page, which provides links to playable and downloadable audio and video files and enables you to search for others.

　● **Copy from CD** enables you to select tracks to play or to copy to the Media Library on your computer.

　● **Media Library** displays the set of folders called Media Library, where you can store, copy, and organize media files and links to Internet media content, as well as create audio and video playlists.

　● **Radio Tuner** connects to WindowsMedia.com's Internet radio page, which provides links to radio stations on the Internet and enables you to search for others by type of music. You can store links to stations you like to quickly access them in the future.

Features taskbar   Playlist selection controls   Playlist pane

Visualization controls   Playback controls

Figure 7-1 Windows Media Player playing a music CD

- **Copy to CD or Device** allows you to copy music tracks in the Media Library to a writable CD (CD-R or CD-RW) or to a solid-state storage device or card.

- **Skin Chooser** allows you to choose a different look, or "skin," for Windows Media Player.

- **Visualization controls** enable you to choose the type of visualization, the specific one within that type, and whether to display it over the full screen or just within the Media Player.

- **Playback controls** provide the standard tape deck–like controls, including play/pause, stop, previous, next, and volume control across the bottom, and rewind, seek slider, and fast forward on top.

- The **Playlist pane** lists the pieces on the current playlist, the tracks on the current CD, the movie on the current DVD, or the radio station being played.

- The **Playlist selection controls** enable you to select a playlist or other items, such as your radio stations, from which you can choose what you want to play. From the left, there are controls to display the menu bar, randomize the play of pieces or tracks in a playlist, display the Now Playing tools, and display the playlist pane.

The playlist selection controls allow you to display or not to display two optional areas that give you additional controls. These are the menu bar, which appears when you display the full window, and the Now Playing tools pane, which can contain several different sets of controls, including a graphic equalizer shown here:

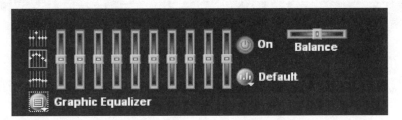

Listen to Internet Radio Stations

If you have a broadband connection (as described in Module 6) of at least 128 Kbps and a sound card with speakers, you can listen to radio stations around the world that have added an Internet connection. Windows Media Player gives you access to these stations through the Radio Tuner feature, which you can see in Figure 7-2. Radio Tuner gives you several ways of finding and playing a particular station. These are

- Choosing from a featured set of stations or an editor's picks of the day

Figure 7-2 Media Player's Radio Tuner allows you to listen to Internet radio stations.

- Selecting a type of music or genre on which to search, or searching on a keyword, the station's call letters, for instance, or the ZIP code where it is located

- Choosing a station you have recently played or that you have added to a list of your favorite stations

Ask the Expert

Q: I know that a radio station is on the Internet (KING in Seattle), but I can't find it using Media Player. How come?

A: KING and some other radio stations are set up to use Real Networks' RealPlayer and cannot be heard with Windows Media Player.

Build and Manage a Music Library

On most CDs, there are tracks you like and those that you don't, and it has long been desirable to put together just the music you want to hear. Media Player gives you that ability by providing the means to copy tracks that you like to your hard disk and to build and manage a library of your favorite music.

NOTE

The material on most CDs and DVDs is owned and copyrighted by some combination of the composer, the artist, the producer, and/or the publisher. The copyright law prohibits using the copyrighted material in ways that are not beneficial to the owners, including giving or selling the content without giving or selling the original CD or DVD itself. To back that up, most CDs and DVDs are protected to make copying difficult. Media Player provides the ability to copy copyrighted material to your hard disk and then to a recordable CD or a solid-state device with the understanding that it is solely for your own personal use and you will not sell or give away the copies. This is both a great gift, to be able to copy the material, and a responsibility. As one who makes his living on copyrighted material, I ask you not to abuse it.

Copy Tracks from CDs

In Media Player, you copy tracks from a CD using the Copy From CD feature (shown in Figure 7-3) with the following steps:

1. Insert into your computer a CD from which you want to copy tracks. Click OK to open Windows Media, Player and when it opens, click Copy From CD in the features taskbar.

2. Select the tracks you think you want to copy to your hard disk by checking the check boxes on the left of each track. Click Play in the playback controls to listen to the track and make sure your choices are correct.

3. When you are satisfied that you have selected the correct tracks, click Copy Music. A message box will open asking if the copy on your disk should be copy protected so that it cannot be played on other computers and reminding you that you are responsible.

4. Make the copy protection choice that is correct for you and click OK. The selected tracks will be copied to your hard disk.

Figure 7-3 Creating a music library by copying tracks from CDs

NOTE

The process of copying a music track from a CD to a digital file on your hard disk is very time consuming, and even on a relatively fast computer, it can take a significant amount of time; it also produces large files. To see the copying progress, look at the Copy Status column in the top pane of the Copy From CD window, as shown here:

	Title	Length	Copy Status	Artist	Composer	Genre
1	Blue Rondo a la Turk	6:47	Copied to Library	Dave Brubeck	Dave Brubeck	JAZZ
☑ 2	Strange Meadowlark	7:26	Copying (99%)	Dave Brubeck	Dave Brubeck	JAZZ
☑ 3	Take Five	5:28	Pending	Dave Brubeck	Paul Desmond	JAZZ

Dave Brubeck Quartet - Time Out   ⊗ Stop Copy

Manage a Media Library

To better organize the media on your hard disks, as well as media-related Internet links, Media Player has the Media Library feature and screen, shown in Figure 7-4, which provides a Windows Explorer view. The Media Library copies media from a CD. Once in the library, contents are automatically indexed alphabetically by album, artist, and genre. In addition, you can combine them in a playlist to allow you to play pieces from several albums. Here is how to build a new playlist:

1. Click Media Library in the features taskbar and then click New Playlist in the toolbar. Enter the name you want to use for the new playlist and click OK.

2. Open an album, artist, or genre, identify a piece you want in the new playlist, and either drag it there or click Add To Playlist in the toolbar and select the playlist.

3. When you have added all the pieces that you initially want to add (you can always add more later), start listening to the pieces by clicking Play in the playback controls.

TIP

When playing a playlist, you can randomize the play among the pieces by clicking Turn Shuffle On in the Playlist Selection toolbar, third button from the right.

Ask the Expert

Q: Why do I need to use Media Player's Media Library to manage and organize media when I can use Windows Explorer for the same task?

A: It depends on what you want to do. You can work with playlists only in Media Player, but you can add pieces to playlists from Explorer, although it opens Media Player to do it. If you are working for a period of time with media on your hard disk, it is easier and more productive to do it in Media Player.

NOTE

For easy access, selections copied to playlists in Media Player show up under My Documents | My Music | *CD Title* | *Song title.*

Figure 7-4 Media Library provides a way to manage the media you store on your computer.

CRITICAL SKILL
7.3 Write Your Music Library on a CD

To make the most of your music library, you can write it to a writable or rewritable CD or to a solid-state music device such as an MP3 Player. Media Player provides this capability in the Copy To CD Or Device feature shown in Figure 7-5. Here are the steps to use it:

1. Put a blank recordable disk in the CD-R or CD-RW drive or connect your solid-state music device to the computer.

2. While still in the Media Library, make sure your new playlist is selected and then click Copy To CD Or Device in the features taskbar.

3. Make any corrections to the list of pieces that will be copied to the CD or solid-state device by selecting or deselecting the check boxes. You can also change the playlist by opening the playlist drop-down list (in Figure 7-5, this says "My Jazz").

4. When you are sure you have the list of pieces you want to copy, click Copy Music. The digital files will first be converted to analog music files and then written to a CD or device. The Status column will show you the progress (it is not very fast!).

   The resulting CD should be playable in most music CD players.

Change Skins

Just to be "way cool," you can change how Media Player looks by clicking Skin Chooser in the features taskbar, choosing one of the 20 skins, and click Apply Skin. If you don't like any of the 20 skins that are included with Windows XP, click More Skins. You will be connected to the WindowsMedia.com Skins page, where there are many more skins to choose from. Some of the skins are very inventive and take a bit to figure them out. Those that are quite small have an anchor window that you can hide, but it gives you some important controls including switching back to full mode (the default look in all the previous figures), which you can also do by pressing CTRL-1.

Progress Check

1. How do you play a music CD in Windows XP?

2. What are the playback controls for?

3. What is the principle benefit of using playlists?

---

1. Simply insert in it in the CD drive.
2. Playback controls provide the standard tape deck–like controls used to play, pause, and stop playing a particular piece or track, to move to previous or next piece or track, and to control the volume.
3. Playlists allow you to select just the tracks you like from several CDs, put them in a single playlist, and, optionally, copy them to a recordable CD or device.

Figure 7-5 Copying a playlist to a writable CD

7.4 Use Windows Movie Maker

Windows Movie Maker lets you take video from a camcorder or import an audio or video file, store it on your hard disk, edit both the video and audio, and produce a movie from the result. You can also create a narrated "slide show" by capturing a series of still pictures and adding sound to them.

Video can come into Windows Movie Maker either directly from a digital camcorder using an IEEE (Institute of Electrical and Electronic Engineers) [standard number] 1394 FireWire interface card or indirectly through a file on your computer created by playing an analog recording into a video capture card. In the digital case, Movie Maker records the signal coming into the computer and creates the file. In the analog case, either Movie Maker or software that comes with the video capture card creates the file. Once the video file is on your hard disk,

Movie Maker divides it into short video segments, or *clips*. You can delete unwanted clips, rearrange them, and combine them in any way you want. Between clips, you can create a transition of one clip fading into another. You can use the audio on the original tape or record and use a new sound track of narration and/or music. When you are done, you can save the file and then play it back.

NOTE

One major drawback with Windows Movie Maker is that you can save your movie files only in the Windows Media Video file format, which can be played only with Windows Movie Maker on Windows Me, 2000, and XP systems.

Prepare for Movie Maker

To make movies using a computer takes more hardware than any other task. The faster your CPU, the more memory, and the larger your disk, the smoother the task will go. The beauty is that today's new computers have most of what you need. Table 7-1 shows what Microsoft says are the minimum requirements, what I say they are, and what I believe is the recommended configuration.

NOTE

If you are going to do digital video camera capture, Microsoft recommends a 400 MHz or higher processor.

Component	Microsoft Minimum	My Minimum	My Recommended
CPU	300 MHz Pentium II (see following note)	600 MHz Pentium III	1 GHz Pentium III
RAM memory	64MB	128MB	256MB
Hard drive free space	2GB	10GB	40GB
Video recording from DV camcorders		IEEE 1394 FireWire card, OHCI-compliant	
Video capture from analog VCR /Camera		Windows XP–compatible Video Capture card	
Audio capture from microphone, tape		Windows XP–compatible Audio card	

Table 7-1 Minimum and Recommended Hardware for Movie Maker

Of all the components, memory is the most important. With less than 128MB it may work, but you will not be happy using it. If you have access to a digital video (DV) camcorder with an IEEE 1394 FireWire interface, it is strongly recommended that you get a FireWire interface card (make sure it is OHCI compliant) for your computer (they are available for under $70). With it, you can digitally transfer video information between the camera and the computer without losing anything. The alternative is to use a video capture card where you can plug in an analog video signal from a TV, a VCR, an analog camcorder, or in most cases a DV camcorder, which normally also has an analog output to directly play on a TV. In "capturing," the analog signal is converted and stored as a digital file, but the process is less than perfect, and the result is not as good as the original recording.

TIP

If you are trying with Movie Maker to record an analog signal coming from a video capture card and are having problems, which is common, don't fight it. Use the software that comes with the video capture card to create a file on your hard disk and then import that file into Movie Maker (you'll see how in a moment).

In almost all cases, you will want to add narration and music to the sound that is recorded on the original videotape. You are going to be cutting the original recording up, discarding some segments, and using others. As a result, you will want music and narration to carry you from clip to clip of recorded sound. Movie Maker lets you increase and decrease the volume of the recorded sound. To do this, you will need a Windows XP–compatible sound card, a microphone, and a CD player or tape deck with the music you want. You can then directly record a sound track in Movie Maker, or you can copy the music to a file using Windows Media Player and then import that file into Movie Maker.

NOTE

There can be some copyright issues using music from professionally recorded CDs and tapes. If you are making a movie solely for your own use and you are not going to put it on the Internet, sell it, or otherwise distribute it, then there are no issues. If you are going to use your movie in any of the prohibited ways and it has someone else's copyrighted material (either audio or video) in it, you need to get permission from the copyright holder.

Capture a Video Image

As you have read, you can capture a video image either by directly recording it using Windows Movie Maker or by importing files that you recorded with other programs. In many, maybe even most cases, you will use a combination of recording and importing to create a movie. Look at both methods next.

Record in Movie Maker

Recording video directly from your camcorder through Movie Maker to your hard disk is simple and can often give you the best results. You can start the process in one of two ways: plug your camera into a FireWire port where Windows XP will detect it or start Windows Movie Maker and direct it to record.

Plug into FireWire   When you plug in to an OHCI-compliant FireWire port, Windows XP will detect it, install the necessary software, and ask you if you want to start Windows Movie Maker, like this:

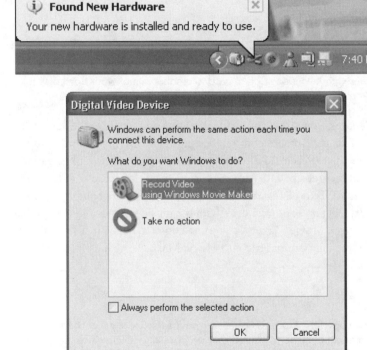

Accept the default Record Video and click OK. Movie Maker will start and open the Record dialog box.

Start Movie Maker   If plugging in your camera didn't start Movie Maker or you are recording from a video capture card, then you need to manually start it by opening the Start menu and choosing All Programs | Accessories | Windows Movie Maker. When Movie Maker completes loading, click Record in the toolbar. The Record dialog box will open.

Prepare for the Recording   In the Record dialog box, there are several settings you want to consider before starting to record. In the upper left, you should see the device from which you are recording. If it isn't correct, you can change it. Beneath that, you can change the time limit you want to allow for recording. The reason for this is that if you have a limited amount of disk space (see the bottom left of the dialog box), you can prevent the recording from using it all up.

Next you can decide if you want to create clips or just one solid block of video. The default is to create clips, which Movie Maker does by looking at where the original taping was discontinued and breaking at that point. This is an imperfect process, and there may be breaks where you don't intend them. The point of clips is to give you more manageable pieces to edit and allow you to easily delete segments you don't want by simply not using clips that don't hold anything of interest. I would recommend that you use clips unless you know that you want to use the entire segment that you are recording.

If you have a limited computer, toward the Microsoft minimum, then you may want to turn off the preview of what you are capturing. If you do that, you will want to keep close track of the time, using notes you make ahead of time on the elapsed time of specific segments you want to record.

Selecting the quality of the recording is largely dependent on what you want to do with it and the amount of disk space you have. If you want to use it on the Internet or send it to someone using e-mail, you will want to select Low or Medium quality. If you want it for viewing directly from a computer and you have plenty of disk space, then you may want to use High quality.

Record   With the Record dialog box open, the process is to play the tape and record what you want of it. You can start recording immediately and record the entire tape, or you can just record portions of the tape. What I like to do is to play the tape through looking for what I want to use. If there are just certain large segments that I want, I'll just record those segments. If I want clips sprinkled throughout the tape, I'll record the entire tape. Remember that what you are doing here is getting the tape onto the hard disk; the real cutting and editing are done later.

If you using a DV device coming in through a FireWire port, then you use the DV controls at the bottom of the Record dialog box to start, stop, advance, and rewind the tape in the camera. Otherwise, you must control the camera or VCR and tape using the controls on the camera or VCR.

If you want to record the entire tape, click Record and then start the camera or VCR. If you want to record just segments of the tape, start the camera or VCR and when you reach the first segment, click Record. In the latter case, you may want to stop and back up the tape just a bit, start recording, and then restart the tape.

While the recording is in process, you can see the elapsed time and, if you didn't turn it off, watch what you are recording in the preview window, as shown in Figure 7-6. When you are done recording, click Stop. The Record dialog box closes, and you are returned to the Movie Maker window, which will show your newly recorded video and begin the creation of clips out of your video.

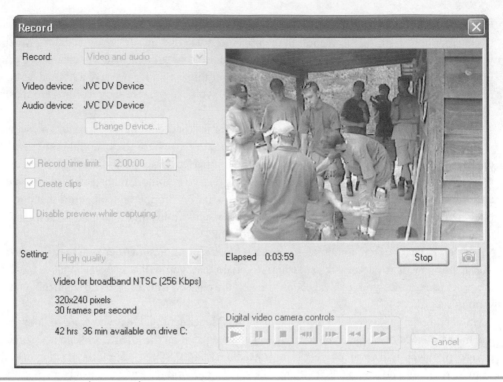

Figure 7-6 Recording a video

Import Files

Windows Movie Maker can import a number of file formats including video, audio, and still pictures, as shown in Table 7-2. These files can be used alone or combined with recorded clips. The following steps will show you how this is done:

1. If it isn't already open, start Windows Movie Maker by opening the Start menu and choosing All Programs | Accessories | Windows Movie Maker.

2. In Movie Maker, open the File and choose Import. The import dialog box will open.

3. Select the file you want to import, make sure Create Clips For Video Files is checked, and click Open. If you are importing a video file, it will be divided into clips. If you are importing either still images or audio, it will simply go into Movie Maker.

   In all cases, the material you imported will appear in the center area of Movie Maker for use in editing and assembling a movie.

Type of File	File Formats
Audio	AFC, AIF, AIFF, AU, MP3, SND, WAV, WMA
Still images	BMP, DIB, GIF, JFIF, JPE, JPEG, JPG
Video	ASF, AVI, M1V, MP2, MPA, MPE, MPEG, MPG, WMV

Table 7-2 File Formats That Can Be Imported into Movie Maker

CRITICAL SKILL
7.5 Create a Movie

The final process is that of actually creating a movie out of the captured and imported material. This is the process of selecting and editing the available material and then assembling it into the final product. The window you have for doing this has three main sections, shown in Figure 7-7:

● **Collections** on the left of the window, which normally has two panes: a folders pane on the left and a clips pane on the right. If you want more room for the clips pane, you can turn off the folders pane by clicking Close in the upper right of the pane.

● **Monitor** on the right of the window, which displays or plays the current clip or the entire movie and displays still images.

● **Workspace** on bottom of the window, which has two views:

  ● **Storyboard view** (shown in Figure 7-7) is the default and allows you to easily sequence your clips and rearrange them by dragging.

  ● **Timeline view** gives you a precise time measurement of your clips and allows you to trim them, adjust the transitions between clips, and add music and narration.

NOTE

To clarify the Movie Maker terminology, what you record is called a *collection* of clips. Think of a collection as a folder. A *clip* is a small segment of video, generally one episode of turning the camera on and then off. A clip is made up of a series of frames, where each *frame* is a still image that when viewed in rapid succession creates the illusion of motion. As you build a movie, during the in-process stages, it is called and saved as a *project*. Only when you are done and satisfied with the finished project do you save it as a *movie*.

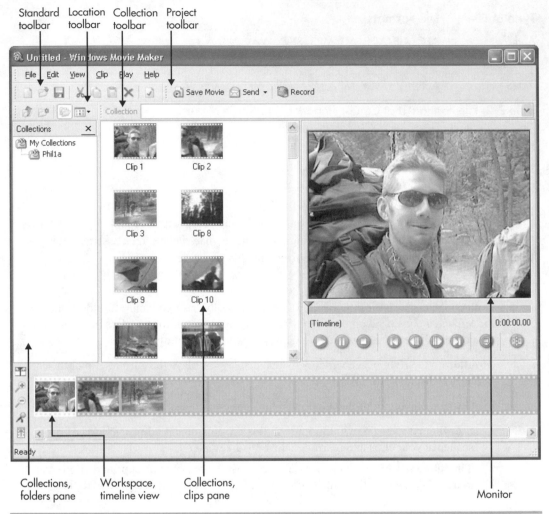

Figure 7-7 The Movie Maker window

In the Movie Maker window, there are many tools to help you convert the video clips, sound, and still images into a movie. In addition to a complete set of menus, there are four toolbars that you can display:

- The **Standard toolbar** with new, open, save project and cut, copy, paste, delete, and clip properties
- The **Project toolbar** with save movie, send, and record

- The **Collections toolbar** with up-one-level, new collection, toggle collections, and view
- The **Location toolbar**, which allows you to choose the collection

In the workspace, especially in timeline view there are also a number of tools that will be discussed under "Edit Clips." Additionally, Movie Maker provides a full set of shortcut keys as described in Table 7-3.

Function	Shortcut Keys
Clear trim points	CTRL-SHIFT-DELETE
Combine clips	CTRL-SHIFT-C
Copy	CTRL-C
Create new project	CTRL-N
Cut	CTRL-X
Delete	DELETE
First clip	HOME
Full screen	ALT-ENTER
Help topics	F1
Import	CTRL-I
Last clip	END
Next clip	CTRL-ALT-RIGHT ARROW
Next frame	ALT-RIGHT ARROW
Next pane	F6 or TAB
Open project	CTRL-O
Paste	CTRL-V
Play/Pause	SPACEBAR
Previous clip	CTRL-ALT-LEFT ARROW
Previous frame	ALT-LEFT ARROW
Previous pane	SHIFT-F6 or SHIFT-TAB
Record	CTRL-R
Rename	F2
Return from full screen	ESC

Table 7-3 Movie Maker Shortcut Keys

Function	Shortcut Keys
Save movie	CTRL-M
Save project	CTRL-S
Save project as	F12
Select all	CTRL-A
Set end trim point	CTRL-SHIFT-RIGHT ARROW
Set start trim point	CTRL-SHIFT-LEFT ARROW
Split clip	CTRL-SHIFT-S
Stop playback	PERIOD
Zoom in	PAGE DOWN
Zoom out	PAGE UP

Table 7-3 Movie Maker Shortcut Keys *(continued)*

Select Clips

There are, of course, many ways to produce a video using the Movie Maker tools. I start out by playing each clip and deciding if the clip holds anything I want to use. If so, I select it and drag it to the workspace at the bottom of the window. As I do that, I make a note about what I ultimately want to do with the clip: trim the beginning, trim the end, split the clip to trim the middle, or combine short clips. I use this as a time to organize. While working through the clips, I determine if the order of the clips should be changed, whether later clips should go before earlier clips and vice versa. This is a very laborious phase, but it is time will spent because it provides the foundation of your project, determining what it is you have to work with in the editing phase. Here are the steps to select and organize your clips:

1. Double-click the first clip you want to want to look at. As it plays, decide if you want to use the clip, if it needs to be trimmed at the beginning, the end, or in the middle and make a note of it.

2. If you want to use the clip, drag it to the workspace, dropping it where you want it in the string of existing clips, either at the end of the existing clips, or somewhere among them.

3. When you have a series of clips in the workspace, periodically right-click the workspace and choose Play Entire Storyboard/Timeline to see how the selection and organization is coming along.

4. If desired, rearrange the clips by dragging them in either direction, or by deleting a clip you no longer want in the project/movie.

NOTE

Deleting a clip in the workspace does not delete in the collection; you can add it back at a later time if desired.

Edit Clips

Editing consists of combining, splitting, and trimming the clips to just what you want and then adjusting the transitions between clips so that they produce the effects you want.

While selecting and organizing clips, the storyboard view of the workspace is the probably the best to use. It is the easiest to see the progression of clips and to drag the clips around the storyboard. For editing clips, the timeline view is probably the best. In timeline view, which is shown in Figure 7-8, clips are shown in proportion to the amount of time they take, and there are a number of tools to work with the editing of a project.

The zoom in and zoom out in the timeline view of the workspace are time-oriented, not visual, zooming. In other words, when you zoom in each timeline division uses a smaller increment of time and each clip takes more space. This is useful for trimming a clip, as you'll see in a moment.

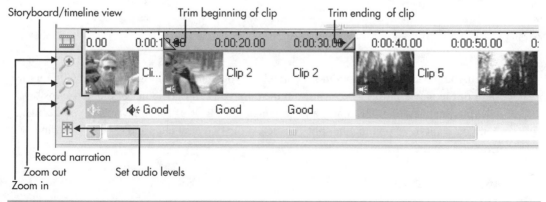

Figure 7-8 Tools available in timeline view

Combine and Split Clips

Movie Maker's automatic division of a recorded tape into clips is on a "best guess" basis, looking at transitions in the recorded tape and breaking a clip at those points. Some work well and provide a good segmentation, while others are not right, either too short or too long, including material in the middle that you want to delete. To handle this, Movie Maker gives you the capability both to combine two or more clips and to split a clip. See how with these steps:

1. Pick a short clip that is obviously part of an adjacent clip and that you will always want to move and handle with the adjacent clip. Click that clip.

2. Hold down SHIFT and click the adjacent clip to which the first clip will be combined. If you want to combine additional adjacent clips, continue to hold SHIFT and click them.

3. When all the clips have been selected, right-click them and choose Combine from the context menu. The selected clips will become one clip. Press SPACEBAR to play the combined clip. If for some reason you made a mistake in combining clips, you can split them again with the next steps.

4. Select timeline view and click a clip that you want to split. Press SPACEBAR to start playing the clip. When it approximately reaches the point where you want to split it, press SPACEBAR again to pause the play. You can then use the play controls under the monitor, shown next and described in Table 7-4, to go forward or backward by varying amounts.

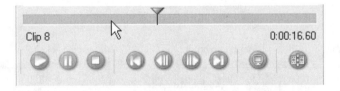

5. When you have found the spot in the clip where you want to split it, click Split Clip on the right of the play controls. Once you split the clip, you can play either of the new clips by clicking the one you want to play and pressing SPACEBAR. If for some reason you decide that you want to recombine the split clip, select the two new clips and choose Combine from the context menu.

TIP

The principle reason to split a clip is to delete or trim frames in the middle of the clip.

Icon	Name	Function
	Pointer	Indicates the current point within a frame, can be dragged to any point.
	Seek Bar	Indicates the span of time in a clip, can be clicked to move the pointer and view to that point.
	Play	Begin playing the clip.
	Pause	Pause playing the clip, leave the pointer where it is in the clip.
	Stop	Stop playing the clip, return the pointer to the beginning of the first clip.
	Back	Return to the previous clip if play is stopped or to the beginning of the current clip otherwise.
	Previous Frame	Return to the previous frame.
	Next Frame	Go to the next frame.
	Forward	Go to the next clip in all cases.
	Full Screen	Display the monitor full screen.
	Split Clip	Split the clip at the current point indicated by the pointer.

Table 7-4 Clip Play Controls

Trim Clips

The reason that Movie Maker breaks a video into clips is to make it easier to locate and remove unwanted segments. You can do this in two ways, by deleting or not using clips, and by *trimming*, deleting frames, at the beginning or end of a clip. There is no way to delete individual frames in the middle of a clip, so you need to split a clip where you need to delete frames in the middle. Here's how to trim frames at the beginning and end of a clip:

TIP

Using the shortcut keys, identified in Table 7-4, in this process might help with the fine selection of frames for trimming.

1. Select timeline view, if it isn't already selected, and click the clip you want to trim. It will appear with *trimming handles* or small triangles in the upper corners of the beginning and end of the clip, like this:

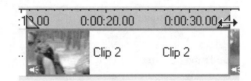

2. Click Zoom In to increase the level of detail displayed and give you greater accuracy in trimming.

3. To trim the beginning of the clip, drag the left trimming handle or triangle to the right the desired amount. When you think you have an initial trim, play the clip and see how you like the results. If you don't like the results, you can adjust the trim in either direction, even recovering the part you trimmed away, by dragging the trim handles in the direction desired.

4. To trim the end of the clip, drag the right trimming handle to the left as you did with the right trimming handle in the preceding step.

NOTE

So long as you are working in the project, even after saving, closing, and reopening it, you can adjust the trim backward or forward; recovering the part you trimmed away.

Adjust Transitions

When you drag a clip to the workspace, it simply abuts the preceding clip. The last frame of the preceding clip shows for a short period of time (1/30th or 1/15th of a second, depending on the resolution with which it was recorded by Movie Maker), and then the first frame of the new clip is displayed. Movie Maker allows you to partially overlap one clip with another and in the process cause a fade out, fade in transition between the two clips. You do this by simply dragging the rightmost clip of a pair to the left over the other clip. You can do this for as much of the clip as you want. I suggest, though, that it be for less than a second, probably no more than half a second, although it is totally up to you.

Assemble the Final Product

Once you have the video clips organized and edited the way you want them, you can add sound, narration or music, titles, and any still pictures that are desired. When you are finished and happy with you project, you can it as a movie file.

Add Sound

There are two ways to add sound to a project, inserting an audio clip and recording narration. The audio clip is an audio file that has been imported into Movie Maker. It can be of any length, from any source, and in any of the formats identified earlier in the module. Once you have imported it into Movie Maker, it will be in the parent collections folder and can be dragged to the workspace in timeline view (if you try to add an audio clip in storyboard view, you'll get a message that the view needs to change, and if you click OK, it will be).

To record narrative, make sure your microphone is connected to your computer and working properly. Then click Record Narration on the left of the timeline view of the workspace. The Record Narration Track dialog box will open, as you can see here.

Talk into your microphone and adjust your Record Level so the bar fills about half of the column. When you are ready, click Record, record the narration you want to add, and when you are finished, click Stop. Enter the filename of the audio file that is created from the recorded narration. The recorded sound clip will appear on timeline.

Once a sound clip is in the workspace, it can be selected and trimmed, dragged anywhere in the timeline, and overlapped in the same way a video clip can be.

If you add a sound clip, either an imported file or a narrated one, you have two sound tracks, one that was on the original recorded tape and one that you have added. By default, the volume level of both tracks is the same unless you click Mute Video Soundtrack in the Record Narration Track dialog box. You can adjust the relative level between the two sound tracks by clicking Set Audio Levels at the bottom left of the workspace in timeline view. The Audio Levels dialog box will open, as you can see next. Dragging the slider one way or the other sets the relative level between the two racks for the entire project.

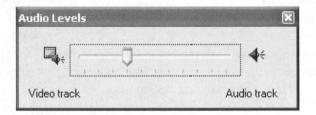

Add Titles and Still Images

Titles and still images are discussed together because Movie Maker does not have its own titling capability; the way that you make titles is to create them in some other product, such as Paint, CorelDraw, Adobe Illustrator, or Microsoft PowerPoint. Then save the title page in one of the still image formats that can be imported into Movie Maker. Here are the steps to make a title page, import it into Movie Maker, and drag it to a project. I'll use Paint, but you can use any drawing or paint program. The last two steps of importing the image and dragging it to the project are the same for any still image:

1. Open Paint, create the title that you want, and save it in a format that can be imported into Movie Maker (BMP, DIB, GIF, JFIF, JPE, JPEG, JPG—JPEG/JPG is my choice).

2. In Movie Maker, open the File menu and choose Import, locate and select the title file to be imported, and click Open. The title image will be imported.

3. Drag the image to the workspace at the point in the project where you want it. By default, the title slide is played for five seconds, but you can drag the right trim handle to the right to lengthen it to be as long as you wish. This will overlap the clip to the right, but if you don't want that, you can drag that clip to the right and all the clips to the right will move.

Titles and still images can be trimmed and overlapped just like video clips.

Save the Finished Project

The final step in making a movie is to save it as a Windows video file that can be played by Windows Media Player. This is done very simply. When you are happy with your project, click Save Movie in the project toolbar. The Save Movie dialog box will open. Select the quality you want, enter a name and any other information you want, and then click OK. Enter the filename and click Save. The saving process will take a bit of time, depending on the speed of your computer and the amount of memory. When it is complete, you will be asked if you want to play the movie. If so, click OK. You can also double-click the resulting file, which is stored by default in the My Videos folder, and Media Player will play the movie. Be sure to save the project one last time by following the prompts when you close Movie Maker.

NOTE

Opening a project opens the media in Movie Maker, where they can be edited; whereas opening a movie sets it up for playback in Media Player.

Ask the Expert

Q: How does Windows Movie Maker compare with other video editing products?

A: Movie Maker is definitely a "first-time" product. If you do more than very occasional video editing, you will want to purchase another product (Adobe Premier is just one of several full-featured products that are available). The primary weaknesses of Movie Maker are

- Lack of an ability to save back to a digital tape
- Ability to save only to WMV format
- Clip making and trimming being not very precise
- Lack of multiple add-on audio tracks
- Lack of an ability to continuously vary the volume level of each track

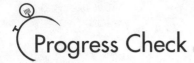

Progress Check

1. If you have a DV camcorder, what should you have on your computer in order to transfer your digital video to it?

2. What are the three main sections of the Movie Maker window and what are they used for?

3. What are the components of video editing in Windows Movie Maker?

4. What does the final assembly phase of video production consist of?

CRITICAL SKILL
7.6 Use CD Writer

Earlier in this module, you saw how Windows Media Player could copy audio tracks to a recordable CD. A new feature in Windows XP allows you to copy both data and smaller video files to a writable or rewritable CD. Many computers now come with a CD-ROM drive that can "burn" or record information on a CD. There are two types of these drives: CD-Rs, the writable drives on which you can write once, and CD-RWs, the rewritable drives on which you can erase older information and write over the same area. Blank CD-R disks are very inexpensive (20 to 50 cents), can store up to 700MB, and, once recorded, can be played in most CD-ROM and CD audio drives. CD-RW disks cost $1 to $1.50, store up to 650MB, and in many cases can be read only on other CD-RW drives by the same manufacturer. A CD-RW drive, though, can write to either CD-R or CD-RW disks.

---

1. An OHCI-compliant IEEE 1394 FireWire card

2. Collections, which holds the clips; the monitor, which displays the or plays the clips; and the workspace, which shows the project as a work in progress

3. Combining, splitting, and trimming the clips and adjusting the transitions between clips

4. Adding sound (narration or music), titles, and still pictures, and then saving the movie

Given that you have a CD-R or CD-RW drive and blank media, the first step is to determine what you want to store on them. With that in mind, here are the steps to carry it out:

1. Place a blank recordable disk in the drive. A dialog box will open asking if you want to open the writable CD folder using Windows Explorer, do nothing, or start some other CD writing software (if you have any installed).

2. Choose to open the writable CD folder using Windows Explorer and click OK. An Explorer window will open for the CD-ROM drive. The easiest way to get a file to this window is to open another Windows Explorer window, locate the files, and drag them to the CD-ROM drive window. Do that next.

3. Create any folders you want on the CD in the CD-ROM drive window and drag the files from the second Explorer window to those folders. When all the files and folders are shown the way you want them, such as in Figure 7-9, click Write These Files To CD in the task pane. The CD Writing Wizard will open.

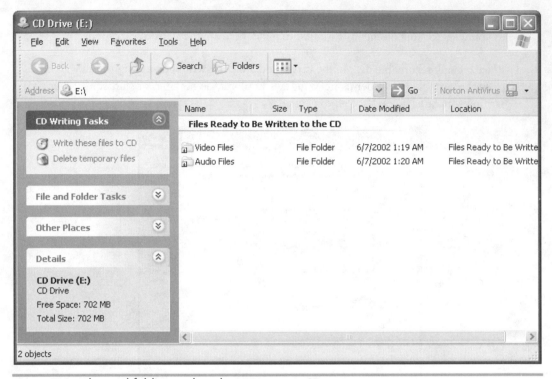

Figure 7-9 Files and folder ready to be written to a CD

 4. Enter a CD Name and click Next. The data will be prepared, and then it will be written to the CD. When it is finished, you will be told it was successful, and the drive will eject the disk. Click Finish to complete the process.

 5. Test the new CD by taking to another computer and make sure it can be read.

Project 7 Set Up and Use Media Player and Movie Maker

This exercise will quickly go through the steps to fully utilize both Windows Media Player and Windows Movie Maker, including

● Playing a music CD

● Listening to Internet radio

- Copying music tracks to a hard disk

- Building a music playlist and writing it to a CD

- Recording a movie

- Selecting and editing video clips

- Assembling and completing a movie

Step by Step

1. Insert a music CD into its drive and click OK to have Windows Media Player play the disk. Media Player will open and begin playing the disk.

2. Click Radio Tuner in Media Player, select a featured station or one of your preselected or recently played stations, or search and select a station to listen to Internet radio.

3. Click Copy From CD in Media Player and insert a music CD with tracks you want to copy to your hard disk. Select the tracks to be copied, click Copy Music, and click OK on the copy protection warning. The music will be copied.

4. Click Media Library in Media Player, click New Playlist in the toolbar, enter the name for the playlist, and click OK. From your Media Library, select and drag the pieces or tracks you want in the new playlist.

5. Click Copy To CD Or Device in Media Player. Select the pieces to copy to a CD, insert a blank CD in the recording drive, and click Copy Music. The music will be copied to analog and written on the disk.

6. To start recording a movie from a digital camcorder, plug it in to an OHCI-compliant IEEE 1394 FireWire connection, click OK to record video using Windows Movie Maker, click Record, and start the playback of the camera. When you have recorded what you want, click Stop. Clips will be created from the recorded video.

7. Select the clips you want in the final movie and drag them to the workspace at the bottom of the Movie Maker window. Select timeline view and trim the beginning and/or end of a clip using the trim handles. If you want to trim the interior of a clip, select and then play the clip to the point where you want it split, click Split Clip, and then trim the ends of the new clips.

8. Click Record Narration on the left of the timeline view of the workspace, adjust the record level, and click Record. When you are finished, click Stop and enter the filename of the audio file.

9. Prepare or obtain still and titles images in any other product and then in Movie Maker open the File menu and choose Import, locate and select the files to be imported, and click Open. The images will be imported.

10. Drag the images to the workspace at the point in the project where you want them. Trim or lengthen the images as desired. When you are finished, click Save Movie in the project toolbar. Select the quality you want, enter a name and any other information you want, and then click OK. Enter the filename and click Save.

Project Summary

Windows Media Player and Windows Movie Maker are both fun and entertaining, and they are also at the heart of the current digital media revolution of using digital music players and digital camcorders. Media Player may do all that you want in its area and be the only product you use for that purpose. Movie Maker will probably be only your introduction to movie making, but it is a good place to start to see what you can do.

✓ Module 7 Mastery Check

1. What are three functions you can perform with Windows Media Player?

2. What are three primary control areas of Windows Media Player and what are they used for?

3. What do you need in order to listen to the radio on your computer?

4. Your friend just noticed that you can get music off a CD and burn it onto a new CD, and asked you to make him a copy. What should you do?

5. What are the formats in which a final movie can be saved?

6. What are two ways you can get video into Windows Movie Maker?

7. What are the tools Windows Movie Maker provides for converting clips into finished movies?

8. What do the terms collections, clips, and frames mean, and how do they relate?

9. What are three types of objects that you can bring into a movie file, and what are some of the acceptable formats?

10. What are three differences between CD-R and CD-RW?

Part III

Advanced Uses of Windows XP

Module 8

Setting Up and Using a Network

Networking, the ability to connect computers and allow them to share information and resources, is at the forefront of today's push for improved productivity and is even becoming important in the home as more and more families have more than one computer. The first part of this module provides a comprehensive foundation on networking by describing the schemes, hardware, and protocols or standards that are used to make it function. The balance of the module describes how networking is set up and managed in Windows XP.

CRITICAL SKILL
8.1 Understand Networking

Windows XP is a *network operating system*. This allows the interconnection of multiple computers for the purpose of

- Exchanging information, such as sending a file from one computer to another
- Communicating by, for example, sending e-mail among network users
- Sharing information by having common files accessed by network users
- Sharing resources on the network, such as printers and Internet connections

Networking is important to almost every organization (including families) of two or more people who communicate and share information. Exchanging information allows multiple people to easily work from and utilize the same data and prevent errors caused by not having the latest information. Communicating facilitates the fast and easy coordination among people of current information, such as meeting arrangements. Sharing information allows multiple people to update and maintain a large database. Sharing resources allows an organization to purchase better (more capable and expensive) devices (for example, a color laser printer) than if they purchased one for each user. Networking is a primary ingredient in the computer's contribution to improved productivity and is critical to virtually every business.

Networking is a system that includes the physical connection between computers that facilitates the transfer of information, as well as the scheme for controlling that transfer. The scheme makes sure that the information is transferred correctly (to the correct recipient) and accurately (the data is exactly the same on both the receiving and sending ends) while many other transfers are occurring simultaneously. To accomplish these objectives while other information is being transferred—generally, a lot of other information—there must be a standard way to correctly identify and address each transfer and to stop one transfer while another is taking place. This is the function of the networking hardware and software in your computer and the protocols or standards they use. This is further complicated by the type of networking and the technology it employs.

Network Types

The network type is determined by whether the network is confined to a single location or is spread over a wide geographic area.

A network that is spread over a wide geographic area is called a *wide area network (WAN)*. WANs can use telephone lines, both shared and private, satellite links, microwave links, and dedicated fiber-optic or copper cabling to connect offices across a street or on the other side of the world. WANs with reasonable amounts of bandwidth (1 Mbps and above) are expensive, on the order of one to several thousand dollars per month, and demand sophisticated technology. They are therefore a major undertaking for a larger organization. A simpler and less expensive, although still not cheap, use of WANs is to interconnect smaller networks within a building or within a campus of closely located buildings. WANs are generally outside the scope of this book but will be touched on in several other places in this module.

NOTE

Many companies are using the Internet to do what WANs once handled, such as e-mail and private information exchange using virtual private networking, or VPN, which is discussed in Module 11, so the growth in WANs is very modest.

A network that is confined to a single location is called a *local area network (LAN)*. LANs use dedicated cabling or wireless channels and generally do not go outside of a single building; they may in fact be limited to a single floor of a building or a department within a company. LANs are much more common than WANs and are the type of network primarily discussed in this module. LANs have two subcategories, peer-to-peer LANs and client/server LANs, which are distinguished by how they distribute networking tasks.

Peer-to-Peer LANs

All computers in a peer-to-peer LAN are both servers and clients and therefore share in both provision and use of resources. Any computer in the network may store information and provide resources, such as a printer, for the use of any other computer in the network. Peer-to-peer networking is an easy first step to networking, accomplished simply by joining existing computers together, as shown in Figure 8-1. It does not require the purchase of new computers or significant changes to the way an organization is using computers, yet resources can be shared (as is the printer in Figure 8-1), files and communications can be transferred, and common information can be accessed by all.

Peer-to-peer LANs tend to be used in smaller organizations that neither need to share a large central resource, such as a database, nor need a high degree of security or central control.

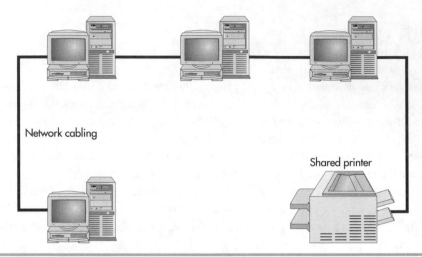

Figure 8-1   A peer-to-peer LAN with a bus topology

Each computer in a peer-to-peer LAN is autonomous and often is joined together with other computers simply to transfer files and share expensive equipment. As you'll read later in the module, under "Understand Networking Hardware," putting together a peer-to-peer LAN with existing computers is fairly easy and can be inexpensive (less than $30 per station).

Client/Server LANs

The computers in a client/server LAN perform one of two functions: they are either servers or clients. *Servers* manage the network, centrally store information that is to be shared on the network, and provide the shared resources to the network. *Clients,* or workstations, are the users of the network and are normal desktop or laptop computers. To create a network, the clients and server(s) are connected together, possibly with stand-alone network resources such as printers, as shown in Figure 8-2.

NOTE

The difference in network cabling between Figures 8-1 and 8-2 is not a function of one network being peer-to-peer and the other client/server, but rather is a function of the cabling topology used. See "Choose Network Topologies" later in this module.

The management functions provided by the server include network security and managing the permissions needed to implement security, communications among network users, and management of shared files on the network. Servers generally are more capable than clients in

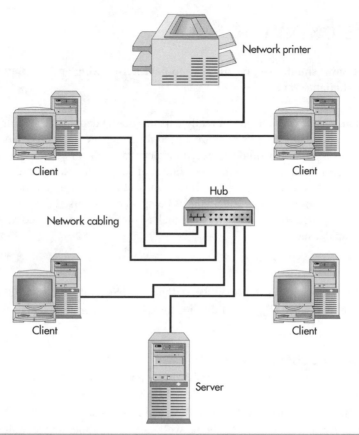

Figure 8-2 A client/server LAN with a star topology

terms of having more memory, faster (and possibly more) processors, larger (and maybe more) disks, and more special peripherals, such as large, high-speed tape drives. Servers generally are dedicated to their function and are infrequently used for normal computer tasks, such as word processing.

Clients generally are less capable than servers and, infrequently, may not even have a disk. Clients usually are normal desktop and laptop computers that perform the normal functions for those types of machines, in addition to being part of a network. Clients can also be "miniservers," by sharing out some or all of their disk drives or other resources. Therefore, the principle difference between peer-to-peer networks and client/server networks is the addition of a dedicated server.

Windows XP and Windows.NET or Windows 2000 servers work together to form a client/server network operating environment, with the Windows server performing their

Ask the Expert

Q: At what point should we give up peer-to-peer networking and go play in the big leagues of client/server?

A: There is no one answer for that; it really depends on the demands of the organization. The reasons for using client/server are a need for a large centralized database and its attendant processing, as would be needed for a central accounting, ordering, or personnel system, and/or the need for centralized control of shared files and permissions. One indication that you are nearing the time to make the switch is that one or more computers in your peer-to-peer network is being so heavily used for group functions that it can no longer be used by an individual as a workstation. This computer should be designated a server.

function and Windows XP Professional being the client. Several Windows XP Professional workstations or Windows XP Home Edition computers can operate in a peer-to-peer network.

LAN Technologies

LAN technologies are standards that span hardware and software, to handle a large part of the dedicated networking task. Windows XP LANs principally (over 90 percent) use the Ethernet technology, although both Token Ring and Fiber Distributed Data Interface (FDDI) technologies are still available. In this book, we'll talk about Ethernet technology and two recent arrivals, wireless networking and home networking technologies.

Ethernet Networking Technology

Ethernet was developed in the early 1970s and was made into a standard first in the United States and then worldwide. There are now three Ethernet standards: the original Ethernet standard operating at 10 Mbps; Fast Ethernet, operating at 100 Mbps; and Gigabit Ethernet, operating at 1,000 Mbps. These will be referred to as "Ethernet," "Fast Ethernet," and "Gigabit Ethernet," respectively throughout the book.

Ethernet is relatively inexpensive, works well interconnecting many different computer systems, and is easy to expand to very large networks. It therefore has become the dominant LAN technology by a wide margin, completely eclipsing some other early technologies. As a result, Ethernet-related equipment and Ethernet support in software, including Windows XP, has become pervasive. This fact has brought many vendors into the market to supply equipment, causing the pricing to become most reasonable. As a result, Ethernet (and now Fast Ethernet) has become the technology of choice for almost all new networks.

Ethernet Hardware   Ethernet LAN technology defines seven alternative hardware standards that can be used with Ethernet. Each hardware standard uses a specific type of cable and cable layout, or *topology,* and provides a rated speed on the network in Mbps, a maximum segment length, and a maximum number of computers on a single segment. The hardware standards are as follows:

NOTE

In the names for the Ethernet hardware standards, such as 10Base5, the "10" is the speed in Mbps, the "Base" is for baseband, a type of transmission, and the "5" is the maximum segment length in hundreds of meters. In more recent standards, such as 10BaseT, the "T" stands for the type of cabling (twisted-pair in this case).

- **10Base5 (also called Thicknet)**   The original hardware specification. It uses a thick coaxial cable in a bus topology (see earlier Figure 8-1) with a fairly complex connection at each computer to produce a 10 Mbps speed over a 500-meter (1,640-foot) maximum segment with up to 100 computers per segment and three segments. 10Base5 is expensive and cumbersome to use, and it is very seldom used today.

- **10Base2 (also called Thinnet or Cheapernet)**   Uses RG-58 A/U thin coaxial cable in a bus topology (see earlier Figure 8-1) with a simple BNC barrel type of connector to produce a 10 Mbps speed over a 185-meter (606-foot) maximum segment with up to 30 computers per segment and three segments. Until a few years ago, 10Base2 was the least expensive form of Ethernet networking for small (30 or less stations) organizations.

- **10BaseT (also called Twisted-Pair)**   Uses unshielded twisted-pair (UTP) telephone-like cable in a star topology (see earlier Figure 8-2) with a very simple RJ-45 telephone-like connector to produce a 10 Mbps speed over a 100-meter (328-foot) segment with one computer per segment and 1,024 segments. Several years ago, 10BaseT came down in price to a level below that of 10Base2 and, with its exceptional expandability, eclipsed that earlier product. Now it is being eclipsed by 100BaseT due to the latter's speed and equal cost.

- **10BaseF**   Uses fiber-optic cable in a star topology running at 10 Mbps to connect two networks up to 4,000 meters (13,120 feet, or about 2.5 miles) apart. This has been all but replaced by 100BaseF.

- **100BaseT (also called Fast Ethernet)**   Has the same specifications as 10BaseT except that the cabling requirements are a little more demanding (requires Category 5 cable in place of Category 3) and it goes ten times as fast. 100BaseT is virtually equal in cost to 10BaseT, and with its significant added speed, it has become the Ethernet hardware standard of choice. With the appropriate connecting hardware (see "Understand Networking Hardware," later in the module), you can mix 10BaseT and 100BaseT hardware in the same network to slowly upgrade a 10BaseT network. There are two subspecifications to

100BaseT: 100BaseTX, the most common, which runs over Category 5 UTP using two twisted pairs, and 100BaseT4, which runs over Category 3 UTP using four twisted pairs.

- **100BaseF**   Uses fiber-optic cable running at 100 Mbps to connect two networks up to 412 meters (1,351 feet) apart; if full duplex (separate fibers for sending and receiving) is used, that distance can be extended to as much as 2 kilometers (over 6,500 feet or a mile and a quarter). Like 10BaseF, 100BaseF is primarily used to join two networks.

- **1000BaseT and F (also called Gigabit Ethernet)**   Uses standard Category 5 or fiber-optic cable to run at 1,000 Mbps. There are several distance standards, ranging from 25 meters (82 feet) to 100 meters (328 feet) for copper UTP, and 550 meters (1,800 feet) for fiber. In mid-2002, Gigabit Ethernet equipment is on the market at about three times the price of high-quality, name-brand 100BaseT equipment for ten times the speed. If this follows the pattern of 100BaseT, these prices will drop by up to 50 percent in the next few years.

The section "Understand Networking Hardware," later in this module, goes into more detail about the Ethernet hardware standards and the options that are available to connect Ethernet networks.

Wireless Networking Technologies

Wireless networking technologies cover a broad spectrum of networking capabilities without wires, including

- Broadband wireless topologies used in WANs and metropolitan area networks (MANs)

- Cellular wireless networking

- Microwave communications used in WANs

- Satellite communications systems

- Wireless LANs

Broadband wireless and microwave are used between buildings to connect LANs, are fairly expensive, and are generally used only by larger organizations. Satellite communications are relatively expensive, slow, and still quite a ways outside any mainstream use. Cellular systems are just starting to get interesting. For some time, cellular networking was very slow, 9.6 to 16 Kbps. Recently, this value has been increased to 64 Kbps, and there are technologies, including Qualcomm's HDR (high data rate), just coming into use that will offer data rates of up 2.4 Mbps.

Wireless LANs or WLANs by 2001 became well implemented, widely available, and reasonably priced. They are based on a standard that provides data transfer of up to 11 Mbps, and they use a transmission scheme that is reasonably secure. A WLAN uses a fixed *access point* that is connected to the wired Ethernet network by, for instance, being plugged into a hub, a switch, or a DSL router; and it uses a transceiver (transmitter and receiver) to communicate wirelessly with cards that are added to computers wishing to use the WLAN (see Figure 8-3). These computers operate on the network in exactly the same way as they would with a cable connection. There are some significant benefits to a WLAN over a normal wired LAN:

NOTE

In addition to the WLAN standard, there is a WIFI wireless fidelity standard that makes sure that the hardware from different manufacturers is compatible; thus, you can walk into any office, airport, or other building with a WIFI standard wireless system and be able to connect if you have the appropriate permissions.

- You do not have the expense of cabling and the even higher expense of installing and maintaining cabling.

- It is extremely easy to add and remove users to the network.

- It is very easy for users to move from office to office.

- Users can roam within an area, say, carrying their laptops to a meeting

- Visitors can easily get on the network.

Figure 8-3   A selection of 3com® 11 Mbps Wireless LAN products, including the Access Point 6000, PC Card with XJACK® Antenna, and the AirConnect® PCI Card (Photo courtesy of 3Com Corporation, http://www.3com.com)

Setting Up and Using a Network

8

The downside is of course cost and speed. A good standard 10/100 network interface card (NIC) to connect a computer to a wired network costs less than $20, a cable for one station, again being generous, is $10, and its installation is $15 (average cost when installing a number of stations). Therefore, the cost of connecting a computer by wire to a network is at most $50. An inexpensive access point is about $150 (they go over $400) and, remembering that you are dividing up 11 Mbps of bandwidth, is good for at most 10 people or $15 per station. The connecting cards for each computer are $80 to $150, so the total wireless cost of connecting a computer to a network is $95 and up, about two times the cost of using a wire. The speed difference is not just the difference between the 11 Mbps access point and a 100 Mbps NIC, it's the net rate of dividing the 11 Mbps access point by the number of people trying to use it. Despite these drawbacks, there is a great amount of interest in WLANs and a number of systems are being sold for both offices and homes.

NOTE

Wireless technology is changing rapidly. As this book is being written, new wireless standards are being promulgated that allow transfer rates up to 22 Mbps and 55 Mbps and wideband access points that do not reduce the communication rate to some fraction of 11 Mbps. These are of course more expensive, and I would be a slow adopter until a number of manufacturers have compatible systems at these higher speeds.

Small/Home Office Networking Technologies

Small/home office networking technologies generally refer to one of two type of networking systems that share existing cabling in a home, either telephone cabling or power cabling. In both cases, the objective is to get around installing separate networking cable.

Ask the Expert

Q: How many people can you realistically get on a wireless access point?

A: This depends on how much each user is using the network. With light use, like several times a day checking for e-mail or occasionally transferring smaller files, you can get quite a few users, say 20 to 25. At the other extreme, where the average user is working full time transferring information to a central application across the network, then two or three users might max it out. Remember that the normal wireless access point has a single 11 Mbps connection to the wired network and so all users going through that access point share that 11 Mbps. In a normal wired network connection, each user has full 10 or 100 Mbps.

Home Phone-Line Networking   Networks using telephone lines simply plug into the phone jacks already installed in many homes and transmit over a frequency that does not interfere with voice communications, so they can be used at the same time a phone conversation is going on. An industry group, the Home Phoneline Networking Alliance (HPNA) (http://www.homepna.org), has developed a set of specifications and two versions of a standard. The original systems operated at a slow 1 Mbps, whereas the more recent ones operate at a rate of 10 Mbps and allow up to 25 devices in a network, up to 1,000 feet between any two devices, and not more than 10,000 square feet of total area covered.

Home phone-line networking uses a special NIC that plugs into the computer and uses a cable that plugs into a telephone outlet, similar to an internal modem. Alternatively, you can use a USB adapter that plugs into a computer's USB port on one side and into a telephone outlet on the other. A home phone-line network does not need a hub or switch, just the NICs or USB adapters, cables to connect to a telephone outlet, and software drivers. Once installed, they look and operate like any other type of networking. The home phone-line NICs cost two or more times what standard Ethernet NICs cost, and the USB phone-line adapters cost about twice what the phone-line NICs cost. Several of the normal network equipment manufacturers, including 3Com, D-Link, Intel, and SMC, make home phone-line networking equipment.

Considering the cost of hubs, cabling, and the installation of cabling, a home phone-line network costs the same as or a little more than an Ethernet network and does not require the physical disruption caused by installing the cable. On the other side, the most commonly installed Ethernet today, 100BaseT, is ten times as fast and very readily available and serviced.

The word "home" has been included in the last several paragraphs because most homes have two to four pairs of wires that run throughout a house so that any jack in the house can get on any of the lines. This allows phone-line networking to work anywhere in the house. Most business phone systems are not wired in that way and instead have a separate line or lines run to each office, which has its own phone number(s). These lines are tied together at a local switch, which would block phone-line networking.

Power-Line Networking   Power-line networking uses the existing power lines that are throughout almost all buildings for networking. Although there may be rooms or areas in rooms without phone lines, there are very few without a power outlet. Like phone-line networking, power-line networking has a manufacturer's group called HomePlug Alliance; this group has set a new technology standard called PowerPacket that is just now being implemented. There is also an older technology available called Passport that is very slow, under 500 Kbps, works only in Windows, has security problems, and is susceptible to power fluctuations. Passport, though, was very cheap, in the neighborhood of $25 per computer. The new PowerPacket runs at 14 Mbps, has improved security, can work with other operating systems, and is not as susceptible to power fluctuations.

Setting Up and Using a Network

Ask the Expert

Q: From the comments here, it sounds like phone-line and power-line networking are not really that much of a benefit over either wireless or standard cable networks. Is that a correct assumption?

A: That certainly was the case a year or so ago. There are now products here or almost here that could change that. A lot depends on how important it is to you to avoid cabling. I happen to not mind the cabling running in the three rooms of my house where I have computers. In addition, I happen to think that wireless networking provides a better solution at a reasonably close price because it is a much more widely used product that is on a developmental fast track.

The PowerPacket uses a NIC-like card that plugs into a computer and an ordinary looking power cord to plug into any power socket. The cost of the PowerPacket NICs is not yet known (the first ones are supposed to be shipping as this is written, summer 2002), but they are expected to initially cost around $75; given enough interest, this will come down. If PowerPacket has truly solved the power fluctuation problems (whereas with PassPort if a garbage disposal was turned on, the network was liable to be scrambled), and if the price per station can come down well under $50, then power-line networking will really take off. It will easily surpass phone-line networking because of the ubiquitousness of power outlets. When we get to the point of networking refrigerators, microwaves, and dishwashers, power-line networking will be the way to go.

CRITICAL SKILL
8.2 Understand Networking Hardware

In its simplest form, computer networking needs only a cable to join two computers and two NICs that plug into the computers and onto which the cable connects, as shown in Figure 8-4.

For both the NICs and the network cable, there are several choices in the types and features, and when you go beyond two computers, there are additional components for which there are multiple choices. The first and major decision in making these choices is the LAN technology you are going to use because that, in many cases, will determine your cabling and NIC, or at least put you in a certain category of cabling and NIC. Therefore, begin this look at hardware with a summary, shown in Table 8-1, of what has been described earlier in this module regarding the alternative LAN technologies.

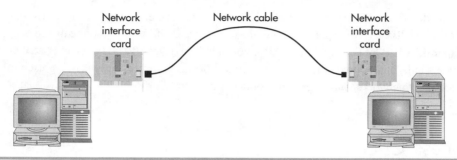

Figure 8-4 Components needed for simple networking

 NOTE

UTP categories are further explained later in this module, under "UTP Categories."

In choosing a LAN technology, Ethernet 10BaseT and 100BaseT are the predominant choices. Probably well over 98 percent choose it, with 100BaseT getting the lion's share of new installations and many upgrades. There probably have been no new installations of 10Base5 for a number of years, and very few legacy installations remain. 10Base2 is also all but gone because there is no longer a cost advantage over 10BaseT.

Ethernet Tech-nology	Max. Speed (Mbps)	Type of Cabling (See Note)	Max. Network Stations	Max. Stations/ Segment	Max. Segment Length	Min. Segment Length	Max. Network Length
10Base5	10	Thick coax	300	100	1,640 ft	8.5 ft	8,200 ft
10Base2	10	Thin coax	90	30	606 ft	2 ft	3,035 ft
10BaseT	10	UTP-Cat 3	1,024	2	328 ft		
10BaseF	10	Fiber-optic		2	2.5 mi		
100BaseT	100	UTP-Cat 5	1,024	2	328 ft		
100BaseF	100	Fiber-optic		2	1,351 ft		
1000BaseT	1,000	UTP-Cat5e		2	328 ft		
1000BaseF	1,000	Fiber-optic		2	1,800 ft		

Table 8-1 LAN Technology Specification Summary

The decision between 10BaseT and 100BaseT has been erased by the steep decline in the prices for 100BaseT components where, in some cases, 100BaseT components are actually cheaper than 10BaseT components. Also, you can always get 10/100 NICs and use them with 10 Mbps hubs and upgrade those at a later time. 100BaseF increasingly is being used to interconnect networks, buildings, and floors within a building.

Progress Check

1. What are the two types of networks, and how do they differ?

2. What are the two types of LANs, and how do they differ?

3. What are the two most common Ethernet hardware standards, and what are their predominant characteristics?

CRITICAL SKILL

8.3 # Select Network Interface Cards

Even though you have decided on Ethernet 100BaseT, the decision on which NIC to buy still has several considerations:

● Which bus will the card use?

● What type of card to use?

● Do you want it to be able to wake up the computer?

● Which brand should you buy?

---

1. The two most common network types are LANs for local area networking within a single building or organizational unit, and WANs for wide area networking outside the bounds of a LAN. The Internet is a WAN.

2. The two types of LANs are peer-to-peer LANs and client/server LANs. In a peer-to-peer LAN, all computers are both clients and servers and share all functions on the network. In a client/server, LAN some computers are servers, which serve as the network controllers and depository of large databases, and others are clients, which utilize the resources of the servers.

3. The two most common Ethernet hardware standards are 10BaseT and 100BaseT. 10BaseT operates at 10 Mbps, uses UTP Category 3 or higher cabling, has a maximum segment length of 100 meters, or 328 feet, and can have up to four levels of hubs. 100BaseT operates at 100 Mbps, uses UTP Category 5 or higher cabling, has a maximum segment length of 100 meters, or 328 feet, and can have up to two levels of hubs.

Which Card Bus

NIC manufacturers provide NICs that plug into either ISA (Industry Standard Architecture) or PCI (Peripheral Component Interface) card slots. (Figure 8-5 shows a 3Com 10/100 Managed Network Interface Card [3C905CX-TX-M] that is used with either 10BaseT or 100BaseT and that plugs into the PCI bus.) You may not have a choice on which bus to use in the computers you are adding to the network, but if you do (most computers built in the last five or six years have both ISA and PCI slots or just PCI slots), you want to choose PCI. ISA slots are either 8 or 16 bits wide (NICs generally use 16 bits), whereas PCI slots are 32 bits wide and thus have a wider data path and are noticeably faster. Another of PCI's major benefits is that you don't have to worry about the IRQ (interrupt request line) because it is uniquely handled in PCI slots. In ISA slots, you have to figure out what IRQs other cards are using, and hopefully have one left over for the NIC. So if it is available, you want to choose PCI-bus NICs.

What Type of Card to Use

Most manufacturers, especially the larger name brands, make several different types of 10/100BaseT NICs in addition to cards for different buses and special features. These

Figure 8-5   3Com 10/100 Managed Network Interface Card (3C905CX-TX-M)
(Photo courtesy of 3Com Corporation, http://www.3com.com)

differences include whether a NIC is full-duplex or half-duplex, whether it is made for a server, and whether it is multiport. All of these features add to the speed and efficiency of the board, but they may also add to the cost, so you need to give them some consideration.

Half-Duplex vs. Full-Duplex

Half-duplex means that when a card is receiving, it can't transmit, and vice versa. *Full-duplex* allows the card to transmit and receive at the same time. Obviously, full-duplex is faster, but it does not double the speed as you might expect; rather, it offers 30–50 percent improvement over half-duplex. Currently, most name-brand 10/100 NICS are full-duplex, but it wouldn't hurt to check this factor when you are researching which ones to buy.

Use Server NICs

Server NICs are developed for use in servers, and they supply several features to support that role. Among these features are higher reliability and greater intelligence. The higher reliability is usually a combination of better parts and higher quality control. The greater intelligence means that there is a processor and even memory on the NIC so that it doesn't have to go out to the computer's CPU and memory to handle its processes. This makes the card faster, allowing it to handle a higher volume of information. These features, of course, cost money, so you need to determine whether they are worthwhile. The higher-reliability cards cost about 30–50 percent more than a normal name-brand NIC. The intelligent NICs cost two to three times the cost of a normal name-brand NIC. Although that sounds like a lot, it translates to less than $100 additional per card, and you do not have to buy very many of them. When you compare this to the cost of upgrading a CPU, it's reasonable. My recommendation is that an intelligent NIC made for a server is worth the price in a server.

Multiport NICs

NICs are available for servers that have two or four ports, the equivalent of two or four NICs in the server. Given that PCI card slots are generally at a premium in most servers, these multiport boards may be attractive. The problem is that a dual-port NIC costs over two times the cost of a name-brand server NIC, and a four-port NIC costs over four times the cost of a name-brand server NIC. If you don't have the PCI slots, then this might be a solution, but another solution is to use an interconnection device in front of the NIC (see "Select Interconnection Devices," later in this module). This is one of those situations in which there is no one right answer. It depends on the network design you are trying to construct.

Wake on LAN and Other Special Features

Several manufacturers, 3Com and Intel among them, have NICs with a "Wake on LAN" feature that will power up a computer to full operating status after it has been turned off. This allows a network administrator or support person to update a computer after hours. Wake on LAN requires a *motherboard* (the main system circuit board in a computer where a NIC plugs in) that implements the PCI bus standard 2.2 or later. Most computers produced in the last two to three years use this standard.

There are at least two other special features that are in some NICs and may prove useful: remote management and remote booting. Remote management allows a network administrator or a server with the appropriate software to monitor the activity and do remote management on a computer across a network. Remote booting allows a server to start a computer without depending on the operating system in the computer. This is important for diagnosing problems in the computer and for the remote installation of Windows and other applications. Remote booting also requires PCI bus standard 2.2 or later.

If these features are of interest to you, look carefully before buying a NIC and make sure the motherboard you are intending to use it with supports the feature(s) you are getting on the NIC. Remote booting in particular may require special support on the motherboard that is *not* included on most motherboards.

Which Brand

If you look at computer product catalogs and web sites, you will see that there are at least three approximate pricing levels of NICs:

- Name brand (3Com, Intel) with the special features previously mentioned: $60 to $100

- Name-brand basic boards (without the special features): $30 to $75

- Generic basic boards (without the special features): $15 to $35

Although some of the price range in each of the three levels is caused by differences in features, much of the differential is caused by differences in what suppliers charge for the same board. You can see that by looking at PriceWatch (http://www.pricewatch.com) and PriceScan (http://www.pricescan.com), which compare the prices of the same item from different suppliers. In any case, make sure you know what you are buying and what the handling and freight charges are.

The pertinent question is whether the name-brand boards are worth the $15 to $30 differential. From my viewpoint, the answer is clearly yes. In the ten-plus years I have been working with PC networking, I have worked with approximately an equal number of generic and name-brand NICs. I have had troubles with both, but I have had to throw away several of the generic boards, whereas I have always been able to get the name-brand boards fixed or replaced. The backing and support of a name brand is comforting (3Com's lifetime warranty in particular), and sometimes they have added features such as diagnostics that may be valuable. Granted, the lower prices of the generic boards are also attractive, but when a network goes down, that price may not look so good. If you buy a generic from a better supplier to get the supplier's support, your price is very close to the name brand. My recommendation is to choose the name-brand board with the thought that it is going to be more easily recognized in software, such as Windows XP, and provide better support should it be needed.

Select Cabling

Unshielded twisted-pair or UTP cable used in 10/100BaseT is similar to, but generally not the same as, telephone wiring. For 10BaseT, this cable contains two pairs of wires, or four wires, first twisted in pairs, and then the pairs are twisted together. An RJ-45 modular connector is placed on each end. Although only two pairs are used, the actual cable in both Category 3 and Category 4 cabling has four pairs, as shown in Figure 8-6. The RJ-45 connector, which can handle four twisted pairs of wires, is similar to but slightly larger than the RJ-11 connector, which can handle two pairs of wires and is used in a normal phone connection. 100BaseT and 1000BaseT use four pairs or all eight wires in Category 5 cable and the same RJ-45 connector.

The pairs of wires in a UTP cable are twisted because that reduces the electrical interference that is picked up in the cable. The number of twists per foot has become a very exact science, and it is important to keep the cable properly twisted up close to the connector. An alternative to UTP is shielded twisted pair or STP, with various degrees of shielding: shielding around

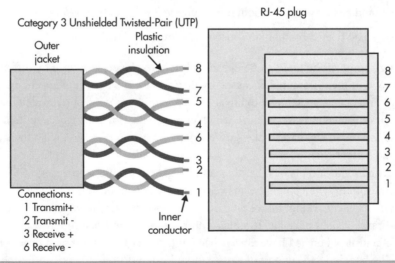

Figure 8-6 Unshielded twisted-pair (UTP) cabling used with an RJ-45 plug

each pair, around both pairs, or shielding around both the individual pairs and around the combination. STP is considerably more expensive than UTP and is more difficult to handle. To avoid potential interference problems without using STP, there are several rules to follow when running the cable:

- Don't run the cable near a fluorescent light fixture.

- Don't run the cable near an electrical motor, such as those in machines, fans, water coolers, and copiers.

- Don't run the cable alongside a power cable.

- Don't make tight turns that can crimp the cable.

- Don't use a staple gun, which can crimp the cable.

NOTE

Crimping network cabling can change the spacing between individual wires and therefore change its electrical characteristics and performance.

Between voice and data (phone and network), a number of different types of UTP cable exist. These differences lie in the degree of fire resistance, in the type of inner core, and in the grade or category of cable, which also specifies the number of twisted pairs.

Degree of Fire Resistance

UTP cables come in two degrees of fire resistance: _plenum_ cable, marked "CMP" on the side of the cable, and _PVC_ or _riser_ cable, marked "CMR." Plenum cable is more fire resistant and doesn't give off dangerous fumes if it does burn. PVC or riser cable, although reasonably fire resistant, is made with polyvinyl chloride (PVC), which gives off potentially dangerous fumes if it does burn. Plenum cable costs between two and two and a half times what PVC cable costs, but it can be used in air passages such as raised floors and suspended ceilings, whereas PVC cable can be used only in walls and out in the open (check your own local codes for the type of cable you should use).

Type of Inner Core

The inner core of UTP cable can be stranded or solid. Stranded wire is more flexible and less prone to breaking when bent a number of times. It is used in situations where it is frequently moved, such as in a patch panel and between a wall outlet and a computer. Solid wire has lower signal loss and therefore is better for longer runs where it won't be moved frequently, such as in walls and ceilings.

UTP Categories

The following are the seven categories of UTP cable that are used with voice and data communications:

● **Category 1**   Used in telephone installations prior to 1983 and has two twisted pairs.

● **Category 2**   Used in telephone installations after 1982 and has four twisted pairs; used in some early data networks with speeds up to 4 Mbps.

● **Category 3**   Used in many data networks and most current phone systems, has four twisted pairs, generally has three twists per foot (not in the specs), and easily handles speeds of 10 Mbps.

● **Category 4**   Used in Token Ring networks, has four twisted pairs, and can handle speeds up to 16 Mbps.

● **Category 5**   Used in most networks until recently, has four twisted pairs, has eight twists per foot, can handle 100 Mbps, and in bulk (1,000 feet) is under 12 cents per foot for solid PVC and about 30 cents a foot for solid plenum.

● **Category 5e (enhanced Category 5)**   Used in almost all current network installations, has the same physical characteristics as Category 5 but with a lower error rate, and in bulk (1,000 feet) is approximately 10 cents per foot for solid PVC and 28 cents a foot for solid plenum.

● **Category 6 (really STP)**   Used where electrical interference is a problem, and has four twisted pairs with a foil wrap around each pair and another foil wrap around all pairs. It is planned to handle Gigabit Ethernet, and in bulk (1,000 feet) is approximately 25 cents per foot for solid PVC and 55 cents a foot for solid plenum.

Connecting UTP

UTP cabling simply plugs into a NIC and then into a wall outlet or hub, making 10/100BaseT installation very simple, as you can see in Figure 8-7. For UTP to work between two computers without a hub, the wires must be *crossed over*—the transmitting wires on one computer must become the receiving wires on the other computer. This is one of the functions of a hub, so the wires connecting a computer to a hub must be the same on both ends. When two computers are directly connected to each other, a special cable must be used that has the end connections reversed.

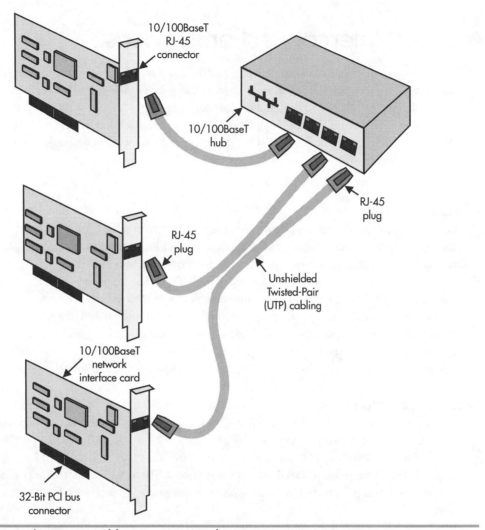

Setting Up and Using a Network

8

Figure 8-7 10/100BaseT cabling in a star topology

TIP

In order to stay within the 100-meter (328-foot) limit for a 10BaseT or 100BaseT segment, the rules of thumb are to keep the cable run from an interconnecting device in a wiring closet to the wall outlet at less than 300 feet, the run from the wall outlet to the computer at less than 20 feet, and the patch panel at less than 8 feet.

CRITICAL SKILL

8.5 Select Interconnection Devices

If you have more than two computers in a 10/100BaseT network, you need some device to which you connect the additional computers. The simplest of these devices is a hub, but you might also use a switch, a router, or a bridge, depending on what you want to do. Each of these devices has a particular use, although there is overlap, and each has several variations. These devices act as building blocks that allow you to expand a network segment and interconnect multiple segments.

Hubs

Hubs are used to connect other devices on the network. Normally these are workstations, but they can also be servers, printers, other hubs, and other interconnection devices. A hub is a repeater device that takes whatever comes in on one line and puts it out on all other lines without any filtering or intelligence applied to the information stream or where it is going. This means that every computer connected to the hub can see what every other computer has put on the network. As the traffic grows, multiple computers will try to put information on the network at the same time, causing a "collision" and a resulting significant degradation in the network throughput because when there is a collision, both computers must resend their information. There are three types of hubs: stand-alone hubs, stackable hubs, and modular hubs.

Stand-Alone Hubs

Stand-alone hubs, shown in Figure 8-8, are used in smaller networks and the final workgroup segment of larger networks. Stand-alone hubs come in 4-, 8-, 12-, 16-, and 24-port models for 10BaseT, 100BaseT, and auto-switching 10/100BaseT. 10BaseT hubs are $8 to $15 per port, 100BaseT hubs and 10/100BaseT hubs are under $10 to $35 per port. There is a lot of variability in this pricing, but generally speaking, the price per port goes down with more ports in the hub.

Most stand-alone hubs are simple devices into which you plug in the 4 to 24 other devices, and that's it. If you want to make a change in the configuration, you have to physically unplug and replug in the devices as needed to make the change. You can get smart stand-alone hubs with a management capability that is most often found in stackable and modular hubs. This allows a hub to be monitored and configured remotely using a software package that normally comes with the hub and either SNMP (Simple Network Management Protocol) or RMON

Figure 8-8   3Com OfficeConnect® Dual-Speed Hub 8 (3C16753) (Photo courtesy of 3Com Corporation, http://www.3com.com)

(Remote Monitoring). The software generally works with only one brand of hub, so it might be worthwhile to standardize on one brand if you are getting the additional management capability. Stand-alone hubs that can be managed cost $5 to $10 more per port and then have a separate charge for the management capability of $250 to $450.

Stackable Hubs

As you build a network with 10/100BaseT's star topology, you do so with a hierarchical structure, as shown in Figure 8-9. Such a structure has a maximum of four hubs (called "repeaters") or levels and five cable lengths between any workstation and the server for 10BaseT, and a maximum of two hubs or levels and three cable lengths for 100BaseT. When you daisy-chain one stand-alone hub to another at any level to simply attach more workstations at that level, each hub counts as an additional level, and you can't exceed these limits. To get around this limitation, stackable hubs were developed, which add ports at the same level by joining the backplanes of the hubs as if they were one hub. Therefore, any two devices connected anywhere in the stack have only a single hub between them.

Stackable hubs, shown in Figure 8-10, are similar in appearance to stand-alone hubs, and the only real difference is that the backplanes of stackable hubs can be connected. Stackable hubs can be stacked six to eight hubs high and cost from $10 to $30 per port. These hubs include the option to be managed with the additional management capability, which costs $200 to $750 for the stack.

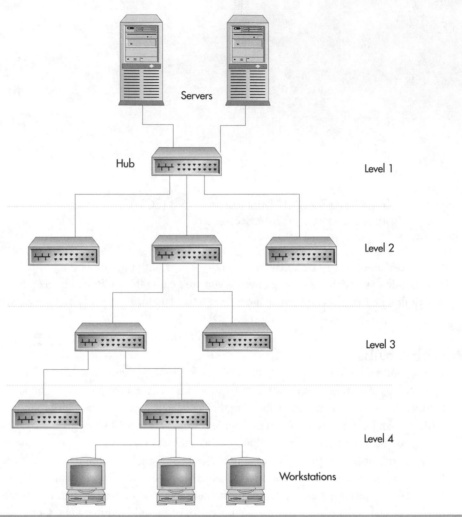

Figure 8-9 Hierarchical structure of a 10BaseT network

Modular Hubs

A modular hub, also called an *enterprise hub,* a *modular switch,* or an *enterprise switch,* is really a large chassis or cabinet with a power supply and backplane into which you can plug many different boards, including hubs, switches, bridges, and routers, as shown in Figure 8-11. By using a single backplane, modular hubs get around the two- or four-layer limit, as do stackable hubs. Modular hubs actually preceded stackable hubs, and in the lesser-demanding

Figure 8-10   3Com SuperStack® 3 Baseline Dual-Speed Hub (3C16592B) (12- and 24-port models) (Photo courtesy of 3Com Corporation, http://www.3com.com)

roles (where all you need are the hub functions), stackable hubs are now being used where modular hubs once were because a stackable hub is much cheaper.

Figure 8-11   3Com Switch 4007R Chassis (3C16817) (Photo courtesy of 3Com Corporation, http://www.3com.com)

There are many forms of modular units because you can buy the modules you want to use (hubs, switches, bridges, or routers) and plug them in to a modular backplane that can span one network segment, multiple network segments, or multiple networks. Basically, you buy a chassis with a power supply and then buy the modules you need to build the device that fits your network requirements. Modular hubs provide a lot of flexibility, but at a steep price.

In addition to flexibility, modular switches provide another very significant benefit, called a *collapsed backbone.* If the modules were separate devices, you would connect them with a high-speed backbone running at, at least, 100 Mbps or 1 Gbps, and maybe double those figures if you run at full-duplex. If you move all of these devices into a single modular hub where they are connected by the backplane, what in a stackable switch is a backbone connection is now collapsed onto the backplane and runs at between 100 Gbps and 600 Gbps (that's a "G," not an "M").

Bridges

A *bridge* is used to either segment a network or join two networks, as you can see in Figure 8-12. A bridge looks at the address in the information on the network. If the address is on the other side of the bridge, the information is passed on to the other side. If the information has an address on the originating side of the bridge, the bridge ignores the information because all devices on the originating side already can see it.

The purpose of the bridge is to reduce the traffic in a network by segmenting it, although it is still one network. If a hub replaced the bridge, the entire network would have all the traffic on both sides of what was the bridge, increasing the collisions and decreasing the throughput.

When you join two networks with a bridge, the result is one network with two segments, but only the traffic that is addressed to the other segment gets through the bridge. Traffic that is addressed within the originating segment stays within its segment. A bridge also lets you have additional hub layers above the two- or four-hub limit in a simple Ethernet network. Information can travel through two 100BaseT hubs, cross a bridge, and then travel through two more hubs. The bridge, in essence, takes information from one side and, if it is properly addressed, re-creates it on the other side.

The bridging discussed so far has described local bridging within a single facility. Bridges can also be used to connect a local network with a remote one and, in so doing, produce a single network with two segments where the traffic between them is limited to that destined for the other network. In this remote scenario, there would be a bridge on either side of the line connecting the two segments so that the local traffic in each segment stays in that segment.

Bridges are basically simple devices and are limited to a single network (both the source and destination addresses must be in the same network) and to a single cabling or media type. Theoretically, a 10BaseT network cannot be joined to a 10BaseF network with a bridge, but by building converters into the bridge, you can join them. Bridges range in price from around $300 to over $1,500, depending on their capabilities and brand.

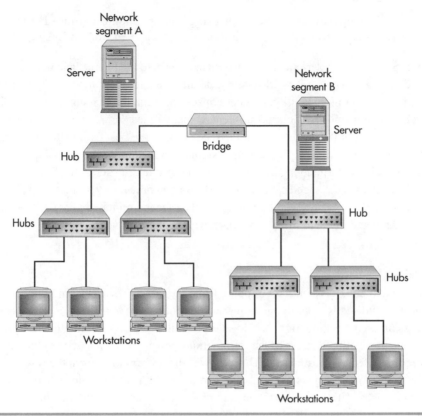

Figure 8-12 A bridge joining two network segments

NOTE

Bridges are becoming hard to find because you can generally perform the same function, plus others with a router or a switch for close to the same price.

Routers

Routers can perform the same segmenting and joining functions as a bridge, but do so at a higher level of sophistication. The resulting added capabilities of a router are significant:

- Routers connect separate networks, leaving them independent with their own addressing.

- Routers connect different types of networks; for example, 100BaseF and 100BaseT.

- Routers select from among alternative routes a path through a complex network in order to get to an end destination.

Setting Up and Using a Network   **8**

- Routers clean up network traffic by checking if information is corrupted or lost (traveling endlessly in the network); if so, the information is removed from the network.

For these reasons, routers are routinely used to connect to the Internet and within the Internet, and to connect a WAN to a LAN. Routers generally are intelligent devices with a processor and memory. With this capability, a router unpacks information that comes to it, looks at each part determining if it is valid, checks to see how many times the information has been around the network, looks at the destination address, determines the best path to get there, repackages the information with the new physical address, and sends it on its way. In addition, routers talk to other routers to determine the best path and to keep track of routes that have failed. Routers do all of this at amazing speeds. At the low end, routers process over 250,000 packets per second, and they go above several million packets a second on the upper end. Routers begin at around $200 and go up to many thousands, depending on what they do.

Switches

A *switch,* like a hub, has a number of ports, from 2 to 24, and takes information that comes into one port and sends it out to one or more other ports. Unlike a hub, which does no filtering or processing on the information that flows through it, a switch is an intelligent device that looks at the destination address of the information flowing into it and directs the information to the correct port for that destination. This removes that information from the rest of the network because the information goes over only the part of the network that connects the sending and receiving devices. This is similar to the maturing of the telephone system from the original party-line system to the modern direct-dial system.

Switches, like bridges and routers, segment a network to reduce the traffic and collisions, and ultimately improve the throughput. Switch segmentation can be done at any level where you would otherwise have a hub, a bridge, or a router. Such a switch functions as a multiport bridge. Further intelligence can be added to some switches so that they become multiport switching routers that unpack information and operate on the address in the packets.

NOTE

If the top two hubs in Figure 8-12 were switches, you could join the two network segments without a bridge simply by running a cable between the two switches, getting the same segmentation.

Switches, like hubs, come in stand-alone and stackable models with and without management capability. The simplest switches cost under $10 a port; switching routers may go over $200 a port.

Ask the Expert

Q: **When should a switch replace a hub?**

A: There are two situations where a switch should be used in place of a hub. First, when the traffic on the network reaches such a level that collisions are starting to really slow down the network, then you need to add a switch to keep traffic just to the links that actually need to be crossed. Second, if you need more than four levels of hubs in a 10BaseT network or more than two levels in 100BaseT one, you can use a switch to add more levels.

CRITICAL SKILL
8.6 Choose Network Topologies

Topology is the design of a network, the way it is laid out. In the figures in this module, you have seen several different topologies. 10Base2 and 10Base5 both use a *bus* topology, wherein all the network devices are attached to a single long cable, as you saw in Figure 8-1. 10BaseT and 100BaseT both use a *star* topology, where the network devices fan out on separate cables from a central hub, as you saw in Figures 8-2, 8-7, and 8-12. Finally, when the backbone cabling is added to a 10/100BaseT network, you have a *star/bus* topology.

The bus topology was the original Ethernet topology, but it has the major disadvantage that a break in any part of the network brings the entire network down. In a star topology, a break in a line takes out only those parts of the network connected to the line, potentially only one station.

There are disagreements as to whether a bus or a star is easier to cable, but although a star takes more cable, it is cheaper cable, and it is easier to manage. You can put the cable for a star topology in the wall and not connect it to a hub or switch if it is not being used. Also, it is easy to move a station from one network segment to another simply by changing a jumper cable that connects the station from one hub to another.

Lay Out a Network

Once you have decided on the network technology and the type of NIC, cabling, and interconnection devices that you want to use, you still have to figure out how to lay out the network. This includes a lot of questions, such as

● Which workstations are grouped with which hubs?

● Do you stack several hubs, or immediately use a switch?

● Should the servers be centralized in one location or decentralized in each department?

● When do you need a switch, a router, or a bridge?

● How do you connect two buildings separated by 1,500 feet or more?

There is no one right answer to any of these questions, and there is a lot of difference between the impact of the first question and that of the last question. You can easily alter the connections to change how workstations are grouped, but setting up a wide area network is a job for professionals because you are talking about serious money to purchase the equipment and install it, and significant expense if you want to change it.

In an Ethernet 10BaseT or 100BaseT network, there are several rules that should be followed in a layout. These vary slightly with different manufacturers, but the general rules of thumb are shown in the following table:

Rule of Thumb	Ethernet 10BaseT	Fast Ethernet 100BaseT
Maximum cable length between hub and workstation	100 meters or 328 feet	100 meters, or 328 feet
Minimum cable type	Category 3	Category 5
Maximum number of hubs between two workstations or a switch and a workstation	Four hubs	Two hubs
Maximum number of cable segments between two workstations or a switch and a workstation	Five cable segments	Three cable segments with a maximum total distance of 205 meters, or 672 feet

CRITICAL SKILL
8.7 Use Network Protocols

Protocols are the standards or rules that allow many different systems and devices to interconnect and operate on a network, be it a small office network or the worldwide Internet. Protocols specify *how* and *when* something should happen, and *what* it is that should happen.

Numerous protocols deal with computer networking, but "networking protocols" normally refers to the addressing and transfer of information. Within Windows XP and over the Internet, one protocol is used to handle this function: TCP/IP.

TCP/IP

Transmission Control Protocol/Internet Protocol is a set of networking protocols that grew out of the Internet and has been refined over 15 years to be an excellent tool for transmitting large amounts of information reliably and quickly over a complex network. The two components, TCP and IP, were originally combined and then were separated to improve the efficiency of the system.

IP

The Internet Protocol controls the assembly and routing of information, its principle function being addressing the information. As it is passed across a network, information always carries with it its final destination address, called the *logical* address. In addition, the information is placed in a wrapper or envelope with the *physical* address of the next piece of hardware to receive the information. In a very simple LAN without routers, the physical and logical addresses describe the same device. In a complex network such as the Internet, the physical address is the next router the information needs to go to. In each router, the information is taken out of its wrapper or envelope *(unpacked),* the logical address is examined, the next best link is determined to get the information to its final destination, and the information is repackaged and given the physical or hardware address of that link. This process is controlled by IP, which allows the information to follow any path through the network, with the decision on which path to take made by the local router on the basis of its knowledge of the local situation; IP is therefore called a *connectionless* service.

The logical addresses used in IP are called *IP addresses* and are assigned worldwide by a consortium of committees. Some IP addresses are permanently assigned, and some are assigned every time the computer logs on to the server.

TCP

The Transmission Control Protocol handles connections. Its purpose is to assure the reliable delivery of information to a specific destination. TCP is a connection-oriented service, in contrast with IP, which is connectionless. TCP makes the connection with the final destination and maintains contact with the destination to make sure that the information is correctly received. Once a connection is established, though, TCP depends on IP to handle the actual transfer. And because IP is connectionless, IP depends on TCP to assure delivery.

The sending and receiving TCPs (the protocol running in each machine) maintain an ongoing, full-duplex (both can be talking at the same time) dialog throughout a transmission to assure a reliable delivery. This begins by the sending TCP making sure that the destination is ready to receive information. Once an affirmative answer is received, the sending TCP packages a portion of the information to be transmitted with control information and sends it to IP. TCP packages the remaining information while watching for an acknowledgment that the previous information has been received. If an acknowledgment is not received, it is re-created and handed off. This process continues until the all the information is sent and acknowledged, at which point the sender tells the receiver that it's done. In the process of transmission, the two computers are constantly talking to make sure that everything is going smoothly.

The functions performed by TCP and IP—the packaging, addressing, routing, transmission, and control of the networking process in a very complex environment—are mind-boggling. When you add to that the ease and reliability of networking, it is truly stunning. Now that you know all the networking ingredients presented here, isn't it amazing that networking works even in a small workgroup, let alone the Internet? That the Internet is such a worldwide success has to be one of the great wonders of the modern world.

Progress Check

1. What are some of the important characteristics to look for in NICs?

2. What type of wire would you install today for a 100BaseT network to run in the wall, in the ceiling, and from the wall to the computer?

3. In a 100BaseT network, how many levels of hubs (hubs plugged into hubs) can you have?

CRITICAL SKILL
8.8 Set Up Basic Networking

When you installed Windows XP, a basic set of networking services was installed and configured using your input and system defaults. This setup may, but doesn't always, provide an operable networking system. In any case, there is a wide spectrum of networking alternatives that can be reviewed and set to provide the networking environment best suited to your needs. The purpose here is to do that by looking at how to set up basic networking in either Windows XP Professional or Windows XP Home Edition.

Basic networking means that the computer can communicate with other computers in the network. To do that, you must do the following:

1. Assure the network interface card (NIC) is properly set up.

2. Install the networking functions that you want to perform.

---

1. Some of the important characteristics to look for when buying a NIC for a workstation are that it be 100BaseT, for the PCI bus, full-duplex, and name brand.

2. In all cases, you should use Category 5e. In the wall, you should use solid-core PVC, in the ceiling, solid-core plenum, and from the wall to the computer, stranded-core PVC.

3. You can have two levels of hubs in a 100BaseT network.

3. Choose and configure a networking protocol.

Set Up Network Interface Cards

In a perfect world, the computer you are setting up has a NIC that is both on Microsoft's Hardware Compatibility List (HCL) and fully Plug and Play–compatible. If this describes your computer, then your NIC was installed by Setup without incident and you don't need to read this section. As is known by anyone who has installed an operating system on more than two computers, this is an imperfect world. Therefore, this section looks at how the NIC was installed and what you need to do to make it fully operational.

If you installed Windows XP using the instructions in Module 13, then you can skip this section if you believe your NIC is operating correctly. If you had problems with networking in Module 13 or did not go through it, then this section will be worthwhile to you.

Assuming that a NIC *is* properly plugged into the computer, any of these three things could be causing it to not operate:

● The NIC driver is either missing or not properly installed.

● The required resources are not available.

● The NIC is not functioning properly.

Look at each of these possibilities in turn in the next several sections.

Check on the NIC Driver

During installation, you may have gotten a message stating that a driver could not be found (although Setup often completes without telling you it skipped network setup because of the lack of a driver). Use the following steps to check whether you have a driver installed and, if you don't, to try to install one:

NOTE

In the previous modules when the Control Panel was discussed, both Category and Classic view instructions were given. It is my opinion that Classic view is more efficient, so throughout Part III of this book on advanced uses of Windows XP, I will give only Classic view instructions.

1. Open the Start menu, choose Control Panel, and double-click Network Connections in Classic view. The Network Connections window opens. If you have an icon in the window labeled Local Area Connection, as shown next, you probably have the NIC driver properly installed and you can go on to the next major section, "Install Networking Functions."

TIP

You can change the name Local Area Connection (for example, if you install two NIC cards, you can give each of them a descriptive name), so it may be named something else in Step 1.

2. If you do not have a Local Area Connection icon, you cannot create one by clicking New Connection Wizard. You must first install the NIC using the Add Hardware control panel.

At this point, it is highly likely that you will need a Windows XP driver for the NIC, so it is best to get it before proceeding. If one did not come with the NIC, then you need to get onto another computer attached to the Internet, bring up the manufacturer's web site, locate and download the driver (you need to know the make and model of the NIC) for Windows XP, and then copy it onto a disk.

NOTE

I went through the process of downloading a driver for an older 3Com card and found it painless. The hard part is figuring out what the card is because often it is not written on the card, so you have to locate purchase records or documentation—if you know which records go with the card.

3. Again open the Start menu, click Control Panel, and double-click Add Hardware in Classic view. The Add Hardware Wizard opens.

4. Click Next. When asked if the hardware is connected, click Yes (given that the NIC is already in its slot), and click Next again. A list of installed hardware will appear. You may

or may not see your NIC on the list (with or without a problem icon—an exclamation point), as shown in Figure 8-13.

   If you see your NIC and it doesn't have a problem icon, then Windows thinks that it is installed and running properly. If you double-click the device, you should get a message saying that "This device is working properly," and you can click Finish to close the Add Hardware Wizard. Your problem may be in software.

5. If you don't see your NIC, click Add A New Hardware Device at the end of the list of Installed Hardware. Click Next. Choose Install The Hardware That I Manually Select From A List, you don't want Windows to search for new hardware (if it was going to find it, it would have), and click Next. Skip to Step 7.

6. If you see your NIC with a problem icon, double-click it, and you will most likely get a Device Status telling you that a driver was not installed. Click Finish to close the Add Hardware Wizard and start a troubleshooter. The Upgrade Device Driver Wizard opens. Click Next. Choose Display a List of Known Drivers and click Next.

7. Independent of whether you saw your NIC, double-click Network Adapters in the list of Common Hardware Types. A list of network adapters appears. If your NIC had been on the

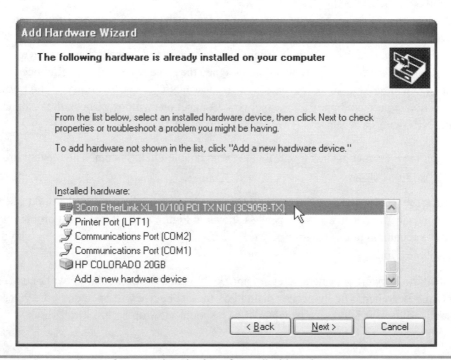

Figure 8-13 Network interface card in the list of installed hardware

list, Setup would have found it, so you need to insert and use the disk you made prior to Step 3 or a disk that came with the NIC.

8. Click Have Disk. Accept the default of the A drive (assuming that is the floppy drive and you want to use a floppy) and click OK. When it is displayed, select the driver for your adapter and click Next. When told that the device will be installed, click Next again.

9. You may get a message stating that the driver you are about to install does not have a Microsoft digital signature. Click Yes to go ahead and install it anyway. The driver and its necessary supporting software will be installed.

10. Click Finish. The Network Connections window should now show the Local Area Connection icon. If you see the Local Area Connection icon, go to the next major section, "Install Networking Functions."

If you still do not have a Local Area Connection, or some other problem occurred in the preceding process that does not point to an obvious solution, continue through the next two sections to see if a solution is presented.

Check NIC Resources

Most interface or adapter cards in a PC require dedicated resources in order to operate. The resources include interrupt request (IRQ) lines, I/O ports, and direct memory access (DMA) lines. Generally, two devices cannot share the same resources, except that PCI devices can share IRQs. Therefore, if two devices are assigned the same resource, a conflict occurs and the device will not operate properly. This will cause a NIC to not function and the Local Area Connection icon to not appear in the Network Connections window. Check the resources used by the NIC, with these steps:

1. Open the Start menu, click Control Panel, and double-click System. The System Properties dialog box opens.

2. Click the Hardware tab and then click Device Manager on the right of the middle section. The Device Manager window opens as shown in Figure 8-14. If you see a problem icon (an exclamation point) on your network adapter, then there may be a problem with the resource allocation.

3. Open the Network Adapters category and double-click the particular network adapter that is being researched. The Properties dialog box for that device will open and give you a device status. If there is a resource problem, then it should show up here.

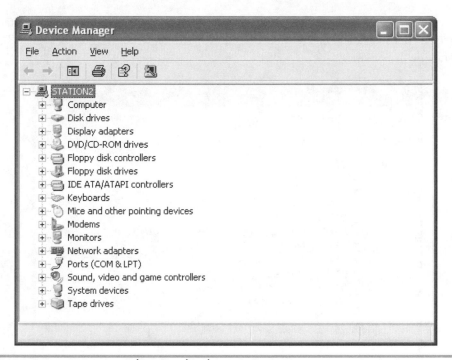

Figure 8-14 Device Manager showing the devices in a computer

4. Click the Resources tab. In the Conflicting Device List at the bottom of the dialog box, you will see the specifics of any resource conflicts.

5. If you have a conflict, click Use Automatic Settings to turn that setting off, and then go through each of the configurations in the Setting Based On drop-down list to see if any of them cure the problem.

6. If none of the canned configurations cures the problem, click the problem resource, clear the Automatic Setting check box, and click Change Setting. Click the up or down arrow to change the setting and click OK to see if that fixes the problem. Try several settings.

7. If you are having a hard time finding a solution, go back to the Device Manager (you can leave the NIC Properties dialog box open), open the View menu, and choose Resources By

Type. Here, you can see all of the assignments for a given resource, as shown for interrupt request lines next, and find an empty resource to assign to the NIC (for example, IRQs 5 and 7 in this case).

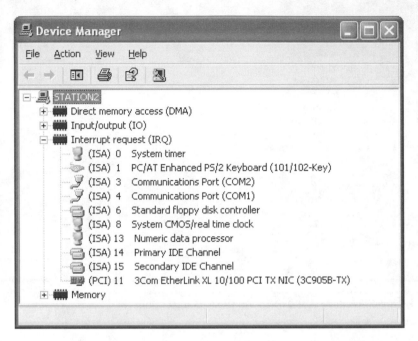

8. If you find an unassigned resource, go back to the NIC Properties dialog box and assign it to the NIC. If you cannot find an unassigned resource, you may have to make a tough choice between the NIC and a conflicting device. Networking is a pretty important service, and if it is conflicting with a sound card, for example, you may have to remove the sound card to get networking. If both of the cards are ISA cards and you have PCI slots available, you may be able to get a new PCI card and remove the conflict.

9. If none of the previous suggestions works, return to the NIC Properties dialog box, click the General tab, and then click Troubleshoot. Windows XP Help will open and lead you through a series of steps to try to resolve the problem.

10. When you have solved the resource problem as best you can, close the NIC Properties dialog box and close the Device Manager. If you made changes in the resources, you may be told that you need to restart your computer and asked whether you want to do it now. Click Yes, and the computer will restart.

11. If you successfully made a change to the resources, you should now see a Local Area Connection icon in the Network Connections window (if necessary, reopen it by clicking

Ask the Expert

Q: If my NIC is not on the HCL, does that mean it doesn't work with Windows XP?

A: No, it just means that Microsoft hasn't checked it out. Also, be sure to look under both "Network/Ethernet" and "Network/Fast Ethernet" in the HCL. A lot of Fast Ethernet cards are listed only under Ethernet. If you can't find your card, check with the manufacturer to see if they believe it works with XP.

Start | Control Panel and double-clicking Network Connections). If you do, go to the next major section, "Install Network Functions." If you don't see a Local Area Connection icon, continue with the following section.

NIC Not Functioning

If neither installing a NIC driver nor changing its resource allocation caused the Local Area Connection icon to appear, it is very likely that the NIC itself is not functioning properly. The easiest way to test that is to replace the NIC with a known good one, ideally one that is both on Microsoft's HCL and Plug and Play–compatible. It is wise to have several spare NICs; they are not terribly expensive (see "Network Interface Cards" earlier in this module), and switching out a suspected bad one can quickly solve problems.

NOTE

For the very latest HCL update, look at Microsoft's web site at http://www.microsoft.com/hcl/.

Install Networking Functions

Networking functions provide the software for a computer to access other computers, and, separately, for other computers to access the computer you are working on. In other words, the two primary functions allow the computer to be a client (it accesses other computers) and to be a server (other computers access it). Make sure that these two services are installed by following these steps:

1. In the Network Connections window, double-click Local Area Connection. The Local Area Connection Status dialog box opens, as shown next. In the particular case shown here, the computer thinks it is connected to the network and it is sending and receiving information.

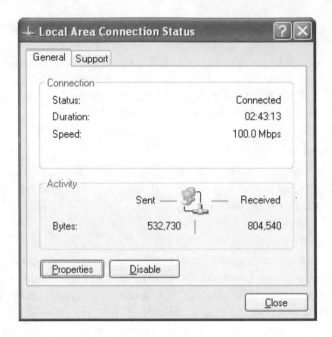

2. Click Properties. The Local Area Connection Properties dialog box, shown in Figure 8-15, opens and displays the services and protocols that have automatically been installed. Under the default circumstances, this includes two services—Client for Microsoft Networks, and File and Printer Sharing for Microsoft Networks—and one protocol—Internet Protocol (TCP/IP). If you have the two services installed, you have achieved the objective of this section, but in any case, continue and explore the alternatives.

3. Click Install. The Select Network Component Type dialog box opens, in which you can add clients, services, and protocols.

4. Double-click Client. If you already have Client for Microsoft Networks installed, you will have only Client Service for NetWare in the list.

5. If Client for Microsoft Networks is not installed, select it and click OK. If you also need to access a NetWare server, select Client Service for NetWare and click OK.

6. Back in the Select Network Component Type dialog box, double-click Service. If you already have File and Printer Sharing for Microsoft Networks installed, you may have QoS (quality of service) Packet Scheduler available to be installed. QoS helps balance a network and alleviate bottlenecks when one part of the network is fast and another part is slow.

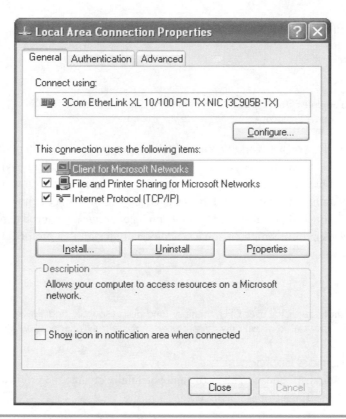

Figure 8-15   Services and protocols installed to support networking

7. If File and Printer Sharing for Microsoft Networks is not installed, select it and click OK. If you need QoS, select it, and click OK.

This should assure that you have the two primary services installed.

Choose and Configure a Networking Protocol

As you read earlier in this module, networking protocols are a set of standards used to package and transmit information over a network. The protocol determines how the information is divided into packets, how it is addressed, and what is done to assure it is reliably transferred. The protocol is therefore very important to the success of networking, and its choice is a major one. Windows XP offers two protocols:

● **Internetwork Packet Exchange/Sequenced Packet Exchange (IPX/SPX)**   For use with networks running Novell NetWare

● **TCP/IP** For use with the Internet and most newer systems

NOTE

IPX/SPX is implemented in Windows XP with the NWLink IPX/SPX/NetBIOS Compatible Transport Protocol.

If the computer you are working on is or will be connected to the Internet, it will require TCP/IP. TCP/IP is a very robust protocol that's suitable for a demanding environment (is there a network environment more demanding than the Internet?) and accepted worldwide. Because of this, it is recommended that TCP/IP be installed as your protocol of choice for both your LAN and the Internet. If you also need the other protocol because you need to network in a Novell NetWare environment, then you can additionally install that protocol.

TIP

Each protocol that you install uses CPU, memory, and disk resources and slows startup, so it is important to install only the protocols that are truly needed.

Check and Change Protocols

Use the following instructions to check on and potentially change the protocols that have been installed and the settings that are being used:

NOTE

In the Local Area Connection Properties dialog box, you should see at least one protocol installed, as shown previously in Figure 8-15. In most cases, TCP/IP should already be installed, and possibly NWLink IPX/SPX if that need was identified during setup.

1. Click Install and then double-click Protocol. The Select Network Protocol dialog box opens, shown next. This lists the available protocols. If necessary, double-click Microsoft TCP/IP. If you want to install another protocol, do so now by double-clicking that protocol. Otherwise, click Cancel to close the Select Network Protocol dialog box.

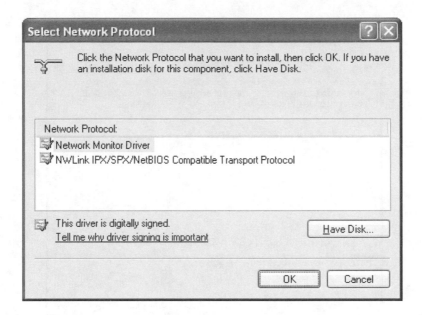

2. Select the TCP/IP protocol in the Local Area Connection Properties dialog box and click Properties. The Internet Protocol (TCP/IP) Properties dialog box opens, shown in Figure 8-16, in which you can choose to use either a dynamic IP address automatically assigned by a server or DSL router running the Dynamic Host Configuration Protocol (DHCP), or a static IP address that you enter in this dialog box.

   If you have a server or a DSL router that automatically assigns IP addresses, then you need to leave the default of Obtain An IP Address Automatically. If the server is down or nonexistent, Automatic Private IP Addressing (APIPA) assigns an IP address from the block of 65,000 numbers 169.254.0.0 through 169.254.255.255. It also generates a subnet mask of 255.255.0.0. APIPA is limited insofar as a computer using APIPA can talk only to other computers in the same subnet with an address in the same range of numbers. If all computers in a small network are using Windows 98/Me or Windows 2000/XP and have Obtain An IP Address Automatically selected, without a DHCP server, they will automatically use the 169.254.0.0 through 169.254.255.255 range of IP numbers.

3. If you are working on a computer that you know you must assign a static IP address, then do so by clicking Use The Following IP Address and entering an IP address. The IP address that you use should be from the block of IP addresses that your organization has been

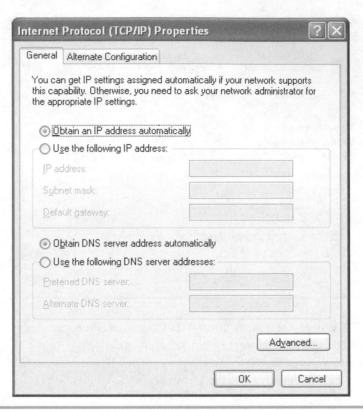

Figure 8-16 Choosing the method of setting the IP address

assigned by its Internet service provider (ISP) or other authority (see the discussion under "Get Blocks of IP Addresses," later in this module). If your organization is small and doesn't plan to access an outside network, then the static IP address can be from the block of APIPA numbers (but manually entered; refer to the limitations in Step 2) or from several other blocks of private IP addresses (see "Get Blocks of IP Addresses").

4. If you entered a static IP address, you must also enter a subnet mask. This mask tells the IP which part of an IP address to consider a network address and which part to consider a computer or *host* address. If your organization was assigned a block of IP numbers, it was also given a subnet mask. If you used the APIPA range of addresses, then use 255.255.0.0 as the subnet mask.

5. If you don't have a specific reason to use a static IP address, click Obtain An IP Address Automatically, and use the addresses from either a server or DSL router on the network or APIPA.

6. Click OK to close the Internet Protocol (TCP/IP) Properties dialog box, click Close to close the Local Area Connection Properties dialog box, click Close to close the Local Area Connection Status dialog box, and click the close button to close the Network Connections window.

7. Open the Start menu, choose Turn Off Computer, and select Restart from the dialog box that appears.

8. When the computer restarts, reopen the Network Connections window (Start | Control Panel, double-click Network Connections). Double-click Local Area Connection to open the Local Area Connection Status dialog box. You should see activity on both the Sent and Received sides.

9. If you do not see both send and receive activity, open the Start menu, click My Computer, and click Search in the toolbar. In the Search pane on the left, click Computers Or People, click A Computer On The Network, enter a computer name in your same subnet, and then click Search. You should see the computer appear with its location on the right, as shown next. If it does appear, then the computer is networking. If it doesn't work, then you have a problem.

10. If you think you have a problem, double-check all the possible settings previously described. If you are using APIPA, make sure that the computer you are trying to contact is also using that range of numbers either as a static assigned address or with automatic assignment. If all the settings are correct, then check the cabling by making a simple connection of just several computers (if you do a direct UTP connection between two computers, remember that you need a special *crossover* cable with the transmit and receive wires reversed) and, finally, replace the NIC. With a good NIC, good cabling, and the correct settings, you'll be able to network.

Get Blocks of IP Addresses

The block of IP addresses you use with the Internet Protocol depends on whether the computers to be assigned the addresses will be public or private. If the computers will be interfacing directly with the Internet, they are *public* and thus need a globally unique IP number. If the computers will be operating only on an internal network, where they are separated from the public network by a router, bridge, or firewall, they are *private* and need only organizational uniqueness. Three blocks of IP addresses have been set aside and can be used by any organization for its private, internal needs without any coordination with any other organization, but these blocks should not be used for directly connecting to the Internet. These private-use blocks of IP addresses are as follows:

- 10.0.0.0 through 10.255.255.255

- 172.16.0.0 through 172.31.255.255

- 192.168.0.0 through 192.168.255.255

In addition is the APIPA range from 169.254.0.0 through 169.254.255.255, discussed earlier in this module. Remember, though, that APIPA works only with computers within its own subnet and with IP addresses from the same range.

If you want a block of public IP addresses, you must request it from one of several organizations, depending on the size of the block that you want. At the local level for a moderate-sized block of IP addresses, your local ISP can assign it to you. For a larger block, a regional ISP may be able to handle the request. If not, you have to go to one of three regional Internet registries:

- American Registry for Internet Numbers (ARIN), at http://www.arin.net/, which covers North and South America, the Caribbean, and sub-Saharan Africa

- Réseaux IP Européens (RIPE), at http://www.ripe.net/, which covers Europe, Middle East, and northern Africa

- Asia Pacific Network Information Centre (APNIC), at http://www.apnic.net/, which covers Asia and the Pacific

Test a Network Setup and Connection

There are several command-line utilities that can be used to test a TCP/IP installation. The more useful of these commands are the following:

- **Ipconfig**   Used to determine if a network configuration has been initialized and an IP address assigned. If an IP address and valid subnet mask are returned, then the configuration is initialized and there are no duplicates for the IP address. If a subnet mask of 0.0.0.0 is returned, then the IP address is a duplicate.

- **Hostname**   Used to determine the computer name of the local computer.

- **Ping**   Used to query either the local computer or another computer on the network to see whether it responds. If the local computer responds, you know that TCP/IP is bound to the local NIC and that both are operating correctly. If the other computer responds, you know that TCP/IP and the NICs in both computers are operating correctly and that the connection between the computers is operable.

Use the following steps to test a network setup with these utilities. Figure 8-17 shows the results on my system:

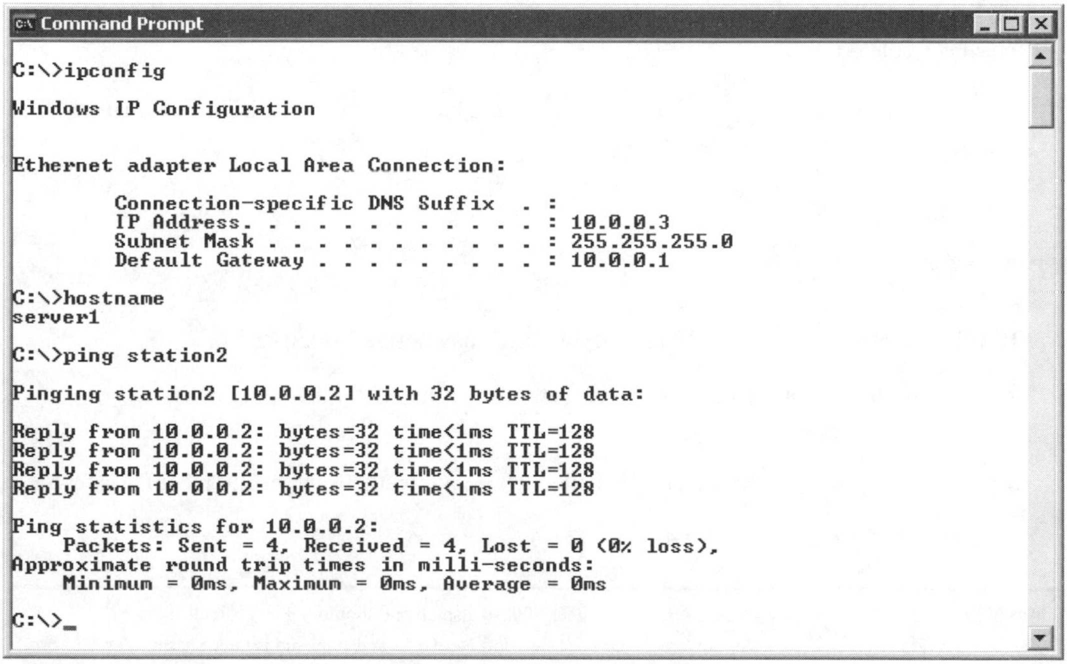

```
C:\>ipconfig

Windows IP Configuration

Ethernet adapter Local Area Connection:

        Connection-specific DNS Suffix  . :
        IP Address. . . . . . . . . . . . : 10.0.0.3
        Subnet Mask . . . . . . . . . . . : 255.255.255.0
        Default Gateway . . . . . . . . . : 10.0.0.1

C:\>hostname
server1

C:\>ping station2

Pinging station2 [10.0.0.2] with 32 bytes of data:

Reply from 10.0.0.2: bytes=32 time<1ms TTL=128
Reply from 10.0.0.2: bytes=32 time<1ms TTL=128
Reply from 10.0.0.2: bytes=32 time<1ms TTL=128
Reply from 10.0.0.2: bytes=32 time<1ms TTL=128

Ping statistics for 10.0.0.2:
    Packets: Sent = 4, Received = 4, Lost = 0 (0% loss),
Approximate round trip times in milli-seconds:
    Minimum = 0ms, Maximum = 0ms, Average = 0ms

C:\>_
```

Figure 8-17 Testing a network with TCP/IP utilities

1. Open the Start menu and choose All Programs | Accessories | Command Prompt. The Command Prompt window opens.

2. Type **ipconfig** and press ENTER. The IP address and subnet mask of the current computer should be returned. If this did not happen, there is a problem with the current configuration.

3. Type **hostname** and press ENTER. The computer name of the local computer should be returned.

4. Type **ping** *computer name* and press ENTER, where *computer name* is the name of another computer on your network. You should get four replies from the other computer.

5. If Ping did not work with a remote computer, try it on the current computer by typing **ping 127.0.0.1** and pressing ENTER. Again, you should get four replies, this time from the current computer. If you didn't get a reply here, then you have a problem with either the network setup or the NIC. If you did get a reply here, but not in Step 4, then there is a problem either in the other computer or in the line connecting them.

NOTE

The 127.0.0.1 IP address is a special address set aside to refer to the computer on which it is entered.

If you do find a problem here, use the steps in the earlier section "Check and Change Protocols" to isolate and fix the problem.

Progress Check

1. What is the ultimate test if you think your NIC may not be working?

2. What are the two networking services that must be installed for a computer to fully function on a network?

3. What is the protocol that must be installed to operate on the Internet and most LANs?

---

1. Install a spare NIC that you know works. NICS cost under $20, so a spare one should not be difficult.

2. The two services required for networking are Client For Microsoft Networks and File And Printer Sharing For Microsoft Networks.

3. The protocol needed to access the Internet and most LANs is TCP/IP.

Project 8   Make Sure Networking is Properly Set Up

This exercise will quickly go through the steps to make sure networking is properly installed and working, including determining if

- You have a network connection
- Your computer recognizes your NIC
- The correct driver is installed for your NIC
- The appropriate networking services are installed
- The correct protocol is installed and properly configured
- Your computer can talk to itself and the rest of the network

If the sum of these items says that networking is not working properly, then you need to return to the section "Set Up Basic Networking" and follow the instructions there.

Step by Step

1. Open the Start menu, click Control Panel, and double-click Network Connections. If the Network Connections window shows a Local Area Connection, you have a network connection. If not, you need to return to the section "Set Up Basic Networking."

2. Double-click the Local Area Connection to open the Local Area Connection Status dialog box. If this shows you are connected and that bytes are being both sent and received, then your connection is operating properly and you can skip to Step 7.

3. Click Properties. In the Local Area Connection Properties dialog box that opens, you should see your NIC listed. If so, your computer recognizes your NIC; if not, you need to return to the section "Set Up Basic Networking."

4. Click Configure. In your NIC's Properties dialog box you should see under Device Status "This Device Is Working Properly." If so, the correct driver is installed for your NIC and you can skip to Step 6.

5. Click the Driver tab, click Update Driver, and follow the directions in the Hardware Update Wizard. When the Wizard is finished, click the Resources tab and make sure that in the box under Conflicting Device List it says "No Conflicts." If not, you need to return to the section "Set Up Basic Networking."

6. Close the NIC's Properties dialog box and reopen the Local Area Connection's Properties dialog box by right-clicking it and choosing Properties. In the middle box, you should see at least the following two services and one protocol

    Client For Microsoft Networks

    File And Printer Sharing For Microsoft Networks

    Internet Protocol (TCP/IP)

If so, the appropriate networking services and protocol are installed. If not, you need to return to the section "Set Up Basic Networking." Close the Local Area Connection Properties dialog box and close the Network Connections window.

7. Open the Start menu and choose All Programs | Accessories | Command Prompt. Type **ipconfig** and press ENTER. If you get a response with an IP address and a subnet mask, then your network components can talk to themselves. Type **ping** *computername*, where *computername* is the name of another computer on your network. If you get a response, then your network components can talk to the rest of the network. If you do not get a response, you need to return to the section "Set Up Basic Networking."

Project Summary

For an organization of any size, networking is extremely important because it allows that organization to share information, communicate, and share resources. Therefore, to make sure that the network is set up and running properly is equally important. If the information in this module is not sufficient, check out my *Windows .NET Server, A Beginner's Guide* or Tom Sheldon's *Encyclopedia of Networking and Telecommunications,* both published by McGraw-Hill/Osborne.

✓ Module 8 Mastery Check

1. What are three purposes of a network?

2. What is the dominant networking technology, and what are some of the reasons for its dominance?

3. What are two reason in favor of wireless networking and two reasons against it?

4. What are two small/home office networking technologies, and how do they compare?

5. What are the two primary card buses used with NICs, which should you use, and why?

6. What are three different types of interconnection devices, and how do they differ?

7. What is the primary topology used today, and what are its components?

8. What are the rules of thumb for laying out a 100BaseT network?

9. What is the primary protocol used in Windows networking, and what do its components do?

10. What are three things to check if you think networking is not working properly?

Module 9

Controlling Security

Computer security is like an onion with many layers. No matter how many you peel away, there always seem to be more. One way to try to understand it is to look at the demands for security in a computer. Once the demands are defined, you can look at how Windows XP handles the demands. Security demands include the following:

- **Authenticating the user**   Knowing who is trying to use a computer or network connection

- **Controlling access**   Placing and maintaining limits on what a user can do

- **Securing stored data**   Keeping stored data from being used, even with access

- **Securing data transmission**   Keeping data in a network from being misused

Windows XP uses a multilayered approach to implementing security and provides a number of facilities that are used to handle security demands. In each of the following sections, a security demand is further explained and the Windows XP facilities that address that demand are discussed, as are the ways to implement those facilities.

NOTE

Many network security issues are addressed at the server level, especially with a domain controller, and are beyond the scope of this book. To learn more about these, see my server books *Windows 2000, A Beginner's Guide* and *Windows .NET Server, A Beginner's Guide,* both published by McGraw-Hill/Osborne.

CRITICAL SKILL
9.1 Authenticate the User

Authentication is the process of verifying that users or objects (documents or e-mail messages) are as they are represented to be. In its simplest form, computer user authentication entails validating a username and password against a database entry in a stand-alone computer. In its fullest form, user authentication entails using the *Kerberos* authentication protocol to validate a potential user, possibly using a smart card or biometric device, such as a fingerprint reader, anywhere in a network against credentials in a server. For objects, such as documents, programs, and messages, authentication requires using Kerberos certificate validation. In Windows XP, all three forms of authentication are available, and both user forms employ a single sign-on concept that allows a user, once authenticated, to access other services within the local computer or the network, depending on their environment, without having to reenter his username and password.

In the default installation, when a Windows XP computer is started, there may be a request to select a username and possibly enter a password if two or more people use the same computer; otherwise, it is assumed that the sole user is at the keyboard. This may or may not be a good assumption. If a username and password are entered, they must be authenticated. This can be done either at the local computer, where the user will be limited to that computer, or at a server supporting a network, in which case the user will have access to the network.

NOTE

If you are using or are going to use a domain, it is important to set up domain user accounts rather than local user accounts on computers within the domain. Local user accounts are not recognized by the domain, so a local user cannot use domain resources and a domain administrator cannot administer the local accounts. Using domain accounts is one of the subjects that is left for server books.

Plan for Usernames and Passwords

Before setting up local user accounts, your organization should have a plan for the usernames and passwords that the company will use and should probably not let everybody have total freedom to select their own. The objectives are to be consistent and to use prudent practices. Here are some considerations:

- For usernames, are you going to use first name and last initial, first initial and last name, or full first and last names?

- How, if at all, are you going to separate the first and last name? Many organizations don't use any separation, whereas others use either periods or the underscore.

- How are you going to handle two people with the same first and last name? Adding a number after the name is a common answer, or use a middle initial.

- Do you need a special class of names for, for example, subcontractors in your organization? If so, how, if at all, do you want to differentiate them from other users? One method is to precede their names with one or more characters to indicate their position, such as "SC" for subcontractor.

- Names must be unique, cannot be over 20 characters long (or 20 bytes long if a character takes over one byte), are not case-sensitive, cannot contain " / \ [ ] : ; | = ,+ * ? < >, and cannot consist solely of periods, the @ character, or spaces. Leading or trailing periods or spaces are ignored.

- Passwords must be unique, cannot be over 127 characters, can use both upper- and lowercase letters, should use a mixture of letters, numbers, and symbols, and should be at least 7 characters long.

NOTE

If your password is over 14 characters, you will not be able to log on to the network from a Windows 95/98/Me computer.

Create Local Computer User Accounts

To have a username and password accepted on a local stand-alone computer, a *user account* with that username and password must have been previously entered into the Local Users and Groups database. Here are the steps to set up a user account:

NOTE

Most sets of steps in this module require that you be logged on as Administrator. You'll know if you are an Administrator by opening the User Accounts window with the steps that follow and seeing whether your account is labeled "Computer Administrator" or "Limited Account."

1. While logged on as an Administrator, open the Start menu, choose Control Panel, switch to Classic view if needed, and double-click User Accounts. The User Accounts window opens.

2. Click Create New User and enter a name of up to 20 characters. It cannot contain just periods, spaces, or the @ symbol; it can't contain " / \ [ ] : ; | = ,+ * ? < >; and leading spaces or periods are dropped. Click Next.

3. Choose either Computer Administrator or Limited as the account type. The default is Computer Administrator and its privileges are shown. If you move the mouse over Limited (you don't have to click), you can see the privileges there.

NOTE

Normally the first user is the Computer Administrator and then the remaining users have either administrator or limited accounts. The administrator can change passwords and install programs. Limited accounts can change only their own passwords and may or may not be able to install software, depending on the program.

4. Click Create Account. You are returned to the main User Accounts window. Click the new account to change its properties; the window changes to that shown in Figure 9-1.

5. Click Create A Password. Enter a password and its confirmation, and then enter a phrase or word that will help you remember the password. The hint, though, is available to everybody, so it should be only a hint for you and not indicate to others what the password is.

CAUTION

As you can see in the warning at the top of the Create A Password window, creating a
password wipes out any other passwords and other security elements for that user, including
logon password, passwords for web sites, personal certificates, and encrypted files.

6. When you have successfully entered the information, click Create Password. If you wish,
you can change the picture by clicking that option, either selecting a new picture from those
presented or browsing for one, and then clicking Change Picture. When you are ready, click
Close. You will now be able to log off and log on as your new user. Try that to make sure
it works.

With the entry of this single username and password, the new user will be able to do
anything that is within that user's level of permission on that single computer. If the computer
subsequently is connected to a network, the account has to be reestablished there for the user
to be able to use the network.

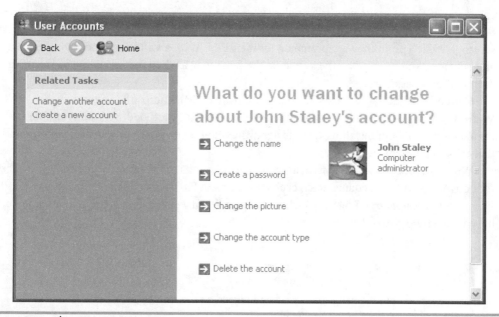

Figure 9-1 Changing a user account

Replacements for Passwords

The weakest link in the Windows XP security scheme is probably the use of passwords. Users give their passwords to others or forget them, and passwords are stolen or just "found" in many different ways. There is nothing to tie a password to an individual. With someone's password in hand, nothing can stop you from impersonating that person on a password-protected system. Two potential means of replacing passwords are smart cards and biometric devices.

Smart Cards   *Smart cards* are credit card–sized pieces of plastic that have a tamper-resistant electronic circuit embedded in them that permanently stores an ID, a password, a digital signature, an encryption key, or any combination of those. Smart cards require a personal identification number (PIN), so they add a second layer (smart card plus PIN in place of a password) that an impersonator would have to obtain to log on to a system. Also, smart cards can be configured to lock up after a few unsuccessful attempts to enter a PIN.

Windows XP supports smart cards and lets them be used to log on to a computer or network or to enable certificate-based authentication for opening documents or performing calculations. Smart cards require a reader attached to the computer through either a serial port or a PCMCIA slot. With a smart card reader, users only need to insert their card at the logon screen, at which point they are prompted for their PIN. With a valid card and PIN, users are authenticated and allowed on the system in the same way as they would be by entering a valid username and password.

Currently, Windows XP lists 23 smart card readers that Microsoft has tested with Windows XP. The drivers for these 23 devices are either included with or available for Windows XP, and installing them is not difficult; you need only follow the instructions that come with them.

With a smart card reader installed, set up new accounts (as previously described) and then, for both new and old accounts, open each user's Create Password page and click Smart Card Is Required For Interactive Logon, which will appear when a smart card is present. You do not have to enter a password.

NOTE

In case you wondered, the PIN is encrypted and placed on the smart card when it is made. The PIN is not stored on the computer.

Smart cards are particularly valuable for remote entry to a network and can be used by a traveling staff member with a laptop, possibly using virtual private networking (VPN) over the Internet. Smart cards are also frequently used in the issuance of certificates of authenticity for documents and other objects (see the discussion of certificates later in the module under "Implement Secure Data Transmission").

Biometric Devices   Smart cards do provide an added degree of security over passwords, but if someone obtains both the card and the PIN, she's home free. The only way to be totally sure that the computer is talking to the real person is to require some physical identification of the person. This is the purpose of *biometric devices,* which identify people by physical traits, such as their voice, handprint, fingerprint, face, or eyes. Often, these devices are used with a smart card to replace the PIN. Biometric devices are just moving into the mass production stage, and nothing is built into Windows XP specifically to handle them. Devices and custom installations are available from around $100 for a fingerprint scanner to several thousand dollars for a face scanner. In the next few years, these devices will be everywhere, so depending on your needs, you may want to keep them in mind.

Certificate Authentication

If you want to bring users into a network over the Internet, but you are concerned that sending usernames and passwords in that public way might compromise them, then you can replace them with a digital certificate. A *digital certificate* (or just "certificate") is issued by a certification authority (CA), who digitally signs it and says that the bearer is who he or she says they are, or that an object and sender are as represented. There are both private and public CAs. An organization can be its own private CA and issue certificates to its employees, vendors, and/or customers, so that those people can be authenticated when they try to enter the organization's network. Also, a well-trusted public CA, such as VeriSign (http://www.verisign.com/), can issuc a certificate to a person, object, organization, or web site. A person or organization receiving the certificate, if they trust the CA, can be reasonably certain that the presenter is as represented. Besides a certificate, most CAs provide the bearer with an encryption key in the certificate, so that secure data transmissions can occur.

Request a Certificate   Users, computers, and other services can request certificates to identify themselves. Some certificates are automatically given to computers and users who are known and trusted entities on the network, such as the administrator for the CA and the computer on which the CA resides. It is also possible to explicitly request a certificate over either an intranet or the Internet. In doing this, you access a web page that is created and maintained by Certificate Services. Use these steps to request a certificate over an intranet (it is assumed that a domain controller/server on which Certificate Services has been installed is available on the local area network):

1. Open your browser and enter the URL or address of the server with Certificate Services. The address should look something like http://*servername*/certsrv/. If requested, enter a username and password and click OK for access to the server. The page should appear as shown in Figure 9-2.

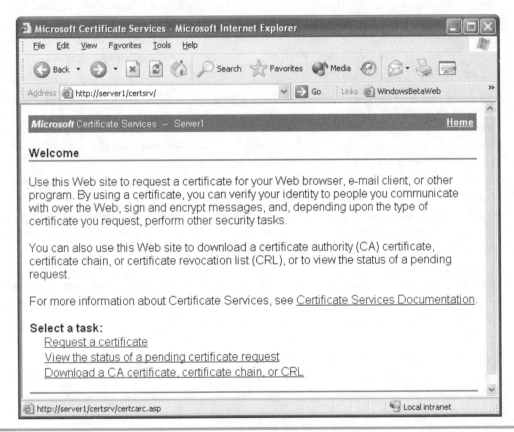

Figure 9-2 Requesting a certificate over an intranet

2. Click Request A Certificate. Choose User Certificate for the request type.

3. Click Submit. If the user and/or computer are already known to the server, a certificate will be issued. Otherwise, you will be told that the request is pending.

4. When you get the certificate, click Install This Certificate. You are asked if you want to add this certificate to the Root Store.

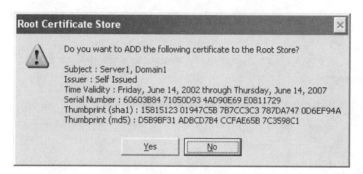

5. Click Yes. You are told that the certificate is installed and you can close your browser.

The core of Windows XP's user-oriented security consists of user accounts, which can require a username and password to log on and are the basis for the permission system that controls access to computer and network resources. When someone comes into Windows XP with a certificate, they don't have a username and password to be attached to a user account and the permissions that go with it. The solution is to map or relate a certificate to a user account, so that when someone presents an acceptable certificate, he will be attached to a user account and

Ask the Expert

Q: I have a stand-alone computer in my home. Why should I have to sign on and use a password?

A: The quick answer is that you don't. Windows XP gives you that option. Only you can determine what the risks are, who else is in or might come into your home, and what sort of information is on the computer. If you have thought that through and are comfortable, then there is no need.

given the permissions he would possess if they had logged on with a username and password. Certificate mapping is done on a server through Active Directory services.

Progress Check

1. Should an organization let everybody have total freedom to select their own usernames and passwords?

2. What are the two types of computer user accounts in a stand-alone system and what are their differences?

3. What are two possible replacements for passwords?

Control Access

User accounts identify people and allow them to log on to a computer and possibly to a network. What they can then do depends both on the permissions given to them or given to groups to which they belong and on the ownership of the object they want to use. Windows XP, when using the NT File System (NTFS), allows an administrator to assign various levels of permission to use an object (a file, a folder, a disk drive, a printer), as well as assign ownership and the rights of ownership. (You cannot do this with the FAT or FAT32 file system.)

When you initially install Windows XP, the default is to use *Simple File Sharing,* where most files, folders, disk drives, and printers give permission for all registered users on the local computer to do almost anything with these objects, but prevent everyone not a local registered user. (There are some files and folders related to the operating system that by default have withheld some permission for users who are not administrators.) You can turn off Simple File Sharing and change the initial settings rather quickly by using a property called *inheritance* that says all files, subfolders, and files in subfolders automatically inherit (take on) the permissions of their parent folder. Every file, folder, and other object in Windows XP NTFS, though, has its own set of *security descriptors* that are attached to it when it is created, and with the proper permission, these security descriptors can be individually changed.

---

1. An organization should not let everybody have total freedom to select their own usernames and passwords; they should have definite policies in place in order to be consistent and to use prudent practices.

2. The two types of computer user accounts in a stand-alone system are Administrator, which can change passwords and install programs; and Limited, which can change only their own passwords and may or may not be able to install software.

3. Two possible replacements for passwords are smart cards and biometric devices.

NOTE

Simple File Sharing is turned on permanently in Windows XP Home Edition and can be turned off only in Windows XP Professional.

Share Files and Folders

Initially, with Simple File Sharing, all permissions, most importantly sharing, are granted by the creator of an object or by an administrator. The creator of an object is called its *owner*. The owner of an object has the right to grant and deny permission, such as sharing or not sharing the object. You can change how an object is shared, both locally and over the network, through the object's Properties dialog box. Leave Simple File Sharing turned on and see how file or folder sharing is changed in the Properties dialog box opened through Windows Explorer with these steps:

1. Open the Start menu and choose My Computer. Click Folders in the toolbar.

2. In the left pane, open the disk and folders necessary to see in the right pane the folder or file that you want to change the ownership for.

3. In the right pane, right-click the subject folder and choose Properties. In the Properties dialog box, click the Sharing tab, which will open as shown in Figure 9-3.

   In the Sharing tab, you can make the folder private to the local computer users and you can share it on the network; in other words, you can reverse the defaults. The first two lines of the top box imply that the folder is not shared on the local computer by default and that you must drag it to the Shared Documents folder to be shared. That is *not* correct. All files and folders are by default shared among all users on the computer unless you change that status.

NOTE

When you share or make private a folder, all folders and files within it are given the same sharing status due to inheritance. If that is not what you want for a particular file or folder, you must individually change its sharing status.

4. To share the file or folder over the network, in the lower box Under Network Sharing And Security click Network Setup Wizard (the link at the end of the first paragraph), which will open. Click Next twice. Select the type of Internet connection you have and click Next. Enter the computer description, click Next, enter the workgroup name, click Next twice, select whether you want a network setup disk for other computers, click Next again, and finally click Finish.

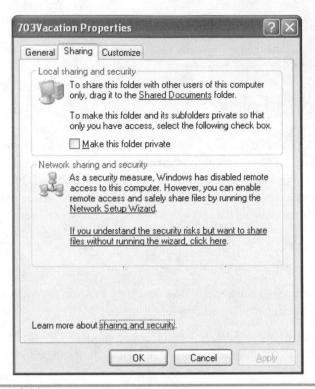

Figure 9-3 Sharing a folder

5. Back in the file or folder Properties dialog box, you can choose to share the file or folder, give it a share name, and determine if you want to allow network users to change it. When you are finished, click OK and then Close.

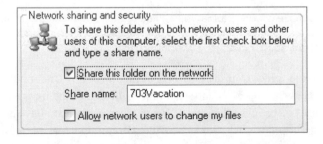

Groups

Groups, or *group accounts,* are collections of user accounts and can have permissions granted to them. Most permissions are granted to groups, not individuals, and then individuals are made members of the groups. (See the next section on permissions.) It is therefore important that you have a set of groups that handles both the mix of people in your organization and the mix of permissions that you want to establish. A number of standard groups with preassigned permissions are built into Windows XP, but you can create your own groups, and you can assign users to any of these.

NOTE

Windows XP Home Edition offers limited security and permissions and doesn't support groups.

Look at the groups that are a standard part of Windows XP, see what permissions they contain, and then create your own if you need to. As with user accounts, you look at groups differently depending on whether you are on a stand-alone Windows XP Professional computer or on a domain controller. Here we will consider only the groups in Windows XP Professional where you need to use the Computer Management window, as follows:

1. Open the Start menu and choose Control Panel, double-click Administrative Tools, and double-click Computer Management.

2. In the Tree pane on the left, open System Tools | Local Users and Groups and click Groups. The list of built-in groups will be displayed, as shown in Figure 9-4.

3. Double-click a few groups to open the Properties dialog box for each, in which you can see the members of that group.

4. Click the white space in the right pane so no group is selected, open the Action menu, and choose New Group. The New Group dialog box opens.

5. Enter a group name of up to 60 characters (Windows XP lets you enter more, but if you ever want to use the group in Windows 2000 or NT systems, it will not work). It cannot contain just numbers, periods, or spaces; it can't contain " / \ [ ] : ; | = ,+ * ? < >; and leading spaces or periods are dropped. Enter the description of what the group can uniquely do, and click Add. The Select Users dialog box opens.

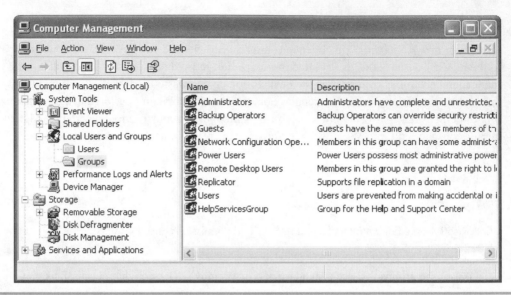

Figure 9-4 Built-in groups in a stand-alone computer

6. Either type a name in the text box and click Check Names or click Advanced, click Find
   Now, hold down CTRL while clicking the user to include in the group, and click OK. When
   you have selected all you want to include, click OK. Your new group should appear with
   the new members added to it.

7. When your group is the way you want it, click Create and then click Close. The new group
   will appear in the list on the right of the Computer Management window. Close the Computer
   Management window.

Permissions

Permissions authorize a user or a group to perform some function on an object. Objects, such
as files, folders, disks, and printers, have sets of permissions associated with them that can be
assigned to users and groups. The specific permissions depend on the object, but all objects
have at least two permissions: Read, and either Modify or Change. Permissions are initially set
in one of three ways:

- The application or process that creates an object can set its permissions upon creation.

● If the object allows the inheritance of permissions and they were not set upon creation, a parent object can propagate permissions to the object. For example, a parent folder can propagate its permissions to a subfolder it contains.

● If neither the creator nor the parent sets the permissions for an object, then the Windows XP system defaults will do it.

Once an object is created, its permissions can be changed by its owner, by an administrator, and by anybody else who has been given the permission to change permissions. The following sections look at the default permissions for both folders and files and at how those defaults are changed. In order to see, set, and change permissions, you must first turn off Simple File Sharing.

Turn Off Simple File Sharing

Simple File Sharing is meant to make life easier in an uncomplicated environment, but it takes away a large amount of your control. In order to work with permissions, you must first turn it off. Here are the steps:

NOTE

You cannot turn off Simple File Sharing in Windows XP Home Edition.

1. Open the Start menu and choose My Computer. Open the Tools menu and choose Folders Options.

2. Click the View tab, scroll to the bottom of the Advanced Settings, and click the check box opposite Use Simple File Sharing to uncheck it or turn it off.

3. Click OK to close the Folder Options dialog box and then close My Computer.

With Simple File Sharing turned off, an additional Security tab appears in dialog boxes for both the files and folders, as you'll see in a moment.

Folder Permissions

Folder permissions are set in the Security tab of a folder's Properties dialog box, shown in Figure 9-5. You can open this tab and change the permissions with these steps:

1. Open the Start menu, choose My Computer, and click Folders in the toolbar.

2. In the Folders pane on the left, open the drives and folders necessary to see the folder for which you want to set permissions.

3. Right-click that folder and choose Properties. In the Properties dialog box, click the Security tab.

Figure 9-5 Default folder permissions

NOTE

If you do not have a Security tab, you are not connected to a domain, since the features described here are available only in a domain.

You can see the default permissions that have been granted to one or more groups and at least one individual. You can change some of the permissions that are preassigned, and you can add new users and groups to the permission list. Some of the assignments are inherited from the parent folder, so you can turn inheritance on or off if you wish. That is done by clicking Advanced to open the Advanced Security Settings dialog box shown in Figure 9-6.

Turning off inheritance is accomplished by unchecking the check box in the lower left of the Advanced Security settings dialog box. When you do that, you are warned that you will prevent any inheritable permissions from propagating to this folder.

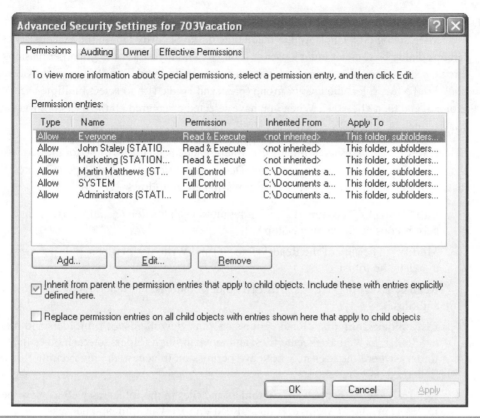

Figure 9-6 Detailed permission information is available in Advanced Security Settings.

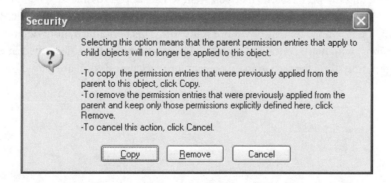

4. Click OK to close the Advanced Security Settings dialog box and return to the folder's Properties dialog box. Click Add in the middle of the Security tab. In the Select Users Or Groups dialog box, either enter a user or group to whom you want to grant permissions and click Check Name (if it comes back with the name underlined, it is OK) or click Advanced, click Find Now, select the user or group (press and hold CTRL to select multiple users or groups), and then click OK. When you have selected or entered all the users or groups you want to include, click OK again.

5. Select one of the new users or groups that you just added and click Allow for the permissions that you want that entity to have, or click Deny to specifically exclude a permission. The tasks that can be performed with each permission are as follows:

- **Full Control**   The sum of all other permissions, plus delete subfolders, change permissions, and take ownership

- **Modify**   The sum of the Read & Execute and Write permissions, plus permission to delete the folder

- **Read & Execute**   The same as List Folder Contents, but inherited by both folders and files

- **List Folder Contents**   Read permission, plus view the list of subfolders and files in a folder, as well as execute files, and move through folders to reach other files and folders, where the user may not have permission to access the intervening folders (inherited only by folders)

- **Read**   View the contents of subfolders and files in the folder, as well as view the folder's attributes (Archive, Hidden, Read-only), ownership, and permissions

- **Write**   Make subfolders and files inside the folder, plus view the ownership and permissions for the folder and change its attributes

6. After selecting the permissions that you want to use, click Advanced. The Advanced Security Settings dialog box opens. Select a user or group and click Edit. The Permission Entry dialog box appears, as shown in Figure 9-7. This contains a more detailed level of permissions, which are contained within the primary permissions described in Step 2. The detailed permissions that are granted by each primary permission are shown in Table 9-1.

NOTE

Synchronize isn't available unless the folder is set up for it.

7. Make any changes that you want to the detailed permissions, check the check box at the bottom if you want the permission to be propagated to the subfolders and files of this folder, and click OK three times to close all dialog boxes.

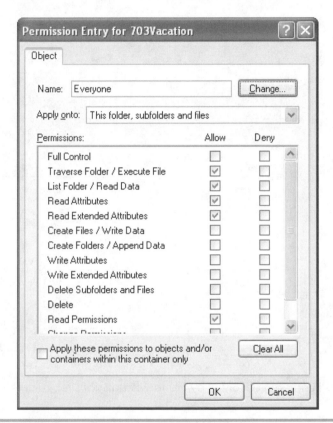

Figure 9-7 Detailed permissions that are available if needed

Detailed Permission	Primary Permission					
	Read	**Write**	**List Folder Contents**	**Read & Execute**	**Modify**	**Full Control**
Traverse Folder/ Execute File			Yes	Yes	Yes	Yes
List Folder/ Read Data	Yes		Yes	Yes	Yes	Yes
Read Attributes	Yes		Yes	Yes	Yes	Yes
Read Extended Attributes	Yes		Yes	Yes	Yes	Yes
Create Files/ Write Data		Yes			Yes	Yes
Create Folders/ Append Data		Yes			Yes	Yes
Write Attributes		Yes			Yes	Yes
Write Extended Attributes		Yes			Yes	Yes
Delete Subfolders and Files						Yes
Delete					Yes	Yes
Read Permissions	Yes	Yes	Yes	Yes	Yes	Yes
Change Permissions						Yes
Take Ownership						Yes
Synchronize	Yes	Yes	Yes	Yes	Yes	Yes

Table 9-1 Detailed Permissions Granted by Primary Permissions for Folders

CAUTION

Denying Everyone the Full Control permission prevents anybody from doing anything with the folder, including administrators. The folder is permanently locked from everybody, and the only thing you can do to get rid of the folder is to reformat the hard drive.

File Permissions

File permissions are set in the Security tab of the file's Properties dialog box, which is very similar to what you saw in Figure 9-5 for a folder. You can open this tab and change the permissions with these steps:

1. Open My Computer and click Folders. Locate and right-click the file for which you want to set permissions and choose Properties. In the Properties dialog box, click the Security tab.

2. Click Add to open the Select Users or Groups dialog box, either enter a user or group to whom you want to grant permissions and click Check Name (if it comes back with the name underlined, it is OK), or click Advanced, click Find Now, select the user or group (press and hold CTRL to select multiple users or groups), and then click OK. When you have selected or entered all the users or groups you want to include, click OK again.

3. Select one of the new users or groups and then click Allow for the permissions that you want that entity to have or click Deny to specifically exclude a permission. The following are the tasks that can be performed with each permission:

   - **Full Control**   The sum of all other permissions, plus change permissions and take ownership

   - **Modify**   The sum of the Read & Execute and the Write permissions, plus delete and modify the file

   - **Read & Execute**   The Read permissions, plus execute applications

   - **Read**   View the contents of the file, as well as view its attributes (Archive, Hidden, Read-only), permissions, and ownership

   - **Write**   Write to the file, plus view the file's permissions and ownership, and change its attributes

   - **Special Permission**   Allow unique activities that are related to a particular type of file

4. After selecting the permissions that you want to use, click Advanced. The Advanced Security Settings dialog box opens. Select a user or group and click Edit. The Permission Entry dialog box appears. This contains a more detailed level of permissions, which are contained within the primary permissions described in Step 3. The Special Permissions that are granted by each primary permission are shown in Table 9-2.

5. Make any changes that you want to the detailed permissions, and click OK three times to close all dialog boxes.

Detailed Permission	Primary Permission				
	Read	Write	Read & Execute	Modify	Full Control
Traverse Folder/ Execute File			Yes	Yes	Yes
List Folder/ Read Data	Yes		Yes	Yes	Yes
Read Attributes	Yes		Yes	Yes	Yes
Read Extended Attributes	Yes		Yes	Yes	Yes
Create Files/ Write Data		Yes		Yes	Yes
Create Folders/ Append Data		Yes		Yes	Yes
Write Attributes		Yes		Yes	Yes
Write Extended Attributes		Yes		Yes	Yes
Delete				Yes	Yes
Read Permissions	Yes	Yes	Yes	Yes	Yes
Change Permissions					Yes
Take Ownership					Yes
Synchronize	Yes	Yes	Yes	Yes	Yes

Table 9-2 Detailed Permissions Granted by Primary Permissions for Files

Ask the Expert

Q: Under what circumstances should Simple File Sharing be turned off and the individual permissions be used?

A: The reason you would go from Simple File Sharing to working with the individual permissions is when you need to fine-tune the specific tasks an individual or group can perform. The specific reasons depend on the organization and how its computers are being used. To begin with, by turning off Simple File Sharing you can go in and see what permissions are being granted to whom. Then if necessary, you can change them or create a new group with a unique set of permissions to fit the particular needs at hand. Many, maybe even most organizations will not need to do this, but there is always the exception, and this gives you the flexibility to handle it.

Progress Check

1. What are the default Simple File Sharing file and folder access permissions in Windows XP?

2. How are the contents of a folder affected by sharing it?

3. What do you accomplish by turning off Simple File Sharing?

---

1. The default file and folder access permissions in Windows XP give all local users permission to access local files and folders and prevent outside users who come in over the network or Internet from such access.

2. If a folder is shared, the subfolders and files it contains are also shared unless they are specifically and individually made private.

3. Turning off Simple File Sharing allows you to work with the individual permissions granted to a group or user and to turn off the inheritance of permissions from the parent folder.

CRITICAL SKILL
9.3 # Secure Stored Data

User authentication puts a lock on the outside doors of the computer, and controlling access puts locks on the inside doors, but if someone breaks through or gets around those barriers, the data inside is available to anyone who wants it. For example, someone may take a disk drive and access it with another operating system, or steal a laptop and methodically break through the passwords. Or, what is much simpler and more common, an employee either purposefully gets or mistakenly is given access to data she should not have and decides to misuse it.

The answer to all of these scenarios is to make the data itself unusable without a key. This is done by encrypting a file or folder so that no matter how it is accessed, by another operating system or a low-level utility, it is encrypted and cannot be read without the key, and the key is itself encrypted so that it is exceptionally difficult to obtain and use.

File and Folder Encryption

File and folder encryption has been built into Windows XP Professional (but not Home Edition) using NTFS and is called the *Encrypting File System (EFS)*. Once EFS is turned on for a file or a folder, only the person who encrypted the file or folder will be able to read it, with the exception that a specially appointed administrator will have a recovery key to access the file or folder. For the person who encrypted the file, accessing it requires no additional steps, and the file is reencrypted every time it is saved. All of the encrypting and decrypting is done behind the scenes and is not obvious to the user.

NOTE

Neither system files or folders nor compressed files or folders can be encrypted. You can decompress a compressed file or folder and then encrypt it.

The Encryption Process

The actual encryption of a file or folder is done with a *symmetric encryption key,* which is the same for both encryption and decryption and is very fast. The symmetric encryption key (also called a *private key*) is itself encrypted using the file owner's public key that is contained in her EFS certificate. (See "Understand Private/Public Key Encryption," later in this module.) Therefore, the owner with her private key matching the public key is the only one who can open the encrypted file—except for the recovery administrator. When the file is created or recreated and a symmetric key is made, the key is actually encrypted twice, once for the owner and once for the recovery administrator. Then if the need arises, the recovery administrator can use his private key to decrypt the file.

The encrypted symmetric key is stored as a part of the file. When an application requests the file, NTFS goes and gets it, sees that the file is encrypted, and calls EFS. EFS works with the security protocols to authenticate the user, use her private key to decrypt the file, and pass a plain text file to the calling application, all in the background, without any outward sign that it is taking place. The encryption and decryption routines are so fast that on most computers that can run Windows XP, you seldom notice the added time.

TIP

Because many applications save temporary and secondary files during normal execution, it is recommended that folders rather than files be the encrypting container. If an application is then told to store all files in that folder where all files are automatically encrypted upon saving, security is improved.

Encryption Considerations

Several requirements must be met to use file and folder encryption:

- Windows 2000 or XP Professional NTFS must be in use. Any other file system, whether Windows NT 4 or Windows XP Home Edition NTFS or FAT, will not work with EFS.

- Certificate Services should be installed and running either on a stand-alone computer or within a domain. If Certificate Services is not running, EFS will issue its own certificates, but these are considered "not trusted" by Windows XP, although they will work as an interim solution.

- The user of the file or folder must have an EFS certificate. If one does not exist, it is automatically created.

- There must be one or more certificated recovery agent administrators. If one does not exist, a default administrator is automatically appointed and a certificate is issued. The default administrator on a stand-alone computer is the local administrator, while in a domain, it is the domain administrator on the first domain controller that is installed.

CAUTION

If a user encrypts a file on a domain and then attempts to open it on a local computer, the file will not be available, because the public key used to encrypt the file on the domain is contained in a certificate there. When the same user signs on to a local computer (maybe the same physical computer, just disconnected from the network, such as a laptop might be), his user account and resulting certificate will be different because it no longer has the domain qualifier, so the private key in the certificate will not open the file.

Recovery Agent Administrators   The reason a recovery agent administrator is required is shown by the situation in which someone leaves an organization, maybe through an accident, and her encrypted files are needed. Another situation is one in which a disgruntled employee encrypts shared files before leaving the organization. EFS is disabled without a recovery agent, so that files cannot be encrypted without a means to decrypt them. Several recovery agents may be assigned to an EFS file or folder, but there must be at least one. For each recovery agent, as well as the user, a copy of the symmetric encrypting key encrypted with the person's public key is stored with the encrypted file. Whoever decrypts the file reveals only the data and not any of the other keys.

Copying and Moving EFS Files   Copying and moving EFS files and folders has special significance. Here are the rules:

●   If you copy or move a file or folder to an encrypted folder, the item copied or moved will be encrypted.

●   If you copy or move a file or folder to an unencrypted folder, the item moved remains as it was prior to moving. If it was unencrypted, it remains so, and if it was encrypted, it is still encrypted after moving.

●   Someone other than the owner trying to copy or move encrypted files or folders to a different computer gets an error message that access is denied.

●   If the owner copies or moves an encrypted file or folder to another file system, such as Windows NT 4 NTFS or Windows 98 FAT32, the encryption is removed, but a warning message is generated before the copy or move is complete.

●   Backing up encrypted files or folders with Windows XP Backup leaves the items encrypted.

NOTE

When you back up encrypted data, make sure that both the user and the recovery agent keys are also backed up, which can be done with Certificate Services.

Use File and Folder Encryption

The actual process of encrypting a file or folder is very easy; you simply turn on the Encrypted attribute. Given that there is a certificated recovery agent administrator and that the user turning on the encryption has an EFS certificate, there is very little else to do. Look at the full process in the next sections.

Encrypt a File and a Folder

Encryption of either files or folders can be done from Windows Explorer or from the command prompt.

Encrypt a File from Windows Explorer   Here are the steps to encrypt a file from Windows Explorer:

1. Open the Start menu, click My Computer, and click Folders in the toolbar.

2. In the folders tree on the left, open the drive and folders necessary to display on the right the file you want to encrypt.

3. Right-click the file and choose Properties. In the General tab, click Advanced. The Advanced Attributes dialog box opens.

4. Click Encrypt Contents To Secure Data.

5. Click OK twice. You get an Encryption Warning that the file is not in an encrypted folder, which means that when you edit the file, temporary or backup files might be created that are not encrypted.

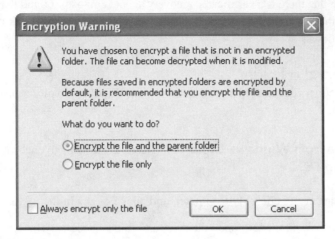

6. Choose Encrypt The File Only. If you don't want to see this warning in the future, click Always Encrypt Only The File. Click OK.

7. Log off as the current user and log on as another user. Open My Computer and open the drive and folders necessary to display on the right the file you encrypted. You can see that the file exists, but when you try to open it, edit it, print it, or move it, you will get a message that access is denied.

Encrypt a Folder from Windows Explorer

Encrypting a folder from Windows Explorer is very similar, as you can see in these steps:

1. Open the Start menu, click My Computer, and click Folders in the toolbar.

2. In the folders tree on the left, open the drive and folders necessary to display on the right the folder you want to encrypt.

3. Right-click the folder and choose Properties. In the General tab, click Advanced. The Advanced Attributes dialog box opens, as you saw in Step 3 in the preceding section.

4. Click Encrypt Contents To Secure Data and click OK twice. The Confirm Attribute Changes dialog box opens.

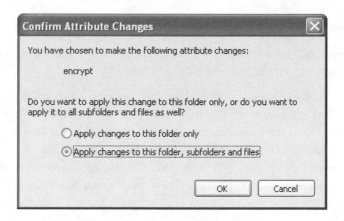

5. You are asked whether you want to apply the encryption to this folder only or to the folder, its files, and its subfolders. If you choose This Folder Only, *existing* files and folders in the folder being encrypted will *not* be encrypted, while files and folders created or copied to the encrypted folder after the fact will be encrypted. If you choose This Folder, Subfolders, and Files, existing files and folders, as well as those created or copied in the future, will be encrypted.

6. Choose the setting that is correct for you and click OK. To decrypt a file or folder, simply clear the Encrypt Contents To Secure Data check box.

CAUTION

If you choose This Folder, Subfolders, and Files for a shared folder that has files or subfolders belonging to others, you will encrypt those files and subfolders with your key, and the owners will not be able to use their property.

Encrypt a File and a Folder from the Command Prompt   At the command prompt, you can use the Cipher command to encrypt and decrypt files and folders. The following exercise encrypts a file and then a folder that contains the file plus another unencrypted file, looks at the results, and then decrypts the folder and its contents:

NOTE

Close Windows Explorer before you use the command prompt, and make sure your file and folder names do not have embedded spaces. Failure to follow either of these guidelines can cause problems with the following steps.

1. Open the Start menu and choose All Programs | Accessories | Command Prompt.

2. Type **cipher /?** and press ENTER to see the parameters that are available with the command. Read down through this to get a feel for the command.

    In the Cipher parameters, using /E by itself encrypts only the folder, not the files and subfolders it contains. This is the same as choosing Folder Only in Windows Explorer. If you want to encrypt the folder and its subfolders, you must use both **/E** and **/S** with a space between them. If you want to encrypt the folder, its subfolders, and the files they contain, use **/E /S /A** (be sure to complete entering **/S** in the form of /s:*path\foldername* before entering **/A**. To encrypt a file by itself, you must use **/E /A** with a space between them; /E/A will not encrypt the folder.

3. Type **cipher /e /a** *path\filename* and press ENTER to encrypt just the file *filename*.

4. Type **cipher /e** *path\foldername* and press ENTER to encrypt just the folder *foldername*.

5. Open My Computer and look at the attributes for the two files and the folder. When you are done looking at these files and this folder, close Windows Explorer.

TIP

Encrypted folders and files have their names in green in Windows Explorer.

6. Type **cipher /d /s:***path/foldername* **/a** and press ENTER to decrypt both the folder and the file it contains, as shown in Figure 9-8.

7. Type **Exit** and press ENTER to close the command prompt and then open My Computer to check out the attributes on the files and folder you have been using.

Test File Encryption

A you saw in Step 7 under the earlier section "Encrypt a File from Windows Explorer," when you try to open a file encrypted by another user, it looks like it's going to open, and then this little message appears:

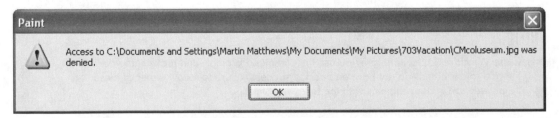

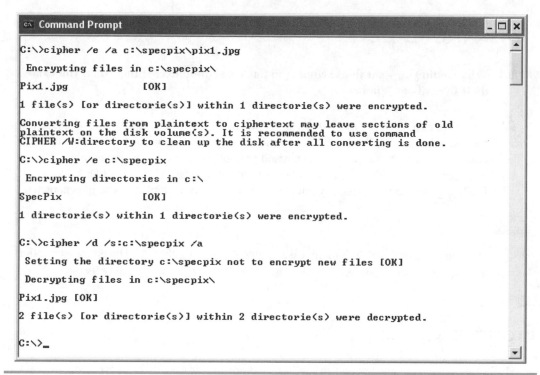

Figure 9-8 Encrypting a file, then a folder, and then decrypting them both

This is purposely understated—"one of those little access problems; call the network administrator and she'll work it out." If access is appropriate, the recovery agent administrator can solve the problem and no one is offended.

Okay, what about copying the file to a non–Windows XP NTFS file system, such as a Windows 98 FAT32 machine on the network? The file is no longer encrypted when you do that, correct? Try it, first while logged on as the one who encrypted the file. Everything will work as it is supposed to—you will get a warning message, and if you go ahead, the file will be copied and will no longer be encrypted. Then, log off and log back on again as someone else and try copying the file. Once more, it looks like it's going to work, and then another little message appears:

Ask the Expert

Q: Why would you want to use command line encryption/decryption when you can do it so easily in Windows?

A: There are two reasons. One is that you might not be able to get into Windows, and the second is that in Windows you can encrypt only one file or one folder (plus its contents) at a time, but from the command prompt you can encrypt any number in one command by either listing the objects or using wildcard characters like *.doc or file??.jpg, where * replaces any number of characters and ? replaces a single character.

This too is understated, and in my case, nothing was using the file. The entire encryption system is meant to be unobtrusive, remaining in the background while doing its job.

Progress Check

1. If the person who encrypts a file leaves the company, can the file be decrypted, and if so, how?

2. What method is used to encrypt files and folders?

3. What are two ways to encrypt a file?

---

1. An encrypted file or folder can be opened only by the person who encrypted it or the recovery agent administrator.

2. Files and folders are encrypted with the Encrypting File System (EFS) using symmetric encryption or a private key in which the key to encrypt the file or folder is the same as the key used to decrypt the same file or folder.

3. The ways to encrypt a file include opening a file's advanced attributes and selecting encrypt, using the command-line cipher command, and dragging a file to an encrypted folder.

CRITICAL SKILL
9.4 # Understand Private/Public Key Encryption

The discussion so far in this module has dealt with securing computers and their contents and has been silent about securing the transmission of data among computers, using e-mail, or otherwise transferring information either within a LAN directly or using an intranet or the Internet. Yet, the need to extend a network to outlying parts of an organization and to customers and suppliers is very real and requires secure data transmission. Securing data transmission means the encryption of the information being transmitted so that it cannot be read and misused by those who don't have the ability to decrypt it. Encrypting information is probably as old as the human race and has really blossomed with the advent of computers. Data encryption has become so sophisticated that the U.S. government, worried that it won't be able to decrypt the data (can you imagine that!), hasn't until very recently allowed the better technology to be exported (everyone was getting it over the Internet anyway).

Several encryption schemes for securing data transmission are in use: private key encryption, public key encryption, and combinations of the two. The set of these three schemes and the technology and standards or protocols that surround them collectively is known as the *public key infrastructure (PKI)*. Windows XP has made PKI an integral part of the operating system. Windows XP has implemented all three encryption key schemes and fully supports them with Certificate Services.

Private Key Encryption

Private key encryption, or *symmetric cryptography* (which is also what is used with file and folder encryption, as previously discussed), is relatively old and uses a single key to both encrypt and decrypt a message. This means that the key itself must be transferred from sender to receiver. If this is done over the phone, the Internet, or even a courier service, an unauthorized person simply needs to intercept the key transfer to get hold of the key and decrypt the message. Private key encryption, though, has a major benefit in that it is much faster (as much as 1,000 times faster) than the alternatives. Private key schemes are therefore valuable in situations where you do not have to transfer the key or can do so securely—for example, for personal use such as data encryption, as just discussed, or sending information to someone that you first met face to face. Several private key encryption schemes are being used with the Internet, including the U.S. government's Data Encryption Standard (DES) and the private RC2 ("Rivest Cipher" or "Ron's Code" [for Ron Rivest] 2) and RC4, both from RSA Laboratories.

Public Key Encryption

Public key encryption, or *asymmetric cryptography,* was developed in the mid-1970s and uses a pair of keys—a public key and a private key. The public key is publicly known and transferred and is used to encrypt a message. The private key never leaves its creator and is used to decrypt the message. For two people to use this technique, each generates both a public and a private key, and then they openly exchange public keys, not caring who gets a copy of it. Each person encrypts their message to the other by using the other person's public key and then sends the message. The message can be decrypted and read only by using the private key held by the recipient. The public and private keys use a mathematical algorithm that relates them to the encrypted message. By use of other mathematical algorithms, it is fairly easy to generate key pairs, but with only the public key, it is extremely difficult to generate the private key. The process of public key encryption is relatively slow compared to private key encryption. Public key encryption is best in open environments where the sender and recipient do not know each other. Most public key encryption uses the Rivest-Shamir-Adleman (RSA) Public Key Cryptosystem, called RSA for short, developed and supported by RSA Laboratories.

Combined Public and Private Key Encryption

Most encryption on the Internet actually is a combination of public and private key encryption. The most common combination, Secure Sockets Layer (SSL), was developed by Netscape to go between HTTP and TCP/IP. SSL provides a highly secure and very fast means of both encryption and authentication.

Recall that private key encryption is very fast but has the problem of transferring the key, whereas public key encryption is very secure but slow. If you were to begin a secure transmission by using a public key to encrypt and send a private key, you could then securely use the private key to quickly send any amount of data you wanted. This is how SSL works. It uses an RSA public key to send a randomly chosen private key using either DES or RC4 encryption, and in so doing sets up a "secure socket" through which any amount of data can be quickly encrypted, sent, and decrypted. After the SSL header has transferred the private key, all information transferred in both directions during a given session—including the URL, any request for a user ID and password, all HTTP web information, and any data entered on a form—is automatically encrypted by the sender and automatically decrypted by the recipient.

Several versions of SSL exist, with SSL version 3 being the one currently in common use. SSL 3 is both more secure than, and offers improved authentication over, earlier versions.

Another combination of public and private key encryption is Transport Layer Security (TLS), which is an open security standard similar to SSL 3. TLS was drafted by the Internet Engineering Task Force (IETF) and uses different encryption algorithms than SSL. Otherwise, TSL is very similar to SSL and even has an option to revert to SSL if necessary. Both SSL 3 and TLS have been proposed to the World Wide Web Consortium (W3C) standards committee as security standards.

Encryption Keys and Certificates

The PKI in Windows XP and in general use on the Internet depends on digital certificates to issue, authenticate, and maintain encryption keys. (See "Certificate Authentication," earlier in this module, for a discussion of certificates and how to issue and use them.) To get an encryption key, you get a certificate, of which the key is a part. To authenticate the key, you use the certificate that it is a part of. The key is stored in a certificate, which is the means by which keys are maintained in an organization. Certificate Services in Windows XP provides all of these services.

CRITICAL SKILL
9.5

Implement Secure Data Transmission

You may be thinking that SSL and TLS sound great but also sound complex to use. In fact, both are easy to use, either across the Internet or internally in a LAN.

Implement Secure Internet and Intranet Transmissions

To implement secure Internet and intranet transmissions, you need a web server that supports SSL or TLS, such as Microsoft IIS 6, plus a supporting web browser, such as Microsoft Internet Explorer 6, both of which are included in Windows XP Professional (IIS is not available in Windows XP Home Edition). From the browser, to visit a web site that has implemented SSL or TSL, you simply need to begin the URL with **https://** rather than http://. SSL will then kick in, and without your even being aware that it's happening, the browser and server decide whether to use DCS or RC4, use RSA to transfer a private key, and then use that key and the chosen private key encryption scheme to encrypt and decrypt all the rest of the data during that session. The only thing that you see is a message saying you are about to begin to use a secure connection, similar to this:

Once you are connected using SSL, your browser will indicate that a secure connection is established. Netscape and Microsoft display an icon of a closed padlock in the browser's status bar.

NOTE

Even though the combination of public and private encryption is relatively fast, it is still significantly slower than no encryption. For that reason, it is recommended that you use SSL only when you send sensitive information, such as financial or credit card data, and not for an entire web site.

Implement Secure LAN Transmission

Although SSL can be used within a LAN and in an intranet, it requires a security server (which function IIS fulfills) and can get in the way of applications that are working across a LAN. The answer to this is *Internet Protocol Security (IPSec),* which works between any two computers over a network to supply encrypted transmission of information without a security server and without getting in the way of applications. IPSec is a part of IP and works below any applications; it therefore seldom interferes with them.

The IPSec Process   IPSec is almost totally automated, and once group policies are established for its operation, network users don't realize that their network communication is taking place securely. The process for establishing and carrying out IPSec is as follows:

1. Domain or local computer policies are established that specify what network traffic needs to be secure and how that security will be handled.

2. Based on the policies, IPSec establishes a set of filters to determine which network packets require secure transmission.

3. When IPSec receives from a sending application a series of network packets that require secure transmission, the sending computer passes this fact to the receiving computer. The two computers exchange credentials and authenticate each other according to IPSec policies.

4. Given authentication, the two computers work out an algorithm whereby each computer can generate the same private key without having to transmit the key over the network, again based on IPSec policies.

5. The sending computer uses the private key to encrypt the packets it is transmitting, digitally signs them so that the receiving computer knows who is sending the packets, and then transmits the packets.

6. The receiving computer authenticates the digital signature and then uses the key to decrypt the packets and send them on to the receiving application.

Setting Up IPSec   To set up and use IPSec, you need only establish or revise default IPSec policies. You can do that through the IP Security snap-in to the MMC with these steps:

1. Open the Start menu, choose Run, type **mmc**, and press ENTER. The MMC shell opens.

2. Open the File menu, choose Add/Remove Snap-In, click Add, scroll down, and double-click IP Security Policy Management.

3. Select whether you want to manage security policy for a domain or a computer, select which domain or computer, and click Finish.

4. Close the Add Standalone Snap-In dialog box and click OK to close the Add/Remove Snap-In dialog box. Open the Console Root and select IP Security Policies On [either] Local Computer [or] Active Directory, so that your MMC looks like this:

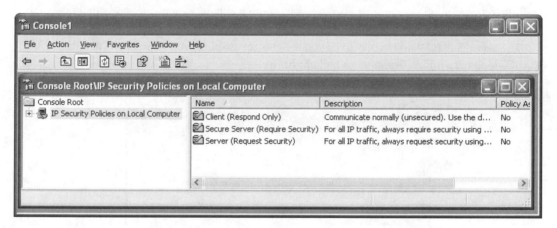

5. Right-click Secure Server and choose Properties. In the Rules tab, you will see a list of IP Security Rules, as shown in Figure 9-9.

6. Select the All IP Traffic rule and click Edit. The Edit Rule Properties dialog box opens. Look at each of the tabs and then return to the Filter Action tab.

7. Select Require Security and click Edit, which displays a list of security methods. Select each of these and click Edit again to select the particular security method you want for a given situation.

8. When you are done, click OK twice and then click Close twice to return to the IPSec console, where you can also click the Close button, answering Yes to save the console settings, giving the settings the name IPSec.

You can see that the Windows XP IPSec default is to require security on all IP traffic. This is a safe default; your data will be better protected. The negative side of this default is that the security negotiation between the computers, encrypting and decrypting the data, and the extra

Ask the Expert

Q: What makes modern encryption keys so hard to crack?

A: They are very sophisticated mathematical algorithms, and the hardest of them are quite long so that even a supercomputer working for a long time cannot break them.

bits to transmit all take time. It also uses a lot more bandwidth on the network. Only you and your organization can determine which is more important—time and bandwidth, or security. The point is that Windows XP gives you the choice, enabling you to make the determination of which networking aspect has a higher priority.

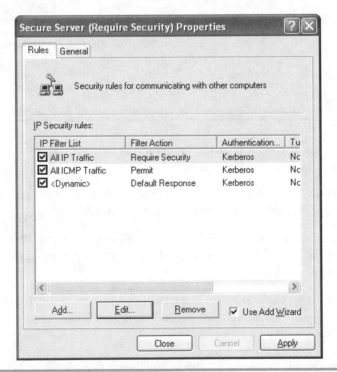

Figure 9-9 IPSec rules for filtering network packets

Progress Check

1. What are three encryption schemes for securing data transmission in Windows XP?

2. Which is faster and which is safer to use on the Internet, public key or private key encryption, and how is the resulting dichotomy handled?

3. What is the primary item needed to use public or private encryption keys?

Project 9 Set Up Security in Windows XP Professional

Use this exercise to review how security is set up and managed on Windows XP Professional computer in a network environment, including

- Setting up a local user account
- Requesting a certificate
- Sharing a folder
- Creating a group
- Assigning permissions
- Encrypting a folder

Step by Step

1. To create a new user account, open the Start menu, choose Control Panel, switch to Classic view if necessary, and double-click User Accounts. On a workstation not part of a domain, click Create A New Account, enter a username, click Next, click the desired account type, and click Create Account. Close User Accounts and the Control Panel. (In a domain, new users must be added to the domain controller.)

(continued)

---

1. The three encryption schemes for securing data transmission are private key encryption, public key encryption, and the combination of the two. The set of these three schemes is known as the public key infrastructure (PKI).

2. Private key encryption is much faster, but public key encryption is much safer. To get around this dichotomy, public key encryption is used to send a private key, which is used to send the data.

3. Both public and private encryption keys used in Windows XP and on the Internet depend on digital certificates to issue, authenticate, and maintain them.

2. To request a certificate, open your browser and enter the URL or address of the server with Certificate Services in the form http://*servername*/certsrv/. If requested, enter a username and password, and click OK for access to the server. Click Request A Certificate, choose User Certificate, and click Submit. When you get the certificate, click Install This Certificate, and click Yes to add it to the Root Store. Close your browser.

3. To share a folder, open the Start menu, choose My Computer, click Folders, open the disk and folders so that you can right-click the folder or file that you want to share, choose Properties, and click Sharing. If this is the first time network sharing has been done on this computer, go through the Network Setup Wizard; then click Share This Folder On The Network, give it a share name, and click OK.

4. To create a new group, open the Start menu, choose Control Panel, double-click Administrative Tools, and double-click Computer Management. On the left, open System Tools | Local Users And Groups and click Groups. Right-click the white space on the right and choose New Group. Enter a group name, enter a description, and click Add. Click Advanced, click Find Now, hold down CTRL while clicking the users to include in the group, click OK twice, click Create, and then click Close. Close the Computer Management window, and Administrative Tools.

5. To assign permissions, open the Start menu, choose My Computer, click Tools | Folder Options, open the View tab, scroll to the bottom of Advanced Settings, uncheck Use Simple File Sharing, and click OK. Right-click the file or folder whose permissions you want to assign, click Properties, open the Security tab, click Add, type the name of your new group or user, click Check Name, click OK, select the permission you want for the group or user, and click OK.

6. To encrypt a folder, with My Computer open, right-click the folder that you want to encrypt, choose Properties, and click Advanced, click Encrypt Contents To Secure Data, click OK three times, and close My Computer.

Project Summary

At a time when security is high on everybody's mind, it is good to know that Windows XP has a number of features and tools to enable you to keep your computer and data secure at several levels. Of course, it is up to you to implement and manage that security and to work closely with whoever is handling security at the server level.

Module 9 Mastery Check

1. What are three forms of authentication that are available in Windows XP?

2. What are three considerations to take into account when setting up usernames and passwords?

3. How can you tell if you are an administrator?

4. What are two factors that must be true in order to work with permissions?

5. What are groups and how are they used?

6. What are three requirements that must be met to encrypt a file or folder?

7. How are encrypted files different to work with from normal files for the person with the encryption key, and what does a person without the key see when he or she tries to open an encrypted file?

8. What are three rules to remember when copying and moving encrypted files and folders?

9. What are the differences between private and public key encryption, and how does the combination of the two work?

10. What do you need to implement secure Internet and intranet transmissions?

Module 10

Managing a Windows XP System

One of Windows XP's greatest strengths is the variety of management tools that are available to control the many facets of the operating system. The purpose of this module is to look at the general-purpose tools, those that are not part of setting up, networking, file management, printing, communications, security, or multimedia. The discussion of these tools is broken into system management tools, disk management tools, and user management tools.

System management tools are those tools that facilitate running the parts of the operating system and the computer that are not discussed elsewhere. These tools include the following:

- The Control Panel
- The Task Manager
- The boot process

CRITICAL SKILL
10.1 Use the Control Panel

The Control Panel, which is shown in Classic view in Figure 10-1, has been a part of Windows for at least since Windows 3.1. It is a folder that holds a number of tools that control and maintain configuration information, mainly for system hardware. Control Panel tools are

Figure 10-1 The Control Panel in Classic view is a Windows management tool chest.

discussed in many places in this book. Here, we'll look at those that are not discussed elsewhere:

- Date And Time
- Regional And Language Options
- Scanners And Cameras
- Scheduled Tasks
- System

The other Control Panel tools are discussed in the modules shown in Table 10-1.

Control Panel Tool	Module
Accessibility Options	Module 3
Add Hardware	Module 14
Add Or Remove Programs	Module 14
Administrative Tools	Module 9 and later in this module
Display	Module 3
Folder Options	Module 3
Fonts	Module 5
Game Controllers	Module 14
Internet Options	Module 6
Keyboard	Module 3
Mouse	Module 3
Network Connections	Module 8
Phone And Modem Options	Module 6
Power Options	Module 3
Printers And Faxes	Module 5
Sounds And Audio Devices	Module 7
Speech	Module 7
Taskbar And Start Menu	Module 3
User Accounts	Module 9

Table 10-1   Control Panel Tools Discussed in Other Modules

Managing a Windows XP System

10

Before looking at any of the specific tools, open your Control Panel and look at the tools you have available. You may have slightly different tools than those shown in Figure 10-1, depending on the hardware and software you have and the components of Windows XP that you have installed. Open the Control Panel by opening the Start menu and clicking Control Panel.

NOTE

As has been mentioned in earlier modules, I believe that the Classic view of the Control Panel is easier to use, so throughout Part III of this book it will be the view that I use in all the discussions and exercises. If your Control Panel is not in Classic view, change it now by clicking Switch To Classic View in the tasks pane.

Date And Time

Date and Time

Date And Time is where those values are set for the computer on which you are working. You can open the Date And Time dialog box, which is shown in Figure 10-2, either by double-clicking the Date And Time icon in the Control Panel or by double-clicking the time in the notification area of the taskbar in the lower right of the screen. In the Time Zone tab, you can not only select the time zone you are in but also choose whether or not to automatically adjust for daylight saving time if you are in a time zone that adjusts for it. In the Internet Time tab, you can automatically synchronize the computer's clock with an Internet time server you choose.

Regional And Language Options

Regional and Language ...

Regional And Language Options lets you determine how numbers, dates, currency, and time are displayed and used on your computer, as well as the languages that will be used. When you choose the primary language and locale, such as French (France), all the other settings, including those for formatting numbers, currency, times, and dates, are automatically changed to the standard for that locale. If you wish, you can customize these settings by clicking Customize and going into the individual tabs for numbers, currency, time, and date, and customize how you want items displayed. The Languages tab lets you select the languages in which you will be typing and how you want to switch among them.

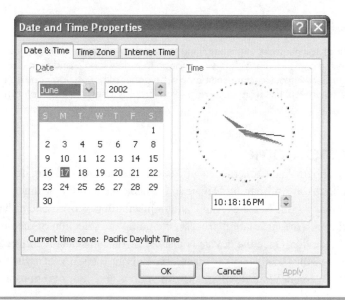

Figure 10-2 Setting the date and time

Ask the Expert

Q: I am multilingual and often work with several languages. How is that done?

A: First, select your dominate language in the Regional Options tab. Then, in the Languages tab, click Details to open the Text Services And Input Languages dialog box, where you should click Add. Select the Input Language, which will automatically change the Keyboard Layout, but you can change that yourself to anything else. Click OK when you are ready. You can select as many languages as you wish. This process works for European, Latin American, and African languages that come preinstalled in the English version of Windows XP. For Arabic, Hebrew, Chinese, Japanese, and other script and right-to-left languages, you must install the language. This is done by enabling Supplemental Language Support in the middle of the Languages tab of the Regional And Languages Options dialog box.

NOTE

The custom settings for numbers, currency, time, and dates will remain set only as long as you maintain the same locale. When you change to a new locale and then change back to the original one, your custom settings will be gone, although you can use a separate profile to prevent this from occurring. See "Employ User Profiles," later in the module.

Scanners And Cameras

Scanners and Cameras

Scanners And Cameras lets you set up and control imaging devices. When you click Add An Imaging Device in the tasks pane of the Scanners And Cameras windows, the Scanner And Camera Installation Wizard opens. This leads you through the installation process, including the selection of the port being used by the device. Once the device is installed, you can select it and a set of imaging tasks will appear in the tasks pane, as you can see in Figure 10-3. When you click Get Pictures, the Scanner And Camera Wizard will open with options and controls appropriate for the device you selected.

Scheduled Tasks

Scheduled Tasks

Scheduled Tasks allows you to set up certain tasks, such as performing a backup or disk defragmentation, on a periodic basis, and have those tasks carried out automatically. Double-clicking Scheduled Tasks in the Control Panel opens the Scheduled Tasks window, where, after they are identified, you see the scheduled

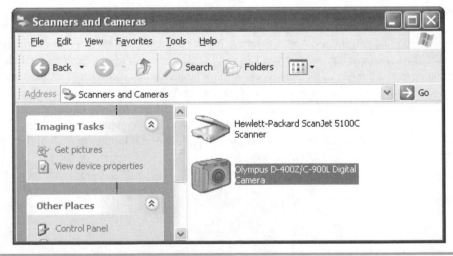

Figure 10-3 Imaging tasks for a digital camera

tasks. Double-clicking Add Scheduled Task in the Scheduled Tasks window opens the Scheduled Task Wizard, with which you can select the program you want to run from among all the installed programs that are either part of the operating system, such as Backup, or independent, such as Veritas's Backup Exec. Then, you select the frequency with which you want to run the program, the time of day and day of the week to do it, and finally the user name and password of the person authorizing the running of this program. You then are shown what you have scheduled. If you made an error, click Back and make the correction; otherwise, click Finish to establish the scheduled task. An icon for the newly scheduled task will appear in the Scheduled Tasks window. If you want to make a change in the task, double-click its icon, which opens a dialog box that allows you to change everything ranging from the program that is run to the schedule, date, and time.

System

System

Double-clicking System in the Control Panel opens the System Properties dialog box, the central place to establish, view, and change hardware settings. The System Properties dialog box can also be opened by right-clicking My Computer and choosing Properties. The first two tabs provide general and network identification, where you can change the computer name and join a workgroup or domain by clicking Change, or use the Network Identification Wizard to join a domain by clicking Network ID.

Hardware

The Hardware tab enables you to start the Add Hardware Wizard, which also can be started by double-clicking Add Hardware in the Control Panel. You can also open the Hardware Profiles dialog box, in which you can set up and manage multiple hardware profiles, such as those used with laptops and their docking stations. The Driver Signing option opens a dialog box where you can determine whether you want to be prevented from using, be warned about, or ignore files that are not digitally signed. Driver digital signing gives you assurance of who created the driver and other installation files, and that they have not been changed.

Device Manager

The Device Manager, shown in Figure 10-4, is the most important facility in System, enabling you to look at and configure all of your hardware in one place. You can immediately see whether you have a hardware problem; for example, the Audio Adapter in Figure 10-4 has a problem, as indicated by the exclamation mark icon. You can then directly open that device by double-clicking it, and attempt to cure the problem. In most cases, a Troubleshooter will lead you through a problem search. Two common problems that often can be cured with a Troubleshooter are a wrong or missing driver (the case in Figure 10-4), or incorrect resources being used, often because the correct ones weren't available. If you open the Properties dialog box for a device and look at the General tab, you will get a quick device status. The Driver tab

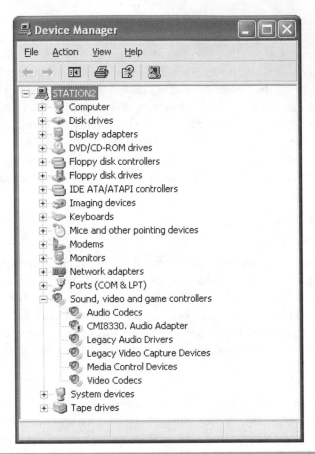

Figure 10-4 Access all hardware resources in the Device Manager.

will then allow you to reinstall or update the driver, and the Resources tab will show you where the problem is and allow you to select different resources (resources include interrupt request lines, or IRQs, and input/output ports). If you opened the Device Manager, close it to return to the System Properties dialog box.

NOTE

You can print a System Resource Summary that shows all the resource assignments (IRQs, DMAs, and I/O ports) on the computer by opening the Action menu and choosing Print.

Advanced Tab

The System Properties dialog box's Advanced tab provides access to the settings for four operating system features:

NOTE

If you have installed multiple user profiles, you will also have a Users Profiles section, which is discussed later in this module under "Employ User Profiles."

- **Performance Options**   Optimize performance between running applications or running background services, as are required in a file or print server; you also can determine the amount of disk space you want to set aside for temporary page files, the storing of memory on disk. The Visual Effects tab adds options to the appearance of Windows in addition to those we talked about in the Display Properties dialog box described in Module 3 in the section "Alter the Desktop."

- **Startup and Recovery**   Select the default OS to use on startup, how long to wait for a manual selection of that OS, and what to do on a system failure.

- **Environment Variables**   Add and change both user and system variables, such as Temp, that tell the OS where temporary items are stored on disk.

- **Error Reporting**   Determine whether to report operating system and/or program errors to Microsoft.

TIP

The Startup area is where you can change the amount of time the computer sits idle during startup waiting for you to pick an OS. You might want to change it to something shorter, such as five seconds.

System Restore

System Restore keeps track of the changes you make to your system, including the software you install and the settings you make. If some change or software installation causes the system to fail, you can use System Restore to very easily restore the system to what it was before you made the change. The System Restore tab allows you to turn off System Restore and to determine how much disk space to allocate to it. Module 14 will discuss this further.

Automatic Updates

Automatic Updates downloads and installs quick updates to Windows XP on a periodic basis, giving you the advantage of the latest fixes from the manufacturer. The Automatic Updates tab allows you to turn off Automatic Updates and to determine how automatic to make the downloading and installation. Module 14 will discuss this further.

Remote

The Remote tab allows you to turn on or off Remote Assistance and Remote Desktop. Remote Assistance allows someone to remotely log on to your computer and control it for purposes of assisting you or repairing the software. Module 14 will discuss Remote Assistance. Remote Desktop (available in Windows XP Professional only) allows someone, possibly yourself, to remotely log on to your computer and use it as a normal user, for example, to log on to your office computer from home. Module 11 will discuss Remote Desktop.

CRITICAL SKILL
10.2 Employ the Task Manager

Windows Task Manager allows you to look at and control what is running in Windows XP. You can start Task Manager, shown in Figure 10-5, either by right-clicking a blank area of the

Figure 10-5 Looking at the applications that are currently running

taskbar and choosing Task Manager or by pressing CTRL-ALT-DELETE and, if necessary, choosing Task Manager. The Applications tab shows you the application tasks that are currently running and allows you to end a task, switch to a task, or start a new task by using the Run command.

The Processes tab shows the processes that are currently loaded. These include the programs needed for the applications that are running, as well as the OS processes that are active. You can display a large amount of information for each of the processes, and you can select what you want to display by choosing View | Select Columns, as shown next. After you choose the columns you want to display, you can arrange the columns by dragging the column headers, and you can sort the list by clicking the column you want sorted. You can end any process by selecting it and clicking End Process.

The Performance tab, shown in Figure 10-6, shows you how the tasks being performed by the computer are using the CPU and page file memory, and what are the components of that usage. This information is particularly important in heavily used computers. You can see if either the CPU or memory (or both) is reaching its limit and what the system is doing to handle it. If you have multiple CPUs, you can see how each is being used, and assign processes to particular processors by right-clicking the processes in the Processes tab and clicking Set Affinity. You can also set the priority of a process by right-clicking it in the Processes tab.

The Networking tab, which you can see in Figure 10-7, allows you to see the percent usage of the local area network connection on the computer you are looking at. This is very useful in

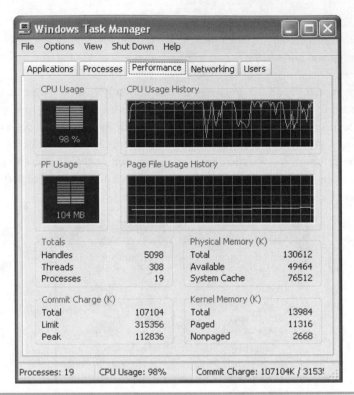

Figure 10-6 Watching how the CPU and page file memory are being used

analyzing a heavily used network. You can choose what is displayed at the bottom of the tab by opening the View menu and clicking Select Columns.

CRITICAL SKILL
10.3 Utilize the Booting Process

Numerous situations can cause a computer to not boot. To counter this fact, Windows XP has several features to help you work around the problem and to help you fix it. Among these features are the following:

- Return to the Last Known Good Configuration
- Use Safe Mode and other Advanced Options
- Use Automated System Recovery

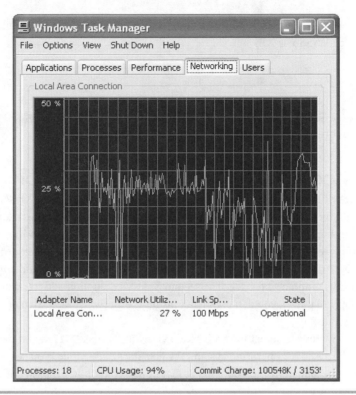

Figure 10-7   Analyzing network usage

Return to the Last-Known Good Configuration

If a computer doesn't successfully complete the boot process, and you have just tried to install a new piece of hardware or software or have otherwise changed the system, the problem often is due to the system's trying to load a device driver that doesn't work properly, or the result of some other system problem. You would normally learn of this problem late in the boot process. The fastest cure is to return to the last-known good configuration by following these steps:

1. Restart the computer, and press F8 when you see the message For Troubleshooting And Advanced Startup Options For Windows, Press F8. This message flashes by so fast that you might not see it. You'll find it immediately after the messages about booting from a floppy and/or CD-ROM.

2. Use the arrow keys to select Last Known Good Configuration, and press ENTER. The last-known good files will be used to start up Windows XP.

The last-known good files were saved the last time you successfully completed booting and logged on to Windows XP.

NOTE

The Last Known Good Configuration is not the same as (and much simpler in concept than) System Restore. It therefore works even if System Restore is turned off.

Use Safe Mode and Other Advanced Options

Safe Mode uses only minimal default drivers to start the basic Windows XP services, with the idea that, in that mode, you can fix the problem that's preventing the full startup. You start Safe Mode with the same steps used to start Last Known Good Configuration, except that you choose one of three Safe Modes: Safe Mode, Safe Mode With Networking, or Safe Mode With Command Prompt. Basic Safe Mode does not include networking and comes up with a minimal Windows graphics interface. The second Safe Mode option adds networking capability, and the third option places you at a command prompt; otherwise, these two options are the same as Safe Mode.

Use the arrow keys to select the Safe Mode you want, press ENTER, and then press it again to select the Windows XP operating system. As you start Safe Mode, you see a listing of the drivers as they are loaded. If the boot fails at that point, you are left looking at the last drivers that were loaded.

Just before opening Windows, you are reminded you are running in Safe Mode and asked whether you really want to do that or would rather use System Restore to return to the last-known good configuration. Click Yes to continue in Safe Mode. Once you get into Windows, you may not have a mouse available, so you'll need to remember the shortcut keys for important functions, as shown in Table 10-2.

While working in Safe Mode, the System Information window is very handy, as shown in Figure 10-8. Start the System Information window by opening the Start menu and choosing All Programs | Accessories | System Tools | System Information. Within System Information, Hardware Resources | Conflicts/Sharing, Components | Problem Devices, and Software Environment | Running Tasks are particularly of value.

In addition to Safe Mode and Last Known Good Configuration, the Advanced Options menu has the following options (these are in addition to the options Start Windows Normally, Reboot, and Return To OS Choices Menu, which do not need explanation):

- **Enable Boot Logging** Logs all the events that take place during startup in the file Ntbtlog.txt, located by default in the root (C:/) folder. The loading of all system files and drivers is logged so that you can see if one failed while it was being loaded. Boot logging is done in all advanced startup options except Last Known Good Configuration.

Function	Shortcut Key
Open Start menu	CTRL-ESC
Open context menu	SHIFT-F10
Close active windows	ALT-F4
Open Help	F1
Open Properties	ALT-ENTER
Search for files or folders	F3
Switch tasks	ALT-ESC
Switch programs	ALT-TAB
Switch tabs	CTRL-TAB
Turn on MouseKeys	LEFT SHIFT-LEFT ALT-NUM LOCK
Undo last operation	CTRL-Z

Table 10-2 Shortcut Keys for Use in Safe Mode

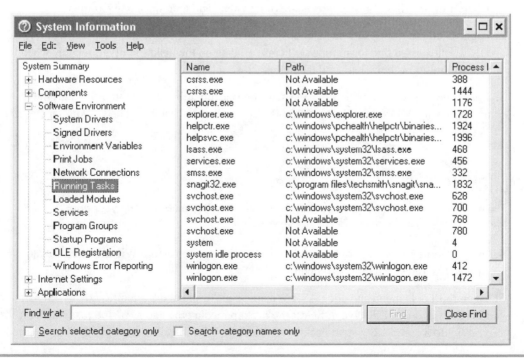

Figure 10-8 The System Information window is useful for correcting startup problems.

- **Enable VGA Mode** Sets the display for a minimal video graphic adapter (VGA) with 640×480 resolution using a known good default driver. All other drivers and capabilities are loaded normally. The VGA mode is also used in Safe Mode.

- **Directory Services Restore Mode** Restores Active Directory in domain controllers, which excludes all Windows XP computers, so it is not applicable.

- **Debugging Mode** Turns on the debugger and then boots up into the normal configuration for the computer. This allows you to work on scripts that might be getting in the way of a proper startup.

Use Automated System Recovery

The final way to repair a problem starting the operating system is to use Automated System Recovery (ASR) to replace all the operating system files. To do this, though, you need to prepare for it ahead of time by making an ASR disk and doing a special system backup, as well as a data backup. The ASR disk and the special system backup are done in the Backup utility. Create the ASR disk and do the backup here so that you have it ready. First, you need to format a floppy disk:

1. Insert a floppy disk whose contents are of no value, and then open My Computer.

2. Right-click the floppy disk icon, choose Format in the context menu, click Start, and click OK when warned that formatting will erase all data on the disk. Finally, click OK when told that formatting is complete, and then click Close.

3. Leave the floppy disk in its drive and start the Backup utility by opening the Start menu and choosing All Programs | Accessories | System Tools | Backup. The Backup Or Restore Wizard will open.

CAUTION

The process described here backs up only the system files. You must back up your data files separately. See the discussion of that in Module 4.

4. In the middle of the Welcome message of the Backup Or Restore Wizard, click Advanced Mode. The Backup Utility will open.

5. Open the Tools menu and click ASR Wizard. The Automated System Recovery Preparation Wizard will open. Click Next. Select the backup media type and filename that is correct for you (to do a complete system backup of Windows XP Professional on my system required

about 2.5GB), click Next, and then click Finish. The Backup Progress window will open, and you will see how the backup is going, as shown in Figure 10-9.

6. If you haven't already done so, when asked, insert a blank 1.44MB formatted floppy disk in drive A. In any case, click OK. After the floppy is created, you are told to remove and label both it and your other backup media containing the full system backup. Click OK when you have finished, and then click Close twice to close the Backup Progress dialog box and the Backup Utility window.

You use the ASR when you cannot boot your computer. To do so, you will need the floppy and system backup media you just created, as well as your Windows XP installation CD. With those items, restart the computer and boot from the Windows XP CD. Early in the text-mode process, press F2 when you see a prompt to do so. When requested, insert the ASR floppy and follow the instructions on the screen. Your system will be re-created as it is now, but you must separately restore your programs and data files.

Figure 10-9 Doing a system backup

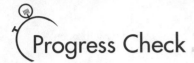

Progress Check

1. How do you switch to daylight saving time in Windows XP?

2. How can you easily determine if a piece of nonobvious hardware is not working?

3. How do you start up in Safe Mode or use Last Known Good Configuration?

CRITICAL SKILL
10.4

Manage the File System

Windows XP provides several different types of storage, as well as a couple of different file systems in an environment that is friendly to the end user. Within this environment, file system management provides the means to look at the health of drives, to change both the type of storage and the file system, and to add and remove both drives and partitions within drives.

Types of Storage

Prior to Windows 2000, there was only one type of storage, called *basic storage,* which allowed a drive to be divided into partitions. Windows 2000 added *dynamic storage,* which allows the dynamic creation of volumes. On a disk-by-disk basis, you must choose which type of storage you want to use, because you can use only one type on a drive. You can have both types in a computer that has two or more drives.

Basic Storage

Basic storage, which provides for the partitioning of a hard disk, is the default type of storage in Windows XP and is the type of storage used in earlier versions of Windows, Windows NT, and MS-DOS. Partitioning uses software to divide a single disk drive into *partitions* that act as if they were separate disk drives. There are primary partitions and extended partitions.

Primary partitions are given a drive letter, are separately formatted, and are used to boot or start the computer. There can be up to four primary partitions on a single drive. One partition at a time is made the *active* partition that is used to start the computer. You can put different

---

1. If you have left the default option in the Date And Time dialog box, the computer will automatically switch to daylight saving time for you. Otherwise, you have to manually change the clock.

2. From the Control Panel, open the System Properties dialog box, choose the Hardware tab, and click Device Manager. In the Device Manager that opens, look for an exclamation point on one of the hardware devices. Double-click that device. In the Device Status box, you can see what the problem is.

3. To boot into Safe Mode or use Last Known Good Configuration, you press F8 early in the boot process, use the arrow keys to select the option you want, and press ENTER.

operating systems on different partitions and start them independently. Because each partition is formatted separately, another use of partitions is to put data on one partition and the programs and operating system on another partition, allowing you to reformat the applications/OS partition without disturbing the data.

Partitions are usually created and changed while you are doing a clean install of an OS. In Windows XP, though, you can use the Disk Management pane (see "Disk Management," later in this module) to create a new partition if there is enough unpartitioned space, or you can delete a partition to create more unpartitioned space. If you delete a partition, you lose all of its contents and must reformat any new partition that is created.

Dynamic Storage

Dynamic storage uses a single partition spanning an entire disk that has been upgraded from basic storage. This single partition can be divided into volumes. *Volumes,* which in their simplest form are the same as partitions, may also have additional features. In addition to simple volumes, you can use volumes that span drives, are mirrored or contain the same information, or that spread information over several volumes to protect from a disk failure.

Unlike basic storage, dynamic storage can be changed in real time without rebooting the computer. Using Dynamic Volume Management (discussed later in the module), you can convert basic storage to dynamic storage and add, delete, and change the size of volumes, all without rebooting. You cannot convert to dynamic storage on either portable computers or removable storage.

File Systems

File systems determine the way data is stored on a disk; they are the data structure or format of the data. When you format a disk, you must specify the file system that will be used. In Windows XP, you have a choice of three file systems: FAT (file allocation table), FAT32, and NTFS (new technology file system).

FAT and FAT32 File Systems

FAT was the original file system used in MS-DOS and early versions of Windows through Windows 3.*x* and Windows for Workgroups. The initial releases of Windows 95 used VFAT (virtual FAT), and Windows 95 OSR2 (original equipment manufacturers, or OEMs, service release 2) and Windows 98 used FAT32. FAT is a 16-bit file system with a maximum disk partition size of 512MB and uses a maximum eight-character filename with a three-character extension. VFAT is also a 16-bit file system, but it supports disk partitions up to 2GB and allows long filenames of up to 255 characters. FAT32 is a 32-bit file system, allows disk partitions of over 2TB (terabytes or trillion bytes), and allows long filenames. In Windows NT and 2000, FAT partitions can go up to 4GB.

FAT, VFAT, and FAT32 store information using a fixed-sized increment of the disk, called a *cluster*. Clusters range in size from 512 bytes to 32KB, depending on the size of the disk partition, as shown in Table 10-3. Therefore, as the size of the partition increases, the minimum cluster size increases. A large cluster size can be very inefficient if you are storing a lot of small files. FAT32 made a big improvement in the minimum cluster size and is therefore a major benefit with today's large disks.

Because most files are substantially larger than the cluster size, a number of clusters are necessary to store a single file. The FAT has an entry for each file, containing the filename, the creation date, the total size, and the address on the disk of the first cluster used by the file. Each cluster has the address of the cluster after it, as well as the address of the preceding cluster. One cluster's getting corrupted can break cluster chains, often making the file unreadable. Some utilities occasionally can restore the file by several techniques, including reading backward down the cluster chain. The common end result is orphaned clusters, which can only be deleted.

Clusters can be written anywhere on a disk. If there is room, they are written sequentially; but if there isn't room, they can be spread all over the disk. This is called *fragmentation,* which can cause the load time for a file to be quite lengthy. As you saw in Module 4, utilities are available, including one in Windows XP, to defragment a partition by rearranging the clusters so that all the clusters for a file are contiguous.

Disk Partition	FAT and VFAT Cluster	FAT32 Cluster
0–31MB	512 bytes	512 bytes
32–63MB	1KB	512 bytes
64–127MB	2KB	512 bytes
128–255MB	4KB	512 bytes
256–511MB	8KB	4KB
512–1,023MB	16KB	4KB
1024–2,047MB	32KB	4KB
2–4GB	64KB	4KB
4–8GB		4KB
8–16GB		8KB
16–32GB		16KB
33GB and above		32KB

Table 10-3 Cluster Sizes Resulting from Various Partition Sizes

NTFS File System

NTFS was developed for Windows NT and contains features making it much more secure and less susceptible to disk errors than FAT or FAT32. NTFS is a 32-bit file system that can utilize very large (in excess of 2TB) volumes or partitions and can use filenames of up to 255 characters, including spaces and the preservation of case. Most important, NTFS is the only file system that fully utilizes all the features of Windows XP, such as encryption.

One of the most important features of NTFS is that it provides file- and folder-level security, whereas FAT and FAT32 do not. This means that with FAT or FAT32, if someone gets access to a disk, every file and folder is immediately available. With NTFS, each file and folder has an *access control list (ACL),* which contains the *security identifiers (SIDs)* of the users and groups that are permitted to access the file.

The sum of all this is that NTFS is strongly recommended. The only situations in which you would not want to use NTFS are if your software requires FAT or FAT32, or if you want to dual-boot with an older operating system that requires FAT or FAT32.

Convert a FAT or FAT32 Drive to NTFS

Normally, you would convert a drive from FAT or FAT32 to NTFS while you are installing Windows XP. Module 13 has instructions to do that. You can also convert a FAT or FAT32 partition, volume, or drive at any other time in either of two ways:

- By formatting the partition, volume, or drive

- By running the program Convert.exe

Formatting deletes everything on the partition, volume, or drive. Using Convert.exe preserves the partition, volume, or drive. Use the following instructions to use Convert.exe.

NOTE

Many of the steps in this module require that you be logged on either as the Administrator or as someone with Administrator permissions.

1. Open the Start menu and choose All Programs | Accessories | Command Prompt. The Command Prompt window opens.

2. At the command prompt, type **convert** *drive:* **/fs:ntfs** and press ENTER, where *drive* is the drive letter of the partition, volume, or drive that you want converted. If you would like to see a list of the files that are being converted, you can add /v after /fs:ntfs and a space. The partition, volume, or drive will be converted.

3. When you see Conversion Complete, at the command prompt, type **Exit** and press ENTER.

Convert.exe has only three switches:

● **/fs:ntfs**   Specifies a file system conversion to NTFS.

● **/v**   Specifies verbose mode, which displays all the files being converted.

● **/nametable:*filename*.log**   Creates a log in the root directory of the filenames that are converted.

The only way to return a partition, volume, or drive to FAT or FAT32 after converting it to NTFS is to reformat it.

Disk Management

Disk Management provides a means for managing both local and remote network drives, including partitioning. Disk management is handled by the Disk Management pane of the Computer Management window. Use the following steps to open Disk Management:

1. Open the Start menu, click Control Panel, double-click Administrative Tools, and then double-click Computer Management. The Computer Management window opens.

2. Open Storage in the left pane and click Disk Management. The Disk Management pane appears, as shown in Figure 10-10.

NOTE

If you use it often, you can add Administrative Tools to the All Programs menu by right-clicking the Start menu, choosing Properties, and clicking Customize. In the Advanced tab, scroll the Start Menu Items to the bottom; under System Administrative Tools, click Display On The All Programs menu and click OK twice. This gives you a flyout menu where you can directly select Computer Management.

Disk Management Pane

The Disk Management pane has two main sections: a character-based listing of partitions, volumes, and drives at the top, and a graphic display of the same objects at the bottom. Explore the Disk Management pane with the next set of steps:

1. Right-click an object in the character-based listing to open its context menu. From this menu, you can look at the contents in either My Computer or Windows Explorer; mark the

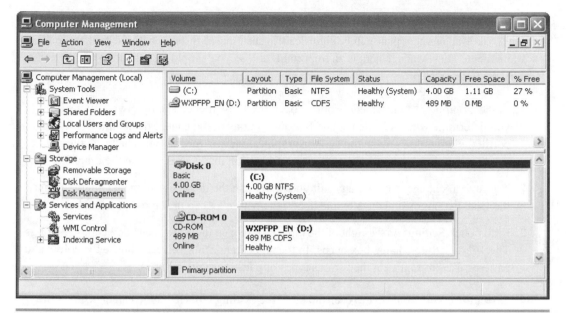

Figure 10-10 The Disk Management pane

drive, partition, or volume as active, if it isn't already so; change the drive letter and path; format or delete the partition or volume if it isn't the active or system partition or volume; open the partition's or volume's Properties dialog box; and get Help.

2. Right-click a partition or volume on the right of the graphic display at the bottom of the pane. You'll see a menu similar to that in Step 1 (depending on the type of partition, you may see some differences).

3. Right-click a drive on the left of the graphic display. You will see a drive menu that allows you to upgrade to a dynamic disk, if you click a basic disk that is not removable and you are in a desktop computer, not a laptop. This menu also allows you to open the drive's Properties dialog box and open Help.

4. Click the Action menu to open it. Here, you can quickly refresh the current status of the storage objects; rescan all drives, which is usually done only when the computer is restarted, and is used to display a drive that has been added or removed without restarting the computer *(hot swapping)*; display the menu for the partition, volume, or drive that is currently selected (All Tasks); and access Help.

Customize the Disk Management Pane

The Disk Management pane can be significantly customized through both the toolbar and the View menu. Disk Management is an important tool, so you should take the time to customize it by using these steps:

1. In the Computer Management window, open the View menu. The first two options let you determine what is in the top and bottom sections of the pane. The default is a list of partitions or volumes at the top and the graphical view at the bottom. The third alternative is a list of disk drives, which is the same information that is presented in the graphical view.

2. Try several changes to see if any suit you more than the default. A compact alternative has the Disk list on top and the Volume list on the bottom. Keep the layout you like best.

3. Either click Settings on the right of the toolbar or reopen the View menu and choose Settings. The View Settings dialog box opens. In the Appearance tab, you can choose the colors and patterns used to represent the various types of partitions and volumes.

4. Select the colors you want to use, and click the Scaling tab. Here, you can choose the way that disks and disk regions (partitions and volumes) are graphically displayed relative to each other. To show capacity logarithmically is probably the best choice if you have drives and regions of substantially different sizes.

5. Make the choices that are correct for you and click OK. Reopen the View menu and choose Customize. The Customize View dialog box opens. Here, you can customize the Computer Management window (called MMC in the dialog box, for Microsoft Management Console).

6. Try several changes to see if you like them, and configure the window the way that is best for you. When you have finished, click OK to close the Customize View dialog box.

NOTE

The Drive Paths option of the View menu will be discussed in "Dynamic Volume Management," later in this module.

Drive and Partition Properties

There are separate Properties dialog boxes for drives and for partitions. What many people have thought of as the drive properties are really the partition or volume properties. See this for yourself next:

1. Right-click a drive on the left side of the graphic view and choose Properties. The Disk Properties dialog box opens. Click and look at each of the tabs.

From the General tab, you can start the Troubleshooter; and from the Policies tab, depending on the type of drive, you can choose how to optimize it and whether to enable write caching. In the Volumes tab, you can see information about the partitions or volumes on the drive and open the Properties dialog box for a partition or volume.

2. Select a partition or volume in the lower part of the Disk Properties dialog box Volumes tab and click Properties. The Properties dialog box for the partition or volume opens, as you can see in Figure 10-11. This dialog box also provides some information, but unlike the Disk Properties dialog box, it is primarily a place to perform tasks on partitions and volumes.

3. When you have finished looking at the Properties dialog box for the partition or volume, click OK to close it.

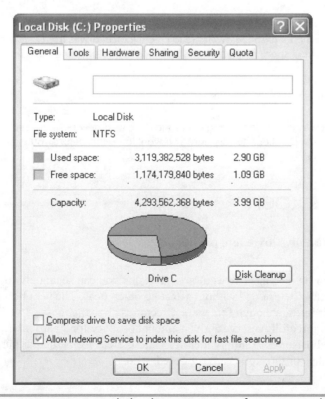

Figure 10-11   A partition's Properties dialog box gives you information and a number of tools to work on the partition.

NOTE

The Properties dialog box for a partition or volume can be opened by right-clicking a drive, partition, or volume in Windows Explorer and choosing Properties.

Use Partitioning and Formatting

The first step in preparing a disk for use is to partition it and then format it. Partitioning can be done only when there is unallocated space on the drive—space that is not currently used for an existing partition. If you have no unallocated space, then the only way to create a new partition is to delete an existing one (although there are third-party tools available such as Partition Magic that can create free/unallocated space from an existing partition). Therefore, start out looking at deleting partitions, then adding partitions, formatting them, adding logical drives, and changing drive letters.

TIP

Free space is the amount of space available to create logical drives from extended partitions. Unallocated space is space that is not allocated to anything.

CAUTION

Deleting a partition and then formatting either the drive or a new partition eliminates all information in the partition. Be very sure you want to do this before you execute the commands.

Ask the Expert

Q: Why divide a disk drive into partitions?

A: The best reason is to have areas of your disk that you can separately format, and therefore really "clean-up" without affecting other areas. The next best reason is for security purposes, although folders or directories do that almost as well now. Another reason is to forcefully reserve a given amount of space for a particular purpose. A not-so-good reason is to simply identify various areas for particular purposes, which is what folders or directories are supposed to do.

Delete Partitions   To delete a partition, as with the rest of the partitioning and formatting functions, you should have the Disk Management pane open in the Computer Management window. From that point, right-click the partition to be deleted and choose Delete Partition. You are warned that all data will be lost. Click Yes if you are sure you want to do that. The partition is deleted.

Add Primary Partitions   Adding a primary partition is a little more complex and has its own wizard. To add a partition:

1. Right-click an unallocated area of a disk and choose New Partition. The New Partition Wizard opens.

2. Click Next. Choose the type of partition you want, either a primary partition or an extended partition. You need to use a primary partition to start an operating system, but you can have only four primary partitions. If one of the four partitions is an extended partition, you can then divide it into up to 23 logical drives. After making the decision, click Next.

3. Select the size of the partition. The maximum is the size of the unallocated space; the minimum is 2MB. When you have selected the size, click Next.

4. Assign a drive letter. The drop-down list shows you the options available, which is the alphabet less the other drives already in the computer. There are two other options: you can make this partition a folder on any other drive that supports drive paths (most do), and you can leave the drive letter unassigned. Make your choice and click Next.

5. Choose how you want the partition formatted (if at all), the label to use, and whether you want to use file and folder compression, as shown in Figure 10-12. Then, click Next.

6. Review the options that you have chosen and use Back to correct any that are not what you want. When all the choices are the way you want them, click Finish. The partition will be created and formatted as you instructed.

TIP

One good reason to attach a new partition to an existing drive and folder is to increase the space available in an existing shared folder ("a share") so that users can continue to use an existing path for storing or accessing files.

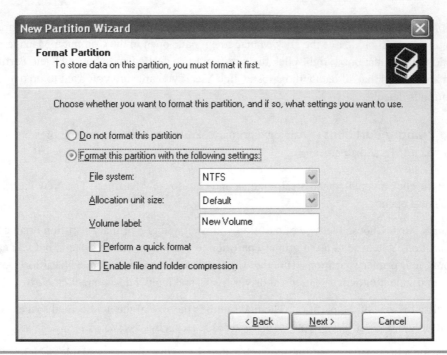

Figure 10-12 Formatting a partition

Format Partitions   Often, you'll format a partition when you create it, as described in the preceding section, but you can also separately format the partition, if either it was not done when the partition was created or you want to replace an existing format. The following steps show you how.

NOTE

If you try to format a partition that contains Windows XP, you'll get a message box that says you can't.

1. Right-click the partition that you want to format, and choose Format. A small Format dialog box opens, asking for the label, the file system, and the allocation unit size.

2. Make the choices that are correct for you and click OK. You will be warned that all data on the partition will be erased. Click OK. The drive will be formatted.

Add Logical Drives   To add logical drives, you must first have an extended partition, so do that first. Then, add logical drives, as follows:

1. Right-click an unallocated area of a disk and choose New Partition. The New Partition Wizard opens. Click Next.

2. Select Extended Partition and click Next. Specify the partition size and again click Next. Click Finish to actually create the partition. The partition will be created.

3. Right-click the free space in the new partition and choose New Logical Drive. The New Partition Wizard again opens. Click Next. The Select Partition Type dialog box opens, with Logical Drive as your only option.

4. Click Next. Enter the size of the logical drive and again click Next. Assign a drive letter (see the discussion on assigning a drive letter or path in the earlier section "Add Primary Partitions") and click Next.

5. Choose the way you want the logical drive formatted, click Next, review the choices you have made, and click Finish. The logical drive will be created as you described it and as shown in Figure 10-13.

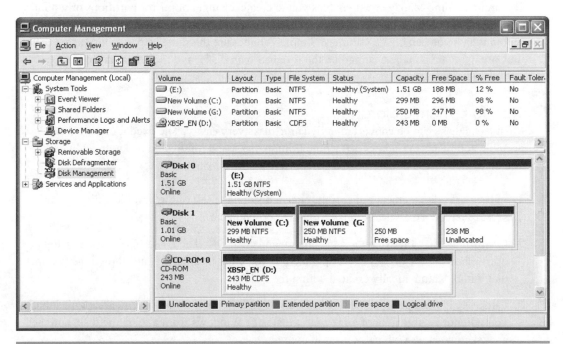

Figure 10-13 A new logical drive G: on Disk 1

6. Repeat Steps 1–5 for as many logical drives (up to 23) as you want.

Change Drive Letters   Changing a drive letter is similar to the previous functions:

1. Right-click the partition or logical drive whose drive letter you want to change, and select Change Drive Letter And Paths. The Change Drive Letter And Paths dialog box opens.

2. You can add additional drive letters and paths on existing drives, change existing drive letters, and remove (delete) existing drives and/or paths.

3. Click Add, Change, or Remove, fill in the necessary information, click OK, and click Close.

NOTE

You can have several drive letters and/or paths for a single partition or logical drive.

Dynamic Volume Management

Dynamic Volume Management enables you to create, change, or mirror partitions or volumes without rebooting, by using dynamic storage and disks. A dynamic disk has a single partition within which you can create volumes. Simple volumes are the same as partitions except that they are dynamic (can be changed on the fly), can span disks, and include additional types for advanced hardware.

Convert to Dynamic Storage

Most basic disks can be converted to dynamic disks very easily. The exceptions are disks on portable computers, Windows XP Home Edition disks, and removable disks. In addition, the disk must have 1MB of unallocated space. Here's how to convert:

1. In the Disk Management pane, right-click a disk on the left of the graphical display and select Convert To Dynamic Disk from the pop-up menu.

2. Confirm the disk that you want to convert, and click OK. The Disks To Convert dialog box opens showing the disk(s) to be upgraded. If you click Details, you are shown the volumes that will be automatically created within the disk.

3. Click OK if you opened the Convert Details and then click Convert. You are warned that you will not be able to boot a previous version of Windows from a dynamic disk, and then are asked whether you really want to upgrade.

4. If you in fact want to upgrade, click Yes. You are then told that the file systems on the disk(s) to be upgraded will be dismounted, meaning that the system will be restarted, and again you are asked whether you want to continue.

5. If you do want to continue, click Yes and then click OK to restart the computer. After restarting (may be a minute or two) you get a message that Windows XP "…has finished installing new devices…" and are asked if you want to restart the computer a second time. Click Yes.

NOTE

The only way to change a dynamic disk back to a basic disk is to delete all dynamic volumes, and therefore all files, and then right-click the drive and choose Revert To Basic Disk.

Create Volumes

You can create a new volume within the unallocated space of a dynamic drive. Do that with these steps:

1. Right-click the unallocated space of a dynamic drive and choose New Volume. The New Volume Wizard appears.

2. Click Next. The Select Volume Type dialog box is displayed. Accept the default Simple volume and click Next.

3. Select the drive on which you want the volume (or accept the default), enter the size of the volume, and click Next.

4. Assign a drive letter, and click Next. Choose how you want the drive formatted, and again click Next.

5. Confirm the steps you want taken, going back and fixing those that are not correct if necessary, and then click Finish.

Extend Volumes

Volumes that are created on a dynamic disk, but not those that were upgraded from basic disks, can be extended. Here's how:

1. Right-click a volume you want to extend and choose Extend Volume. The Extend Volume Wizard opens.

Ask the Expert

Q: I don't expect to need to change my partitioning very often (I don't use it); is there any other reason I should use dynamic storage?

A: No, not really. Dynamic storage enables you to do sophisticated partitioning and that is all. If you don't need partitioning, you don't need dynamic storage.

2. Click Next. Select the drive on which you want to extend the volume (or accept the default), enter the size of the extended volume, and click Next.

3. Confirm the steps you want to perform, and click Finish.

In the graphical section of Disk Management, this looks like two separate volumes, as shown by the two New Volume areas of Drive 0 in Figure 10-14, but they have the same drive letter and appear as one volume (New Volume (H:)) in the Volume section.

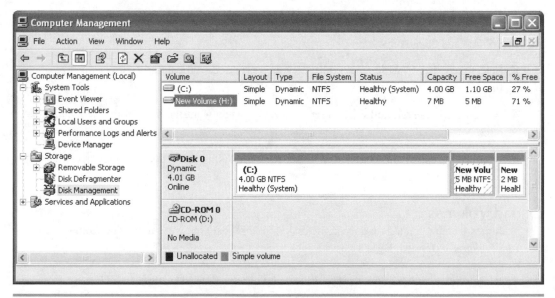

Figure 10-14 An extended volume looks separate, but it isn't.

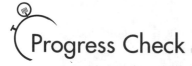

Progress Check

1. What are the two types of storage in Windows XP and what is their primary difference?

2. What is a reason for partitioning?

3. What is the purpose for extended partitions?

CRITICAL SKILL
10.5 # Manage Users

Managing computer users with their varying needs and peculiarities is an issue to which Windows XP has committed considerable resources. The key areas for this are the following:

● Using local user accounts

● Employing user profiles

Local user accounts were discussed in depth in Module 9.

Employ User Profiles

An individual who is the only user of a computer can tailor the desktop, Start menu, folders, network connections, Control Panel, and applications to his individual taste and needs. If several users are on the same computer, however, they could potentially upset each other by making those changes. There are two interrelated ways to address this: create local user accounts, as discussed in Module 9, and create user profiles that contain individual settings and that load when a particular user logs on to a computer.

When a new user account is set up on a Windows XP computer, a user profile is created automatically; and when that user logs off the computer, his or her settings are saved under that profile. When the user logs back on, his or her settings are used to reset the system to the way it was when that user last logged off. When Windows XP is installed, it establishes a default user profile that is then used as the default for all new users and saved with any

---

1. The two types of storage in XP are Basic storage and Dynamic storage. Dynamic storage allows you to change partitioning on the fly without rebooting, while basic partitioning is often done only when a disk is formatted.

2. Some reasons to partition are to have areas of your disk that you can separately format, for security purposes, to dual-boot a second operating system, to forcefully reserve a given amount of space for a particular purpose, and to simply identify various areas for particular purposes.

3. An extended partition allows you to divide a drive into more than the four primary partitions, up to 23 logical drives.

changes under the user's name when the user logs off. A user's profile is a set of folders, files, and information stored in the Documents and Settings folder on the hard disk. Figure 10-15 shows the folders within a user profile for a user named Martin Matthews. In the same figure, you can see a folder for All Users, which contains files, folders, and settings applicable to all users, and folders for two other users.

There are three types of user profiles: local user profiles, roaming user profiles, and mandatory user profiles.

Create User Profiles

Local user profiles are automatically created when a new user account is set up on a computer, and they are changed by the user making changes to his environment, such as changing the desktop or the Start menu. When the user logs off, any changes that were made are saved in the user's profile. This is an automatic and standard process in Windows XP and an integral part of a local user account. A local user account, though, is limited to the computer on which it was established. If the user logs on to a different computer, a new local user profile must be created on that computer. A roaming user profile eliminates the need to have a separate profile on each computer.

Figure 10-15 Set of folders representing a user profile for Martin Matthews

Creating Roaming User Profiles

A *roaming* user profile is set up on a server so that when a user logs on for the first time to a computer on the same network as the server, the user is authenticated by the server and his complete user profile is sent down to the computer, where it is saved as a local user profile. When the user logs off the computer, any changes that he made to the settings in the profile are saved both on the computer and on the server. The next time he logs on to the computer, his profile there is compared to his profile on the server, and only the changes on the server are downloaded to the computer, thereby reducing the time to log on.

The process of creating a roaming user profile has five steps and must be performed on a Windows 2000 or .NET server by a system administrator:

1. Create a folder to hold profiles.

2. Create a user account.

3. Assign the profiles folder to the user's account.

4. Create a roaming user profile.

5. Copy a profile template to a user.

Create a Profiles Folder   Roaming user profiles can be stored on any Windows 2000 or .NET server—they do not have to be on a domain controller. In fact, because of the size of the download the first time a user signs on to a new computer, it might make sense to not store the roaming user profiles on the domain controller. There is not a default folder to hold roaming profiles, so you must create one as follows:

1. Log on as an Administrator to the server where you want the profiles folder to reside, and open Windows Explorer (Start | Windows Explorer).

2. Open My Computer and click the Local Disk (C:) in the folders pane. Right-click in the right pane and choose New | Folder.

3. In the new folder's name box, type the name you want to give to the folder that will hold your profiles. This should be an easily recognized name, such as "Profiles." Press ENTER.

4. Right-click the new folder and choose Sharing And Security. In the Sharing tab, click Share This Folder, accept the folder name as the share name, and click Permissions. For the Everyone group, click Full Control, which will automatically check the Change and Read permissions.

5. Click OK twice to close the Permissions and Properties dialog boxes. Leave Windows Explorer open.

Create a User Account   Every user in a domain must have a user account in that domain. You have seen how to create a local user account in Module 9. Here are the steps to do it in a domain:

1. While still logged on as an Administrator on the server, open the Start menu and click Administrative Tools | Active Directory Users And Computers.

2. Open the domain within which you want to create the account, and then open Users. Scan the existing users to make sure the new user is not already a user.

3. Open the Action menu and choose New | User. The New Object – User dialog box will open. Enter the user's name and logon name and click Next.

4. Enter the user's password, choose how soon the password must change, and click Next. Review the settings that you have made. If you want to change any of them, click Back and make the changes. When you are happy with the settings, click Finish.

For the purpose of these exercises, make a total of three new accounts: one that will have a regular roaming profile, one that will have a preconfigured roaming profile, and one that will be a template for the preconfigured profile. Leave the Active Directory Users And Computers window open when you have finished.

NOTE

In addition to using the Action menu, you can select New | User from the context menu opened by right-clicking either Users in the Folders or left pane, or the white space in the Details or right pane.

Assign the Profiles Folder to a User's Account   To utilize a roaming profile, the user's account must specify that her profile is stored in the profiles folder that you established earlier. Otherwise, Windows XP will look in the Documents And Settings folder of the computer the user is logging on to. The following steps show how to assign the profiles folder to a user's account:

1. In the Users folder in which you added the new users, right-click one of the new users that you added and choose Properties. The user's Properties dialog box opens.

2. Click the Profile tab. In the Profile Path text box, type **\\servername\foldername\ logonname**. For example, if the server name on which the profile is stored is Server1, the folder is Profiles, and the logon name is Marty, then you would type **\\Server1\ Profiles\Marty**, like this:

Martin S. Matthews Properties   ? X

Member Of	Dial-in	Environment	Sessions
Remote control	Terminal Services Profile		COM+
General	Address	Account	Profile	Telephones	Organization

User profile

Profile path: \\Server1\Profiles\Marty

Logon script:

Home folder

⊙ Local path:

○ Connect: ▼ To

3. Close the Properties dialog box and repeat this process for the second and third users you created.

Create a Roaming User Profile

Once you have set up a shared Profiles folder on a server and specified in a user's account that the user's profile is in the specified folder on the server, then the actual user profile will be created and stored on the server simply by having the user log on to any computer within the domain. Try this with these steps:

1. Log on as one of the new users to a computer in the network. Make some changes to the desktop and the Start menu, and then log off that computer.

2. Look at the folder you created on the server to hold profiles. You will see a new profiles folder named after the logon name of the user in Step 1.

3. Log on as this same user to another computer in the network. The changes to the desktop and Start menu will follow you to this computer.

NOTE

To sign on to a Windows XP computer with a roaming user profile, you must change the sign-on procedure: Open the Start menu, click Control Panel, double-click User Accounts, click Change The Way Users Log On Or Off, turn off or uncheck Use The Welcome Screen, click Apply Options, and then close both User Accounts and the Control Panel.

The preceding technique is fine for someone to whom you want to give free rein to the system and who is knowledgeable about how to tailor it to his needs and desires. However, if you want to put limits on a user or on someone who does not have a lot of knowledge about how to change the system, you want to create a template profile and then assign it to one or more users.

To build a template, you simply log on the user account that you want to be the template profile, and then make the necessary changes that you want reflected in the profile. If the template will be assigned to several people, be sure that the hardware and applications are the same both among the group that will use the profile and on the computer you used to create the template.

Copy or Assign a Profile Template to a User

You can handle a template in one of two ways. You can "copy" it to create a new profile that you assign to a user, or you can assign the template as is to several users. See how both of these are done in following steps:

NOTE

The "copying" in this case uses a special technique and cannot use the Windows Explorer or My Computer Copy command. In addition, you cannot copy the user account to which you are currently logged on.

1. On the server, open the Start menu, click Control Panel, and double-click System. The System Properties dialog box opens.

2. Click the Advanced tab; in the User Profiles area, click Settings, select the template profile, and click Copy To.

3. In the Copy To dialog box, browse to or enter the path to which you want the template profile copied, and click OK.

4. To assign a template to several users on the server, open Start | Administrative Tools | Active Directory Users And Computers, and open the domain and users in the tree on the left.

5. Scroll the list of users until the first of the users who will share a profile is shown, and then double-click that user.

6. In the user's Properties dialog box, click Profile and enter the full path to the template profile that you created. Click OK to close the Properties dialog box, and close the Active Directory Users And Computers window.

7. Log on as one of the new users to one or more computers and make sure they work. One possibility if the logon doesn't work is that there is a typing error in the path of the profile in the user's Properties dialog box.

Use Mandatory User Profiles

A *mandatory* user profile is a roaming user profile that cannot be changed; it is read-only. This is particularly valuable when several users are sharing the same profile. When a user logs off a computer where a mandatory profile has been used, the user's changes are not saved. The profile does not prevent the user from making changes while they are logged on, but the changes aren't saved. A mandatory user profile is created by taking a roaming user profile and, in the folder with the user's name, renaming the hidden file Ntuser.dat to Ntuser.man. Here is how to do that:

1. In the server, open the Start menu and click Windows Explorer. Open My Computer | Local Disk (C:) | Profiles | *User Name*. Your Windows Explorer should look like Figure 10-16.

2. If you don't see the file Ntuser.dat, open the Tools menu and click Folder Options. Open the View tab, click Show Hidden Files And Folders, and click OK.

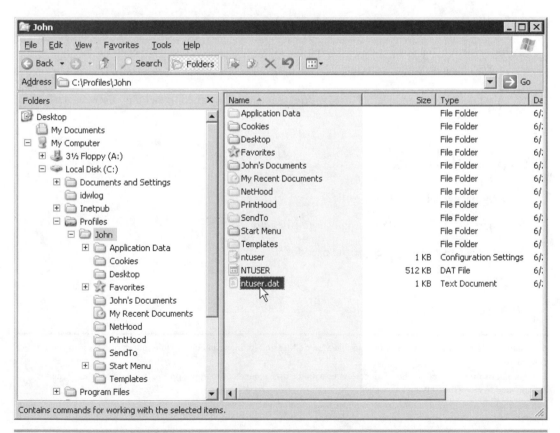

Figure 10-16 Change Ntuser.dat to Ntuser.man to make a mandatory profile.

Ask the Expert

Q: After reading all of the preceding information on user profiles, I'm still not sure how to relate user accounts to user profiles.

A: Think of a user profile as nothing more than the set of folders and information files with settings that are created as a normal part of creating a user account. If the person is using only a single machine, then you never have to separately deal with the set of files and folders dedicated to that user. But if that user wanted her folders and files to follow her from computer to computer, then her folders and files need to be available to all the computers she uses. First, to make discussion easier, call her "folders and files" her "profile." It is still an integral part of her account. Second, store this profile on a server so that each time she logs on to a computer, the computer can go out to the server and get the profile required to use the account.

3. In the details pane, right-click Ntuser.dat, choose Rename, type **Ntuser.man**, and press ENTER. Restart your computer.

You now have a mandatory user profile that can be assigned to as many users as desired.

Progress Check

1. Why have a roaming user profile?

2. Where are normal and roaming user profiles stored?

3. What is a mandatory user profile used for?

---

1. The reason for a roaming user profile is so that a user's files and settings can be available to him or her on any computer in a network.

2. A normal profile is stored on the client computer with the user account. A roaming profile is stored on a server and is downloaded to clients' computers as needed.

3. A mandatory user profile is used by several users who cannot change the profile.

Project 10 Review Windows XP Management Techniques

Use this exercise to review the management techniques discussed in this module, including

- Changing the time or date
- Adding another language to Regional settings
- Checking to see if your printer port is working properly
- Using Disk Management to delete, add, and format a partition
- Converting a drive to dynamic disk storage and adding a volume

Step by Step

1. Open the Start menu, click Control Panel, and then double-click Date And Time. Use the drop-down list boxes under the month and year to change them, and click the date to change it. Click the Time Zone tab and, if necessary, use the drop-down list to select the correct zone. Click the Internet Time tab and click Update now to download the correct time. Click OK to close the Date And Time Properties dialog box.

2. From the Control Panel, which should still be open, double-click Regional Settings And Language Options, click the Languages tab, and click Details. Click Add, select the input language you want, and click OK three times to close all dialog boxes. Leave the Control Panel open.

3. To see if your printer port is working properly, from the Control Panel, double-click System, click the Hardware tab, and click Device Manager. Open Ports (COM and LPT) and double-click Printer Port (LPT1). In the Printer Port (LPT1) Properties dialog box, under Device Status, it should say "This device is working properly" if all is well with the printer port. Click Close three times to close all open dialog boxes. Leave the Control Panel open.

4. To use Disk Management for partitioning, from the Control Panel, double-click Administrative Tools, double-click Computer Management, open Storage and click Disk Management in the left column, select a partition that can be deleted (CAUTION, all data will be lost), right-click it, choose Delete Partition, and click Yes to continue. Right-click the resulting unallocated area and choose New Partition. Work through the New Partition Wizard choosing the type of partition, the size, the drive letter, and the type of formatting. Then click Finish.

5. To convert to a Dynamic Disk, from the Disk Management graphical display, right-click a disk on the left of the display and select Convert To Dynamic Disk, confirm the disk that

you want to convert, and click OK. Click Convert, click Yes you really want to, click Yes, and then click OK to restart the computer. After restarting and waiting a bit, click Yes to again restart. Close the Computer Management window and also the Control Panel.

Project Summary

The management tools in Windows XP are very extensive and give you the ability to make major changes in how it looks and behaves, as well as how to look for and cure problems. Your task is to make sure you know what tools exist and how to use them. If you do that, they will be a significant asset.

Module 10 Mastery Check

1. How do you determine the format used to display numbers, currency, and dates, as well as the use of characters unique to a particular language?

2. If you are having a problem with a system, what is an easy way to go back to an earlier setup of Windows XP to see if that cures the problem?

3. How do you open the Task Manager, and what does it do?

4. What are two alternative ways to start your system and their uses when you have problems booting?

5. What are the three file systems available in Windows XP, and what are their differences?

6. How do you convert a FAT or FAT32 disk to NTFS?

7. What are the two types of partitions, and how do they compare?

8. What is the purpose of Dynamic Volume Management?

9. Can you change a dynamic disk back to a basic disk? If so, how?

10. What are the three types of user profiles, and how do they differ?

Module 11

Using Remote Desktop, Remote Access, and VPN

W indows XP includes a number of ways for you to work remotely—from another computer to your own office computer (Remote Desktop connection), from a home computer or laptop to an office server (remote access service, or RAS), or from a laptop over the Internet to an office server (virtual private networking, or VPN). The objective in all cases is to transfer information and utilize resources from a distance, not necessarily using a local area network (LAN) connection.

As you read this module, you'll see that Remote Desktop, RAS, and VPN are interrelated; and although the module's flow will be in that order, Remote Desktop could also go last because it can use either RAS or VPN. Here, though, we'll first look at Remote Desktop as a tool for remotely controlling a computer, and then look at RAS and VPN, which are both ways to access remote computers. Although RAS and VPN can be used for functions other than Remote Desktop, we'll come back in both sections and look at how Remote Desktop works with each access method.

Set Up a Remote Desktop Host

Suppose for a minute that you are in a negotiation and badly need to run a financial modeling program that is on the computer in your office. If you get up and go to your office, you will interrupt the negotiation and possibly harm it; but without running the modeling program, you can't tell if the concession you are being asked to make will be harmful to your company. The answer is to run the computer in your office from the negotiation using the laptop you brought with you. Remote Desktop allows you to do that.

Remote Desktop, with appropriate permissions, enables you to literally take control of another computer and do everything you could do if you were sitting in front of that computer. Remote Desktop can be run over a LAN, a dial-up connection, or the Internet—and in this module, you'll look at all three. In Remote Desktop, there is the computer you are sitting at and the computer you are accessing. Call the computer you are accessing the *remote host* because it is hosting the programs you want to run and is remote from you, and call the computer you are sitting at the *local client* because it is local to you and a client to the host. The host may or may not be a server in real life, so I am using the word "host" to not confuse the issue. In the next several sections, you'll look at setting up the host, then setting up the client, and finally using the Remote Desktop over a LAN. In later sections, you'll see how to use Remote Desktop with first a dial-up connection and then an Internet connection.

Set Up User Accounts for Remote Desktop

To use Remote Desktop, the host must have user accounts that are established for that purpose, and the user account must have a password; so the first step in setting up the account is to set up one or more such accounts. Second, there are both LAN-based hosts and Web-based hosts, so we'll look at setting up both of them.

NOTE

Windows XP Home Edition cannot be a Remote Desktop host, but it can be a Remote Desktop client.

The process of setting up a normal user account is not complex, as you saw in Module 9. Here are the steps for doing it for Remote Desktop:

1. Open the Start menu, click Control Panel, and double-click User Accounts.

NOTE

As I have mentioned in the previous three modules, in Part III of this book I am assuming that the Control Panel is in Classic view because it is a little faster to use that way.

2. Click Create A New Account, enter the name for the account (I'm using "Remote"), click Next, select the type of account you want, and click Create Account.

3. Click the new account, click Create A Password, enter the password, press TAB, type the password again, press TAB twice, enter a hint if you wish (anyone can see the hint), and press ENTER. Close the User Accounts window.

4. In the Control Panel, double-click Administrative Tools, and double-click Computer Management.

5. In the left pane, open Computer Management | System Tools | Local Users And Groups and click Users. In the detail or right pane, double-click the new user you just created, as shown in Figure 11-1.

6. Click the Member Of tab and click Add. In the Select Groups dialog box, click Advanced and then click Find Now to search for groups. Select Remote Desktop Users, click OK three times, and close both the Computer Management and Administrative Tools windows.

TIP

In the Computer Management window, with Users selected in the left pane, you can right-click the right pane, select New User, enter the user name and password twice, and click Create and Close to quickly create another user. You can then double-click the new user and repeat Step 6 to make it a member of the Remote Desktop Users group.

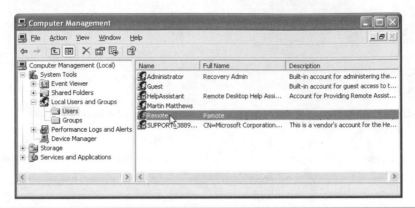

Figure 11-1 Selecting the user account to make a member of the Remote Desktop Users group

Set Up a LAN-Based Host

To set up the LAN-based host for Remote Desktop, use these steps:

1. Open the Start menu, click Control Panel, and double-click System. Click the Remote tab and, in the bottom Remote Desktop panel, click Allow Users To Connect Remotely To This Computer, as you can see in Figure 11-2.

2. If you are reminded that accounts to access Remote Desktop need passwords, click OK. Click Select Remote Users. The users that you added to the Remote Desktop Users group are displayed.

3. If you want to add more users to the Remote Desktop Users group, click Add, click Advanced, and click Find Now. Select the users to include by pressing and holding CTRL while clicking the users, and then click OK four times to close all open dialog boxes.

NOTE

The process in Step 3 adds users from the host computer to the Remote Desktop Users group. If you want to add users from other computers, you need to enter them in the Enter The Object Names To Select in the form *computername\username,* as shown next.

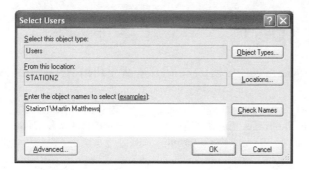

Set Up a Web-Based Host

The Web-based host requires that Windows XP Professional's Internet Information Services (IIS) be installed (IIS is also available on all recent Windows server products, but it is not

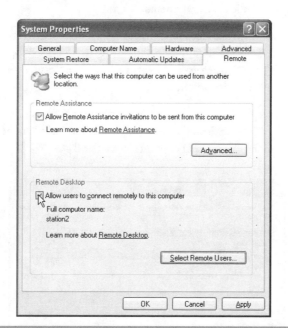

Figure 11-2 Turning on Remote Desktop

Ask the Expert

Q: Why would I want to use a web connection over the LAN when I can directly use the LAN?

A: You wouldn't. The reason to set it up here is to test it on the LAN so that you know you can come in and use it from the Internet.

available on Windows XP Home Edition). In the steps that follow, IIS will be installed first, followed by the Web-based Remote Desktop host:

1. Open the Start menu, click Control Panel, double-click Add Or Remove Programs, and select Add/Remove Windows Components.

2. Click Internet Information Services, click Details, select World Wide Web Service, and again click Details. If it isn't already selected, click Remote Desktop Web Connection and leave the Printers Virtual Directory and World Wide Web Service selected, as shown in Figure 11-3; click OK twice; and click Next.

3. Insert your Windows XP Professional CD when requested, click OK, and close the Setup Welcome window. When IIS installation is complete, click Finish, close Add Or Remove Programs, and close the Control Panel and remove the CD.

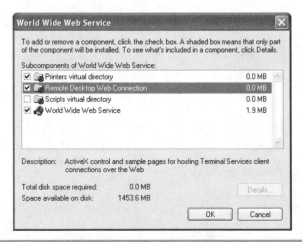

Figure 11-3 Install IIS and Remote Desktop Web Connection.

CRITICAL SKILL
11.2 Set Up a Remote Desktop Client

The Remote Desktop Connection program is probably already installed on the computer you will be sitting at while using this service, the local client. Although this is normally the case because Remote Desktop Connection is a part of the default installation, you should check on it and, if it is not installed, do so with these steps:

1. Open the Start menu, click All Programs | Accessories | Communications. You should see Remote Desktop Connection, like this:

2. If you do see Remote Desktop Connection, skip to Step 2 in the next section, "Use Remote Desktop in a LAN."

3. If you do not see Remote Desktop Connection, insert the Windows XP installation CD in its drive. In the Welcome window, click Perform Additional Tasks, and then click Set Up Remote Desktop Connection. The Remote Desktop Connection – InstallShield Wizard opens.

4. Click Next, click I Accept The Terms In The License Agreement, and click Next. The current User Name and Organization are displayed, as is the default Anyone Who Uses This Computer can use Remote Desktop Connection. Accept or change these as needed, click Next, and then click Install.

5. When the installation is complete, click Finish, close Setup's Welcome window, and remove the CD.

   You are now ready to use Remote Desktop.

CRITICAL SKILL
11.3 Use Remote Desktop in a LAN

Given that the preceding steps have been carried out as described, actually using the remote desktop is anticlimatic. Once again, there are both LAN-based and Web-based techniques.

LAN-Based Technique to Connect to a Remote Desktop

When you are sitting at the local client computer and connected to the host with a LAN, follow these steps to connect to a LAN-based Remote Desktop host:

1. Open the Start menu, click All Programs | Accessories | Communications.

2. Click Remote Desktop Connection. The Remote Desktop Connection dialog box opens like this:

3. Enter the name or IP address of the computer to which you want to connect. If you are not sure of the computer name, click Browse For More in the Computer drop-down list box. This lists the computers in your immediate domain or workgroup. If you want to connect to a computer outside your local domain or workgroup, you may be able to find the name by opening My Network Places | Entire Network | Microsoft Windows Network, which will show you the domains and workgroups that are available to you and within each of those the computers. If that doesn't work, see the discussion of using an IP address in the next section, "Web-Based Technique to Connect to a Remote Desktop."

4. When you have entered the computer name, click Connect. The Remote Desktop toolbar appears in the top center of the screen. Enter the user name and password for the Remote Desktop host computer and click OK. If someone is logged on to the host computer, you will get a message to that effect and be told that if you go ahead, the other user's Windows session will be discontinued and any unsaved data will be lost. If you choose to go ahead, click Yes; and if there is actually a user on the host computer, they will be given a brief warning and then summarily thrown off, all that user was doing will be lost, and you will be logged on. This allows you to use a computer that no one is currently using, but whoever last used it didn't log off. If someone comes along and tries to log on to the host computer, they will get a message that it is locked and only the current user or an Administrator can unlock the system.

Web-Based Technique to Connect to a Remote Desktop

The use of a web connection can be across a local intranet within an organization or across the Internet. The steps are really the same for making the actual connection; the major difference is in the security desired. For an Internet connection, you will probably want to use VPN, which is discussed later in this module. Here, we'll look at a simpler and less secure approach that might be used with an intranet:

1. Open the Start menu, click Internet Explorer, and enter the Uniform Resource Locator (URL) for the host computer whose desktop you want to take over and the name of the Remote Desktop web program to use, which in most cases is Tsweb. The form of the URL is http://*hostname*/tsweb, and the "http://" is frequently not required. The Remote Desktop Web Connection page will open, as shown in Figure 11-4.

2. Enter the remote host's computer name or IP (Internet Protocol, see the upcoming Note) address, select the screen size to use, and click Connect. Enter your User Name and Password and click OK. If you get the message that someone is currently logged on to the remote host, decide whether you can disconnect them and click the appropriate choice. You will be logged on as you were in the LAN-based technique.

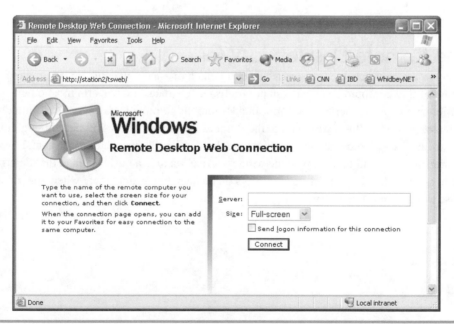

Figure 11-4 Connecting to a remote desktop using a web connection

NOTE

The Internet Protocol (IP) address is either temporarily or permanently assigned to every computer on the Internet or every computer on a LAN that uses the TCP/IP protocol. It is, of course, simpler just to enter the computer name; but when you are outside of your network—for example, at home—you will probably have to use the computer's IP address. You can find out a computer's IP address by opening the Start menu, clicking Control Panel, and double-clicking Network Connections. Right-click the connection you use to connect to your intranet or the Internet and choose Status. In the LAN Status dialog box, click the Support tab. You will see the IP address of the computer you are on, like this:

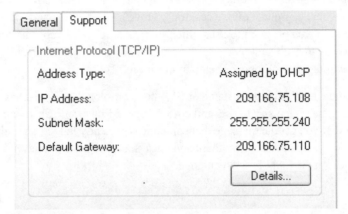

Put the Remote Desktop to Work

Once you are connected to the host, you can do much of what you could do if you were sitting in front of that computer. You can run programs, access data, and perform most other functions you could otherwise perform. In addition, the Remote Desktop toolbar, called the "Connection Bar," allows you to close the Remote Desktop window without logging out, so your programs will keep running, to minimize the window, so you can see the actual machine you are sitting at, and to maximize the window. Also, there is a push-pin icon that determines whether or not the Connection Bar is always on the desktop or only there when you move the mouse to the top of the screen.

The Remote Desktop also gives you the capability of transferring information between the host computer and the local client computer you are using. This means that you can print to a local printer connected to the client, the default; work with files on both the remote host and the local client in the same window, not the default; and cut and paste between both computers and documents on either one, also not the default. The local client resources that are available in a Remote Desktop session are controlled by the Remote Desktop Connection dialog box options. Use the following steps to explore these settings:

1. Open the Start menu and choose All Programs | Accessories | Communications | Remote Desktop Connection. The Remote Desktop Connection dialog box opens. Click Options and the box expands to give you a number of controls for Remote Desktop.

2. Click the Display tab. The default for a LAN is to use Full Screen and up to True Color (24 bit) if your computer can handle it, and to display the Connection Bar. If your LAN has particularly heavy traffic and is slow, you might want to lower the screen size and colors.

3. Click the Local Resources tab. As you can see in Figure 11-5, you can determine if you want sound brought to the client and the ability to use shortcut keys. Again, if you have a slow network, you might not want to do either of these. If you want to transfer information, even cut and paste, between the two computers, select Disk Drives; if you want to print on the printer attached to the local client, leave the default Printers selection; and if you intend to use a modem or other serial device on the local client, choose Serial Ports.

NOTE

To cut or copy and paste, you must have the local client's disk drives available, and therefore they must be selected in the Remote Desktop Connection dialog box Local Resources tab.

4. If you want to start a program when you open the Remote Desktop Connection, open the Programs tab, click the check box, and enter the path and filename of the program and the starting folder to use.

5. Click the Experience tab and select the connection speed you are using. This will determine which of the items below the drop-down list box are checked. You can change the individual items if you want.

6. Click the General tab. If you will use several settings, save the ones you just made by clicking Save As, entering a name, and clicking Save.

7. Finally, enter your password and click Connect.

Figure 11-5 Controlling the resources that are available

8. When you have finished using Remote Desktop, leave it in any of three ways:

   ● Click the Close button in the Connections Bar. This leaves you logged on, and any programs you have will remain running. If you restart Remote Desktop Connection with the host computer and no one else has logged on locally, you will return to the same session you left.

   ● Click Start | Log Off. This terminates your Remote Desktop session, and all programs are stopped. If you restart Remote Desktop Connection with the host computer and no one else has logged on locally, you will begin a new session.

   ● Click Start | Disconnect. This is the same as clicking the Close button in the Connections Bar.

Progress Check

1. What are the three ways you can access a remote desktop?

2. Can you use Windows XP Home Edition with Remote Desktop?

3. What essential element must a user account have to use Remote Desktop?

CRITICAL SKILL

11.4 Establish a Remote Access Connection

Remote Access Service, or RAS, provides the means for one computer to use a dial-up phone line to directly connect to another computer without using the Internet. The receiving computer, or host, can allow the calling computer, or client, to utilize the network to which the host is connected and to use Remote Desktop.

TIP

RAS is a foundation service behind VPN, and making sure that RAS is operating properly will significantly help you set up VPN. I therefore recommend that you set up RAS before attempting VPN.

Set Up RAS on the Host

Setting up RAS and use of the host's connection to the network has both hardware and software components. The correct hardware must be installed and operating properly with the correct drivers, and Windows XP must be configured appropriately.

---

1. You can access a remote desktop over a LAN, through the Internet or an intranet, or with a dial-up phone connection.

2. Windows XP Home Edition can be a Remote Desktop client, but not a host.

3. To use Remote Desktop, the user account must have a password.

Check RAS and Networking Hardware

RAS and networking hardware include, at a minimum, a modem and a network interface card (NIC). Assuming that this hardware has been installed in accordance with the manufacturer's instructions, it was most likely automatically set up in Windows XP either when the operating system (OS) was installed or when the hardware was installed and detected by the OS, as described in Module 13. Here, you should only need to make sure that the correct driver has been installed and that the device is operating properly. You can do both of these through the Device Manager and these instructions:

1. On the host computer, open the Start menu, click Control Panel, double-click System, open the Hardware tab, and click Device Manager in the middle right.

2. Open the local computer and Network Adapters, and double-click the NIC that you want to check. The Properties dialog box for that device will open, as shown in Figure 11-6.

Figure 11-6 Checking to see if a NIC is operating properly

3. If the device is operating properly, you should see a statement to that effect, as you can see in Figure 11-6. If so, click OK to close the Property dialog box. If the NIC is not operating, turn to Module 8 and review setting up a network.

4. When you have the NIC properly installed, close its Properties dialog box and open the Properties dialog box for the modem. Again, you should see an affirmative device status. Open the Diagnostics tab and click Query Modem. After waiting a few moments, you should see a list of commands and responses. It does not matter if you get a "Command Not Supported" message, as long as you get other normal-looking responses, such as you see here:

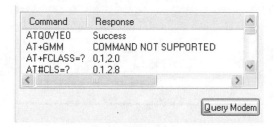

5. If the modem is operating properly, click OK to close the Properties dialog box. Otherwise, turn to Module 6 to isolate and correct the problem(s). When you are done, close the Properties dialog box, the Device Manager window, and the System Properties dialog box. Leave the Control Panel open.

   Although you may think that hardware is not a problem, it is wise to check it out and eliminate it as a possible reason RAS (and VPN) do not work.

Configure Networking on the Host

With your networking hardware installed and operating on the host, it is highly likely that networking itself is also operating. To eliminate any possibility of a problem and to make sure networking is properly configured, check it with these steps:

1. From the Control Panel, double-click Network Connections, and observe whether you have a Local Area Connection. If so, networking has been set up on the host you are looking at.

2. Double-click Local Area Connection. The Status dialog box should open and show Connected with a significant activity of bites sent and received, as shown in the next illustration.

3. Click Properties. The Properties dialog box should open and show the components set up for the connection. These should include, at a minimum, Client For Microsoft Networks, File And Printer Sharing For Microsoft Networks, and Internet Protocol (TCP/IP), as you can see in Figure 11-7.

4. Double-click Internet Protocol (TCP/IP) to open its Properties dialog box. What you see here will depend on the role of this computer in the network. At least one server must have a fixed or static IP address (with Use The Following IP Address selected).

5. Close Internet Protocol (TCP/IP) Properties, Local Area Connection Properties, and Local Area Connection Status, but leave the Network Connections window open.

6. If any of the preceding steps did not produce the expected results or some problem was observed, go back to Module 8 and review setting up a network.

NOTE

For RAS, and especially for VPN, the host needs to have a static IP address assigned by an ISP. In other words, you need an IP address that is acceptable across the Internet—not one, such as 10.0.0.2, that you assigned yourself.

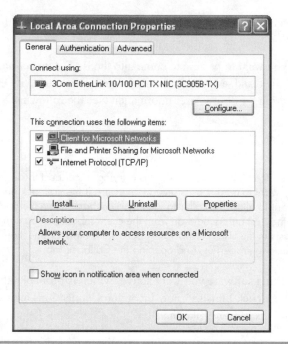

Figure 11-7 Checking the network connection properties

Set Up Remote Access Service in the Host

RAS is installed by default as a part of installing Windows XP Professional, but it is not enabled. So setting up RAS is simply enabling and configuring it. To do this, you must have administrative privileges and use these steps:

1. From the Network Connections window, click Create A New Connection. The New Connection Wizard will open. Click Next.

2. Click the bottom option, Set Up An Advanced Connection, which includes "setting up this computer so that other computers can connect to it." Click Next.

3. Accept the default of Accept Incoming Connections and click Next. Select the modem as the connection device and click Next.

4. Click Allow Virtual Private Connections, because eventually you will be doing that, and click Next.

5. Select the users you want to be able to come into the RAS connection. If you want to add additional users, click Add, enter the person's information, and click OK. When you complete selecting and entering the desired user information (see the following Note), click Next.

NOTE

RAS can be configured to call back a person who is trying to connect through a dial-up connection. You may want to do this as a security measure if the callback number is fixed, or you may want to allow the caller to identify a callback when the cost of the call is cheaper from the host outbound than from the client inbound. You can set this on a user-by-user basis in the User Permissions page of the New Connection Wizard by clicking a user, clicking Properties, and opening the Callback tab.

6. Select the networking software you want active (which is probably already selected) and click Next, and then click Finish. A new Incoming Connections icon will appear in the Network Connections window, like this:

Set Up a Dial-Up Connection in the Client

To use RAS, you must have a dial-up connection in the client. It is assumed that the client is also running Windows XP, either Home or Professional, and that you are using a modem connection that is already installed and running (Module 6 has instructions for installing a modem).

Quickly set a dial-up connection with these steps:

1. On the client computer, open the Start menu, click Control Panel, and double-click Network Connections. In the Network Connections dialog box that opens, click Create A New Connection to open the New Connection Wizard. Click Next.

2. Click Connect To The Network At My Workplace and then click Next. Select Dial-Up Connection and click Next. Enter a name for the connection and once more click Next.

3. Enter the phone number of the server including, if necessary, "1" and the area code, and then click Next. Depending on how the client is set up, you may be asked whether you want the connection for Anyone's Use or for My Use Only, and then you need to click Next.

Office

4. If you want a shortcut to this connection on the desktop, select that option and then click Finish. A new connection will appear in the Network Connections window and, if you chose it, on the desktop, as shown on the left (my connection is called "Office").

Use RAS

With a dial-up connection set up on the client and a remote access server set up and enabled on the server, you can use RAS with these steps:

TIP

Be sure to test this with the two computers near each other so that you can make any necessary adjustments to the settings before trying this at a distance. You will need two phone lines, and be sure to disconnect the client from the network.

1. Log on to the dial-up client with a username and password that can be authenticated by the RAS. Then, on the client, open the Start menu, choose Connect To, and select the dial-up connection you want to use. The Connect dialog box opens, as you can see in Figure 11-8.

2. Enter the appropriate username and password and click Dial. You will see messages stating that the number you entered is being dialed, that the username and password are being checked, that the computer is being registered on the network, and then that the connection is complete. The connection icon will appear in the notification area on the right of the taskbar.

3. Test the connection in the client by opening Windows Explorer; My Network Places | Entire Network | Microsoft Windows Network; and finally the domains or workgroups, computers, and shares that you want to access. If you can see these shares, the remote access connection is working. If you don't see the shares, make sure you have the appropriate permission for dial-up access.

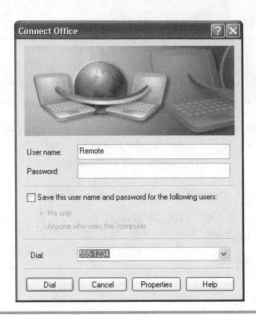

Figure 11-8 Connecting to an RAS host

4. Test the connection in the host by opening the Start menu and choosing Connect To | Show All Connections. In the Network Connections window, you should see 1 Client Connected, like this:

5. Keep the connection for a moment to test Remote Desktop; but when you have finished testing the RAS connection, you can terminate it by clicking the connection icon in the notification area on the right of the taskbar of the client and then clicking Disconnect in the dialog box that opens.

   With RAS fully accessible from a remote dial-up client, you know that all but the unique VPN components are fully operational on the two computers that you tested. If your dial-up to RAS connection did not work, look back at Modules 6 and 8, which discuss communications and networking in more detail.

Use Remote Desktop with RAS

With a RAS connection fully operational, you can open a Remote Desktop connection by first opening the dial-up RAS connection and then starting Remote Desktop. Try that next:

1. With the dial-up connection still functioning, open the Start menu. If Remote Desktop Connection is on the left of the menu, click it; otherwise, click All Programs | Accessories | Communications | Remote Desktop Connection.

2. Click Options. Because you are entering over a dial-up connection using a modem, you need to adjust the Remote Desktop settings to compensate for a low-speed line. Click the Display tab, change the Remote Desktop Size to half of full screen, and change the Colors to 256. Click the Local Resources tab and change Remote Computer Sound to Do Not Play. Click the Experience tab and change the Connection Speed to Modem (56 Kbps). Return to the General tab.

3. If needed, enter the computer to which you want to connect and your username and password, and click Connect. If you are reminded that your local disk drives will be made available, click OK. If asked again, enter your username and password; and if told that there is a user on the host computer, determine whether it is OK to disconnect them, and if it is, click Yes. The Remote Desktop window will open, and you can do the tasks you wish. It will be considerably slower than when you used the LAN.

Ask the Expert

Q: If I have a choice between a VPN/Internet connection and a direct dial-up connection to my office, which is better?

A: There are a number of answers to this, depending on what is meant by "better"—better speed, better cost, better security, better error rate, or better ease of use. If both services are using the same modem and phone line, then the speed is the same. If the dial-up connection requires a long-distance charge, then its cost is probably higher. A dial-up connection may have a slight security edge because far fewer people have access to the connection, although the security that is available over VPN is considerable. Also, the error rate is probably better in a dial-up connection because it is generally more direct. Ease of use is a toss-up. Only you can really answer this question, depending on the factors that are in place for you. Most people choose the VPN/Internet route because a dial-up connection for them means long-distance charges.

4. Open the Remote Desktop Start menu and choose Log Off and then click Log Off again to confirm it. Click the dial-up connection icon in the notification area of the taskbar, and click Disconnect. The modem connection will be dropped.

When you don't have an alternative means of communication, a dial-up to RAS connection is a sure, although slow, way to get the job done.

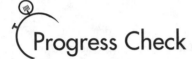

Progress Check

1. What hardware is needed for RAS?

2. To use RAS, what must be set up in the client?

3. With a dial-up connection, what changes need to be made to Remote Desktop?

CRITICAL SKILL
11.5 Implement Virtual Private Networking

Virtual private networking (VPN) uses an insecure public network to handle secure private networking. Most commonly, this means connecting to or extending a LAN using the Internet, and replacing leased lines and/or dial-up connections at a savings in cost. VPN allows a traveling worker to connect to and utilize an organization's LAN by connecting to and utilizing the Internet. The key ingredient in VPN is security. VPN allows one to use a public network with a high degree of certainty that the data sent across it will be secure.

You can think of VPN as a secure pipe through the Internet connecting computers on either end, as you can see in Figure 11-9. Information is able to travel through the pipe securely and without regard to the fact that it is part of the Internet. This concept of a pipe through the Internet is called *tunneling*. The secure "tunnel" is achieved by first encrypting the data, including all its addressing and sequencing information, and then encapsulating or wrapping that in an Internet "envelope" with routing and addressing information. The outer package can then weave its way through the servers and routers of the Internet without the inner information ever being exposed.

---

1. RAS requires that both the client and the host have a modem. If you want the client to be able to connect to the LAN at the host, the host must also have a NIC.

2. To use RAS, a dial-up connection must be set up in the client.

3. Because a dial-up connection is inherently slow, the Remote Desktop options need to be set for a slower service, including screen size, colors, audio, and desktop experience.

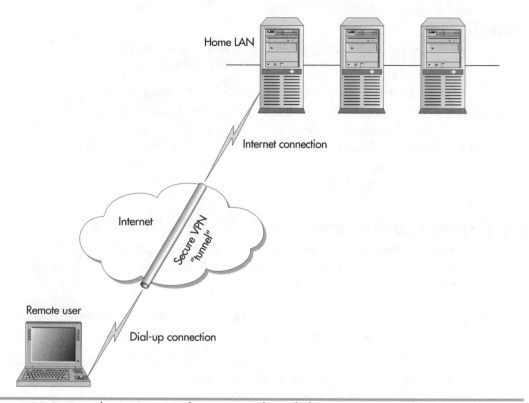

Figure 11-9 Virtual private networking, a pipe through the Internet

VPN replaces both leased lines between facilities and the need for long-distance dial-up connections. For example, before VPN, a company needed a leased line between the headquarters and a branch office in another city. With VPN, each office just needs a local, probably high-speed, connection to the Internet, which is then used with VPN to transmit information between the offices. In another example, before VPN, a traveling worker would make a long-distance call into a RAS host to connect to the company's LAN, incurring a long-distance charge. With VPN, the worker places a local call to an Internet service provider (ISP) to connect to the Internet, which is then used with VPN to connect to the company's LAN. In both cases, significant cost savings are achieved.

To set up VPN, you need to have both networking and Remote Access Service (RAS) set up and running. With that done, setting up VPN is just an enabling and configuration task. The preceding discussion of RAS looked at checking networking and setting up RAS. You may also refer to the primary modules (Module 8 for networking and Module 6 for communications) if you have questions about these topics.

NOTE

It is very important that you know RAS is operating correctly before setting up VPN. Too often, a problem in RAS is the cause for VPN to not operate correctly.

VPN, like RAS, has both client and host components. The most common setup, and the one described here, is for the client (assumed to be running Windows XP, either Home or Professional) to have a dial-up connection to an ISP and travel across the Internet to the host (assumed to be running Windows XP Professional), where a VPN termination is active and allows access to the LAN. See how this is done, first in terms of configuring the host and then the setup that is needed on the client.

Configure a VPN Host

VPN requires that you have an incoming connection (RAS) configured for VPN, which, if you followed the earlier instructions for RAS, you have already done. Use the following instructions to make sure RAS is properly configured for VPN:

1. Open the Start menu, click Control Panel, and double-click Network Connections. If you have an incoming connection, skip to Step 5.

2. Click Create A New Connection and click Next when the New Connection Wizard appears. Click Set Up An Advanced Connection and click Next.

3. Keep the default Accept Incoming Connections and click Next. Because the incoming communications will be over the Internet, you do not want any connection devices selected. Click Next.

4. Click Allow Virtual Private Connections and click Next. Select the users that will be allowed to connect and click Next. Accept the default set of networking software, click Next, and click Finish. An Incoming Connections icon will appear in the Network Connections window.

5. Double-click the Incoming Connections icon. Make sure that no devices are checked and the Virtual Private Network Allow Others To Make Private Connections... box is selected.

6. Make one final check of both the Users and Networking tabs, and then click OK.

Set Up a VPN Client

Setting up a VPN client is a relatively simple task. You need to set up a dial-up connection for the client to connect to the Internet and then a connection between the client and the VPN host.

In Windows 2000 and XP, there is an integrated and automated approach to these two tasks, but it is still done in two steps, connecting to the Internet and connecting to the VPN server.

Establish a Windows 2000/XP Dial-Up Connection

This is the standard dial-up connection done elsewhere in the book, so if you have a dial-up connection to the Internet already that you know works, you can skip this:

1. Open the Start menu, click Control Panel, and double-click Network Connections. Click Create A New Connection to start the New Connection Wizard. Click Next.

2. Click Connect To The Internet and click Next. Choose Set Up My Connection Manually as the method you want to use to connect to the Internet, click Next, choose Connect Using A Dial-Up Modem as the way to connect, click Next, enter the name of the ISP, click Next, enter the phone number of the ISP, and click Next.

3. If you get the Connection Availability dialog box, determine if you want the connection for Anyone's Use or for My Use Only and click Next.

4. Enter the user name and password needed for the Internet connection, confirm the password, determine if the user name and password can be used by anyone using this computer, accept that this will be the default Internet connection, leave on the default firewall, click Next, and then click Finish. The Connect dialog box will open, as you have seen in Module 6.

5. In the Connect dialog box, click Dial to try out the connection. If all your settings are correct, you should connect and get a notification balloon like the one shown next. If not, go back over the preceding steps and make the necessary corrections.

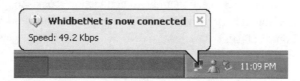

Connect to a VPN Host

The VPN connection is just another network connection:

1. If your Network Connections window is not already open, open the Start menu, choose Control Panel, and double-click Network Connections. In the Network Connections window, click Create A New Connection to start the New Connection Wizard. Click Next.

2. Select Connect To The Network At My Workplace and click Next. Choose Virtual Private Network Connection, click Next, enter the name of the company or connection, click Next, choose whether to automatically dial a connection using the dial-up connection established previously (assumed in these steps) or to use an existing connection, and click Next.

3. Enter a registered host name (such as osborne.com) or an IP address like 123.10.78.100 and click Next. If you get the Connection Availability dialog box again, determine if you want the connection for Anyone's Use or for My Use Only, click Next, and click Finish. The Connect dialog box will open.

TIP

See the Note earlier in this module in the "Web-Based Technique to Connect to a Remote Desktop" section on finding the IP address.

4. Click Dial to establish the dial-up connection. After the dial-up connection is established, enter the user name and password required by the VPN host, choose whether to save the user name and password for you personally or for anyone using this computer, and click Properties. In the General tab, you will see the settings you have already made.

5. In the Options tab, select both Include Windows Logon Domain and Redial If Line Is Dropped. In the Security tab, use Typical settings and check Automatically Use My Windows Logon Name And Password.

6. In the Networking tab, select PPTP VPN as the Type Of VPN, clear File And Printer Sharing For Microsoft Networks, and click OK. You should be connected to the VPN server and be able to browse the portions of the network for which you have permission. A balloon should confirm the connection and two connection icons should appear in the notification area on the right of the taskbar. The Network Connections window should look something like Figure 11-10.

If you did not connect, take heart; I didn't either the first time. There are a number of reasons why that may not happen. If RAS works, that eliminates many of the potential reasons.

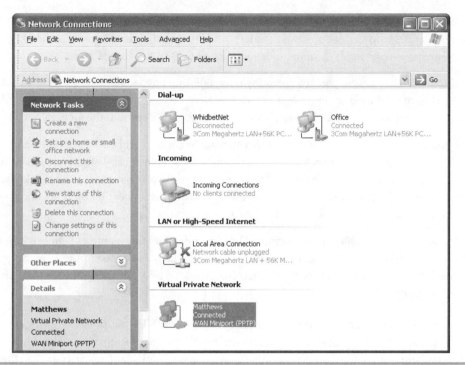

Figure 11-10 Both dial-up and VPN connections are visible in Network Connections.

First, look at whether the firewall is enabled on the host (it shouldn't be) by right-clicking the Internet connection, selecting Properties, clicking the Advanced tab, and making sure the check box is unchecked. Then look at the permissions that have been established for the VPN user in the host by opening Control Panel | Administrative Tools | Computer Management | System Tools | Local Users and Groups | Users, double-clicking the user name, opening the Member Of tab, and looking at the groups assigned to the user. Finally, carefully go over all the preceding steps looking for what you did differently.

Use Remote Desktop with VPN

With your VPN connection operational, you can open a Remote Desktop connection by first establishing that connection and then starting Remote Desktop. Try that by following the next steps.

1. With the VPN connection confirmed as shown in Figure 11-10, open the Start menu. If Remote Desktop Connection is on the left of the menu, click it; otherwise, click All Programs | Accessories | Communications | Remote Desktop Connection.

2. Click Options. Again, you are operating over a dial-up connection using a modem, so the Remote Desktop settings need to compensate for a low-speed line. See Step 2 under the previous heading "Use Remote Desktop with RAS." Return to the General tab.

3. If needed, enter the computer to which you want to connect and your user name and password, and click Connect. If you are reminded that your local disk drives will be made available, click OK. If asked again, enter your username and password; and if told that there is a user on the host computer, determine if it is OK to disconnect them. If so, click Yes. The Remote Desktop window will open for you to use.

4. When you have finished using Remote Desktop, open its Start menu and choose Log Off and then click Log Off again to confirm it. Click the dial-up connection icon in the notification area of the taskbar, and click Disconnect. The VPN and modem connection will be dropped.

There is a great deal of similarity between RAS and VPN, with two significant differences: RAS uses normal phone service, with its lack of security and its long-distance connection fees. VPN uses the Internet, with significant security precautions and no long-distance fees.

Ask the Expert

Q: VPN seems to be overly complex for what we have to do and our needs for security. Why should we use it?

A: VPN is both a security solution and a generally less expensive way to communicate, so you need to look at your security needs, as well as whether you can lower your communications costs. In terms of security, you need to look at not only whether disclosure of your data would be harmful, but also whether someone could change it and harm you.

Progress Check

1. What are the components of a VPN connection?

2. What is the source of the dollar savings inherent with VPN?

3. What should you set up first to make setting up VPN easier?

Project 11   Setting Up Remote Communications

Use this exercise to review setting up the remote communications methods discussed in this module, including

- A Remote Desktop host

- A Remote Desktop client

- A RAS host

- A dial-up client

- A VPN host

- A VPN client

Step by Step

1. To set up a Remote Desktop host, open the Start menu, click Control Panel, double-click System, click the Remote tab, and click Allow Users To Connect Remotely To This Computer.

2. Click Select Remote Users, click Add, click Advanced, and click Find Now. Select the users to include by pressing and holding CTRL while clicking the users, and click OK four times to close all open dialog boxes and then close the Control Panel.

---

1. The components of a VPN connection include a VPN client using a dial-up connection to an ISP and an Internet connection to the host, which has a VPN server.

2. VPN normally replaces leased telephone lines or long-distance dial-up service with much cheaper Internet service.

3. If you set up RAS first and get it running, it will eliminate a number of potential problem areas.

3. The Remote Desktop client is set up by opening the Start menu, clicking All Programs | Accessories | Communications. If you do not see Remote Desktop Connection, install it from the Windows XP installation CD. Otherwise, click Remote Desktop Connection.

4. Enter the name or IP address of the computer to which you want to connect and click Connect. The Remote Desktop toolbar appears in the top center of the screen. Enter the user name and password for the Remote Desktop host computer and click OK.

5. Set up an RAS host by opening the Start menu, clicking Control Panel, and double-clicking Network Connections. Click Create A New Connection. In the New Connection Wizard, click Next, click Set Up An Advanced Connection, and click Next. Keep Accept Incoming Connections, click Next, select the modem as the connection device, and click Next.

6. Click Allow Virtual Private Connections, click Next, select the users you want to be able to come into the RAS connection, and click Next. Select the networking software you want active, click Next, and then click Finish.

7. To set up a dial-up client, open the Start menu, click Control Panel, double-click Network Connections, and click Create A New Connection. Click Next. Click Connect To The Network At My Workplace, click Next, select Dial-Up Connection, click Next, enter a name for the connection, and once more click Next. Enter the phone number of the server, click Next, and then click Finish.

8. A VPN host is set up by opening the Start menu, clicking Control Panel, and double-clicking Network Connections. Click Create A New Connection, click Next, click Set Up An Advanced Connection, and click Next. Keep Accept Incoming Connections, click Next, select your incoming device, and click Next. Click Allow Virtual Private Connections, click Next, select the users that will be allowed to connect, and click Next. Accept the default networking software, click Next, and click Finish.

9. To set up a VPN client, first set up the dial-up connection to the ISP by opening the Start menu, clicking Control Panel, and double-clicking Network Connections. Click Create A New Connection, click Next, click Connect To The Internet, click Next, click Set Up My Connection Manually, click Next, choose Connect Using A Dial-Up Modem as the way to connect, click Next, enter the name of the ISP, click Next, enter the phone number of the ISP, and click Next. Enter the user name and password needed for the Internet connection, confirm the password, turn off the default firewall, click Next, and then click Finish.

10. Set up the VPN client connection itself from the Network Connections window by clicking Create A New Connection, clicking Next, selecting Connect To The Network At My Workplace, and clicking Next. Choose Virtual Private Network Connection, click Next, enter the name of the connection, click Next, choose to use the dial-up connection, and click Next.

11. Enter a registered host name or an IP address, click Next, and click Finish. The Connect dialog box will open. Click Dial; after the dial-up connection is established, enter the user name and password required by the VPN host, and click Properties. In the Options tab, select Include Windows Logon Domain and Redial If Line Is Dropped. In the Security tab, use Typical settings and check Automatically Use My Windows Logon And Password. In the Networking tab, select PPTP VPN as the Type Of VPN, clear File And Printer Sharing For Microsoft Networks, and click OK.

Project Summary

Being able to work remotely and use the information and computer resources at your home office can be very valuable. This module gives you three different means to do that, each of which is applicable under different circumstances. It is important to understand what to use in a given situation and then be able to quickly set it up. It is probably worthwhile practicing this setup so that when you really need it, the setup is down pat.

✓
Module 11 Mastery Check

1. How are Remote Desktop, RAS, and VPN related?

2. What happens to someone who is logged on to the host computer when a Remote Desktop user tries to log on to the same computer?

3. How can you find out what the IP address is for a computer?

4. In a default installation of Remote Desktop, can you cut and paste between the remote host and the local client?

5. What is the difference between disconnecting and logging off a Remote Desktop connection?

6. What are the essential steps to set up an RAS connection?

7. Are RAS and VPN related? If so, how?

8. What is the essence of the VPN concept?

9. Match up the services on the right that should be used in each of the situations on the left:

A. You travel frequently and need to connect to the office to get schedules, planning information, and recent pricing decisions, all of which you consider proprietary.	Remote Desktop
B. You live in the same telephone exchange as your office, so there are no long-distance fees for calls, and you want the same information as in A.	Remote Desktop over VPN
C. You run a branch office in another town, and one of your budget items is a $2,500-a-month leased phone line to the home office that is used solely for data communications.	Remote Desktop over RAS
D. You want to run some analysis programs on your office computer using a large company database from another office in the same building as your office.	VPN
E. Same situation as D, but you want to run it from your home as described in B.	VPN
F. Same situation as D, but you want to run it from the remote office described in C.	RAS

Part IV

Setting Up and Maintaining Windows XP

Module 12

Preparing for a Windows XP Installation

CRITICAL SKILLS

12.1 Review System Requirements

12.2 Check Hardware Compatibility

12.3 Make the Correct Installation Choices

12.4 Prepare Your Computer for Installation

12.5 Plan a Windows XP Migration

Setting up Windows XP is, on the surface, very simple: you put the Microsoft distribution CD in the drive or access the files over a network and follow the instructions on the screen. However, below the surface, the installation isn't necessarily that simple because this simplistic view assumes the following:

- Your computer meets the requirements of Windows XP.

- Windows XP supports the hardware in your computers.

- You know the installation choices that are best for you.

- Your computers have been prepared for an operating system installation.

This module helps you prepare for installation by looking at the system requirements for Windows XP, discussing what you can do to prepare for the installation, and then showing you a number of different ways of carrying out the actual installation.

Review System Requirements

Windows XP Professional and Windows XP Home Edition have the same significant hardware requirements. Review Table 12-1 to make sure your systems meet the minimum requirements.

System Requirement Notes

The requirements in Table 12-1 are generalized, and special situations do exist where different requirements apply. These special situations are noted in the following paragraphs.

System Component	Windows XP Professional and Home Edition
Processor	233 MHz Pentium minimum, 300 MHz recommended
RAM memory	64MB minimum, 128MB recommended, 4GB maximum
Hard disk space	650MB free space minimum, 1.5GB recommended
CD-ROM drive	If a CD installation, a CD-ROM or DVD drive is needed
Floppy disk drive	3.5-inch high-density, optional if CD is bootable
Video display system	SVGA (800×600) or higher resolution
Input devices	Keyboard and mouse
Network device	Compatible network card

Table 12-1 System Requirements

Processors

Windows XP Professional supports up to two processors in a single computer, known as *two-way symmetric multiprocessing (SMP),* whereas Windows XP Home Edition supports only one processor.

RAM Memory

Although Windows XP Professional and Home Edition will both run with only 64MB of memory, you can expect that performance will be limited and some functions may not operate satisfactorily. Memory is so inexpensive today that I would strongly recommend a minimum of 256MB of memory

Hard Disk Space

The amount of free hard disk space required is dependent on a number of factors. Among these factors are the following:

- The Windows components that are installed. Different components require different amounts of space and they are additive, so depending on what you choose to install, you will need varying amounts of disk space.

- The type of file system used. NT file system (NTFS) and FAT32 (file allocation table) are more efficient and are assumed in the minimum requirement. An additional 100–200MB of free disk space is required to use FAT.

- A network-based installation requires 100–200MB of additional free disk space to store additional files during installation.

NOTE

The space required during Setup (as shown in Table 12-1) will probably be greater than the space used after installation.

CD-ROM and Floppy Disk

A CD and a floppy disk are not required if a network-based installation is used. Also, a floppy disk drive is not required if the system can be booted from the CD-ROM drive.

Networking

A network card is not required if networking is not desired and a network-based installation is not used. If a network-based installation is used, it requires a suitable server to deliver the files.

12.2 Check Hardware Compatibility

After you have checked and determined that your system meets the minimum requirements for
Windows XP, you need to check to see if the particular brands and models of computers and
component devices are compatible with the operating system. You can do this with the Check
System Compatibility option from the Welcome screen on the Windows XP CD and by checking
the Hardware Compatibility List (HCL) at http://www.microsoft.com/hcl/. Also, the Readme
file in the root folder of the Windows XP CD contains late-breaking information on hardware
usage and other information you need before you install.

TIP

You can save a lot of problem-resolution time by checking the HCL and making any
necessary adjustments before installing Windows XP.

When you check your hardware compatibility, you need to know the makes and models of
all the devices in your systems, and when you do the actual installation, you may need to know
the settings on those devices. Even if you are fairly certain you know this information, it is a
good idea to take an inventory of your systems before you start the installation.

Note Much of this section of the module assumes that you have a running system with an
older version of Windows that allows you to look at the devices that are installed and to connect
to the Internet.

Take a System Inventory

There are two types of system inventory: a physical look at the devices, and an online look at
how the system sees them.

Physical Inventory

The physical inventory requires that you open the computer and identify the circuit boards,
disk drives, and other components. There are a great many types of computers, circuit boards,
and disk drives, so it is not possible to describe how to do a physical inventory. If you don't
know how, skip it, and the online inventory will have to suffice. If you do a physical inventory,
here are the topics you need to consider, along with sample responses in parentheses (see
"Online Inventory," next in this module, for a complete list of topics that you need to handle
with the system inventory):

TIP

If you have all the manuals and brochures or flyers that came with your equipment, you may be able to answer many of the physical inventory questions without opening the computer.

- Type of adapter card (network interface card, sound card, video adapter)

- Make and model of the adapter card (3Com Etherlink XL PCI, Creative Labs CT3930 Sound Blaster 32, Matrox Millennium II)

- Type and position of card slot (ISA, EISA, PCI, or AGP; 1st, 2nd, or 3rd slot)

- Settings on the adapter cards (interrupt request line, or IRQ; I/O port address; direct memory address, or DMA)

- Type, make, model, and size, if applicable, of disk drive (hard drive, IBM, DGHS-39110, 9.1GB; CD-ROM, Yamaha, CDRW6416SZ; floppy, Teac, 1.44MB)

- Type and position of disk drive interface (Small Computer System Interface [SCSI], position 0 through 7 or 15; primary or secondary Integrated Device Electronics [IDE], master or slave)

Online Inventory

The online inventory is done by recording information about your system that can be displayed on the screen or printed using your old operating system. The type and completeness of information that is available to you depend on the operating system you are using. In most cases, you get an initial startup message generated by the BIOS (basic input/output system) that provides a lot of information.

In Windows 98 or Me, you can get further information by opening the Start menu, selecting Settings | Control Panel, double-clicking System, choosing the Device Manager tab, clicking Print, selecting System Summary, and clicking OK. This gives you a comprehensive report of the devices in your system, the resources (IRQs, I/O ports, DMA, and so on) they use, and the types and sizes of your disk drives. The first page of this report for one of my computers is shown in Figure 12-1.

Ask the Expert

Q: I have a Plug and Play NIC and I don't see any switches or other way to change settings. How is this done?

A: The newer Plug and Play cards do not have settings on the card because they are all handled with software.

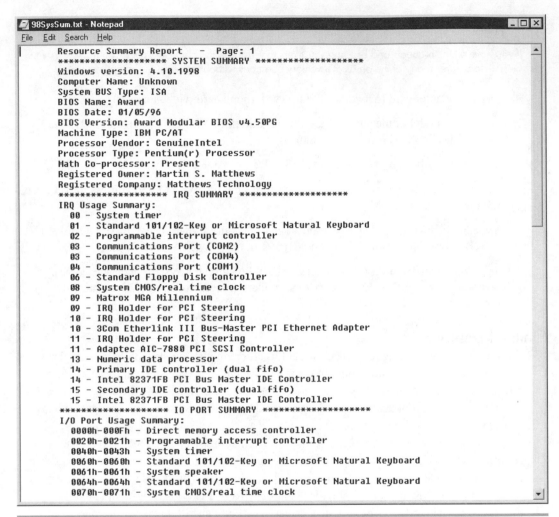

Figure 12-1 First Page of a Windows 98 Resource Summary Report

In Windows 2000 Professional, you can print a Resource Summary report similar to, and possibly an improvement on, the Windows 98 Resource Summary report. This report is available by opening the Start menu and selecting Settings | Control Panel | System | Hardware | Device Manager | View | Print. The first page of the report for my computer is shown in Figure 12-2.

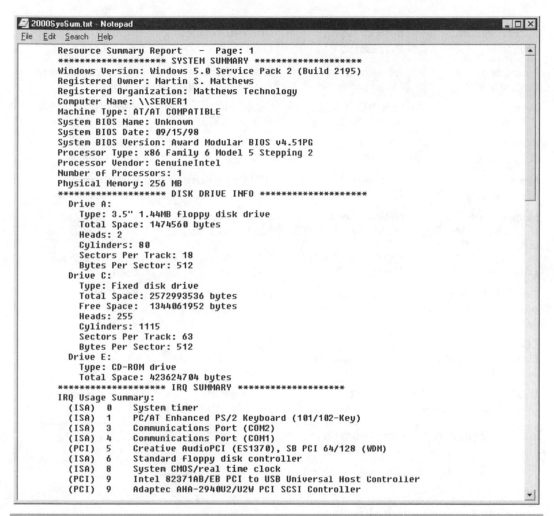

```
2000SysSum.txt - Notepad

File  Edit  Search  Help

    Resource Summary Report    -  Page: 1
    ******************** SYSTEM SUMMARY ********************
    Windows Version: Windows 5.0 Service Pack 2 (Build 2195)
    Registered Owner: Martin S. Matthews
    Registered Organization: Matthews Technology
    Computer Name: \\SERVER1
    Machine Type: AT/AT COMPATIBLE
    System BIOS Name: Unknown
    System BIOS Date: 09/15/98
    System BIOS Version: Award Modular BIOS v4.51PG
    Processor Type: x86 Family 6 Model 5 Stepping 2
    Processor Vendor: GenuineIntel
    Number of Processors: 1
    Physical Memory: 256 MB
    ******************** DISK DRIVE INFO ********************
      Drive A:
        Type: 3.5" 1.44MB floppy disk drive
        Total Space: 1474560 bytes
        Heads: 2
        Cylinders: 80
        Sectors Per Track: 18
        Bytes Per Sector: 512
      Drive C:
        Type: Fixed disk drive
        Total Space: 2572993536 bytes
        Free Space:  1344061952 bytes
        Heads: 255
        Cylinders: 1115
        Sectors Per Track: 63
        Bytes Per Sector: 512
      Drive E:
        Type: CD-ROM drive
        Total Space: 423624704 bytes
    ******************** IRQ SUMMARY ********************
    IRQ Usage Summary:
      (ISA)  0    System timer
      (ISA)  1    PC/AT Enhanced PS/2 Keyboard (101/102-Key)
      (ISA)  3    Communications Port (COM2)
      (ISA)  4    Communications Port (COM1)
      (PCI)  5    Creative AudioPCI (ES1370), SB PCI 64/128 (WDM)
      (ISA)  6    Standard floppy disk controller
      (ISA)  8    System CMOS/real time clock
      (PCI)  9    Intel 82371AB/EB PCI to USB Universal Host Controller
      (PCI)  9    Adaptec AHA-2940U2/U2W PCI SCSI Controller
```

Figure 12-2 First page of a Windows 2000 Resource Summary

The end result of both the physical and online inventory should be a system inventory form containing the information in Table 12-2 (example answers are in italics).

For your systems, you may need to add or remove fields from those shown in Table 12-2, but creating and using such a form will help you prepare for the installation of Windows XP.

System Name: *Station1*	System Type: *Workstation*	Domain Name: *Domain1*	Date: *4-5-2003*
Processor 1: *Pentium II 600*	Processor 2: *Model and speed*	BIOS & Date: *Award, 9-15-98*	Power Management: *Enabled*
Memory: *256MB*	Hard Disk 1: *SCSI-0, 20GB*	Hard Disk 2: *SCSI-1, 10GB*	Hard Disk 3: *Interface and size*
CD-ROM Drive: *SCSI-2, 32x*	Floppy Drive: *1.44MB*	Tape Drive: *SCSI-3, 20GB*	Other Drive: *DVD, CD-RW*
Mouse: *PS/2, Serial, or USB*	Keyboard: *PS/2, Serial, or USB*	SCSI Controller: *Adaptec AHA-2940*	RAID Controller: *Make and model*
Modem Card: *U.S. Robotics 56K Fax, ISA, COM 2, IRQ 3 I/O Port 3E8-3EF DMA – no*	Network Card: *3Com Etherlink III PCI, IRQ 9 I/O Port B800-B81F DMA – no*	Sound Card: *Creative PCI128 PCI, IRQ 5 I/O Port B400-B43F DMA – 1*	Video Card: *Matrox G200 AGP, IRQ 10 I/O Port 3B0-3DF DMA – no*
External Modem: *Make and model, Com 1-3, USB*	PCMCIA Slot 1: *Device, make and model*	PCMCIA Slot 2: *Device, make and model*	Parallel Port: *Device, make and model, ECP*
COM1: *Device, make and model, IRQ*	COM2: *Device, make and model, IRQ*	COM3: *Device, make and model, IRQ*	COM4: *Device, make and model, IRQ*
USB Port 1: *Device, make and model*	USB Port 2: *Device, make and model*	Infrared Port: *Yes/No*	Video In/Out: *Yes/No*

Table 12-2 System Inventory Information

Check Compatibility

Once you know what hardware you have, you can check its compatibility. Do that first using the Check System Compatibility option on the Welcome window of the Windows XP Setup CD and then with the Microsoft HCL web pages using these steps:

1. Place the Windows XP Setup CD in its drive. When the Welcome message comes up, click Check System Compatibility. On the next page that appears, click Check My System Automatically.

2. If you get the message Get Updated Setup Files, click Yes, Download The Updated Setup Files, and click Next.

3. When the system compatibility checking is complete, you will get a message on any problems found. If it finds no problems, you will get a message similar to Figure 12-3. Click Finish.

4. Back in the secondary Welcome message, click Visit The Compatibility Web Site. Click the Hardware tab and then click each of the hardware device types and look up your specific device to see what its status is. "Designed for Windows XP" means that the product is fully compatible.

5. When you are done looking up all your devices, close the Internet Explorer window.

Handle Incompatible Devices

If you find devices in your inventory that are not on the HCL and not mentioned in the Readme or other files, it will often be the case that they will work fine using general-purpose drivers in Windows XP. The only way to know for sure is to try to install Windows XP and see what happens. If there is a problem, you may be told about it while running Setup, or the device may simply not work when you are done. If this is a boot device, such as a SCSI or RAID (redundant array of independent disks) controller, you may not be able to finish the installation. The solution is to contact the manufacturer and obtain a Windows XP driver from them (you may be able to download it from the Internet).

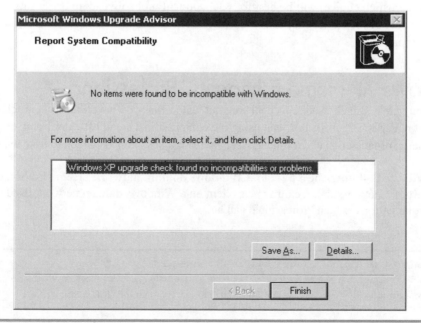

Figure 12-3 Conclusion of a system compatibility check

If you have a third-party driver for hard drives that you want to use with Windows XP, watch for a prompt early in the installation process that asks you to press F6. Then, follow the onscreen instructions to load and install the drivers. Module 14 will further discuss using third-party drivers.

Progress Check

1. What is the recommended amount of memory needed for Windows XP?

2. What is the recommended file system to use with Windows XP in most situations?

3. Where do you need to check to see if your hardware is compatible with XP?

CRITICAL SKILL
12.3 Make the Correct Installation Choices

During the installation process, Setup gives you a number of choices on how you want it installed. If you consider these choices before you do the installation and take the time to determine which choices will be best for you, you will probably end up better satisfying your needs. Some of the choices depend on earlier decisions and may not be available on certain decision paths.

Windows XP Home Edition vs. Professional

You may have already made this decision, but just in case you haven't, take a quick look at it here. It really is a decision between using the computer in a small office or home environment and a large organization environment. Here are the major factors on which to base the decision:

● **Will the computer be a part of a Windows domain network?** Home Edition can be a part of a network, but it cannot be a client on a Windows domain network used in larger organizations, which Professional can be.

---

1. It is recommended that Windows XP have at least 128MB of memory.

2. The NTFS file system should be used in all instances except when installing in a dual-boot situation.

3. To see if your hardware is compatible with XP, you need to look at the Microsoft HCL at their web site, http://www.microsoft.com/hcl/.

NOTE

Although this book does not deal with servers and Windows domains, if I were to install a network for ten or more people, I would use Windows domain networking because of the many advantages it provides, not the least of which is a single user registration covering all the computers in the domain.

- **Is it important to encrypt individual files and folders** or to restrict access to individual files and folders? Windows XP Professional includes both the Encrypting File System (EFS) and Restricted File Access (RFS) that allows you to encrypt and restrict access to selected files and folders, whereas Home Edition does not have these features.

- **Will this computer be accessed remotely by another computer,** for example, accessing an office computer from a home computer? Windows XP Professional includes Remote Desktop, which allows it to be a host to a remote computer. Home edition does not have this capability.

- **Is it important to have a full system restore?** Windows XP Professional includes System Restore as a part of an advanced backup and restore system, whereas Home Edition has a more limited backup and restore system.

- **Will this computer be used to host a web site?** Although hosting web sites is primarily a function of Windows 2000 or .NET servers, Windows XP Professional includes a limited version Internet Information Services (IIS), which allows the computer to host a personal or small office web site.

- **Will this computer be used to work on multiple languages at the same time?** Will it be able to quickly switch between languages?

- **Does this computer have two processors?** Windows XP Home Edition can use only one processor.

If you must have any one of these capabilities, then you must use Windows XP Professional. If any of these features look like something you will want in the near future, then you probably want Professional. If you doubt that you will ever use any of these features, Windows XP Home Edition is what should be installed.

Decide to Upgrade or Do a New Installation

The first decision within Setup that you must make is which type of installation you want to perform, as shown in Figure 12-4. An *upgrade,* in this case, is replacing a currently installed operating system with Windows XP in the same disk partition. A *new installation,* on the other hand, is loading Windows XP Home Edition or Windows XP Professional on to a newly formatted disk or a separate disk partition without an operating system, where either the OS has been removed or the partition has never had one (also called a "clean install").

Ask the Expert

Q: Is there any reason not to mix Windows XP Home Edition and Windows XP Professional and save the added expense of an all-Pro office?

A: So long as you can say that in the foreseeable future the Home machines will not need any of the features mentioned in the preceding list, then there is no reason not to mix the two. Except for the features mentioned and several more minor ones, all of the screens, menus, dialog boxes, and methods of operation are exactly the same, so the training of people is the same on both systems.

You can upgrade to Windows XP only from the following operating systems:

- **Windows XP Home Edition:**
  Windows Me
  Windows 98 and Windows 98 SE

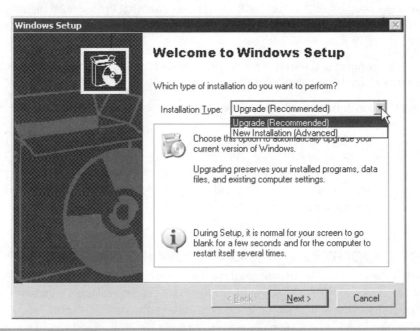

Figure 12-4 Making the first decision between an upgrade and a new installation

- **Windows XP Professional:**
  Windows XP Home Edition
  Windows 2000 Professional (all Service Packs)
  Windows Me
  Windows 98 and Windows 98 SE
  Windows NT 4 Workstation (all Service Packs)

If you are not currently running one of the identified upgradable products, you can either upgrade to one of those products and then upgrade to Windows XP, or you can do a clean install.

The major reasons to upgrade, if you can, are the following:

- To preserve all the current settings (such as users, rights, and permissions), applications, and data on your computer. Your current environment is preserved intact while upgrading to a new operating system.

- To make the installation of Windows XP simpler. Most of the installation decisions are made for you, using the settings in the current operating system.

The major reasons to do a clean install are the following:

- To get around an operating system that cannot be upgraded.

- To dual-boot into both the old operating system and Windows XP. This allows you to use either operating system.

- To really clean up your hard disks, which makes them more efficient, gets rid of unused files, and gives you back a lot of disk space.

If you can either upgrade or do a clean install (setting aside dual-booting for a moment; see the section after next), the decision is between preserving your current system with all of its settings, applications, and inefficient and wasted space, and doing a really clean install. The clean install gives your new operating system an environment not hampered by all that has been done on the computer in the past, *but* it is a *lot* more work. With a clean install, you have to reinstall all of your applications and reestablish all of your settings. This is not an easy decision. It may seem like it is a "no-brainer" to keep your current environment and forgo all the extra work, but are you really that happy with your current environment? Installing a new operating system is an excellent time to clean house and set up your system the way it should be, even if it takes a fair amount of extra time. Consider this decision carefully.

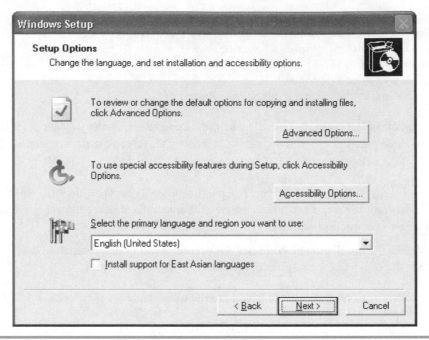

Figure 12-5 Options you can choose to use during setup

Use Setup Options

Early in an installation started from another version of Windows, you are given three setup options (see Figure 12-5):

● **Advanced Options** enables you to choose where to install Windows and its files. This choice allows you to specify from where to copy the installation files, as well as to which drive and folder they should be copied. Except in the case of dual-booting (see the next section), I recommend that the defaults be used.

● **Accessibility Options** provides assistance on seeing or understanding what is presented on the screen. You can choose to turn on a magnifier to make a selected area of the screen easier to read, and you can have the Microsoft Narrator read the contents of the screen.

● **Language Options** allows you to select the primary language and writing practices of a region that you want to use during setup.

Decide Whether to Dual-Boot

Dual-booting allows you to choose from among several operating systems each time you start your computer. If you are unsure if you want to switch to Windows XP, or if you have an application that runs only on another operating system, then dual-booting gives you a solution. For example, if you want to keep Windows NT 4 Workstation and be able to use it after installing Windows XP, or if you have an application that runs under Windows 98, but not Windows XP, then in both of these circumstances, dual-booting provides the means to do what you want. If you are thinking of dual-booting as a disaster recovery strategy for those instances in which you can't boot Windows XP, that is not a good reason because Windows XP has several built-in disaster recovery tools, such as the Recovery Console and System Restore, that assist in repairing the problem that caused the disaster.

You can dual-boot Windows XP with MS-DOS, Windows 3.*x*, Windows 95, Windows 98, Windows Me, Windows NT 3.51 or 4, and Windows 2000. In all cases but Windows 98, Me, and 2000, you must have installed the other operating system before Windows XP. If you are installing Windows XP on a computer that already has a dual-boot environment, Windows XP Setup will create a dual-boot environment with the *last operating system used.* So if you currently dual-boot between Windows 98 and MS-DOS, and MS-DOS was the last operating system used, Windows XP Setup will install dual-booting between Windows XP and MS-DOS.

Dual-booting also has significant drawbacks, such as these:

- You must install Windows XP in a separate partition so that it doesn't overwrite any of the files belonging to the original operating system. This means that you must reinstall all of your applications you want to run under Windows XP and you must reestablish all of your settings.

- You have to handle some complex file-system compatibility issues, and you can't share files that use the latest features of Windows XP. See the discussion following this list of bulleted items.

- Windows NT 4's Defrag and Chkdsk won't work on Windows XP's NTFS partition.

- The Plug and Play features of Windows 95, Windows 98, and Windows XP, in a dual-booting situation, could cause a device to not work properly in one operating system because the other operating system reconfigured it.

- Windows NT 4's Emergency Repair Disk won't work after installing Windows XP.

- Dual-booting takes up a lot of disk space with two complete operating systems.

- Dual-booting makes the operating environment much more complex than it would be otherwise.

When you dual-boot, both operating systems must be able to read the files that you want to share between them. This means that the shared files must be stored in a file system that both operating systems can use. When you install Windows XP, you have a choice of NTFS, FAT, and FAT32 files systems (see the next section, "Choose the File System"). NTFS has significant features in Windows XP, such as improved security, and file encryption, but these features are not usable by Windows NT. Also, Windows NT 4 can only access the latest NTFS (NTFS 5) files if you have installed Service Pack 4 or later, and you still cannot use all the features of NTFS 5. Therefore, if you choose NTFS as your common operating system, you run the risk that Windows NT will be unable to access the files. On the other hand, if you choose FAT, the lowest common denominator, you give up many of the benefits of a more powerful file system, such as file-level security and large disks, and FAT32 cannot be used by Windows NT.

NOTE

Windows XP can't be installed on, or directly access files on, a volume that has been compressed with DoubleSpace or DriveSpace.

One possible file system solution when dual-booting Windows NT and Windows XP is to use FAT for the Windows NT partition where all shared files are stored and use NTFS for the Windows XP partition, knowing that Windows NT probably will not be able to access the files in the NTFS partition.

Dual-booting is a compromise and doesn't give you all that you can get out of Windows XP. It is therefore not recommended unless you have a need that is not handled any other way, such as a needed application that does not run under Windows XP, and even there, you might leave it on a dedicated computer and move most of your work to another computer with Windows XP.

NOTE

Although Windows NT may not be able to access some NTFS files on the same computer in a dual-boot situation, it, along with all other operating systems, can access those same files if the access is over a network (the server translates the files as they are passed to the network).

Choose the File System

If you just read the preceding section on dual-booting, you might think that choosing the file system to use with Windows XP is complex. In fact, it is not. In all but the dual-booting circumstance just described, you want to use NTFS. NTFS provides many significant advantages that far outweigh any consideration for FAT or FAT32. Among the reasons to use NTFS are that it does the following:

- Allows and fully supports the use of disk volumes up to 2TB (terabytes), and files can be as large as the total disk volume. Files on FAT are limited to 2GB, and files on FAT32 are limited to 4GB.

- Provides much more efficient large file and volume handling than does FAT or FAT32.

- Allows the use of file-level security, wherein you can identify how individual files are shared. In FAT and FAT32, this cannot be done below the folder level.

- Supports Active Directory and domains, which are not available with FAT and FAT32, for improved security, flexibility, and manageability.

- Allows the encryption of individual files, which is not available with FAT and FAT32, for a very high level of security.

- Provides for *sparse files,* which are very large files that take up only the disk space needed for the portion of the file that has been written.

- Supports disk quotas that control how much space an individual user can consume.

Unless you have to dual-boot a system, you want to choose to use the NTFS file system. You can convert existing files to it during installation or do it afterward by using the Convert.exe file, which you must expand from Convert.ex_ in the I386 folder on the Windows XP installation CD. Start the expansion process by choosing Start | All Programs | Accessories | Command Prompt to open the Command Prompt window. Then in that window, type the drive letter of the drive on which you have mounted the Windows XP CD, for example **D:**, press ENTER, type **cd\i386** and press ENTER to change the current folder to I386, and finally type **expand convert.ex_ c:\convert.exe** and press ENTER to place the Convert.exe file in the root directory of the C: drive in the computer you are working on. To do the conversion to NTFS, while still in the Command Prompt window type the drive letter of the drive on which you copied Convert.exe, press ENTER, and type **convert *drive*: /fs:ntfs**, where *drive* is the drive letter of the drive to be converted.

Decide on Partitioning

Partitioning divides a single hard disk into two or more partitions, or *volumes*. These partitions are given drive letters, such as *D, E,* or *F,* and so are called *logical drives*. When you do a clean install of Windows XP, you are shown the current partitioning of the boot disk and asked if you want to add or remove partitions. When you have the partitions the way you want, you can determine on which partition you want to install Windows XP. There are two main reasons for partitioning: to have two different file systems on the same drive and to provide a logical separation of information or files. If you dual-boot, you need to use at least two different partitions to keep the two operating systems separate so that the Windows XP installation does not replace any of the original operating system's files.

When you are considering the partitioning you want, you also need to consider the size of each partition. For Windows XP by itself, you need to allocate at least 2GB, and it is wise to leave yourself some extra space, 5GB or more, for swap files, optional components, and future Service Packs.

Under many circumstances, you want only a single partition on a hard disk, to give yourself the maximum flexibility to use the entire disk. There are also ways to manage your partitioning after you complete installation (see Module 10).

Choose Optional Components

There are a large number of optional components in Windows XP, but you cannot install them until after you have completed the installation of the OS, unlike in earlier versions of Windows. Therefore, this discussion will be put off until the end of Module 13.

Prepare Your Computer for Installation

Installing an operating system entails a moderate risk that you could lose some or all the information on the computer, which makes it a good idea to back up the hard disks before the installation. Installing an operating system is also a great opportunity to clean up and make the system more efficient. Additionally, you need to do certain things to the system to make sure that the installation runs smoothly. All of these tasks are included in the following steps to prepare for an operating system installation:

- Back up all hard disks
- Inventory current software
- Clean up current files
- Upgrade hardware
- Disable conflicting hardware and software

Back Up All Hard Disks

Backing up may or may not be a routine task to you. In any case, it is important to perform a thorough backup prior to installing a new operating system. This should include all data files, including mail files, address books, templates, settings, My Documents, favorites, cookies, and history. Backing up application files not only is unnecessary (usually) because you should have copies on the distribution disks, but it is also very difficult because the application files may be in several folders.

The best technique for backing up data files if you don't already have a file list is to work down through a hard disk, folder by folder, looking at each of the files within each folder. This is definitely a tedious task, but very worthwhile not only for backing up, but also for the following cleanup and application inventory tasks. In many cases, you can back up entire folders if you know all the files are data files. In other cases, many of the files in a folder are application files, and you do not want to back them up, although a few files likely are custom templates, settings, or data files that you do want to preserve.

The tools (hardware and software) that you use to do a backup depend on what you have available. Backup within Windows NT 4 is fairly crude, while Windows 98, Me, and 2000 have reasonable Backup programs (Windows XP is better yet, but you need to back up before installing it). The best choice is one of several third-party programs, such as VERITAS's (previously Seagate Software's) Backup Exec (http://www.veritas.com/). Backup media can include tape, removable hard disks, Zip drives, writable or rewritable CDs/DVDs, optical drives, or even a different hard disk on the same or another system. Whatever you use, make sure that you can read it back in your Windows XP system.

TIP

With the very low cost of large hard disks, it might be worthwhile to get one just to hold the latest backup of one or more systems, although you should still also use removable media so that you can store a copy of your data away from the computer in a fireproof container.

Another way to do a backup is to make a mirror copy of a hard disk onto another hard disk using products such as PowerQuest's DriveCopy for a one-to-one copy, or Drive Image for a compressed copy (http://www.powerquest.com). This way, if you have a problem with the installation, you simply have to swap drives or restore a compressed image of the drive.

Another technique of keeping data handy and easy to back up is to put all of your data files in folders within My Documents. This is the default for Windows 98, Me, 2000, XP, and .NET, and it makes it easy to determine which folders contain data. Similarly, if you create a separate partition on your hard drive in which you store only data, you not only can easily determine your data folders, but you also can reformat the partition with your operating system and application files without disturbing your data.

Inventory Current Software

As you are going through the hard disks to back them up, you should also take an inventory of the applications on the disk, so that you know what was there in case you need to reinstall it. Separately from the disk review, note what is on the Desktop, the Start menu, the Programs menu, and the taskbar if the system you are upgrading from is Windows 98, Me, 2000, or XP

(Home Edition to Professional). Additionally, open Add Or Remove Programs from the Control Panel and note what programs it shows as currently installed, as well as the Windows components that are currently installed. For each application, note the installed version, whether it is still used, what its supporting files are (such as templates and settings), and where the files are stored on the hard disk. (This latter information needs to be fed back to the backup process to make sure these files are included.) Finally, you need to make sure you have the distribution disks for each application and note where they are kept. These steps will assure that you have the knowledge, application files, and data files necessary to restore the applications that were running on the computer before Windows XP was installed.

Clean Up Current Files

Most of us mean to clean up the disks we are responsible for, to get rid of the files and applications that are no longer used, but few of us get around to it. It is a very difficult chore, and who is to say that an application or data file will never be needed again? Also, we have all had the experience of either needing a file we recently removed or finding a file that has gone unused for some time.

Given that you have done a thorough job of backing up your data files and have a complete inventory of applications, then the question of whether a file will be needed again is moot because you can always restore the file or application if you need it. That leaves only the objection that it is a long, arduous task—and it is.

The very best way to clean up a hard disk is also the easiest and the scariest because it is so final—reformatting the hard drive and reloading only the applications and files that you know will be immediately used. This puts a lot of pressure on backing up well and making sure you have a good application inventory, but given that you do, then reformatting the hard drive is a very good solution. Also, it is still a fair amount of work because of the time to reload what you want on the hard drive.

Upgrade Hardware

Like cleaning up a hard disk, doing hardware upgrades gets put off because it can disrupt a system. So again, use the "new operating system" excuse to get it done. Use the inventory that you took earlier to determine what hardware you need or want to upgrade, and purchase and install the hardware before installing Windows XP, so the new operating system has the benefit of the new hardware. In doing this, consider upgrading the BIOS on the motherboard by checking the manufacturer's web site to see whether an upgrade is available and, if so, whether it would benefit you.

Disable Conflicting Hardware and Software

Certain hardware and software, if it is running, can cause Setup to fail. For that reason, you need to take the following steps on each computer to prepare for a Windows XP installation:

- Disable any UPS (uninterruptible power supply) device connected to the computer's serial port by removing the serial cable from the computer. The UPS can cause problems with Setup's device-detection process. You can reconnect the cable after Setup is complete.

- If you are using disk mirroring, it needs to be disabled prior to starting Setup. You can restart disk mirroring when Setup completes.

- Windows XP cannot reside on or access either DriveSpace or DoubleSpace volumes, so if you want to use such volumes with Windows XP, they must be uncompressed. Make sure you have backed up and inventoried the volume first because it is possible that uncompressing will lose information.

- Stop all programs that are running, especially any virus-detection programs, before starting Setup. These programs may give you spurious virus warning messages while Setup is writing to the disk. Sometimes these programs are automatically started when the system is booted, so you may have to go to some lengths to find and stop them. Start by opening the Start menu, choosing All Programs | Startup, and removing any programs you see there. Similarly, remove any program in the Autoexec.bat file. Then restart your computer; right-click any icons in the notification area on the right of the taskbar; and select Close, Disable, or Exit if one of those options exist. Finally, press CTRL-ALT-DELETE, and select Task Manager to open the Windows Task Manager shown in Figure 12-6. Select each of the programs in the Applications tab that are running and click End Task. You may want to go to the Control Panel's Add Or Remove Programs and remove any remaining programs that automatically start.

CRITICAL SKILL
12.5 Plan a Windows XP Migration

Going through the tasks described so far in this module for a single computer is a fair amount of work; doing it for a number of computers is a major undertaking. In both cases, having a solid plan for how it will be accomplished is most helpful, and in the large installation case, it is mandatory.

A migration plan must reflect the organization it is designed for, but most plans should cover the following steps:

1. Identify what computers are to be upgraded or installed with Windows XP Home Edition or Windows XP Professional and the order in which they will be completed.

2. Identify the hardware that needs to be acquired and installed so that Step 1 can be accomplished.

Figure 12-6 Applications can be stopped in the Task Manager.

3. Develop a detailed list of tasks needed to complete Steps 1 and 2.

4. Identify who will perform the tasks in Step 3.

5. Develop a timeline for completing the tasks in Step 3 given the labor identified in Step 4.

6. Determine a set of dates on which to do the installation that will provide the minimum amount of disruption to the company's normal activities. A long weekend is often a good idea to everyone except those doing the changeover.

7. Develop a budget for the software, hardware, and labor specified in the preceding steps.

8. Identify realistically the possible disruptions to the company's business and the cost of such disruptions.

9. Identify the benefits of changing over to Windows XP and how those benefits translate into reduced costs and improved revenues.

Most organizations of any size require a plan such as this, and upper management will look long and hard at the results of Steps 7 through 9. It is, of course, not a simple numerical comparison. The dollars in Step 7 are hard, out-of-pocket funds, whereas the dollars in Steps 8 and 9 may be hard to identify. The real question is whether the benefits of Windows XP are worth the costs, and how well could the company get along without the changeover. Every organization has to answer that question for itself.

Carrying out a changeover from one operating system to another is a very serious undertaking. Companies have been significantly harmed when it was poorly done, and have benefited greatly when it was done correctly. There are three key elements to success:

- Have a detailed knowledge of your current computers and networking system and what you want to achieve with Windows XP.

- Have a detailed plan for how you are going to carry out the conversion with minimal cost and disruption to the organization.

- Communicate continually and exhaustively with everyone involved.

It is my opinion that Windows XP provides very significant benefits to most organizations, as discussed in Module 1. Only you can determine if those benefits are worth the cost to your organization and then make sure that the conversion process does not erode the net value.

Ask the Expert

Q: Bottom line, do you believe that the upgrade to Windows XP is worth the cost?

A: If you are running Windows 95, 98, Me, or Windows NT Workstation, then the answer is unquestionably yes. Getting rid of the periodic system crashes alone is worth it, plus the enhancements over those products are substantial. If you are running Windows 2000 Professional, then the improvements in stability (lack of crashes) and the number of enhancements do not make as strong a case, and the factors of cost and effort weigh more heavily. It is my best guess that the next version of Windows for workstations and stand-alone computers will not be available until late 2004 or early 2005.

Progress Check

1. Can you upgrade to Windows XP Home Edition from Windows 95 or upgrade to Windows XP Professional from Windows NT 3.5 Workstation?

2. If you are concerned about Windows XP running your critical applications, should you install XP in a dual-boot environment?

3. What are the principle reasons for preparing a system for installation?

Project 12 Complete an Installation Checklist

Use this exercise to fill in the accompanying checklist that will prepare you for installation of Windows XP.

Step by Step

1. Determine for the system on which you are installing Windows XP:

   a. Processor: Number_____, Type_____, Speed_____ MHz

   b. RAM memory: Amount_____ MB

   c. Primary hard disk: Total size_____ GB, Available Size_____ GB

   d. CD-ROM installed: Yes, No_____

   e. Floppy disk installed: Yes, No_____

   f. Network card installed: Yes, No_____

   g. Keyboard installed: Yes, No_____

   h. Mouse installed: Yes, No_____

2. Compare the results in Step 1 with the system requirements and determine if the system can support XP. Yes, No_____

---

1. The answer in both cases is no. You can upgrade to Windows XP Home Edition from Windows Me, 98, and 98 SE. You can upgrade to Windows XP Professional from Windows XP Home Edition, 2000 Professional, Me, 98, 98 SE, and Windows NT 4 Workstation.

2. Not necessarily. A dual-boot environment is not recommended if at all possible. Take the time to research the applications you are concerned about to determine if they can work under XP or if there is a newer version that can work under XP. If you are installing XP on several machines, try one with just XP and the critical applications to see if that works. Only as a last resort install a dual-boot system.

3. The reasons to prepare for installation include a moderate risk that you could lose some or all the information on the computer, a great opportunity to clean up and make the system more efficient, and the need to make sure that the installation runs smoothly.

3. Inventory for the system on which you are installing Windows XP:

a. Processor 1: _____, Processor 2: _____

b. Memory: _____ MB,

c. Hard Disk 1: Type: _____, Size _____ GB
Hard Disk 2: Type: _____, Size _____ GB

d. CD-ROM Drive: Type: _____, Speed _____ X

e. Floppy Drive: Type: _____, Size _____ MB

f. Tape Drive: Type: _____, Size _____ GB

g. Other Drive (DVD, CD-RW) Type: _____, Speed _____ X

h. Mouse: Type: _____, Keyboard: Type: _____

i. Disk Controller: Type: _____, RAID Controller: Type:_____

j. Modem Card: Type: _____, Speed _____ Kbps

k. Network Card: Type: _____, Speed _____ Mbps

l. Sound Card: Type: _____

m. Video Card: Type: _____

n. External Modem: Type: _____, Port _____

o. PCMCIA Slot 1: Device: _____

p. PCMCIA Slot 2: Device: _____

q. Parallel Port: Device: _____

r. COM1: Device: _____, COM2: Device: _____

s. COM3: Device: _____, COM4: Device: _____

t. USB Port 1: Device: _____, USB Port 2: Device: _____

u. Infrared Port: Device: _____, Video In/Out: Device: _____

4. Compare the inventory prepared in Step 3 with Microsoft's hardware compatibility list and determine if all the components are compatible.

5. Make the following installation choices:

a. Decide to upgrade or do a clean install _____

b. Decide whether to dual-boot _____

(continued)

c. Choose the file system: _____ FAT, _____ FAT32, or _____ NTFS

d. Determine the number of partitions: _____, size of each: _____

6. Carry out the following installation preparation steps:

a. Back up all hard disks: _____ Done

b. Inventory current software: _____ Done

c. Clean up current files: _____ Done

d. Disable conflicting hardware and software: _____ Done

Project Summary

Preparing for many tasks is harder than actually carrying them out, but the preparation assures that the task will go smoothly. Such is the case with Windows XP, but in its case the preparation not only makes it go smoothly, but it also assures it is a success.

✓ Module 12 Mastery Check

1. If you have an older computer that you want to make into a minimal workstation that has a 300 MHz processor, 128MB of memory, 5GB of hard disk, a network card, an SVGA video adapter and monitor, a keyboard and mouse, a floppy drive, but no CD-ROM drive, will it work, and why?

2. What are the steps for checking hardware compatibility?

3. What do you do if you have a component of your system that is not on the HCL or in the Readme files?

4. What are three reasons to use Windows XP Professional over Windows XP Home Edition?

5. What are two reasons each to upgrade or to do a clean install?

6. What accessibility options are available during Windows XP setup?

7. What is dual-booting and why might you want to use it?

8. What are three of the steps in preparing a system for Windows XP installation?

9. What is a low-cost, nonobvious way to do a complete disk backup?

10. What are the three key elements to a successful installation?

Module 13

Installing Windows XP

nstalling Windows XP can be accomplished in a number of possible ways. You can start over a network or locally, you can boot from the installation CD or floppy disks, and you can start from MS-DOS or any version of Windows. You can run a clean install where you completely replace the contents of a disk, or you can upgrade the current operating system (OS) and keep all of the settings, files, and folders that you currently have. When you are done with the installation, you can go back and install a number of optional components if you wish.

In this module, I will address each of the ways to start and run a Windows XP installation, and at the end of the module, I will talk about installing the optional components. In this module, more so than others, you will want to pick and choose the sections that are applicable to you.

TIP

In addition to the methods described here for installing a single copy of Windows XP, there are methods for automating installation of a number of copies both locally at the computer and remotely across the network. These methods are beyond the scope of this book but are included in my book *Windows .NET Server: A Beginner's Guide.*

CRITICAL SKILL
13.1 Start over a Network

If the computer on which you want to install Windows XP is connected to and can access a network where you can see a hard drive or CD-ROM drive on another computer, you can install Windows XP using files on the remote computer. Use these steps to do that:

1. On a server or any other computer on the network (I'll call this the "Setup server"), insert the Windows XP distribution CD in the CD-ROM drive.

2. Either copy the contents from the Windows XP distribution CD to a folder on the hard disk of the Setup server and then share that folder or share the CD-ROM drive on that computer.

3. On the installation computer, using the tools available in its operating system, such as Windows Explorer, locate the other computer over the network (My Network Places and either the folder in which the I386 folder was placed or in the I386 folder on the CD-ROM drive.

4. If you are in DOS or Windows 3.*x* and viewing the I386 folder on the Setup server, run Winnt.exe.

5. If you are in Windows 95, 98, Me, or XP; Windows NT 3.51 or NT 4; or Windows 2000 and viewing the I386 folder, double-click Winnt32.exe, as shown in Figure 13-1.

Figure 13-1 Starting Setup using files on a computer across a network

TIP

It is often advantageous to copy the I386 folder from the Setup server to the local machine and then do a local setup. Sometimes a network hiccup can cause a setup to fail.

Ask the Expert

Q: How is the product key handled when you install over the network?

A: With the new activation policy Microsoft instituted with Office XP and Windows XP, each computer on which you install one of these products must have its own product key. You can buy product keys individually with the product, or you can buy bundles of keys, as small as five.

NOTE

You can upgrade to Windows XP Home Edition from Windows Me, Windows 98, and Windows 98 SE, and you can upgrade to Windows XP Professional from Windows XP Home Edition, Windows 2000 Professional (all Service Packs), Windows Me, Windows 98, Windows 98 SE, and Windows NT 4 Workstation (all Service Packs).

CRITICAL SKILL
13.2 Start Locally

There are a number of ways to start Setup locally, depending on whether

- You want to boot Windows XP Setup directly or start it from an existing system
- Your system can boot from a CD or requires that you use floppies
- You want to start from DOS, Windows 3.x, or a later version of Windows

These alternatives and their resultant starting steps are shown in Figure 13-2 and are further described in the next few sections.

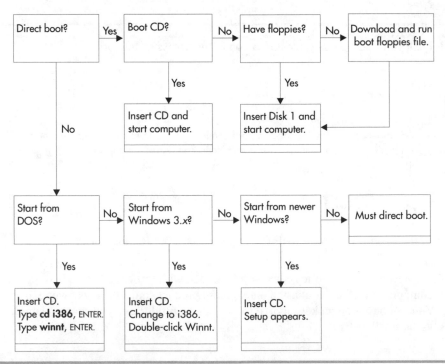

Figure 13-2 Choices in starting Windows XP Setup

NOTE

After starting by directly booting into Setup, you can only do a clean install. If you start Setup from an existing operating system, you can either do a clean install or upgrade from a compatible system (see the preceding Note).

Start by Directly Booting Setup

If you want to directly boot Setup, you can do so with a new unformatted hard drive or one that has any other OS on it. The only questions are whether you can boot from a CD, and if not, you can download a set of boot floppies from Microsoft.

NOTE

If you directly boot Setup, you can only do a clean install, replacing the current OS and all of its settings and files. You cannot do an upgrade.

Boot from a CD

If the system on which you want to do the installation can boot from a CD instead of a floppy or hard disk, then you can start Setup simply by following these steps:

1. Insert the Windows XP CD in the CD-ROM drive.

2. Restart the computer.

3. If necessary, press ENTER or "any key," as suggested, to boot from the CD.

4. Windows XP Setup will begin to load.

If you can't boot from a CD, but believe you should be able to (most computers made after 1996 can boot from the CD), you may need to change one or more settings in the system BIOS (basic input/output system) at the very beginning of the boot process. Depending on the computer, the BIOS can be changed in several different ways. Recent BIOSs from the two most popular third-party BIOS manufacturers, Award and American Megatrends, Inc. (AMI), as well as the Dell Dimension, are changed as follows:

● **Award Version 4.51PG** Press DELETE right after memory check; select BIOS Features Setup; select Boot Sequence; press PGUP until "A, CDROM, C" is displayed; press ESC to quit; select Save & Exit Setup; press ENTER; press Y; and press ENTER.

● **AMI BIOS Version 2.4** Press DELETE right after the memory check; select Advanced Setup; select 1st Boot Device; choose CDROM; select 2nd Boot Device; choose Floppy;

select 3rd Boot Device; choose IDE-0; press ESC twice; select Save Changes And Exit; press ENTER.

● **Dell Dimension 4100**   Press and hold DELETE as the system is first booted until you see Loading Setup, use the arrow keys to first select Boot and then 1st Boot Device, press ENTER, select ATAPI CDROM, press ENTER, similarly choose Floppy for 2nd Boot Device and IDE-HDD for the 3rd Boot Device, press F10 to save and exit, select Yes, and press ENTER.

NOTE

If you have two CD-ROM-type devices such as a DVD or CD-RW, try them both; one may work and the other not.

Boot from Floppies

If you can't boot from a CD, then another alternative is to boot from floppies. A set of six boot floppies can be downloaded from Microsoft. Go to the Knowledge Base article "Obtaining Windows XP Setup Boot Disks" at http://support.microsoft.com/default.aspx?scid= kb;en-us;Q310994&, read about how to download and create the floppies with six blank formatted, high-density (1.44MB) floppy disks, and then follow one of the links to actually do the download and create the floppies with these steps:

1. Start a system that is connected to the Internet with a bootable OS and a 1.44MB floppy drive.

2. Using your Internet browser, connect to http://support.microsoft.com/default.aspx?scid= kb;en-us;Q310994&. Read the instructions and click the link that will start the version (Home Edition or Professional) you want to install in the language you want to use.

3. Click the link under Download Now. When asked, click Save, locate where you want the file stored, and again click Save. The file is a little over 4MB in size. When the download is complete, click Close.

4. With six blank formatted floppies ready, use Windows Explorer to locate the folder and double-click the boot floppies file to begin the creation of the floppies. Click Yes to accept the license agreement.

5. When asked, enter the letter of drive to be used, insert a formatted floppy in that drive, and press any key. The first disk will be written.

6. When prompted, exchange the floppy in the drive for another floppy, press any key, and label the one removed. Repeat this five times.

7. Remove the last floppy and label it.

With a set of floppy boot disks, you can start Setup with these steps:

1. Insert the first Windows XP Setup Boot Disk in its drive.

2. Start or restart the computer.

3. Windows XP Setup will begin to load.

4. Insert the other floppy disks as requested, and press ENTER after each.

If the system does not boot from the floppy, you may have to change the order in which the floppy, CD-ROM, and hard drives boot. See the discussion in the preceding section, "Boot from a CD."

NOTE

The Windows XP Setup floppy disks only start Setup. You still need the CD to do the installation.

Start from Another Operating System

You can start Windows XP Setup from these other operating systems:

- MS-DOS

- Windows 3.1, Windows 3.11, or Windows for Workgroups

- Windows 95, 98, or Me, any version

- Windows NT 3.51, Windows NT 4 (any service packs), Windows 2000, or Windows XP

NOTE

When you start from an upgradable OS, you can either upgrade or do a clean installation.

Start from DOS

With DOS running on the computer on which you want to install Windows XP, use these steps to do the installation:

1. Insert the Windows XP CD in its drive.

2. At the DOS prompt, make the CD-ROM drive current by typing, for example, **d:** and pressing ENTER.

3. Type **cd\I386** and press ENTER. The directory will be changed to I386.

4. Type **winnt** and press ENTER. Windows XP Setup will begin to load.

TIP

Running Setup from DOS or Windows 3.x is much slower than directly booting from either the CD or floppies, or starting from a newer version of Windows. See "Run a Clean Install Started in Other Ways" later in this module, where it discusses using Smartdrive to speed up DOS and Windows 3.x installs.

Start from Windows 3.x

With Windows 3.x running on the computer on which you want to install Windows XP, use these steps to do the installation:

1. Insert the Windows XP CD in its drive.

2. Start File Manager and open the CD-ROM drive.

3. Browse to and open the I386 folder.

4. Browse to and double-click Winnt.exe.

5. Windows XP Setup will begin to load.

Start from a Newer Windows

With Windows 95/98/Me, Windows NT 3.51/4, or Windows 2000/XP running on the computer where you want to install Windows XP, use these steps to do the installation:

1. Insert the Windows XP CD in its drive.

2. The Autorun feature, if active, will load the CD and a Welcome message will appear, as shown in Figure 13-3.

3. If you see the Welcome message, click Install Windows XP.

4. If you don't see the Welcome message, use Windows Explorer to open the CD-ROM drive, browse to the I386 folder, and double-click Winnt32.exe.

Ask the Expert

Q: Why would I want to start Setup from DOS or an early version of Windows if I can't do an upgrade from those products?

A: If you can boot from a CD, then you probably don't want to boot from one of those products because the initial phases of Setup, especially the file copying, will go very slowly. If you cannot boot from the CD, then booting from these products is a simpler, although maybe slower, alternative to downloading and booting from the floppy disks.

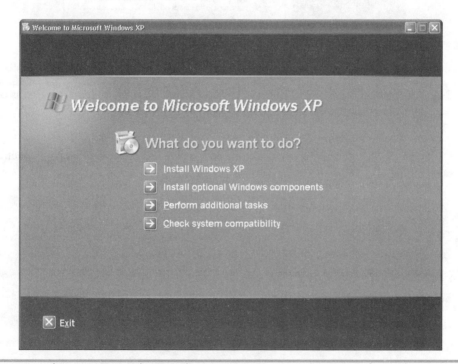

Figure 13-3 When you insert the Windows XP CD in a newer version of Windows, this Welcome message will automatically appear.

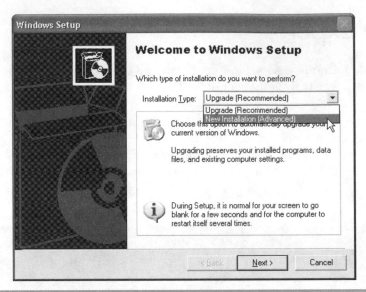

Figure 13-4 You can do a new installation or a clean install from all operating systems and an upgrade from an upgradable version of Windows.

The Windows XP Setup Wizard will launch (as shown in Figure 13-4), asking whether you want to upgrade or do a new installation.

Progress Check

1. What do you need to start over the network?

2. Can you upgrade to Windows XP Home Edition from Windows 95?

3. What are three ways of starting Setup?

---

1. To start over the network, you need to be connected to a network and the Windows XP installation files need to be available on another computer on the network.

2. No. The earliest upgrade to Windows XP Home Edition is from Windows 98.

3. You can start Setup by booting from the Setup CD, by booting from downloaded floppy disks, and from any version of DOS or Windows.

CRITICAL SKILL
13.3 Run a Clean Install Started from a Newer Windows Version

If you start Setup in a newer version of Windows, Setup has three phases:

● An initial GUI phase

● An intermediate character-based Setup Program phase

● A final GUI-based Setup Wizard phase

CAUTION

By definition, a clean install means that anything that was previously on the hard disk partition or volume will be removed and therefore lost during a reformatting process, to give you a clean hard disk.

Initial GUI Phase

Having started from a newer version of Windows, you should have the dialog box shown in Figure 13-4 on the screen. The steps to continue from this point with Setup are as follows:

1. In the dialog box shown in Figure 13-4, choose New Installation (Advanced) (see the discussion in Module 12 under "Decide to Upgrade or Do a New Installation") and click Next. The License Agreement dialog box opens.

2. Click I Accept This Agreement (or forget about installing Windows XP) and then click Next. The Product Key dialog box opens.

3. Enter the product key located on the back of the Windows CD envelope or case and click Next. The Setup Options dialog box opens, shown in Figure 13-5. This allows you to change the way files are copied, select special accessibility options, and change the language used by Setup, as shown by the mouse pointer in Figure 13-5.

4. Complete your selections and click Next. You are asked if you want to get updated Setup files from the Microsoft web site. If you are connected to the Internet, this is a wise idea to utilize any changes since your CD was manufactured, so click Yes. Otherwise, click No.

5. Click Next. Setup will go over the Internet and download the latest files, if you chose that option. Then it will begin copying files. From a CD, this is fairly fast, but over a network, it can take a while, depending on the speed of the network and the traffic on it. When the copying process is complete, the computer is rebooted and the character-based Setup Program is started.

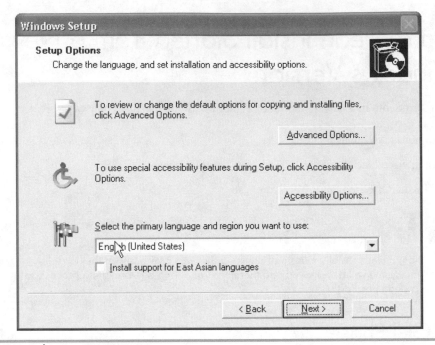

Figure 13-5 Selecting Setup Options

Intermediate Character-Based Setup Program Phase

The intermediate character-based Setup Program phase continues with these steps:

1. Setup inspects your hardware configuration and gives you a chance to press F6 to install a third-party Small Computer System Interface (SCSI) or redundant array of independent disks (RAID) mass-storage driver. If necessary, press F6 and follow the instructions for installing the driver. Setup then loads the files that you need. Upon completion, you are told that Setup will restart your computer. (If you don't press F6, the computer doesn't restart at this point.)

NOTE

You need to press F6 rather quickly if you want to install a driver. You have only about ten seconds to make the decision and press the F6 key. If you are unsure about whether you need to press F6, press it. You can always exit without installing a SCSI or RAID driver.

2. If you pressed F6, press ENTER to restart. You are given a choice of which operating system you want to start. Press ENTER to choose the default Windows XP Professional Setup. You are asked whether you want to set up Windows XP or repair an existing Windows XP installation.

3. Press ESC to continue installing a fresh copy of Windows XP. You are next shown the existing partitions and asked which you want to use for the current installation.

4. Use the UP ARROW and DOWN ARROW keys to select the partition you want to use. You then can press ENTER to install in that partition, press C to create a new partition in unpartitioned space, or press D to delete an existing partition and create a new one in its place.

NOTE

You will not be able to delete in this manner the partition from which you originally booted the computer. You should be able to do this if you direct boot into Setup from the Windows XP CD or floppy disks. If you can boot from the Windows XP CD or floppy disks, start Setup, follow the initial instructions through restarting of the computer, then choose Repair ("R") and Recovery Console ("C"). Here you have a DOS-like interface where you can get a list of commands by typing **help**. Use the Diskpart command to remove partitions (type **help diskpart** to learn how to do to this). Type **Exit** to leave the Recovery Console and reboot.

5. If you have chosen to do a new installation and you are using an existing partition, you will get a message that you are going to copy over all the old operating system's files and settings, removing the old system and requiring reentry of all settings and applications. Press C to continue and then press L to delete the existing files.

6. If you truly want to do a clean install and you did not boot from the partition from which you want to install Windows XP, press D. Confirm that you want to delete a system partition by pressing ENTER and then pressing L. To set up Windows XP in the resulting unpartitioned space, press ENTER (a partition will be created for you).

7. If you created a new partition, select whether you want the new partition formatted using NTFS or the FAT (file allocation table) file system, and press ENTER. If you select NTFS, you are cautioned that it will not be able to be read by the older operating systems. Press C to convert the drive. The new partition will be formatted as you directed, and if you choose NTFS, the computer will be restarted.

Setup then copies the remaining files and begins detecting and installing the hardware devices on the computer. When this is completed, the final GUI-based Windows XP Setup is started.

Final GUI-Based Setup Phase

When Windows XP Setup restarts, you see the Windows Setup window. Setup completes installing devices, and you see a moving bar indicating the progress. When that is completed, the Regional And Language Options dialog box appears. This allows you to choose a system or user locale that determines which language is the default; which other languages are available; and how numbers, currencies, time, and dates are displayed and used. Continue through Setup with these steps:

1. Select the regional settings that you want and click Next. The Personalize Your Software dialog box appears.

2. Enter the person's name and organization to be associated with the computer and click Next. The Computer Name and Administrator Password dialog box appears.

3. Enter a unique name for the computer (it can be up to 63 characters long, but it cannot contain spaces, and pre–Windows 2000 computers will see only the first 15 characters) and enter and confirm a password to be used by the systems administrator.

4. Click Next. If you get the Modem Dialing Information dialog box, enter your area code and, if necessary, the number to dial to get an outside line, and again click Next.

5. You'll see a dialog box for Date and Time Settings. If necessary, set the current date and time and in any case click Next. The Windows networking components will be installed. This allows you to connect to other computers, networks, and the Internet.

   When the networking software is installed, if you have a network card and Setup sees it, you are asked to choose either Typical settings, which creates network connections using the Client for Microsoft Networks, File and Print Sharing for Microsoft Networks, the QoS (Quality of Service) Packet Scheduler, and the TCP/IP protocol with automatic addressing, or Custom settings, which allows you to manually configure the networking components. Choosing Custom allows you to add or remove clients, services, and protocols, such as Client Service for NetWare and the IPX/SPX/NetBIOS protocol.

6. Choose the Network settings you want to use and click Next. The Workgroup or Computer Domain dialog box appears, asking whether you want this computer to e a member of a domain.

7. If you click No and the computer is part of a workgroup, enter a workgroup name. If you click Yes, type the domain name. Click Next when you are done with the domain settings. If you selected Domain, you will need to enter a user name and password and click OK. Setup will install the needed components with the settings you specified.

NOTE

In the Home Edition, you cannot connect to a domain, and you aren't presented with any of the associated questions or dialog boxes.

When component installation is done, Start menu items are installed, components are registered, settings are saved, and all temporary files are removed. The computer is restarted. If the computer is not already connected to the Internet, you will be asked how the computer will do that. Answer Yes if the computer will connect through a network or No if the computer will connect directly to the Internet through a modem.

8. If the Network Identification Wizard appears, click Next. You will be asked if you want to add a user to the computer. If you do (you have already made Administrator a user) and this computer is part of a domain, enter the username and the user's domain, or click that you do not want to add a user. If the computer is not part of a domain, enter the name(s) of the person or persons who will use this computer. In either case, click Next.

9. If you chose to add a user in a domain, you are asked to specify the level of access for that user: Standard, Restricted, or Other. Choose a level of access and click Next.

10. Whether or not you added a user, click Finish to complete Network Identification. Startup will continue.

11. If asked, press CTRL-ALT-DEL, and, if requested, enter the user's name and password you first entered in Step 4 and click OK.

Activate Windows XP

When loading is complete, the default Windows XP desktop will appear and one or more notes will appear in the lower right of the screen. You may be told that you can automatically adjust the screen resolution by clicking the icon being pointed at. You will be told that you can take a tour of XP by clicking an icon, and you will eventually if not immediately be told that you have 30 days to activate Windows and you can do so by clicking another icon. The activation process attaches the copy of the operating system to the set of hardware on which it is installed and then registers that combination with Microsoft. The purpose of this is to prevent one copy of the operating system from being installed on several computers. You do not have to register your name and address if you wish (Microsoft says that no personal information is collected during activation). If you click the activate message, an Activate Windows window opens, as you can see in Figure 13-6. Use the following steps to do the activation:

1. Choose between activation over the Internet and over the telephone and click Next. You are asked if you want to also register with Microsoft by giving them your name and address so

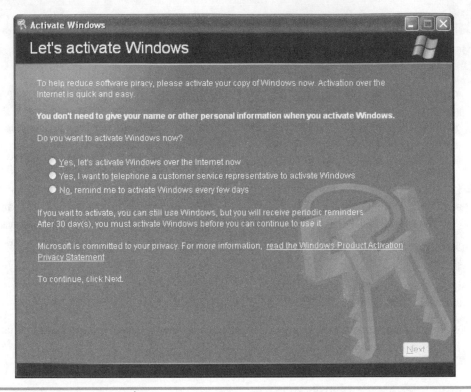

Figure 13-6 Activating Windows

that they can tell you about updates and new products as they come out. This is optional, and there is no problem if you don't want to do it. In most instances, though, it is worthwhile registering.

2. Choose between registering and not and click Next. If you choose to register, you will be asked for your name and address. Do that and click Next. It will then connect to Microsoft over the Internet and both activate and register your installation, given that is what you want. When you are told the process was successful, click OK.

   If you choose to activate over the telephone, you will be asked to select your location, which will give you one or more telephone numbers. You will then be given an installation ID number that you must give to the service representative on the telephone. The service representative in turn will give you a confirming number that you must enter to complete the activation process.

Ask the Expert

Q: I really don't want to activate the product. Is there any way around that?

A: There is no legal way to not activate Windows XP and keep running it after 30 days.

Progress Check

1. Can you do a clean install and preserve any of your current files or settings?

2. How do you change the location of where Windows XP will be installed?

3. If you boot from a newer version of Windows, can you delete the partition from which you booted?

CRITICAL SKILL
13.4 Run a Clean Install Started in Other Ways

When you boot from a CD or floppies, or start from DOS or Windows 3.*x*, you have only two phases: the character-based Setup Program and the GUI-based Setup Wizard. You see none of the startup GUI dialog boxes and go right into the character-based Setup Program.

Character-Based Setup Program

Having started Setup (see the various ways you can do that at the beginning of this module), begin the character-based Setup Program with the following steps:

1. If your boot device does not contain your Setup files, you need to confirm the drive and folder where those files exist. Often, the CD-ROM drive is drive D, in which case the correct response would be **D:/i386**. When the correct drive and folder are displayed, press ENTER.

---

1. No, a clean install by definition cleans off all files on your hard disk, which means that you must reinstall all current applications and copy back all data files that you have backed up.

2. In the initial GUI phase of Setup started from a newer version of Windows, the Setup Options dialog box Advanced Options allows you to specify the location of the Windows XP Setup files and the folder in which you want Windows XP installed.

3. No. you cannot delete the partition from which you booted. You must boot from the CD or downloaded Setup floppies to delete the partition containing the previous OS.

2. If you are starting from an older version (5.x or 6.x) of DOS or Windows 3.x and don't have the DOS SmartDrive disk-caching system loaded, you will be reminded that having it will greatly improve the performance of Setup (although it is still slow compared to other ways of running Setup).

SmartDrive is started with the program Smartdrv.exe that was included with DOS 6.x and Windows 3.x. If you look at the original distribution diskettes for these products, you will see the file Smartdrv.ex_. This is a compressed file that must be expanded with Expand.exe, also on the distribution diskettes (type **expand a:\smartdrv.ex_ c:\smartdrv.exe**, assuming that you are in the directory with Expand.exe). With Smartdrv.exe in the root directory of the hard disk, add the line **smartdrv.exe** to the Autoexec.bat file. After you have started DOS, you can check whether SmartDrive is loaded by typing **smartdrv** and pressing ENTER. If it's loaded, you will see a report of the version, cache size, and status. An initial set of files is copied to the hard disk, which can be a very slow process if you started from DOS or Windows 3.x. When a screen tells you the MS-DOS portion of Setup is complete, remove a floppy if there is one in the drive and then press ENTER to restart.

3. Setup inspects your hardware configuration and gives you the opportunity to press F6 to install a third-party SCSI or RAID mass-storage driver. If needed, press F6 and follow the instructions for installing the driver. Setup then loads the files that you need.

NOTE

You need to press F6 rather quickly if you want to install a driver. You have only about ten seconds to make the decision and press the F6 key. If you are unsure about whether you need to press F6, press it. You can always exit that question without installing a SCSI or RAID driver.

4. If there is an existing operating system, Setup asks whether you want to repair an existing installation of Windows XP or set up a new Windows XP installation. Press ENTER for a new installation.

5. If you started from floppy disks and do not have the Windows XP CD in the drive, you will be asked to insert it.

6. The Microsoft License Agreement is displayed, and you are asked to press F8 if you agree to it or ESC if you don't. If you want to install Windows XP, press F8.

7. If there is an existing Windows installation, you'll be asked again whether you want to repair that installation, which you can do by pressing R, or install a fresh copy of Windows XP by pressing ESC.

8. You are next shown the existing partitions and asked which you want to use for the current installation.

9. Use the UP ARROW and DOWN ARROW keys to select the partition you want to use. You then can press ENTER to install in that partition, press C to create a new partition in unpartitioned space, or press D to delete an existing partition and create a new one in its place.

10. If you want to do a clean install on a previously used partition, press D. Confirm that you want to delete a system partition by pressing ENTER and then pressing L. To set up Windows XP in unpartitioned space, press ENTER (a partition will automatically be created for you).

11. Select whether you want the new partition formatted using NTFS or the FAT file system and whether you want to use the new Quick formatting or the normal formatting (the recommended approach and the default is to use NTFS and normal formatting). Then press ENTER. The new partition will be formatted as you directed.

12. If you have indicated you want to use an existing FAT or FAT32 partition, you will be asked whether you want to convert it to NTFS (recommended) or leave the current file system intact. Select Convert and press ENTER. Confirm that you want to convert the partition by pressing C. When the conversions or formatting is done, the remaining files are copied to the hard disk. Upon completion, Windows XP Setup GUI window will open.

GUI-Based Setup Wizard

When the Windows XP Setup GUI window opens, you see several messages telling you that Windows XP is loading files and then detecting and installing the hardware devices on the computer. When that is done, the Regional And Language Options dialog box appears. This allows you to choose a locale that determines which language is the default; which other languages are available; and how numbers, currencies, time, and dates are displayed and used for the system in general, as well as for the current user. Continue through Setup with these steps:

1. Select the regional and language settings that you want and click Next. The Personalize Your Software dialog box will appear.

2. Enter the person's name and organization to be associated with the computer and click Next. The Product Key dialog box opens.

3. Enter the Product Key that is on the back of the Windows XP CD envelope or case. The Computer Name and Administrative Password dialog box appears in the Professional Edition.

4. Enter a unique name for the computer (it can be up to 63 characters long, but it cannot contain spaces, and pre–Windows XP computers will see only the first 15 characters) and enter and confirm a password to be used by the system administrator.

5. Click Next. If you get the Modem Dialing Information dialog box, enter the area code and number to dial to get an outside line, and again click Next. You'll see a dialog box for Date and Time Settings.

6. If necessary, set the current date and time and click Next. The Windows networking components will be installed, and if you have a network card and Setup sees it, the Networking Settings dialog box will appear. This allows you to connect to other computers, networks, and the Internet.

7. When the networking software is installed, you are asked to choose either Typical settings, which creates network connections using the Client for Microsoft Networks, File and Print Sharing for Microsoft Networks, the QoS Packet Scheduler, and the TCP/IP protocol with automatic addressing, or Custom settings, which allows you to manually configure networking components. Choosing Custom allows you to add or remove clients, services, and protocols, such as Client Service for NetWare and the IPX/SPX/NetBIOS protocol.

8. Choose the Network settings you want to use and click Next. The Workgroup or Computer Domain dialog box appears, asking whether you want this computer to be a member of a domain. (The domain-related information in this and the following steps applies to the Professional version only.)

9. If you answer No and the computer is part of a workgroup, enter a workgroup name. If you answer Yes, type the domain name and click Next. If you entered a domain name, you need to enter a username and password and then click OK. Setup will install the necessary components and the settings you specified.

When component installation is done, more files are copied to the hard drive, Start menu items are installed, components are registered, settings are saved, and all temporary files are removed. The computer is restarted. If the computer is not already connected to the Internet, you will be asked how the computer will do that. Answer Yes if the computer will connect through a network or No if the computer will connect directly to the Internet through a modem.

10. The Network Identification Wizard may appear. If so, click Next. Depending on whether you are a member of a workgroup or a domain, you are asked either if you want to add a user to the computer or if you want to identify who will use the computer. If you add a user, select the type of user and click Next.

11. Whether or not you added a user, click Finish to complete the user identification. Startup will continue.

12. If you are a member of a domain, you will be asked to press CTRL-ALT-DELETE, enter the Administrator's password or select another user and enter their password, and click OK.

When loading is complete, the default Windows XP desktop will appear, and one or more notes will appear in the lower right of the screen. You may be told that you can automatically adjust the screen resolution by clicking on the icon being pointed at. You will be told that you can take a tour of XP by clicking on its icon, and you will eventually if not immediately be told that you have 30 days to activate Windows and you can do so by clicking its icon. See the "Activate Windows XP" section earlier in this module.

CRITICAL SKILL
13.5 Run an Upgrade

You can upgrade to Windows XP Home Edition from Windows Me, Windows 98, and Windows 98 SE, and you can upgrade to Windows XP Professional from Windows XP Home Edition, Windows 2000 Professional (all Service Packs), Windows Me, Windows 98, Windows 98 SE, and Windows NT 4 Workstation (all Service Packs). (MS-DOS, Windows 3.1*x*, Windows 95, Windows NT Workstation 3.51, and OS/2 require a clean install.) Windows XP Setup can therefore be started from any of the upgradable products. Many of the settings for Windows XP are taken from the earlier system, so there are fewer steps and only two phases, both using a GUI.

Initial GUI Phase

Having started from a newer version of Windows, you should have displayed onscreen the upgrade vs. install dialog box shown earlier in Figure 13-4. The steps to continue from this point with Setup are as follows:

1. In the dialog box shown in Figure 13-4, choose Upgrade and click Next. The License Agreement dialog box opens.

2. Click I Accept This Agreement (or forget about installing Windows XP) and then click Next. The Product Key dialog box will appear.

3. Enter the product key that is shown on the back of the Windows XP CD envelope or case and click Next.

4. You may be told that Setup will check your hardware and software for compatibility with Windows XP and prepare an upgrade report, as shown in Figure 13-7. Choose if you want to see only hardware and other serious issues, see all known issues, or not see the report at all, and click Next.

5. You will be asked if you want to get updated Setup files by downloading them from the Microsoft. It is a good idea to do this by clicking Yes and then Next. If you are connected to the Internet, you will be connected to the Microsoft site and the latest files will be

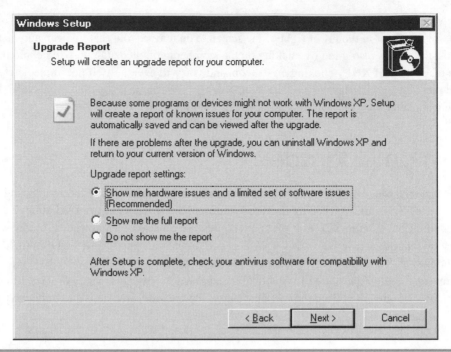

Figure 13-7 Checking for compatibility with Windows XP

downloaded. If you cannot be connected to the Internet, you will be told and Setup will continue. After a bit, if there are issues that need to be addressed, the Upgrade Report will be displayed, as you can see in Figure 13-8.

6. Decide how to handle any incompatible items, as necessary (for example, you may be told that a piece of hardware needs an upgraded driver, which you can install after installation).

7. After you have handled all the issues on the Upgrade Report, click Next. More of the installation files will be copied to the hard disk, and the computer will be restarted.

Final GUI Phase

A new Setup window will appear, and you are told that Setup is preparing for the installation. Setup will continue copying files. From a CD, this is fairly fast, but over a network, it can take a while, depending on the speed of the network and the traffic on it. When the copying process is complete, the computer is rebooted and the same Setup window reappears; now telling you that it is installing Windows.

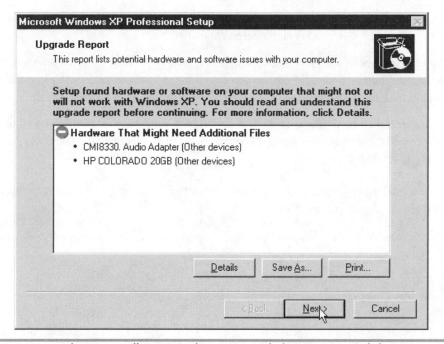

Figure 13-8 Upgrade Report telling you where you might have incompatibilities

In a normal upgrade, the final GUI phase is just a series of messages telling you about Windows XP and indicating what is happening. No installer interaction is needed. Setup will load and install with their original settings the components that were in the previous system. When component installation is done, Start menu items are installed, components are registered, settings are saved, and all temporary files are removed. The computer is restarted, and Windows XP will start to load. After automatically adjusting your screen resolution, you may be asked to press CTRL-ALT-DELETE to begin and to log on with a username and password, and then in all cases the Welcome to Microsoft Windows appears, asking you to spend a few minutes setting up your computer.

1. Click Next in the lower-right corner. You are asked if you want to activate Windows now over the Internet. If so, click Yes and then Next.

2. If you activate now, you are asked it you want to register with Microsoft. See the discussion under "Activate Windows XP" earlier in this module. If you do want to register, click Yes and Next, enter the registration information requested, and again click Next.

3. If you are not already connected to the Internet, you will be asked if you want to do that. If so, follow the instructions on the screen and click Next as needed.

4. Enter the names of the users of this computer and click Next. If you indicated you wanted to activate the computer and you are connected to the Internet, you will be told that you have completed activating and, if selected, registering Windows. Click Finish.

5. If you are asked to enter and confirm an initial password that will be used for all users (these can be changed after starting Windows), do that and click OK. Windows XP will continue to load.

When loading is complete, the Windows XP default desktop will appear with the start menu open, as shown in Figure 13-9.

Figure 13-9 Initial Windows XP Window

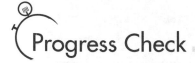

Progress Check

1. If you must boot from DOS or Windows 3.*x*, what program must be run during bootup to speed up the file transfer?

2. What are the typical network settings that are installed by default?

3. To run an upgrade, what is the one primary task you must do?

CRITICAL SKILL
13.6 Choose Optional Components

There are a large number of components in Windows XP, many of which are automatically installed for you. In addition, there a number of optional components that you can choose to install or not, but you cannot make that choice until after you have completed the installation of the OS, unlike in earlier versions of Windows. A simple expedient is to just accept the default selections, but there are so many possible things you might want to do with the computer that it is a good idea to go through the optional components and determine if there are any you need. You install additional components using Add Or Remove Programs in the Control Panel, shown in Figure 13-10. Although additional components add capability to your system, they also take up disk space and possibly utilize resources such as memory and CPU cycles if they are running. It is therefore important to install only the components that you are certain you will need.

Review the Optional Components

The first step is to review the optional components that are available within Windows XP. Many of these are discussed elsewhere in this book, so the following outline simply provides a brief description of each of the components as they are listed by the Windows Components Wizard:

● **Accessories and Utilities**   Tools, small applications, and games that make use of the computer easier and more fun. All installed by default.

---

1. To speed up the file transfer in the initial phases of Setup, run the program Smartdrv.exe, which is included with DOS 6.*x* and Windows 3.*x* as a compressed file Smartdrv.ex_ on the distribution diskettes. This file must be expanded with Expand.exe, also on the distribution diskettes (type **expand a:\smartdrv.ex_ c:\smartdrv.exe**, assuming that you are in the directory with Expand.exe).

2. The typical network settings that are installed by default with Windows XP Setup include Client for Microsoft Networks, File and Print Sharing for Microsoft Networks, QoS Packet Scheduler, and the TCP/IP protocol.

3. To run an upgrade, you must start Setup from an upgradable version of Windows for the product you wish to install.

Accessories:

- **Calculator**   Provides an on-screen calculator for both scientific and general math.

- **Character Map**   Provides special characters and symbols that can be inserted in documents.

- **Clipboard Viewer**   Allows looking at the information on the Clipboard.

- **Desktop Wallpaper**   Provides background images that can be used for the desktop.

- **Document Templates**   Provides document templates for the most common programs.

- **Mouse Pointers**   Provides alternative mouse pointers.

- **Paint**   Provides the means to create and edit simple bitmapped pictures.

Games:

- **FreeCell**   A logical form of the solitaire card game.

- **Hearts**   A card game played against the computer.

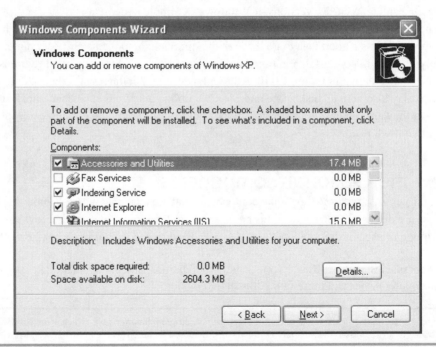

Figure 13-10 Adding or removing Windows components

- **Internet Games**   Games played over the Internet with multiple people including Backgammon, Checkers, Hearts, Reversi, and Spades.
- **Minesweeper**   Provides a strategy game.
- **Solitaire**   Classic card game.
- **Spider Solitaire**   Solitaire with multiple card decks.

- **Fax Services**   Allows the sending and receiving of facsimile transmissions.

- **Indexing Service**   Provides the means to index the text in documents on a hard disk so that full text searches can be done very quickly. Installed by default.

- **Internet Explorer**   Provides the means to access both the World Wide Web on the Internet, as well as web pages on an intranet. Installed by default.

- **Internet Information Services (IIS)**   Allows the distribution of web pages over the Internet or an intranet—a web server (Windows XP Professional only).

  - **Common Files**   Provides files required by IIS components.
  - **Documentation**   Provides information on IIS.
  - **File Transfer Protocol (FTP) Service**   Allows the transfer of files over the Internet or an intranet using FTP.
  - **FrontPage 2000 Server Extensions**   Provides server support for many of FrontPage's features.
  - **Internet Information Services Snap-In**   Allows the management of IIS from the Microsoft Management Console (MMC).
  - **SMTP Service**   Allows the use of the Simple Mail Transfer Protocol (SMTP) in IIS to handle Internet or intranet mail service.
  - **World Wide Web Service**   Provides for the publishing of web pages on the Internet or an intranet.

- **Management and Monitoring Tools**   Allows network performance monitoring and improvement.

  - **Simple Network Management Protocol (SNMP)**   Allows the monitoring and reporting of activity in network devices.
  - **WMI SNMP Provider**   Uses Windows Management Instrumentation (WMI) to allow applications to access SNMP information.

- **Message Queuing Services**   (Professional only) Provides the messaging services needed by applications that are distributed over a network, even when part of the network is down.

- **Active Directory Integration**   Uses Active Directory when the computer is part of a domain.
- **Common**   Provides the core components of Message Queuing Service.
- **MSMQ HTTP Support**   Allows Microsoft Message Queuing Services (MSMQ) to use Hypertext Transfer Protocol (HTTP) to send and receive messages.
- **Triggers**   Notifies an application when a message arrives in a queue.

- **MSN Explorer**   Provides a combination of web browsing and Internet e-mail services. Installed by default.

- **Networking Services**   Allows the transfer of information among both local and remote computers.

  - **RIP Listener**   Uses the Routing Information Protocol to listen for route updates from routers.
  - **Simple TCP/IP Services**   Provides the Character Generator, Daytime Discard, Echo, and Quote of the Day services used in TCP/IP.
  - Universal Plug and Play   Provides for the use of Plug and Play networking devices.

- **Other Network File and Print Services**   Allows Macintosh and UNIX users to access a Windows XP.

  - **Print Services for UNIX**   Allows connected UNIX users to send print jobs to printers on Windows XP.

- **Outlook Express**   Allows the creating, sending, receiving, and storage of e-mail and the use and maintenance of an address book. Installed by default.

- **Update Root Certificates**   Allows secure web browsing, downloads, and e-mail by automatically updating security certificates. Installed by default.

Install the Optional Components

Installing optional components is straightforward, as shown with these steps:

1. Open the Start menu, click Control Panel, in Category view click Add Or Remove Programs (in Classic view double-click Add Or Remove Programs), and click Add/Remove Windows Components in the taskbar on the left. The dialog box that you saw in Figure 13-10 will open.

2. To look at the details within a major component, click the component, such as Accessories And Utilities, and click Details. There can be a second level of details; for example, click Games within Accessories And Utilities to get the list of games that can be installed.

3. To select a component that is not installed, click the check box on its left to add a checkmark. To remove a component that is already installed, click to clear the check box.

Ask the Expert

Q: I don't have a particular need for any of the optional components, but I suspect I will at a later date. Is there any need to install it now?

A: No. It is best to wait until you know you have a need and then install the component.

4. When you have gone through all of the optional components and made the additions and deletions that you want to make, click Next. The Windows Component Wizard will install or remove the necessary software. When it is done, click Finish.

Progress Check

1. When, during an installation, do you install the optional components of Windows XP?

2. How many optional components should you install?

3. If you want to have a small web site on your computer, what component do you need to install?

Project 13 Performing a Clean Install from a CD

Use this exercise to see the complete and concise set of steps to do a clean install when booting from the installation CD.

Step by Step

1. Place the Windows XP installation CD in its drive and restart the computer. When you see the notice Press Any Key To Boot From CD, press ENTER. Windows Setup will begin.

2. Press ENTER to setup Windows XP. Press F8 to agree to the license agreement. If requested, press ESC to continue installing a fresh copy of Windows XP.

(continued)

---

1. The optional components of Windows XP are installed after the installation of Windows XP itself has completed.

2. You should install only the optional components that you truly need. Otherwise, they will only take up space and potentially use up resources.

3. To run a web site under Windows XP (Professional only), you need to install the Internet Information Services (IIS) component.

3. Use the arrow keys to select the partition you want to use and then press D to delete that partition. Press ENTER to confirm the partition deletion. Press L to begin the deletion.

4. Use the arrow keys to identify the partition you want to use and then press ENTER to select that partition.

5. Use the arrow keys to select the NTFS formatting of the partition you selected and press ENTER. The partition will be formatted, files will be copied to the hard disk, and then the computer will be restarted and the Windows XP Setup GUI window will open.

6. When asked about the regional and language options, accept the defaults and click Next. Enter your name and the name of your organization and click Next. Enter the product key and click Next.

7. Enter the computer name, enter and confirm the administrator's password in the Professional Edition, and click Next. If asked, enter the modem dialing information and click Next. Make any needed changes to the date and time and click Next.

8. Select Typical (Network) Settings and click Next. Choose whether the computer is a member of network workgroup or a network domain, enter either the workgroup name or the domain name, and click Next. If you select to be a member of a domain, enter a domain registered user name and password, and click OK. Setup will complete the installation and then restart the computer.

9. If you are in a domain, the Network Identification Wizard will open. Click Next, choose whether to add a user, click Next, and then click Finish. Also, if you are in a domain press CTRL-ALT-DELETE when requested, enter the administrator's password, and press ENTER.

10. If told the screen should be resized, click the icon in the notification area on the right of the toolbar. Click Yes to do the resizing, and click Yes again to accept it.

11. When told you have 30 days to activate the product, click the icon in the notification area. Click Yes, Let's Activate Windows Over The Internet Now and click Next. Click Yes to register while activating, and click Next. Enter your name and other information and click Next. When told you have successfully activated and registered your product, click OK.

Project Summary

If you have done the preparation suggested in Module 12, the actual installation of Windows XP is quite easy, as you have just seen. The key, of course, is to have done the preparation.

Module 13 Mastery Check

1. What are several of the different ways you can start and run Setup?

2. Which of the following are legitimate upgradable products to Windows XP Home? Windows 3.1, Windows for Workgroups, Windows NT 3.*x* Workstation, Windows 95, Windows NT 4 SP2 Workstation, Windows 98, Windows 98 SE, Windows Me, Windows 2000 Professional, Windows XP Professional

3. Which of the following are legitimate upgradable products to Windows XP Professional? Windows 3.1, Windows for Workgroups, Windows NT 3.*x* Workstation, Windows 95, Windows NT 4 SP2 Workstation, Windows 98, Windows 98 SE, Windows Me, Windows 2000 Professional, Windows XP Home

4. Can you do an upgrade of the current OS if you boot from the CD?

5. What is the most likely set of steps to start Setup for a clean install on a new computer?

6. What is the most likely set of steps to start Setup for an upgrade from Windows 98?

7. Why is it beneficial to be connected to the Internet while running Setup?

8. To activate Windows XP, how long do you have and what are the two ways you can do it?

9. If you want to connect to a NetWare server, what must you do while setting up Windows XP?

10. If you are a member of a domain, what unique entries must you make while running Setup?

11. How are the Windows XP optional components installed?

Module 14

Maintaining Windows XP

Maintaining a Windows XP system has many facets. You will most probably want to add and change application and utility software to the system to do everything from word processing, to accounting, to architectural drawing. You may want to add and change some pieces of hardware such as printers, tape drives, sound cards, and scanners. When the system runs into problems, you may want to get remote assistance and you most likely will want to get what information the system can give you about itself. Finally, Windows XP itself has three tools to help you maintain it: an automatic update facility that downloads patches or fixes to the operating system (OS), a system restore capability that restores the system to the last-known good configuration, and a system repair function that replaces damaged pieces of the OS. In this module, we will discuss each of these facets.

CRITICAL SKILL
14.1 Add and Remove Software

Almost all application and utility software today comes in one of two ways: on a CD or downloaded over the Internet.

NOTE

In medium to larger organizations, application software might be available on a server and the installation might be across a LAN. It is generally better to download the software and then do the installation from your computer.

Install Software from a CD

If you get the software on a CD and your computer is less than five years old, all you need to do is put the CD in the drive, wait for the install program to automatically load, and follow the instructions on the screen, which normally are very few. When the installation is complete, you probably have to acknowledge that by clicking OK or Finish and remove the CD from its drive. That is all there is to it.

If you have an older computer, first make sure it can run the software; and if so, open Windows Explorer, locate the CD-ROM drive, and open its root directory by clicking the drive itself. In the root directory, an example of which is shown in Figure 14-1, you should see an Autorun text file. In newer computers, this file is automatically read and executed. If you double-click it, you should see the path and program that needs to be started to begin the installation, like this:

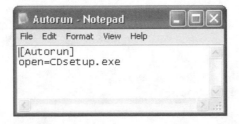

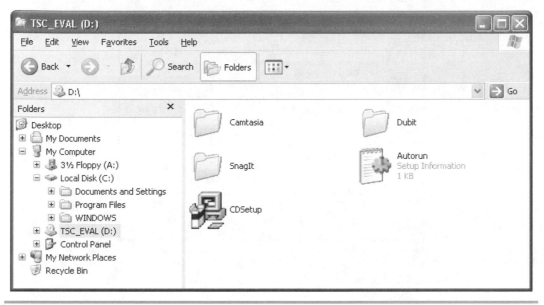

Figure 14-1 The root directories of most recent installation CDs contain an Autorun text file.

Follow the path in the Autorun text file to the program (no path means that it is in the root directory), and double-click it.

TIP

If you are having trouble installing a program for no discernable reason, make sure you are logged on with administrative privileges. Some programs or installation situations require that, and without it the program just refuses to install.

Install Software from the Internet

There are several ways that programs are downloaded from the Internet:

- A large file is downloaded, which you must manually double-click to start the installation.
- A large file is downloaded and automatically starts itself to begin the installation.
- A smaller file is downloaded and either automatically or manually started; it then downloads the remainder of the program as it is being installed.

Look at one example of this with a commonly downloaded program, Netscape Navigator, using these instructions:

1. Open the Start menu and click Internet; in the Address bar, type **http://www.netscape.com** and press ENTER. The Netscape home page will open.

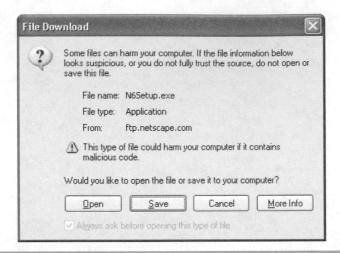

Figure 14-2 The File Download dialog box enables you to choose between saving and opening the downloaded file.

2. Click Downloads in the upper-right corner. Click Download. The File Download dialog box will open, as shown in Figure 14-2. Click Save. The Save As dialog box will open. The default location is the desktop, which is good, at least initially, because you have to double-click the program to get it started. With the desktop open, click Save.

TIP

Unless you are specifically told otherwise, always save a downloaded file to your hard disk and then start it by double-clicking. That way, if there is a problem, you can restart it without having to download it a second time.

3. When you are told the download is complete, click Close. Double-click the program that is now on your desktop and follow the instructions that are presented to you. If, as in the case of Netscape, additional files must be downloaded, the installation process can be fairly slow with several long pauses that you might otherwise interpret as the installation being complete.

4. When the installation is complete, you may be notified, the program may be started, Windows Explorer may be opened to show where the program is installed, and/or one or more shortcuts may be left on the desktop. Netscape does both the last two items, leaving these shortcuts on the desktop if all programs were downloaded:

5. Close the Explorer window and, if you wish, start Netscape by double-clicking its shortcut.

Remove Software

If you want to get rid of a program you have installed, there may be two ways to do that, and at least one way not to do it. You do not want to just locate the main program files in Windows Explorer and delete them. That will leave files stored in other locations that are not obvious, and it will leave all the settings for the program in the Registry. To correctly remove a program, you need to either use the uninstall program that comes with many programs or use Windows XP's Add Or Remove Programs. See how to do the latter with the following set of steps:

1. Open the Start menu, click Control Panel, and click (double-click if in Classic view) Add Or Remove Programs. The Add Or Remove Programs control panel will open, similar to what you see in Figure 14-3.

2. Select the program you want to remove and click Change/Remove. Click Yes, you are sure you want to remove the program. The Remove Programs From Your Computer Wizard will start and display the progress.

3. When Uninstall has successfully completed, you will be told that. Click OK, close the Add Or Remove Programs window, and close the Control Panel.

Ask the Expert

Q: **Why would I want to remove a program?**

A: There are a number of reasons, you may be done with a program, such as an annual tax package, a program may be causing your system problems, or you may want to recover the disk space being used by the program.

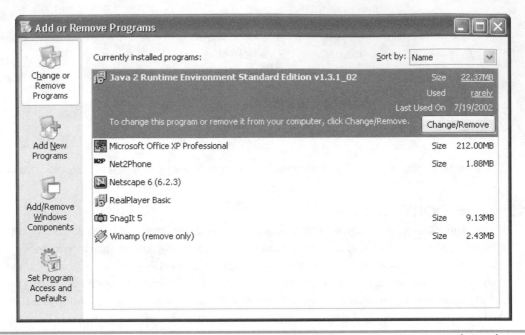

Figure 14-3 Programs are removed through the Add Or Remove Programs control panel.

CRITICAL SKILL
14.2 # Add and Remove Hardware

Much of the hardware, such as the monitor, keyboard, mouse, disk drives, modem, and networking cards that are a common part of a computer, are installed when you install Windows XP. Other devices, such as printers, scanners, and cameras, are added after installation and are a separate and distinct process. These are called *peripheral devices,* and their installation either goes without a hitch or is a major challenge; rarely is there anything in between. If a piece of hardware is Plug and Play and has been certified for use with Windows XP in Microsoft's Hardware Compatibility List (HCL) discussed in Module 12, then it normally installs with great ease: you simply plug it in and you can use it. Often when you first turn on the computer after installing the hardware, you will get a little balloon message telling you that you have new hardware, as shown next. If you click the icon pointed to by the balloon, the installation will proceed or you are told that it has successfully completed.

The problems normally occur when you have older hardware and, even if it is Plug and-Play, the drivers are not included with or are not installed with Windows XP. There are a very large number of such devices and installation situations, so there is not a way to discuss them all. What I will do is to describe two different situations that I encountered and what I did to get the hardware operable, with the hope that the techniques I used will help you get your hardware running.

Installing a Legacy Adapter

I have a six-year-old C-Media CMI8330 audio adapter that Windows XP can see but doesn't know what to do with. When XP first sees it, the balloon you saw in the preceding section is displayed. When I click that balloon, I get the Found New Hardware Wizard. If I accept the default Install The Software Automatically, I get told that the wizard cannot find the correct software, so I must locate the appropriate software or *device driver.*

TIP

The word "legacy" is computer-eze for "old."

Locating Device Drivers

There are three sources of device drivers: the manufacturer, Microsoft, and third-party web sites. The manufacturer is generally the best source; but as hardware gets older, the manufacturer stops writing new drivers. The easiest way to look for manufacturer support is on the Internet. If you know the web site, you can enter it, or you may have to search for it. If you are searching, start out by just typing the name in Internet Explorer's Address bar. This uses MSN Search and gives you a list of sites. When I typed **C-Media**, the eighth entry in the search list was "C-Media Electronics, Inc.," which is the correct manufacturer for my audio card. I clicked Download, selected my card, and, whoops, the latest driver they had was for Windows 2000/Me. I downloaded and tried this driver, but it only partially worked. I e-mailed their technical support, but as of when this book went to press I was still waiting for a reply.

Microsoft has the most popular drivers for recent devices and, as a part of Windows Update (discussed later in this module), the ability to scan your system and see if it has any drivers to help you. The first step with Microsoft is to look in the hardware compatibility list (http://www.microsoft.com/hcl) and see if the device is listed there. In my case, my device was not listed, let alone supported by XP, as you can see in Figure 14-4.

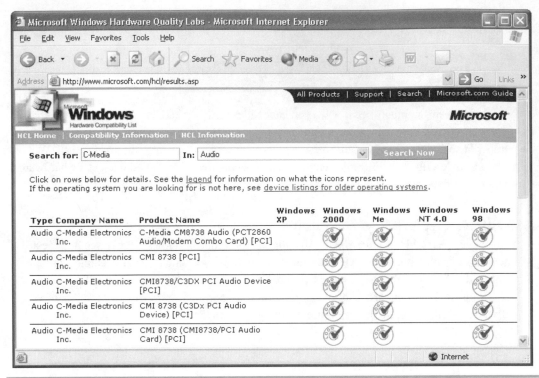

Figure 14-4 Check the Microsoft HCL for support of a device you want to install.

There are a number of third-party sources. I went to Google (my favorite search engine, at http://www.google.com), typed in **device drivers**, and in the first ten entries, got the following sites (in the order presented), which answered my question to varying degrees:

- **Driver Guide** at http://www.driverguide.com requires that you join for a free membership. It has lots of ads, but it has a great new search capability, *and* it has a driver that works with good instructions for installing it, and lots of good comments from others who have installed it.

- **Windows Drivers** at http://www.windrivers.com requires that you register and pay $49.95 per year or $29.95 for six months, and provides a newsletter and other support services. I did not pay to go in to see if they had the driver.

- **The Driver Zone** at http://www.driverzone.com is a free site whose first pages were well done, but I repeatedly got a script error as it was accessing the database for C-Media drivers.

- **Drivers Headquarters** at http://www.drivershq.com is a free site, not very well designed, that after a search gave me the manufacturer's web site to find a driver.

- **Mr. Driver** at http://www.mrdriver.com is a free site overrun with ads that I found hard to use. When I was finally able to search for C-Media, I just got the company's web site.

● **Driver Forum** at http://www.driverforum.com is a free bulletin board where you can post and respond to messages. It also has a link back to Driver Guide for actual driver downloads.

Installing a Device Driver

Once you have found a device driver, it must be installed. Normally, and in my case, the downloaded file is compressed or "zipped," so the first step is to extract the individual files, after which you can install the device. Assume the downloaded file is on your desktop and use these steps:

1. Open Windows Explorer, open the C: drive, right-click the right pane, choose New | Folder, and give the folder the name of the device you are installing (mine's called "C-Media").

2. Drag the file you downloaded to the new folder, double-click the file once it is in the folder, and then click Extract All Files in the tasks pane. The Extraction Wizard will open.

3. Click Next, accept the proposed current folder as the new location for the extracted files, click Next, and then click Finish. Windows Explorer will display the extracted files. Click Close.

4. If the Found New Hardware Wizard is already open, skip to Step 5. Otherwise, open the Start menu, click Control Panel, switch to Classic view if needed, and double-click System. Click the Hardware tab, click Device Manager, double-click the device that needs the driver (it should have an exclamation point over it), and click Reinstall Driver on the General tab. The Hardware Update Wizard opens; it is essentially the same as the Found New Hardware Wizard.

5. Click Install From A List Or Specific Location (Advanced) and click Next. Click Don't Search. I Will Choose The Driver To Install, and click Next. Uncheck Show Compatible Hardware. Click Have Disk.

6. Click Browse and navigate to the new folder containing the files you extracted from the file you downloaded. It should contain an .INF driver information file.

7. Click Open, click OK, and click Next to do the actual installation; when you are told that the wizard has finished installing, click Finish. Close any remaining dialog boxes and windows.

Try out your device to make sure it is working properly. If for some reason it is not working, go back to the second sentence of Step 4 beginning "Otherwise, open the Start menu…," but instead of clicking Reinstall Driver, click Troubleshoot and follow the instructions to try to solve your problems. Also try contacting the manufacturer and using the bulletin board forums to ask and get answers to questions.

Installing a Scanner

I have a Hewlett-Packard (HP) ScanJet 5100C scanner that is between four and five years old. When I tried to install the HP scanner software that comes with the scanner (actually a downloaded update dated 3/20/00), the system would not boot and I had to press F8 and return to the last-known good configuration. Upon rebooting, Windows XP detected that it had crashed and asked if it could send a report to Microsoft, which I approved. When that was complete, the Microsoft Online Crash Analysis web page opened, telling me that the error was caused by a device driver, as shown in Figure 14-5, but otherwise not proving helpful.

I looked up the ScanJet 5100C on the HP web site; what they had for Windows XP was for people that had been running the HP PrecisionScan Software before doing an upgrade to Windows XP. I had done a clean install, so I could not use the downloadable software. I called HP customer support (one of the few companies still providing telephone support) and was told that the ScanJet 5100C "was so old" that HP was no longer supporting and supplying drivers for it, but that Windows XP itself had a basic driver built into it that provided some functionality, which was automatically installed.

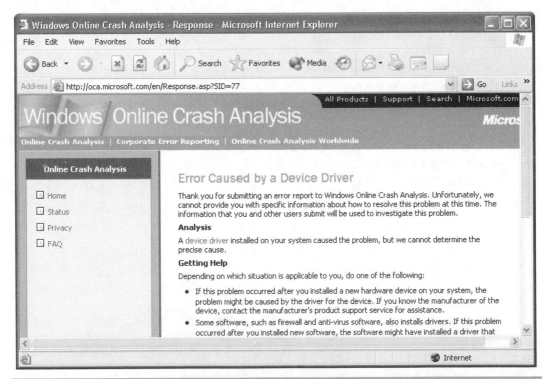

Figure 14-5 Microsoft's Online Crash Analysis trying to identify the cause of a crash

I had been used to using the scanner with HP's software, so I had not tried to use any Windows XP functionality. I opened the Control Panel, double-clicked (in Classic view) Scanners And Cameras, and, sure enough, there was my scanner, like this:

When I double-clicked the scanner, the Scanner and Camera Wizard opened and let me perform the basic function of scanning an image into the computer as an image file. In addition, other programs such as OCR (optical character recognition) and faxing programs can use these scanning functions in Windows XP.

Progress Check

1. What is the most common way today to install software?

2. When downloading software over the Internet, as a general rule, should you choose the Save or Open File download dialog box?

3. If a piece of hardware is "Plug and Play," what does that mean?

4. What are three sources of device drivers?

---

1. Most programs that you buy in a retail outlet and some that you buy over the Internet come on one or more CDs, which you use to install the program.

2. Unless you are specifically given instructions to choose Open, always choose Save because you then have the file on your computer and can reinstall it in the future without downloading it again.

3. Plug and Play means that in the best case, and often, you can plug the device into the computer, turn on the computer, and use the device. In some cases, you may have to go through a couple of installation steps.

4. The three sources of device drivers are the manufacturer, Microsoft, and third-party web sites.

CRITICAL SKILL
14.3 # Get Remote Assistance

Remote Assistance allows someone, at your invitation, to look at what is happening on your computer, control it for purposes of assisting you or repairing software, and chat with you while he or she is doing that. The other person can be an associate at work on your network, or it can be a Microsoft or other software publisher product support person connecting to your computer over the Internet. The other person must also be using Windows XP, and both of you must have Passport accounts and Windows Messenger to chat. The other person can look at and control your computer only if you invite him, you can specify how long he has access, you can determine if he can only look or whether he also can control, and there is a "Kill" button you can click to instantly disconnect the other person. There are three functions connected with using Remote Assistance: setting it up, being the requester, and being the helper.

Set Up Remote Assistance

Remote Assistance is installed and enabled when Windows XP is installed. You can turn it off, turn it back on again, and determine several settings through the Control Panel. Here's how:

1. Open the Start menu, click Control Panel and, if necessary, switch to Classic view; and double-click System. The System Properties dialog box will open.

2. Click the Remote tab and make sure Allow Remote Assistance Invitations To Be Sent From This Computer is checked, and click Advanced. The Remote Assistance Settings dialog box will open, as shown next.

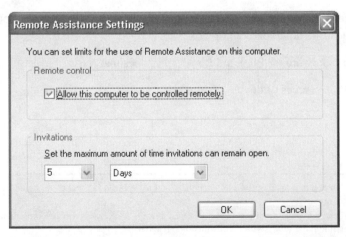

3. Determine if you want the person helping you to also control your computer, and check or uncheck the Remote Control check box accordingly. Then determine how long you want an invitation for remote assistance to remain open and set the period accordingly.

4. Click OK twice to close the two open dialog boxes, and then click Close to put away the Control Panel.

Request Remote Assistance

In order to get remote assistance, you must first have someone willing to provide it, and then you must formally request via e-mail or Windows Messenger that the assistance be provided. Occasionally while you are getting product support, the support person may ask if you would like her to look at your computer. Another situation is that you can be talking to a work associate discussing a problem you are having with your computer and the associate can say "let me see what you are talking about." If you feel comfortable in either of these situations, then you can send out the invitation and begin the remote assistance with these steps:

1. Open the Start menu and click All Programs | Remote Assistance. The Help And Support Center will open, as shown in Figure 14-6.

2. Click Invite Someone To Help You. You are given a choice of using Windows Messenger or either Outlook Express or Microsoft Outlook, whichever is your primary e-mail program. If you use Windows Messenger, you must have a Passport account and the person from whom you are requesting assistance needs to be online to respond. Select that person and

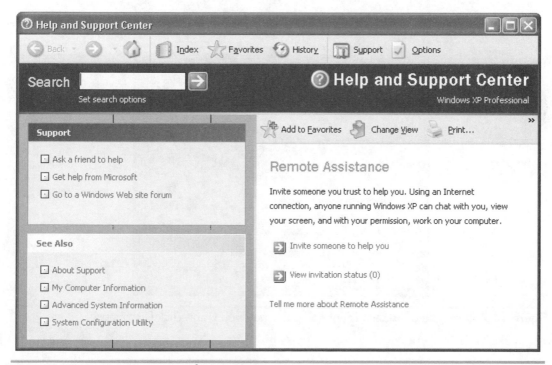

Figure 14-6 Initiating a request for assistance

click Invite This Person. A message will appear telling you that an invitation has been sent and you need to wait for a response, like this:

3. If the other person accepts your invitation, you are told that and asked whether you want to let this person view your screen and chat with you. Click Yes. The Remote Assistance window will open, as you can see in Figure 14-7.

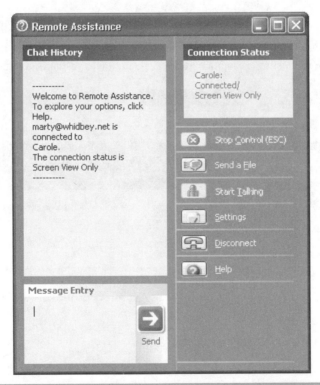

Figure 14-7 If remote assistance is not going the way you want, click Disconnect.

14

4. Type a message to the other person; or if you have speakers and a microphone, you can speak to each other. At this point, the other person can see anything you do on your computer, so you do whatever is causing you a problem.

5. If the other person wants to do something on your computer, she can click Take Control. You then get a message, shown next, asking if you want to share control of your computer. If you want to do that, click Yes. If you become uncomfortable with the other person controlling your computer, you can click Stop Control or press ESC at any time.

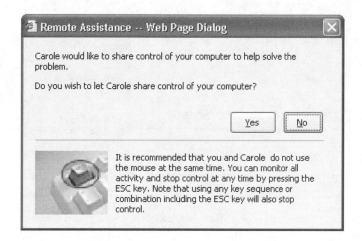

6. When you are ready to end the Remote Assistance session, send a message to that effect to the other person, click Disconnect, and close both the Remote Assistance and the Help and Support Center windows.

NOTE

You are protected from misuse of Remote Assistance in four ways: without an invitation, the person giving assistance cannot come onto your computer; you can limit both the time the invitation remains open and the time the person can be on your computer; you can determine whether the person can control your computer or just look at it; you can click Stop Control or press ESC or any key sequence that includes ESC at any time to immediately cut the other person off.

Provide Remote Assistance

If you want to provide remote assistance, you have a simple set of steps, as follows:

1. When the helper receives a request for assistance, as you can see next, she can either accept or decline it by clicking the appropriate link or pressing ALT-T or ALT-D, respectively.

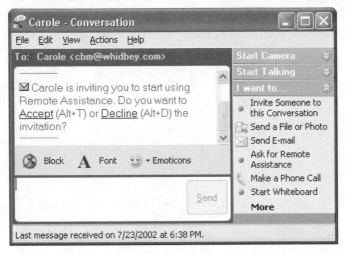

2. If you click Accept or press ALT-T, Remote Assistance loads; and given that the other person approves, you are shown their screen. You can view it actual size, which means that you have to scroll it both horizontally and vertically to see it all, or you can scale it to fit in the window on the right of your screen, as you can see in Figure 14-8.

3. In this position, you can see anything that is displayed on the other screen. If you wish, and the other person agrees, you can take control of the other computer by clicking Take Control and then clicking OK when the other person gives their approval. You can now do anything on that computer within Windows that you could do if you were sitting in front of it.

4. If you want to return sole control to the other person, you can click Release Control or press ESC, and you can click Disconnect to end the session. If you do that or the other person disconnects, click Close in the Remote Assistance window and in the Conversation dialog box.

<table>
<tr><td>CRITICAL SKILL
14.4</td></tr>
</table>

Get System Information

Often as you are working through various situations on your computer, you want information about the computer and its components. In addition, when you are working with a product support professional, he may want or need information about how your computer is configured and what hardware and software you have on it. In Module 10, you read about the Task Manager and the information it supplies, primarily telling you what is running at the current moment on

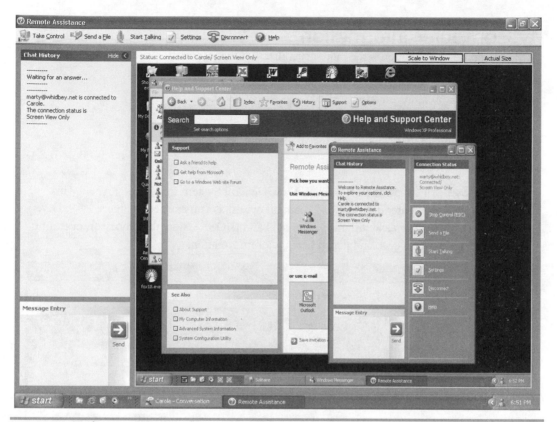

Figure 14-8 The remote screen shown on the assistance provider's screen

your computer and how well it is running. Windows XP has two other, much more extensive, information sources about what hardware and software is installed on your computer and the resources used by the hardware. These two sources of information are My Computer Information and System Information. There are a number of ways to start System Information, but both My Computer Information and System Information can be started from the Help and Support Center by opening the Start menu, clicking Help And Support, and then clicking Support in the toolbar. In See Also in the lower left, you will see the two information sources, like this:

> **See Also**
>
> ☐ About Support
>
> ☐ My Computer Information
>
> ☐ Advanced System Information
>
> ☐ System Configuration Utility

My Computer Information

My Computer Information is the more generalized of the information sources. Click My Computer Information to get a list of the information you can view, including

- General system information
- Status of system hardware and software
- Information about the hardware installed on this computer
- List of Microsoft software installed

General System Information   Click View General System Information About This Computer. My Computer Information—General opens, as you can see in Figure 14-9. Here you can see information about the system model and BIOS version, the processor, operating system, memory, hard disk, and general computer information.

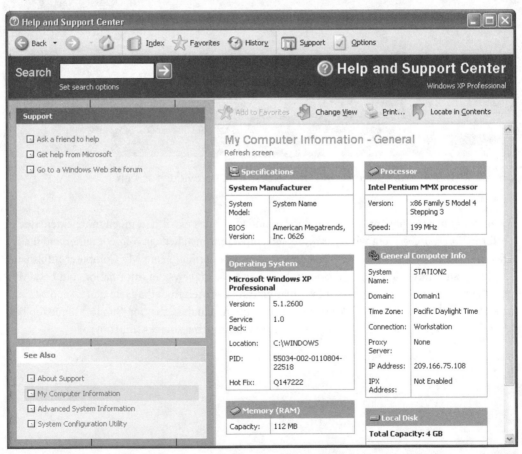

Figure 14-9 General information in My Computer Information

Status of System Hardware and Software   Click Back and then click View The Status Of My System Hardware And Software. This gives you the install date of Windows XP, the creation date of the BIOS, the status of each adapter card in the computer, disk usage, and amount of memory. The adapter card status is handy when you go about installing a card as was discussed earlier in this module. As you can see next, my sound card, even after I got it installed, shows as not being supported.

Hardware			
Component	**Status**	**Update**	**Help**
Video Card	Supported	Not Required	Troubleshooter
Network Card	Supported	Not Required	Troubleshooter
Sound Card	Not Supported	Recommended	Look for driver
USB Controller	null	null	null

Information About the Hardware Installed   Click Back and then click Find Information About The Hardware Installed On This Computer. Additional detailed information is provided on this page about all of the major hardware components, including the disk, display, and various adapter cards.

List of Microsoft Software Installed   Click Back and then click View A List Of Microsoft Software Installed On This Computer. Here you can see not only the Microsoft software installed, but probably most valuably, the programs that are in the Startup Program Group and therefore automatically started when you start Windows XP. Also of value in this page is the crash information. Remember how earlier in the module I said that I tried to install the HP ScanJet software and it crashed my system. Here is the report of that; you can see how it might be valuable to a product support person:

Sunday, July 21, 2002

The application,
C:\SCANJET\PrecisionScan\hpsjbmgr.exe,
generated an application error The error
occurred on 07/21/2002 @ 11:19:33.897
The exception generated was c0000005
at address 00C784DF (hpscnmgr!
PreFreeLibrary)

System Information

System Information provides a wealth of detailed information about everything on your computer. It is the source that you go to for the lowest level of information, as you will see in a moment. Some form of System Information has been in Windows since Windows 98, so it has had significant time to mature. It also means that there are several ways to start System Information, including

- The Help And Support Center Support page, as you saw earlier under "Request Remote Assistance"

- Opening the Start menu and choosing All Programs | Accessories | System Tools | System Information

- Opening the Start menu, clicking Run, typing **msinfo32**, and pressing ENTER or clicking OK

Use one of these techniques now to open System Information. You will see that there are five major sections and a System Summary, as shown in Figure 14-10.

The System Information System Summary is a brief, high-level summary of the operating system, your computer, and the settings on it. The items that may be of more interest are the version of your operating system, the BIOS date, the system name, and the user name. The other five sections all contain a much lower level of detail broken out into several subheadings.

Hardware Resources   Hardware Resources provides detail information about the computer resources being used by the various hardware components in the system. Four of the categories—DMA (Direct Memory Access), I/O (Input/Output port addresses), IRQs

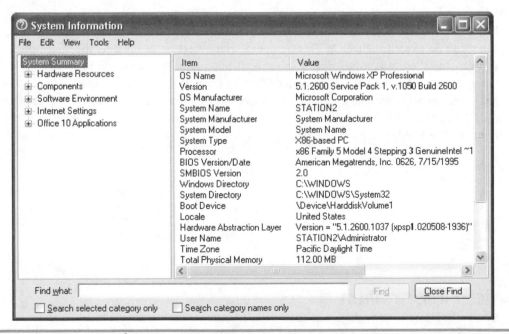

Figure 14-10 System Information System Summary

(Interrupt Request Lines), and Memory—show how hardware components use the specific resource. Conflicts/Sharing identifies any components that use the same resource. If it is a true conflict, it will be identified either as a caution in yellow or an error in red. Forced Hardware is a list of components that you manually installed using settings that Windows would not have otherwise picked.

Components   Components provides detailed information about the hardware components in the computer, the settings and resources they use, and whether there is any problem with them. The devices listed are a standard set of which you may have only a subset, so some components may not have any information. For those components that you do have, a very detailed set of information is displayed, including the resources used and the settings and drivers that have been installed, as shown in Figure 14-11.

NOTE

The Components section of System Information is the best and most concise source of information about a hardware component.

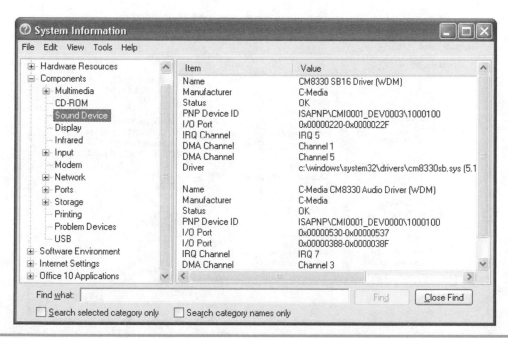

Figure 14-11   System Information Components provides detailed information about hardware.

Software Environment Software Environment provides detailed information about the system and application software that is installed and running, and other information about what is happening in the computer. The installed and running system software information includes Drivers, Running Tasks, Loaded Modules, and Services. The other information includes Environment Variables, Print Jobs, Network Connections, Program Groups, Startup Programs, OLE Registration, and Windows Error Reporting. This is very useful information if you are trying to track down software conflicts.

Internet Settings Internet Settings provides information about how Internet Explorer is set up and other information about it. This includes the version of Internet Explorer that is installed, how it connects to the Internet, how cache is set up and how much disk space is available, how Internet Explorer's content is controlled (if it is), and the level of security that has been set.

Applications Applications—or in my case, Office 10 Applications—provides information about the Microsoft Applications that are installed and considerable detailed information about the document you are currently working on. For example, Figure 14-12 shows information about this module.

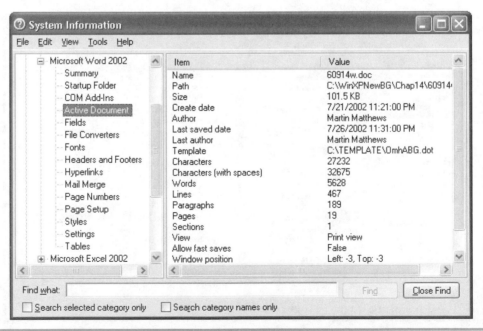

Figure 14-12 Detailed information about a Microsoft Word document

Ask the Expert

Q: I find it really hard to find what I am looking for in System Information. Is there an easy way to do that?

A: Yes. You can use the Find What text box at the bottom of the System Information window to enter what you are looking for and click Find to search for the element you want to find.

Progress Check

1. To use Remote Assistance, what must both parties be using?

2. What is the first action you must take to use Remote Assistance?

3. What are two major sources of information about your computer and how are they accessed?

CRITICAL SKILL
14.5 Update Windows XP

When you finish installing Windows XP, and periodically thereafter if you don't do anything, you are reminded to "Stay current with automatic updates" in a little balloon in the lower right of your screen, like this:

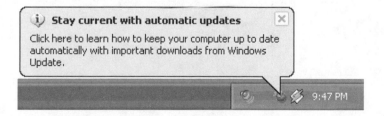

---

1. To use Remote Assistance, both parties must be using Windows XP, Passport, and either Windows Messenger or one of the Microsoft or compatible e-mail handlers.

2. You must locate someone to provide the assistance, and you must invite the person to help you.

3. Two sources of information are My Computer Information and System Information. You can start them both by opening the Start menu, clicking Help And Support, clicking Support in the toolbar, and then clicking one of the information sources in the lower left of the Help And Support window.

If you choose to turn on Automatic Updates, it will automatically determine if any updates are available for your computer, either automatically or manually download the updates over the Internet, and either automatically or manually install updates to Windows XP on a periodic basis, giving you the advantage of the latest fixes from Microsoft. If you choose not to install automatic updates, you can still download and install the updates manually.

Manual Updates

To manually get and install updates, you have to open the Windows Update web site and let it scan your system to determine if updates are needed, downloading and then installing the updates. Use the following steps to do that:

1. Open the Start menu and choose All Programs | Windows Update. You will be connected to the Internet and the Windows Update web page will be displayed, as shown in Figure 14-13.

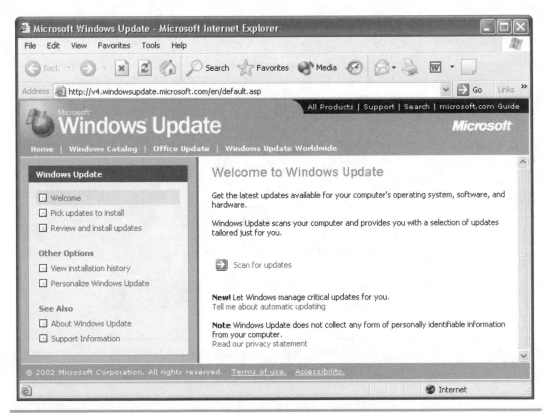

Figure 14-13 Microsoft web site for manually getting updates to download

2. Click Scan For Updates. The system software on your computer will be compared against known updates, and if there are any updates you don't have installed, you will be told, like this:

```
☐ Pick updates to install
   ☐ Critical Updates and Service
      Packs (0)
   ☐ Windows XP (2)
   ☐ Driver Updates (0)
☐ Review and install updates
```

3. If you have updates that need to be or can be installed, click the type of updates (Critical Updates, Windows XP updates, or Driver Updates) to see the explanation of the specific updates and be given the option to download them. For those updates you want to download, click Add.

4. When you have selected all of the updates that you want to download, click Review And Install Updates. Your selections will be displayed, and if you want to go ahead, you can click Install Now.

5. Click Accept when the license agreement is displayed, and then downloading will commence. When downloading is complete, the updates will automatically be installed. When the installation is complete, depending on the update, you may be told that you need to restart your computer. If asked, click OK.

6. If you don't have to restart your computer, close the Internet Explorer window. The updates are in place and ready to use.

Automatic Updates

If Automatic Updates is turned on, Windows detects when you are online and not particularly busy. It then goes out to the Windows Update web site you saw in the preceding section and determines if there are updates you need to download. If so, Automatic Updates will, at your choice, either notify you of the update availability or just automatically download the updates. You can then choose to either automatically install the updates or just be told they have been downloaded and you can install them manually. If you choose to do all three steps (detect updates needed, download them, and install them) automatically, you can schedule a time to do it.

Turn On Automatic Updates

Automatic Updates can be turned on in two ways. Shortly after installing Windows XP, the Stay Current With Automatic Updates balloon appears. This opens the Automatic Updates Setup Wizard. By following its instructions, you can turn on Automatic Updates. You can also access Automatic Updates at any time through the Control Panel. Here's how to turn on Automatic Updates in that way:

1. Open the Start menu, click Control Panel, and double-click System. In the System Properties dialog box that opens, click the Automatic Updates tab, which is then displayed as you can see in Figure 14-14.

2. Determine the amount of automation you want, and click one of the three choices:

   a. The first choice automatically determines if there are updates that are needed and then asks you before downloading, and asks you again before installing them.

   b. The second choice automatically determines if there are updates and automatically downloads them; it then asks you before installing them.

   c. The third choice does everything automatically on a schedule you determine.

3. Click OK when you have finished.

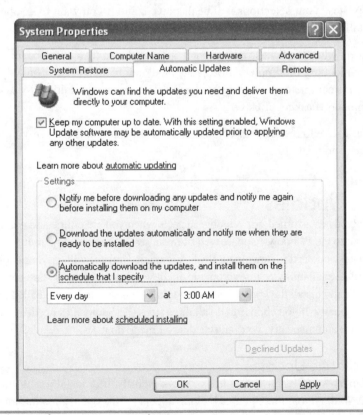

Figure 14-14 Choices for Automatic Updates

Use Automatic Updates

If you choose either the first or second choice in the previous section, you will get a notice when updates are ready to download and/or install. For example, here is the notice that I got with the second choice:

When you click the icon pointed to by this balloon, the Automatic Updates dialog box opens. If you click Details, you will see the specific updates that are being proposed, along with a description of each. You can choose to download and/or install each update by clicking the check box. When you are ready, click either Download or Install, or delay the download and/or installation by clicking Remind Me Later and specifying a time. If you click Download or Install, that process will be carried out.

Maintain Automatic Updates

Once you have installed Automatic Updates, the Automatic Updates tab in the System Properties dialog box (Start | Control Panel | System |Automatic Updates) allows you to maintain Automatic Updates, including turning this feature off and changing your selection of how automatic to make the downloading and installation.

CRITICAL SKILL
14.6 # Restore Windows XP

System Restore is one of the most powerful new features in Windows XP. System Restore keeps track of the changes you make to your system, including the software you install and the settings you make. If a hardware change, a software installation, or something else causes the system not to load, or not to load or run properly, you can use System Restore to return the system to the way it was at some previous time, and do so very easily.

The restore point to which you return the system can either be set by you or automatically determined by the system. Over even a short period of time, like several weeks, you should have several automatic restore points, generally caused by the installation of software or the addition of new hardware. In addition, at any time, you can set a restore point. When the time comes to do a system restore, you can choose which restore point to return the system to. After restoring the system, if you decide that you want to go back to the way the computer was before it was restored, you may also do that.

NOTE

System Restore does not restore or make any changes to data files, only to system and application program files. If you lose or corrupt a data file, such as accounting, spreadsheet, word processing, database, and drawing files, you cannot use System Restore to return those files to a previous state. Data files must be backed up using either the Windows XP or a third-party backup program and then restored from a backup.

In the following sections, you'll see how to

● Set up System Restore

● Create restore points

● Run System Restore

● Undo a System Restore

Set Up System Restore

When you do a default install of Windows XP, System Restore is automatically installed. If you have at least 200MB of free disk space after installing Windows XP, System Restore will be turned on, and the first restore point will be set. If you do not have 200MB remaining, System Restore will be there but not enabled. If at a later date you get more disk space, you can turn it on and set a restore point. Here is how to do that and make other settings, including determining how much disk space System Restore can use:

1. Open the Start menu and click Control Panel; in Classic view, double-click System. In the System Properties dialog box, click the System Restore tab. The System Restore page will appear, as you can see in Figure 14-15.

2. If System Restore is turned off, there will be a checkmark in the check box. Click the check box to turn it on.

3. If you have only one hard disk drive, as is the case in Figure 14-15, you can directly drag the slider to decrease the amount of disk space used by System Restore. If you have multiple drives, you will see the list of them. Click the one you want to change and then click Settings. The Drive Settings dialog box will open. On the System Drive (generally drive C:), all you can do is adjust the disk space usage. On a second or higher drive, you can turn off the System Restore's usage of that drive, as well as the amount of disk space used on that drive.

4. If you have a multiple disk drive situation, when you have adjusted the settings for a given drive, click OK. When you have adjusted the settings for all the drives on the system, click OK.

Figure 14-15 System Restore settings

NOTE

The amount of disk space used by System Restore is dependent on the size of your disk. If you have a relatively small disk, it could use a large amount of the disk to get 200–500MB. Once it has around 500MB, it will back off the percentage of the drive until it gets down to 12 percent. System Restore then takes a fixed 12 percent, at a maximum, whatever that is.

Create Restore Points

If you are planning to do something that might disrupt the system and cause it not to function properly, you probably want to create a restore point so that you can restore your system to where it was immediately before you did the suspect operation. You can use these steps to set a restore point:

1. Open the Start menu and click All Programs | Accessories | System Tools | System Restore. The System Restore window opens, as you can see in Figure 14-16.

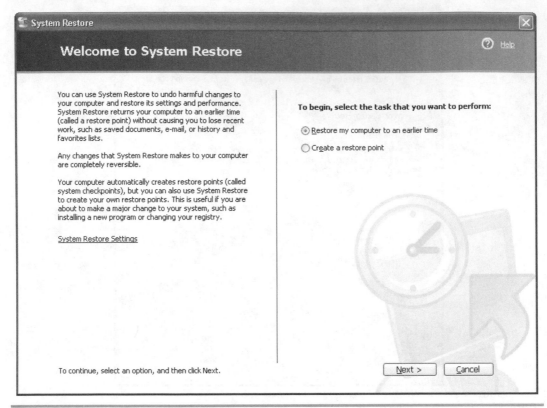

Figure 14-16 The System Restore window is also used to set a restore point.

2. Click Create A Restore Point and click Next. Type a name for the restore name; you don't need to include the date and time because that is automatically added, and you cannot change the name after it is created.

3. When you have a name you are sure you want, click Create. When it is done, you will be told that the restore point was created with the name you gave it and the date and time, like this:

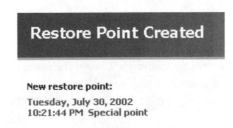

New restore point:
Tuesday, July 30, 2002
10:21:44 PM Special point

4. Click Close.

Run System Restore

When the time comes that you need to run System Restore, the first step is to determine if you can start Windows normally or not. If you can, you run System Restore one way; if you can't, you need to run it another way.

From Normal Windows

If you can start and operate in normal Windows, try to execute the following steps. If you can't make it through these steps without Windows crashing, go to the next section:

1. Open the Start menu and click All Programs | Accessories | System Tools | System Restore. The same windows you saw in Figure 14-16 will open.

2. Accept the default Restore My Computer To An Earlier Time and click Next. The Select A Restore Point window will open, similar to what is shown in Figure 14-17.

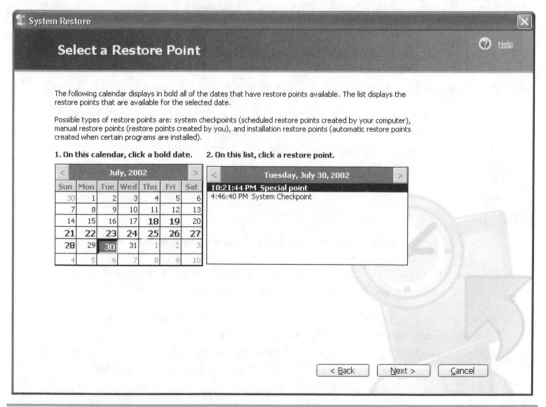

Figure 14-17 Selecting a restore point

3. Select a bold date in the calendar on the left. You can change the month by clicking either < or >. When you have selected a date, click a restore point from the list on the right and click Next.

4. The confirmation window opens telling you that Windows will be restarted, so make sure all documents are saved and other programs are shut down. Click Next. Your system will be shut down and then restarted. As it restarts, you are told you can choose another restore point or undo the restoration. Click OK.

From Safe Mode

Safe Mode is running Windows with the fewest possible drivers and other accessories in an attempt to get it running so that you can fix whatever is preventing it from running in its full form. In Safe Mode, you can start System Restore. Here is how to start in Safe Mode and then start System Restore.

1. If your computer is turned on, turn it off, totally remove all power except for the clock battery, and let it sit for a couple of minutes—at least two full minutes. This allows all of the components to fully discharge and will give you a clean restart.

2. After your computer has sat for at least two minutes without power and with no disks in either the floppy or CD drives, turn it on. As soon as the memory check is complete, press and hold the F8 function key. After a moment, the Windows Advanced Options Menu will appear.

3. Press HOME or use the UP ARROW key to go to the top choice, Safe Mode, and then press ENTER. If the Operating System menu appears, make sure that Microsoft Windows XP is chosen and press ENTER again. You will see many lines of information appear about the drivers that are being loaded, and then Windows will begin loading in Safe Mode.

NOTE

You may or may not have the mouse working, so the instructions here assume you won't.

4. If you are in a domain, press CTRL-ALT-DELETE, enter your password, and press ENTER. Press ENTER to acknowledge you are starting in Safe Mode.

5. Press CTRL-ESC to open the Start menu, use the arrow keys to select All Programs, press ENTER, use the arrow keys to select Accessories, press ENTER, again use the arrow keys to select System Tools, press ENTER, and finally use the arrow keys to select System Restore and press ENTER. The System Restore window will open as you saw earlier.

6. Make sure that Restore My Computer To An Earlier Time is selected; if not, use the arrow keys to select it, and then press ALT-N to go to the next page.

Ask the Expert

Q: I ran System Restore and selected a date that wasn't far enough back. How do I go back and choose an earlier date?

A: To give yourself an extra advantage, undo the restore you just ran (see the next section), and then run the restore again and choose the earlier date. I have actually just run the restore again without running the undo, but infrequently this can cause added problems that are not worth the little time savings.

7. Use the arrow keys to select the restore date you want to use, press TAB to go to the list of restore points, and use the arrow keys to go to the restore point you want to use. Press ENTER. Then press ALT-N to begin the restore.

8. Confirm that no programs are running. If any are, press ALT-TAB to get the list of open programs, then use the arrow keys to select the open program other than System Restore, and then press ALT-F4 to close the program.

9. When you are ready, press ALT-N to begin the restoration. Several messages will appear telling you about the progress and then Windows will be restarted. The System Restore window will appear telling you that the restoration was successful. Click OK.

Undo a System Restore

As good as System Restore is, it is not always the answer, and so you may find yourself in the situation where you want to undo a system restore. Like System Restore, Undo System Restore can be run from normally operating Windows and from Safe Mode.

From Normal Windows

From normal Windows, use the following steps:

1. Open the Start menu and click All Programs | Accessories | System Tools | System Restore. The System Restore window will open.

2. Select Undo My Last Restoration and click Next.

3. The confirmation window opens telling you to make sure all documents are saved and other programs are shut down. Do that and click Next. Your system will be shut down and then restarted. You will then be told that the undo restoration was successful. Click OK.

From Safe Mode

To start in Safe Mode and then start System Restore, use these steps:

1. If your computer is turned on, turn it off for at least two full minutes. Then turn on your computer. As soon as the memory check is complete, press and hold the F8 function key.

2. Press HOME to select Safe Mode, and then press ENTER and press ENTER again if the Operating System menu appears.

3. Press CTRL-ESC to open the Start menu, use the arrow keys and ENTER to select All Programs | Accessories | System Tools | System Restore, and press ENTER. The System Restore window will open.

4. Select Undo My Last Restoration with the arrow keys and press ALT-N. Confirm that no programs are running. When you are ready, press ALT-N to begin the undo restoration. Windows will be restarted, and the System Restore window will appear telling you that the undo restoration was successful. Click OK.

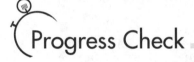

Progress Check

1. What does Automatic Updates do?

2. If you don't use Automatic Updates, is it still possible to get the updates?

3. Before restarting a computer in Safe Mode, what should you do?

---

1. Automatic Updates automatically determines if updates are available for your computer, either automatically or manually downloads the updates over the Internet, and either automatically or manually installs updates to Windows XP on a periodic basis, giving you the advantage of the latest fixes from Microsoft.

2. Yes, if you don't want the updates to be automatically downloaded and/or installed, you can do it manually at a time and in a manner that is most useful to you.

3. Before restarting a computer in Safe Mode, you should power off the computer for at least two minutes and make sure all removable disks are out of their drives.

Project 14 Set Up System Maintenance Procedures

Use this exercise to do a quick review of the major system maintenance procedures discussed in this module, including

- Adding software
- Getting Remote Assistance
- Getting System Information
- Updating Windows XP
- Restoring Windows XP

Step by Step

1. To add most current software purchased in a retail store, place the CD in its drive and follow the instructions on the screen.

2. To add software downloaded from the Internet, use Internet Explorer to locate the download site and then follow the instructions displayed there.

3. To get remote assistance, open the Start menu and click All Programs | Remote Assistance. Click Invite Someone To Help You, select the person from whom you want help, and click Invite This Person. When the person accepts your invitation, click Yes, to indicate that you want to let this person view your screen and chat with you.

4. If the person clicks Take Control, you can accept that by clicking Yes. You can click Stop Control or press ESC at any time. At the end of the Remote Assistance session, click Disconnect, and close both the Remote Assistance and the Help And Support Center windows.

5. To get System Information, open the Start menu, click Help And Support, and then click Support in the toolbar. In the lower left, click My Computer Information, and then click one of the four views on the right. Click Back and another view to see others. Click Advanced System Information and then click View Detailed System Information to open the System Information window. Select categories on the left to see detailed information on the right.

(continued)

6. To turn on Automatic Updates for Windows XP, open the Start menu, click Control Panel, and double-click System. In the System Properties dialog box, select the Automatic Updates tab, click the check box to Keep My Computer Up To Date, and choose how you want to be notified and how automatically you want the updates delivered.

7. To restore Windows XP, open the Start menu, click All Programs | Accessories | System Tools | System Restore, accept the default Restore My Computer To An Earlier Time, and click Next. Select a bold date, click a restore point, and click Next. In the confirmation window, click Next. When the restoration is complete, click OK.

Project Summary

Windows XP provides a number of tools to help you maintain a smoothly running system, including adding and removing software, adding and removing hardware, getting remote assistance, getting information about your system, updating Windows, and restoring Windows.

✓ Module 14 Mastery Check

1. What are the two most common ways today to install a program?

2. What is the most general-purpose way of removing software, and what should you not do to remove software?

3. Where should you look to see if a device is compatible with Windows XP?

4. Where is the best place to look for a device driver, and what are the summary steps to do it?

5. How are you protected from misuse of Remote Assistance?

6. If you are given control while providing remote assistance, what can you do?

7. What are three ways that you can use the information in either My Computer Information or System Information?

8. What are the two ways to get interim updates to Windows?

9. Once you have turned on Automatic Updates, how do you turn it off or change its settings?

10. How is System Restore used to restore data files?

11. If after doing a System Restore you are unhappy with the results, what are the two further steps you can take?

Part V

Appendixes

Appendix A

Mastery Check Answers

Module 1: Exploring Windows XP

1. What does an operating system, such as Windows XP, do?

An operating system, such as Windows XP, performs the central role in managing what a computer does and how it is done. It provides the interface between you and the computer hardware, facilitating your storing a file, printing a document, connecting to the Internet, and transferring information over a local area network without your knowing anything about how the hardware does that.

2. What are three features that are in Windows XP Professional and not in Windows XP Home Edition?

Some of the Windows XP Professional features not in Windows XP Home Edition are

Use with domains

Remote Desktop

Encrypting File System

Restricted File Access

More upgrade options

Enhanced backup and restore

Enhanced automatic updating

Ability to use multiple languages

Built-in support for wireless networks

Support for computers with multiple processors

3. What is the difference between My Computer and Windows Explorer?

Except that they open with different views, there is no difference between Windows Explorer and My Computer.

4. Match up the function on the left with the component on the right.

The correct match of function and component is as follows:

Primary tool for working with files	Windows Explorer
Containers that hold files	Folders
Starts a program from a remote location	Shortcuts
Multimedia playback component	Windows Media Player
Internet web browsing tool	Internet Explorer
Internet e-mail component	Outlook Express

Provides for multiple users on a computer	User Accounts
Allows one computer to take over another	Remote Desktop Connection
Provides automatic and manual updates	Windows Update

5. **What is your primary hard drive normally called, and what is your primary floppy drive always called?**

Your primary hard drive is normally called "drive C:," and your primary floppy drive is always called "drive A:."

6. **Where is printing done in Windows XP?**

Printing is generally done in applications, although it is controlled by Windows.

7. **What is the difference between client/server and peer-to-peer networks?**

In a peer-to-peer network, all computers are both clients and servers; whereas in a client/server network, they are either one or the other.

8. **How are policies and permissions used in Windows XP?**

Policies establish the rules that control many functions within Windows and allow you to promulgate the same rules over many computers. Permissions are used to apply different rules to different groups or individual users.

9. **What does the Control Panel do?**

The Control Panel provides access to many of the hardware and software settings needed for maintenance.

10. **What does "Plug and Play hardware" mean?**

Plug and Play hardware will be automatically detected by Windows XP, and either its driver will be automatically installed if it is in the Windows driver database, or you will be requested to insert a disk containing the driver.

Module 2: Components of Windows XP

1. **When you first turn on the computer, the computer goes through an initial startup procedure and there may be a beep. What is this sequence called and what does it do?**

The initial procedure that a computer goes through when it is first started is called the Power-On Self Test, or POST. The memory and other components will be checked, and you are given a list of the hardware that is found.

2. **If your network is using a domain, what do you have to do to log on?**

Press CTRL-ALT-DELETE.

3. What are two different ways to temporarily stop using the computer, and what is the difference between them?

Logging off and switching users. Switching users keeps all of your programs and network connections active so that you can quickly resume using them. Logging off shuts them down.

4. What does "hibernate" mean?

Hibernate means to save the current state of the computer, including the programs and files that are open and the network connections that are active, and then shut down the computer. This allows you to start up the computer at a later date and resume with exactly the same programs, files, and network connections that you had open when you shut down.

5. What mouse action would you use in each of the following situations? Match the task on the left to the correct mouse action on the right.

The correct mouse commands for each situation are

Open a folder or start a program.	Double-click
Move the mouse to an object.	Point
Move an object around the desktop.	Drag
Select an object.	Click
Open a context or shortcut menu.	Right-click

6. Is the illustration in question 7 a window or a dialog box? Why?

A window because it has a menu bar and a sizing handle.

7. In the illustration, to what does each of the numbers point (match the numbers and the objects)?

The correct names for each of the callouts are

1	Title bar
2	Control Menu icon
3	Menu bar
4	Toolbar
5	Address bar
6	Folders pane
7	Status bar
8	Sizing handle
9	Scroll bar
10	Close button

11   Maximize button

12   Minimize button

8. What is meant by the term "cascading menus" and what is an example of one?

A cascading menu is a series of menus that open one after the other. For example, when you open the Start menu, you can choose All Programs, which allows you to choose Accessories, where you can choose System Tools, and finally you can choose Character Map. In this book, this set of steps is abbreviated as follows: Open the Start menu, choose Programs | Accessories | System Tools, and click Character Map.

9. What are three or four ways you can open Windows Explorer?

Windows XP gives you five ways to open Windows Explorer in the upper right of the Start menu (only four ways if you are not connected to a network). Three of the ways, My Documents, My Pictures, and My Music, open specific folders, whereas My Network Places lets you look for a file on other computers on your network. My Computer opens looking at all the storage devices on your computer.

10. In Windows Explorer, what do you accomplish when you click the plus or minus sign in the folders pane?

Clicking the plus sign next to a folder is called "opening the folder" because it shows the folders beneath it. Similarly, clicking the minus sign is called "closing the folder."

Module 3: Customizing Windows XP

1. What are three changes you can make to the Start menu?

The changes that can be made to the Start menu are these:

- Change the style from Windows XP to the classic Windows Start menu.
- Change the size of the icons on the left.
- Change the number of recent programs kept on the menu.
- Don't show or change the Internet browser and mail programs.
- Change which items are shown on the right side of the menu.

2. What is an icon on the desktop called and what does it do?

An icon on the desktop is normally called a "shortcut," and it is used to start a program or open a folder or file stored in another location. Infrequently, an icon on the desktop is the actual program file.

3. What are two ways to get standard icons on the desktop, such as My Computer and Internet Explorer?

You can turn on standard icons on the desktop, such as My Computer and Internet Explorer, either by turning on the classic Start menu or by turning on these icons through Customize Desktop on the Desktop tab of the Display Properties dialog box.

4. What is the area on the left of the taskbar that you can create and how is it used?

The area you can create on the left of the taskbar is called the Quick Launch toolbar; it contains shortcuts to frequently used programs so that they can be quickly started.

5. What are three changes that you can make to the Windows Explorer window?

Changes you can make to the Windows Explorer window include:

- Adding Address and Links toolbars
- Adding a status bar
- Adding buttons to the Standard Buttons toolbar and changing how they look
- Changing the way files and folders are displayed
- Changing the contents of the left pane from a tasks list to a folders list
- Changing the sorting of files and folders

6. If you are having trouble double-clicking, what can you do?

Use the Control Panel to open the Mouse Properties dialog box and change the double-click speed.

7. What are a couple of the options you have in displaying the mouse pointer?

The options that are available for displaying the mouse pointer include determining how fast the mouse pointer moves for a given hand movement, allowing the pointer to follow very small movements of the mouse, automatically moving the pointer to the default button when you open a dialog box, enhancing your ability to see the mouse on the screen by turning on Display Pointer Trails and Show Location Of Pointer When I Press The CTRL Key, and hiding the pointer while typing.

8. If you get two or more of the same letter when you meant to type just one, what can you do about it?

Use the Control Panel to open the Keyboard Properties dialog box and increase the wait time before producing repeated letters.

9. How do you open the volume control?

Single-clicking the speaker icon in the notification area on the right of the taskbar opens a simple volume control, whereas double-clicking opens a full volume control audio mixer.

10. What are three accessibility options and what do they do?

The accessibility options include

- **StickyKeys** allows you to press SHIFT, CTRL, ALT, or the Windows logo key plus one other key and have the computer interpret it as a single keystroke.
- **FilterKeys** allows a user to quickly press a key twice and have it interpreted as a single keystroke.
- **ToggleKeys** plays a tone when CAPS LOCK, NUM LOCK, or SCROLL LOCK is pressed.
- **SoundSentry** displays a visual indicator when the system makes a sound.
- **ShowSounds** tells compatible systems to display a caption when they make a sound.

- **HighContrast** uses colors and fonts that are easier to read.
- **Cursor Options** makes the cursor easier to see.
- **MouseKeys** allows you to use the numeric keypad instead of the mouse to move the pointer on the screen.

Module 4: Using Files, Folders, and Disks

1. **Can you store a 2,340KB file on a 1.44MB floppy disk?**

No. 2,340KB is 2.34MB, which is larger than the capacity of the floppy disk.

2. **A program you just installed has several .DLL files, an .EXE file, and a .TXT file. Which one do you double-click to start the program?**

The .EXE is the main program file, and you should be able to start the program by double-clicking it.

3. **What is the difference between Tasks view and Folders view in Windows Explorer?**

Tasks view provides a list of tasks, such as Make A New Folder, whereas Folders view lets you see the folder structure on a disk. Folders view allows you to more easily navigate among folders, especially when copying and moving, whereas Tasks view makes performing some tasks easier.

4. **How does Windows' graphical user interface (GUI) help manipulate files and folders?**

The graphical user interface (GUI) allows you to use the mouse to select and drag an object on the screen that represents a file or a folder and have that action accomplish copying or moving a file.

5. **Match up the action on the left with the command on the right. There may be more than one command for one action, and some actions may not have a command.**

The correct matchup between actions and commands is

Action	Command
Copy a file or folder	CTRL-C CTRL-drag (except .EXE file, which creates shortcut)
Back up a file or folder	
Create a shortcut	CTRL-SHIFT-drag
Open a context menu	RIGHT-CLICK
Create a folder	
Move a file or folder	Drag (same drive) CTRL-X then CTRL-V
Rename a file or folder	Slowly click twice Click-F2

Action	Command
Create a zipped file	
Delete a file	Drag it to the Recycle Bin Click-DELETE
Search for a File	

6. What are two ways you can recover deleted items?

To recover deleted items, open the Recycle Bin and drag the items to the folders in which you want them; or open the Recycle Bin, select the items, and click Restore The Selected Items in the tasks pane.

7. What is WinZip and how does it affect Windows zipping?

WinZip is a third-party program for compressing or zipping files. Microsoft uses WinZip technology to do its zipping. If you have WinZip installed, you will get a message box that asks whether you want compressed (zipped) folders to be associated with zipped files. If you say "Yes," you will get a WinZip or other program icon instead of the "zipper" folder.

8. How do file attributes differ between FAT and NTFS files?

NTFS has the Advanced attributes dialog box, where you can encrypt and archive a file; with FAT/FAT32, there is no Advanced dialog box (and therefore no encryption option), but there is an Archive check box in the Properties dialog box.

9. What is the difference between hidden files and read-only files, and what are these properties called?

Hidden files are not displayed in Explorer if the Do Not Show Hidden Files And Folders option is turned on. Read-only files cannot be modified, only read. Hidden and read-only are file and folder *attributes*.

10. What is Backup used for?

Backup is used to make a copy of files and folders on the hard disk to another medium, such as a CD using a CD-RW, or a tape using a tape drive, or even a second hard drive.

Module 5: Printing and Faxing

1. As a general rule, should you use the CD that came with your printer or Windows XP to install your printer?

As a general rule, it is better to use the driver and printer setup provided by Windows than it is to use the CD that comes with the printer. The two exceptions are if the printer came out after Windows XP October, 2001, and if Windows XP does not have a driver for the printer.

2. **What are some of the things you should do before installing a printer?**

Before installing a printer, make sure it is plugged into the correct connector (port) on your computer, is plugged into an electrical outlet, has a fresh ink or toner cartridge (which, along with the print heads, is properly installed), has adequate paper, and is turned on.

3. **What are three kinds of network printers?**

The three kinds of network printers are printers connected to someone else's computer, printers connected to a dedicated printer server, and printers directly connected to a network.

4. **What are the two situations where you would want to print to a file and how do they work?**

The two reasons to print to a file are to take the file to a remote location for printing on a particular printer, and to get information out of one program and into another when the first program has no data export command. In the first case, the information for a printer must be formatted and then sent to a file, so you need to have installed the ultimate printer you want to use. In the second case, you want the "printer" to produce unformatted generic text, so you need to create a "printer" to produce the unformatted generic text.

5. **What are the tasks that are part of controlling a printer queue?**

The tasks that are part of controlling a printer queue include pausing and resuming printing, canceling printing, redirecting documents, and changing a document's properties.

6. **What is a good method of handling several printing priorities?**

One of the best ways to handle ongoing different printer priorities is to have two or more printer definitions for the same printer and to have each definition have a different priority.

7. **What is the one thing you have to do if you have multiple printers?**

With multiple printers, you must pick one as the default to use if you don't specify a printer.

8. **What is a font, what is a typeface, and how do they differ?**

A *font* is a set of characters with the same design, size, weight, and style. A font is a member of a *typeface* family, all members of which have the same design. The font 12-point Arial bold italic is a member of the Arial typeface with a 12-point size, bold weight, and italic style.

9. **What are the three kinds of fonts?**

The three kinds of fonts are outline fonts, which are stored as a set of commands; bitmapped fonts, which are stored as bitmapped images; and vector fonts, which are created with line segments.

10. **What are two of the three ways of loading the Fax Console?**

You can open the Fax Console from the Start menu (Start | All Programs | Accessories | Communications | Fax | Fax Console) by double-clicking the Fax "printer" in the Printers And Faxes window.

Module 6: Using Communications and the Internet

1. What is a modem and what does it do?

A modem is short for "modulator-demodulator" and is used to convert a digital signal (ones and zeros) in a computer to an analog signal (current fluctuations) in a phone line and back again.

2. What are three types of communication services that can be used for an Internet connection, and how do they differ in terms of their speed and cost?

The four primary services are dial-up, DSL or ADSL, cable Internet, and satellite Internet. In terms of download speed, dial-up is around 48 Kbps, ADSL is 768 Kbps, and both cable and satellite are about 1 Mbps. Dial-up pricing is approximately $20 per month, ADSL and cable Internet are around $50, and satellite Internet is about $70.

3. If you use your own ISP, what information do you need from them to connect to the Internet?

To connect to the Internet, you need to have an existing account with an Internet service provider (ISP), and you need to know the phone number for your modem to dial (the ISP's modem phone number) and the username and password for your account. If you want to use Internet mail, you need to know your e-mail address, the type of mail server (POP3, IMAP, or HTTP), the names of the incoming and outgoing mail servers, and the name and password for the mail account.

4. If you know your modem is working properly and you still did not connect to the Internet, what are some of the possible reasons?

If your modem is working and you can't connect to the Internet, the reason might be not having a cable between the modem and a telephone outlet with the outlet being turned on, not correctly entering the username and password that the ISP gave you, not entering the ISP's phone number correctly, or the service on that phone number not being the correct speed for your modem.

5. What is the most common form of DSL and what are some of its characteristics?

The most common form of DSL is ADSL (asymmetric digital subscriber line), where the speed of downloading to your computer is greater than the upload speed. Most purveyors of ADSL have several speed offerings, but a very common combination is 768 Kbps downloading and 128 Kbps uploading. Pricing for this service, including the extra telephone charge as well as the Internet charge to replace a dial-up Internet connection charge, runs from $40 to $80. Faster ADSL service, which can go up to 1.5 Mbps down and 512 Kbps up, can cost as much as $180 a month. With a DSL line, you can also have a full-time telephone or fax on the line at the same time. DSL is on 24 hours a day, seven days a week, is quite reliable, and has become very common in most major cities. DSL is limited to a distance of 18,000 feet or under 3.5 miles from a switch.

6. What are some of the characteristics of cable Internet?

Cable Internet uses the standard TV cable outside most homes and many businesses; a cable modem connects your computer(s) to a TV cable outlet. The newest cable systems have download speeds of up to 1.5 Mbps and upload speeds of up to 500 Kbps. Cable Internet services cost around $40 to $60 per month and may or may not include the cost of the cable modem, which typically adds about $10 per month or can be purchased outright from $150 to $250.

7. What can you do with Internet Explorer?

Internet Explorer allows you to locate, open, and interact with pages of text and images, as well as audio and video files that have been made available on the World Wide Web.

8. What can you do with Outlook Express?

Outlook Express allows you to create, send, receive, and store e-mail messages and attached files both on the Internet and using an in-house mail server. You can also participate in newsgroups.

9. What are newsgroups and how are they used?

Newsgroups are an organized chain of messages on a particular subject sponsored by some organization; they allow people to enter new messages and respond to previous ones. To access a newsgroup, you need to set up a new account for the newsgroup, similar to the account you set up for your e-mail. To set up and use a newsgroup account, you need the name of the news server and possibly an account name and password.

10. What can you do with Windows Messenger?

Windows Messenger allows you to communicate in real-time with others over the Internet (and possibly an intranet) using written messages, voice communications, video images, shared applications, or a whiteboard.

Module 7: Using Audio and Video Media

1. What are three functions you can perform with Windows Media Player?

The four primary functions of Windows Media Player are playing music CDs and DVDs, listening to Internet radio stations, building and managing a music library, and writing your music library on a CD.

2. What are three primary control areas of Windows Media Player and what are they used for?

The primary control areas of Windows Media Player are the features taskbar used for selecting the major functions of Media Player, the visualization controls used to change the visual content in Now Playing, the playback controls used to control what is playing, and the playlist selection controls used to determine what is displayed in the playlist pane.

3. What do you need in order to listen to the radio on your computer?

If you have a broadband connection of at least 128 Kbps and a sound card with speakers, you can listen to radio stations around the world that have added an Internet connection. Windows Media Player gives you access to these stations through the Radio Tuner feature.

4. **Your friend just noticed that you can get music off a CD and burn it onto a new CD, and asked you to make him a copy. What should you do?**

Tell him "no," because it violates copyright law. The copyright law prohibits using the copyrighted material in ways that are not beneficial to the owners, including giving or selling the content without giving or selling the original CD or DVD itself.

5. **What are the formats in which a final movie can be saved?**

Windows Movie Maker files can be saved only in the Windows Media Video file format, which can be played only with Windows Movie Maker on Windows Me, 2000, and XP systems.

6. **What are two ways you can get video into Windows Movie Maker?**

Video can come into Windows Movie Maker either directly from a digital camcorder using an IEEE 1394 FireWire interface card or indirectly through a file on your computer created by playing an analog recording into a video capture card.

7. **What are the tools Windows Movie Maker provides for converting clips into finished movies?**

The Movie Maker tools to convert video clips, sound, and still images into a movie are on four toolbars: the Standard toolbar with new, open, and save project and cut, copy, paste, delete, and clip properties; the Project toolbar with save movie, send, and record; the Collections toolbar with up one level, new collection, toggle collections, and view; and the Location toolbar, which allows you to choose the collection.

8. **What do the terms collections, clips, and frames mean, and how do they relate?**

A collection is similar to a folder and contains a recorded video that has been divided into clips. A clip is a small segment of video, generally one episode of turning the camera on and then off. A clip is made up of a series of frames (where each frame is a still image) that when viewed in rapid succession creates the illusion of motion.

9. **What are three types of objects that you can bring into a movie file, and what are some of the acceptable formats?**

The three types of objects that you can bring into a movie file are audio segments, still images, and video clips. The acceptable formats for each are audio segments: AFC, AIF, AIFF, AU, MP3, SND, WAV, WMA; still images: BMP, DIB, GIF, JFIF, JPE, JPEG, JPG; video clips: ASF, AVI, M1V, MP2, MPA, MPE, MPEG, MPG, WMV.

10. **What are three differences between CD-R and CD-RW?**

CD-Rs are writable drives on which you can write once, and CD-RWs are rewritable drives on which you can erase older information and write over the same area. CD-R disks cost about $0.20, store up to 700MB, and can be played in most CD-ROM and CD audio drives. CD-RW disks cost about $1, store up to 650MB, and in many cases can be read only on other CD-RW drives. A CD-RW drive, though, can write to either CD-R or CD-RW disks.

Module 8: Setting Up and Using a Network

1. **What are three purposes of a network?**

   Network uses include exchanging information, such as sending a file from one computer to another; communicating, such as sending e-mail among network users; sharing information by having common files accessed by network users; and sharing resources on the network, such as printers and Internet connections.

2. **What is the dominant networking technology, and what are some of the reasons for its dominance?**

   The dominant networking technology is Ethernet. It is relatively inexpensive, works well for interconnecting many different types of computer systems, and is easy to expand to very large networks. As a result, Ethernet-related equipment and Ethernet support in software, including Windows XP, has become pervasive. This fact has brought many vendors into the market to supply equipment, causing the pricing to become most reasonable.

3. **What are two reason in favor of wireless networking and two reasons against it?**

   The reasons for wireless networking are that it does not require cabling and that it gives users flexibility in where they are when they are networking: they can sit anywhere in a room, roam from room to room, and even be online in some public facilities such as airports. The reasons against it are expense and lack of speed.

4. **What are two small/home office networking technologies, and how do they compare?**

   Small/home office networking technologies generally refer to one of two types of networking systems that share existing cabling in a home, either telephone cabling or power cabling. Networks using telephone lines simply plug into the phone jacks already installed in many homes and transmit over a frequency that does not interfere with voice communications, so they can be used at the same time a phone conversation is going on. Power-line networking uses the existing power lines that are throughout almost all buildings for networking. Although there may be rooms or areas in rooms without phone lines, there are very few without a power outlet.

5. **What are the two primary card buses used with NICs, which should you use, and why?**

   The two primary card buses used with NICs are ISA and PCI. You want to choose PCI. ISA slots are either 8 or 16 bits wide (NICs generally use 16 bits), whereas PCI slots are 32 bits wide and thus have a wider data path and are noticeably faster. Another of PCI's major benefits is that you don't have to worry about the IRQ (interrupt request line) because it is uniquely handled in PCI slots. In ISA slots, you have to figure out what IRQs other cards are using, and hopefully have one left over for the NIC.

6. **What are three different types of interconnection devices, and how do they differ?**

   The interconnection devices are hubs, bridges, routers, and switches. Hubs simply join other components on the network and pass all information to all components. Bridges are used to divide two segments of the same network so that information addressed within its originating segment stays in that segment, and information addressed to the other segment gets there. Routers are used to join two networks, such as a LAN and the Internet, keeping the traffic within a network there unless it addresses the other network. Switches are used to divide a network into many segments as a bridge does for two segments; for the most part, they have replaced bridges.

7. What is the primary topology used today, and what are its components?

The primary topology used today is a star topology that uses a hub from which clients, servers, other hubs, and other connection devices radiate.

8. What are the rules of thumb for laying out a 100BaseT network?

In a 100BaseT network, the maximum cable length between a hub and a workstation is 100 meters, or 328 feet, the minimum cable type is Category 5, the maximum number of hubs between two workstations or a switch and a workstation is two, and the maximum number of cable segments between two workstations or a switch and a workstation is three, with a maximum total distance of 205 meters, or 672 feet.

9. What is the primary protocol used in Windows networking, and what do its components do?

The primary protocol used in Windows networking is TCP/IP. IP, the Internet Protocol, is used primarily for addressing and the conversion from the logical IP address to the physical hardware address. TCP, the Transmission Control Protocol, establishes the connection with the receiving station, packages the information into digestible packets, and makes sure it is received.

10. What are three things to check if you think networking is not working properly?

If you believe that networking is not working correctly, make sure that the network interface card (NIC) is properly set up, the networking functions you want are installed, the cabling is correct, and the networking protocol is installed and properly configured.

Module 9: Controlling Security

1. What are three forms of authentication that are available in Windows XP?

Three forms of authentication available in Windows XP are simple user authentication with a username and password; sophisticated user authentication using the *Kerberos* protocol with a smart card or biometric device; and object authentication for documents, programs, and messages using Kerberos certificate validation.

2. What are three considerations to take into account when setting up usernames and passwords?

Considerations to take into account when setting up usernames and passwords include whether to use first name and last initial, first initial and last name, or full first and last names; how to separate the first and last name; how to handle two people with the same first and last name; is there a need for a special class of names; that names must be unique and not over 20 characters long; and that passwords must be unique, should not be over 14 characters, can use both upper- and lowercase letters, should use a mixture of letters, numbers, and symbols, and should be at least 7 characters long.

3. **How can you tell if you are an administrator?**

You'll know if you are an Administrator by opening the User Accounts window and seeing whether your account is labeled "Computer Administrator" or "Limited Account."

4. **What are two factors that must be true in order to work with permissions?**

To work with and use individual permissions, you must be using Windows XP Professional and the NTFS file system, and you must turn off Simple File Sharing.

5. **What are groups and how are they used?**

Groups, or group accounts, are collections of user accounts and can have permissions assigned to them just like user accounts. Most permissions are granted to groups, not individuals, and then individuals are made members of the groups.

6. **What are three requirements that must be met to encrypt a file or folder?**

The requirements that must be met to encrypt files or folders include these: Windows 2000 or XP Professional NTFS must be in use; Certificate Services should be installed and running either on a stand-alone computer or within a domain; the person encrypting the file or folder must have an EFS certificate; there must be one or more certificated recovery agent administrators; and the file or folder should be encrypted on the computer or within the domain in which it will be decrypted.

7. **How are encrypted files different to work with from normal files for the person with the encryption key, and what does a person without the key see when he or she tries to open an encrypted file?**

To the person with the key on the computer, working with encrypted files is exactly the same as working with normal files. You do not have to unlock the files, or enter a password, or do anything unusual. Simply open the file and use it. Persons without the key get an innocuous message that access is denied.

8. **What are three rules to remember when copying and moving encrypted files and folders?**

The rules to remember when copying and moving files and folders include these: copying or moving files or folders to an encrypted folder will encrypt the copied or moved items; copying or moving files or folders to an unencrypted folder will leave the items moved as they were prior to moving; someone other than the owner trying to copy or move encrypted files or folders to a different computer will get an error message that access is denied; the owner copying or moving encrypted files or folders to another file system, such as Windows NT 4 NTFS or Windows 98 FAT32, will get a warning message and then the encryption will be removed; backing up encrypted files or folders with Windows XP Backup leaves the items encrypted.

9. **What are the differences between private and public key encryption, and how does the combination of the two work?**

The differences between private and public key encryption are that with a private key, the same key is used to both encrypt and decrypt; whereas with public key encryption, two keys are used: a public one to encrypt and a private one to decrypt. In addition, private key encryption is very fast, compared to public key, which is relatively slow. The combination of the two uses public key encryption to send a private key that will be used for the balance of the transmission.

10. **What do you need to implement secure Internet and intranet transmissions?**

To implement secure Internet and intranet transmissions, you need a web server that supports SSL or TLS, such as Microsoft IIS 6, plus a supporting web browser, such as Microsoft Internet Explorer 6, both of which are included in Windows XP Professional. From the browser, to visit a web site that has implemented SSL or TSL, you simply need to begin the URL with https:// rather than http://.

Module 10: Managing a Windows XP System

1. **How do you determine the format used to display numbers, currency, and dates, as well as the use of characters unique to a particular language?**

Regional and Language Options lets you determine how numbers, dates, currency, and time are displayed and used on your computer, as well as the languages that will be used. When you choose the primary language and locale, such as French (France), all the other settings, including those for formatting numbers, currency, times, and dates, are automatically changed to the standard for that locale.

2. **If you are having a problem with a system, what is an easy way to go back to an earlier setup of Windows XP to see if that cures the problem?**

System Restore keeps track of the changes you make to your system including the software you install and the settings you make. If some change or software installation causes the system to fail, you can use System Restore to restore the system to what it was before you made the change; you can do so very easily.

3. **How do you open the Task Manager, and what does it do?**

Pressing CTRL-ALT-DELETE will open the Task Manager, which is used to look at what is running on your computer; how the computer is performing in terms of CPU, memory, and network usage; and who the current users are.

4. **What are two alternative ways to start your system and their uses when you have problems booting?**

Two alternative ways to start your system when you have problems are Safe Mode and Last Known Good Configuration. Safe Mode starts without most of the device drivers and automatically loaded software, allowing you to fix or uninstall whatever is causing the problem. Last Known Good Configuration rolls back your system software to whatever was loaded the last time you successfully booted.

5. **What are the three file systems available in Windows XP, and what are their differences?**

The three file systems are FAT (File Allocation Table), FAT32, and NTFS (New Technology File System). FAT is a 16-bit file system with a maximum disk partition size of 512MB; it uses a maximum eight-character filename with a three-character extension. FAT32 is a 32-bit file system, allows disk partitions of over 2TB (terabytes or trillion bytes), and allows long filenames of up to 255 characters. NTFS is a 32-bit file system that can utilize very large (in excess of 2TB) volumes or partitions and can use filenames of up to 255 characters, including spaces and the preservation of case. Most important, NTFS is the only file system that fully utilizes all the features of Windows XP, such as encryption.

6. How do you convert a FAT or FAT32 disk to NTFS?

Normally, you would convert a drive from FAT or FAT32 to NTFS while you are installing Windows XP. You can also convert a FAT or FAT32 partition, volume, or drive at any other time in either of two ways: by formatting the partition, volume, or drive, or by running the program Convert.exe.

7. What are the two types of partitions, and how do they compare?

There are two types of partitions: a primary partition and an extended partition. You need to use a primary partition to start an operating system, but you can have only four primary partitions. If one of the four partitions is an extended partition, you can then divide it into up to 23 logical drives.

8. What is the purpose of Dynamic Volume Management?

Dynamic Volume Management enables you to create, change, or mirror partitions or volumes without rebooting, using dynamic storage and disks. A dynamic disk has a single partition within which you can create volumes. Simple volumes are the same as partitions except that they are dynamic (can be changed on the fly), can span disks, and include additional types for advanced hardware.

9. Can you change a dynamic disk back to a basic disk? If so, how?

The only way to change a dynamic disk back to a basic disk is to delete all dynamic volumes, and therefore all files, and then right-click the drive and choose Revert To Basic Disk.

10. What are the three types of user profiles, and how do they differ?

There are three types of user profiles: local user profiles, roaming user profiles, and mandatory user profiles. Local user profiles are on the same computer as the original user account and are available only on that computer. Roaming user profiles are stored on the server and are available to all computers on the network. The roaming user profile can be changed by the user. The mandatory user profile is the same as the roaming user profile except that it cannot be changed by the user.

Module 11: Using Remote Desktop, Remote Access, and VPN

1. How are Remote Desktop, RAS, and VPN related?

Remote Desktop, RAS, and VPN are interrelated. Remote Desktop is used to remotely control a computer, and RAS and VPN are both ways to access remote computers, as is a LAN. While RAS and VPN can be used for functions other than Remote Desktop, Remote Desktop can use both access methods, as well as a LAN to access a remote computer that it will control.

2. **What happens to someone who is logged on to the host computer when a Remote Desktop user tries to log on to the same computer?**

If someone is logged on to the host computer when you try to log on through Remote Desktop, you will get a message about that. If you choose to go ahead, the user on the host computer will be warned and then summarily thrown off, everything that user was doing will be lost, and you will be logged on.

3. **How can you find out what the IP address is for a computer?**

You can find out a computer's IP address by opening the Start menu, clicking Control Panel, and double-clicking Network Connections. Right-click the connection you use for your intranet or the Internet and choose Status. In the LAN Status dialog box, click the Support tab, where you will see the IP address.

4. **In a default installation of Remote Desktop, can you cut and paste between the remote host and the local client?**

In a default installation of Remote Desktop, cut, copy, and paste are not available because the local client's disks are not available. You can activate the local client's disks by selecting Options in the Remote Desktop Connection dialog box.

5. **What is the difference between disconnecting and logging off a Remote Desktop connection?**

Disconnecting from a Remote Desktop connection leaves you logged on, and any programs you have will remain running. If you restart Remote Desktop, you will resume the preceding session. Logging off terminates your Remote Desktop session and all programs are stopped. If you restart Remote Desktop, you will begin a new session.

6. **What are the essential steps to set up an RAS connection?**

To set up an RAS connection, you must make sure the modem is working on both computers, and then set up an incoming network connection on the host computer and a dial-up network connection on the client. If you want the client to get onto a LAN through the host, then the host must have an operating network connection.

7. **Are RAS and VPN related? If so, how?**

RAS is a foundation service behind VPN, and making sure that RAS is operating properly will significantly help you set up VPN. You should therefore set up RAS before attempting VPN.

8. **What is the essence of the VPN concept?**

VPN allows you to use the Internet as a secure extension of your LAN without the expense of a leased phone line or long-distance charges. You can think of VPN as a secure pipe through the Internet connecting computers on either end. Information is able to travel through the pipe securely and without regard to the fact that it is part of the Internet.

9. **Match up the services on the right that should be used in each of the situations on the left.**

Here are the correct matchups:

A. You travel frequently and need to connect to the office to get schedules, planning information, and recent pricing decisions, all of which you consider proprietary. VPN

B. You live in the same telephone exchange as your office, so there are no long-distance fees for calls, and you want the same information as in A. RAS

C. You run a branch office in another town, and one of your budget items is a $2,500-a-month leased phone line to the home office that is used solely for data communications. VPN

D. You want to run some analysis programs on your office computer using a large company database from another office in the same building as your office. Remote Desktop over a LAN

E. Same situation as D, but you want to run it from your home as described in B. Remote Desktop over RAS

F. Same situation as D, but you want to run it from the remote office described in C. Remote Desktop over VPN

Module 12: Preparing for a Windows XP Installation

1. If you have an older computer that you want to make into a minimal workstation that has a 300 MHz processor, 128MB of memory, 5GB of hard disk, a network card, an SVGA video adapter and monitor, a keyboard and mouse, a floppy drive, but no CD-ROM drive, will it work, and why?

The described configuration will work if the Setup files are available on the network and the computer can be booted into a state where it can see the files across the network.

2. What are the steps for checking hardware compatibility?

The steps used in checking hardware compatibility are to first do a system inventory to determine what equipment you have using both physical and online inventories. Then use the Check System Compatibility option on the Welcome screen of the Windows XP CD, check the Hardware Compatibility List (HCL) at http://www.microsoft.com/hcl/, and finally go over the Readme file in the root folder of the Windows XP CD for late-breaking information on hardware usage and other information you need before you install.

3. What do you do if you have a component of your system that is not on the HCL or in the Readme files?

If you find a device in your inventory that is not on the HCL and not mentioned in the Readme or other files, it is often the case that it will work fine using general-purpose drivers in Windows XP. The only way to know for sure is to try to install Windows XP and see what happens. If there is a problem, you may be told about it while running Setup, or the device may simply not work when you are done. If this is a boot device, such as a SCSI or RAID controller, you may not be able to finish the installation. The solution is to contact the manufacturer and obtain a Windows XP driver from them (you may be able to download it from the Internet).

4. What are three reasons to use Windows XP Professional over Windows XP Home Edition?

The reasons to choose Windows XP Professional over Windows XP Home Edition include the need to

- Be a part of a Windows domain network
- Encrypt individual files and folders
- Be accessed remotely by another computer
- Perform a full system restore
- Host a web site
- Work in multiple languages at the same time
- Have two processors

5. What are two reasons each to upgrade or to do a clean install?

The major reasons to upgrade are to preserve all the current settings, applications, and data files, and to make the installation of Windows XP simpler. The major reasons to do a clean install are to get around an operating system that cannot be upgraded, to dual-boot, and to really clean up your hard disks.

6. What accessibility options are available during Windows XP setup?

The accessibility options that are available during Windows XP setup provide assistance on seeing and understanding what is presented on the screen. These include a magnifier to make a selected area of the screen easier to read and the Microsoft Narrator to read the contents of the screen.

7. What is dual-booting and why might you want to use it?

Dual-booting allows you to choose from among several operating systems each time you start your computer. If you are unsure whether you want to switch to Windows XP, or if you have an application that runs only on another operating system, then dual-booting gives you a solution. For example, if you want to keep Windows NT 4 Workstation running and be able to use it after installing Windows XP, or if you have an application that runs under Windows 98 but not Windows XP, then in both of these circumstances, dual-booting provides the means to do what you want. Dual-booting, though, forces you to keep an older file system, which probably does not support all of the potential features of Windows XP.

8. What are three of the steps in preparing a system for Windows XP installation?

The steps to prepare a system for Windows XP installation are: back up all hard disks, inventory current software, clean up current files, upgrade hardware, and disable conflicting hardware and software.

9. What is a low-cost, nonobvious way to do a complete disk backup?

A low-cost, nonobvious way to do a complete disk backup is to use another hard disk. With the very low cost of large hard disks, it can be worthwhile to get one to hold the latest backup of one or more systems. You should still also use removable media so that you can store a copy of your data away from the computer in a fireproof container.

10. **What are the three key elements to a successful installation?**

The three key elements to success are to have a detailed knowledge of your current environment, to have a detailed plan of how you are going to carry out the conversion, and to communicate continually and exhaustively with everyone involved.

Module 13: Installing Windows XP

1. **What are several of the different ways you can start and run Setup?**

You can start Setup over a network or locally, you can boot from the installation CD-ROM or floppy disks, and you can start from MS-DOS or any version of Windows. You can run a clean install where you completely replace the contents of a disk, or you can upgrade the current operating system (OS) and keep all of the settings, files, and folders that you currently have.

2. **Which of the following are legitimate upgradable products to Windows XP Home? Windows 3.1, Windows for Workgroups, Windows NT 3.x Workstation, Windows 95, Windows NT 4 SP2 Workstation, Windows 98, Windows 98 SE, Windows Me, Windows 2000 Professional, Windows XP Professional**

You can upgrade to Windows XP Home Edition from Windows Me, Windows 98, and Windows 98 SE.

3. **Which of the following are legitimate upgradable products to Windows XP Professional? Windows 3.1, Windows for Workgroups, Windows NT 3.x Workstation, Windows 95, Windows NT 4 SP2 Workstation, Windows 98, Windows 98 SE, Windows Me, Windows 2000 Professional, Windows XP Home**

You can upgrade to Windows XP Professional from Windows XP Home Edition, Windows 2000 Professional (all Service Packs), Windows Me, Windows 98, Windows 98 SE, and Windows NT 4 Workstation (all Service Packs).

4. **Can you do an upgrade of the current OS if you boot from the CD?**

No. When you boot from the installation CD you can do only a clean or new installation.

5. **What is the most likely set of steps to start Setup for a clean install on a new computer?**

To start Setup for a clean install on a new computer, insert the Windows XP Setup CD in its drive, reboot the computer, and press any key to boot from CD.

6. **What is the most likely set of steps to start Setup for an upgrade from Windows 98?**

To start Setup for an upgrade from Windows 98, insert the Windows XP Setup CD in its drive and select Install Windows XP.

7. **Why is it beneficial to be connected to the Internet while running Setup?**

It is beneficial to be connected to the Internet while running Setup for two reasons: you can get updates to Setup as you are running it, and you can directly activate the product when you complete Setup.

8. **To activate Windows XP, how long do you have and what are the two ways you can do it?**

   To activate Windows XP, you have 30 days, after which the product will cease to operate. You can activate Windows XP either over the Internet or over the telephone, but the Internet is much easier because you don't have to copy down and enter two very long strings of numbers.

9. **If you want to connect to a NetWare server, what must you do while setting up Windows XP?**

   To connect to a NetWare server while setting up Windows XP, in the final GUI phase after networking is installed, choose Custom settings, which allows you to add Client Service for NetWare and the IPX/SPX/NetBIOS protocol.

10. **If you are a member of a domain, what unique entries must you make while running Setup?**

    If you are a member of a domain, you must identify that, enter the domain name, and enter a domain-recognized username and password; when you have completed Setup and are starting the computer for the first time, you need to press CTRL-ALT-DELETE, enter the Administrator's password or enter another domain-recognized user, enter their password, and click OK.

11. **How are the Windows XP optional components installed?**

    Windows XP optional components are installed after completing the installation of Windows XP itself by opening the Start menu; clicking Control Panel; clicking (double-clicking if in Classic view) Add Or Remove Programs; clicking Add/Remove Windows Components; selecting the components you want to add or remove; and clicking Details, Next, and Finish as necessary.

Module 14: Maintaining Windows XP

1. **What are the two most common ways today to install a program?**

   The two most common ways today to install a program are using a CD and downloading the software over the Internet.

2. **What is the most general-purpose way of removing software, and what should you not do to remove software?**

   Programs are most easily removed through Add Or Remove Programs from the Control Panel and should never be removed by just deleting the files on your hard disk.

3. **Where should you look to see if a device is compatible with Windows XP?**

   To determine if a device is compatible with Windows XP, look in Microsoft's hardware compatibility list at http://www.microsoft.com/hcl and see if and how the device is listed.

4. **Where is the best place to look for a device driver, and what are the summary steps to do it?**

   The best place to look for a device driver is on the Internet, and the summary steps to look for it there are: look at the device's manufacturer's web site and see if they have what you need, then look at Microsoft's site—both the HCL and Windows Update, and finally use a search engine to look up device driver sites to investigate.

5. How are you protected from misuse of Remote Assistance?

You are protected from misuse of Remote Assistance in four ways: without an invitation, the person giving assistance cannot come onto your computer; you can limit both the time the invitation remains open and the time the person can be on your computer; you can determine whether the person can control your computer or just look at it; you can click Stop Control or press ESC at any time to immediately cut the other person off.

6. If you are given control while providing remote assistance, what can you do?

If you are given control through Remote Assistance, you can do anything within Windows that you could do if you were sitting in front of the other computer.

7. What are three ways that you can use the information in either My Computer Information or System Information?

Several of the ways that you can use My Computer Information and System Information are

- To get general system information, such as the BIOS date, the amount of memory, and what hardware is installed
- To assist a product support person with whom you are working
- To get the best and most concise information about a hardware component
- To see what software is automatically started at startup
- To see what software and drivers are currently loaded and/or running
- To see what recent system crashes there have been

8. What are the two ways to get interim updates to Windows?

You can get interim updates to Windows either manually by opening the Windows Update web site or automatically by turning on Automatic Updates.

9. Once you have turned on Automatic Updates, how do you turn it off or change its settings?

The Automatic Updates tab in the System Properties dialog box (Start | Control Panel | System | Automatic Updates) enables you to maintain Automatic Updates, including turning it off.

10. How is System Restore used to restore data files?

It can't be. Data files must first be backed up using a backup program such as the one in Windows XP from which they can be restored. System Restore has no impact on data files.

11. If after doing a System Restore you are unhappy with the results, what are the two further steps you can take?

If you are unhappy after doing a System Restore, you can undo the restoration and/or go back and do another restore using a different restore point.

Appendix B

Shortcut Keys

Shortcut keys provide a way of working in Windows XP without a mouse. There are shortcut keys to do just about anything you can with a mouse, including opening the Start menu, getting around the desktop, using dialog boxes, and even renaming a shortcut. Depending on what you are doing, shortcut keys might be easier to use than a mouse—whereas at other times, the mouse is easier. Of course, in the situations when the mouse is not working, shortcut keys provide the only way to operate.

There are a number of different types of shortcut keys, many of which have been discussed elsewhere in this book. Here, we'll look at shortcut keys that are used on the desktop, in windows and dialog boxes, and to start the accessibility options.

Working with Menus and Controls

Shortcut keys are especially useful for opening and using menus, especially the Start menu, particularly in situations where the mouse isn't working. Table B-1 shows the shortcut keys for working with menus and controls.

NOTE

On most recent keyboards, there are two additional keys to work specifically with Windows: the WINDOWS key that looks like ⊞ and the CONTEXT key that looks like 🗒. There are generally alternatives to using these keys, but they are handy. The CONTEXT key performs the same function as right-clicking the active or selected object and opens its context menu.

To (often for the selected item)	Press
Open the Start menu	CTRL-ESC or WINDOWS
Open a context menu	SHIFT-F10 or CONTEXT
Open a System menu	ALT-SPACEBAR
Open the System Properties dialog box	WINDOWS-BREAK
Open the Task Manager or log on to a network	CTRL-ALT-DELETE
Show the desktop	WINDOWS-D
Open a menu in a menu bar	ALT-underlined letter in a menu name
Carry out a menu command	ENTER or underlined letter in a command name
Activate a menu bar	F10

Table B-1 Shortcut Keys for Working with Menus and Controls

To (often for the selected item)	Press
Open the next menu to the right or left, or open or close a submenu	RIGHT ARROW or LEFT ARROW
Select the menu entry above or below	UP ARROW or DOWN ARROW

Table B-1   Shortcut Keys for Working with Menus and Controls *(continued)*

Working with Dialog Boxes and Windows

Once you can open a menu, you can open windows and dialog boxes and then must handle the elements that they contain. Table B-2 shows the shortcut keys for working with dialog boxes and windows.

To	Press
Open My Computer	WINDOWS-E
Minimize all windows	WINDOWS-M
Restore minimized windows	WINDOWS-SHIFT-M
Search for a file or folder	WINDOWS-F
Search for computers	CTRL-WINDOWS-F
Display Windows Help (F1 is the same as WINDOWS-F1 in Windows; otherwise, it opens the current program's Help)	F1 or WINDOWS-F1
Lock your computer if you are connected to a network domain, or switch users if you are not connected to a network domain	WINDOWS-L
Open the Run dialog box	WINDOWS-R
Carry out the command for the option or button	ENTER
Select or clear a check box	SPACEBAR
Select a button from a group of option buttons	Arrow keys
Display the items in the active list	F4
Display the bottom of the active window	END
Display the top of the active window	HOME

Table B-2   Shortcut Keys for Working with Dialog Boxes and Windows

To	Press
Display all subfolders under the selected folder	NUM LOCK-ASTERISK on the numeric keypad
Display the contents of the selected folder	NUM LOCK-PLUS SIGN on the numeric keypad
Collapse the selected folder	NUM LOCK-MINUS SIGN on the numeric keypad
Collapse the current selection if it's expanded, or select the parent folder	LEFT ARROW
Display the current selection if it's collapsed, or select the first subfolder	RIGHT ARROW
Refresh the active window	F5
Continue through a wizard's pages	ALT-N

Table B-2 Shortcut Keys for Working with Dialog Boxes and Windows *(continued)*

Working with Objects

Objects include icons on the desktop, pieces of text, and pictures, as well as objects in dialog boxes and windows. One of the beauties of Windows is that different types of objects are treated in the same way. Table B-3 shows the shortcut keys for working with objects.

To (the selected item)	Press
Copy	CTRL-C
Cut	CTRL-X
Paste	CTRL-V
Undo	CTRL-Z
Delete	DELETE
Delete permanently without using the Recycle Bin	SHIFT-DELETE
Select all	CTRL-A
Select more than one item	SHIFT with any of the arrow keys
Rename	F2

Table B-3 Shortcut Keys for Working with Objects

To (the selected item)	Press
Open the Properties dialog box	ALT-ENTER
Close, or quit	ALT-F4
Close the active document	CTRL-F4
Switch between open items	ALT-TAB
Cycle through items in the order they were opened	ALT-ESC
Cycle through objects in the active window or on the desktop	F6

Table B-3 Shortcut Keys for Working with Objects *(continued)*

Working with Accessibility Options

Accessibility options help overcome physical difficulties accomplishing tasks on the computer and are described at the end of Module 3. Table B-4 shows the shortcut keys for working with objects.

NOTE:

Some shortcut keys may not work if StickyKeys is turned on.

To	Press
Turn FilterKeys on and off	Right SHIFT for eight seconds
Turn High Contrast on and off	Left ALT-left SHIFT-PRINT SCREEN
Turn MouseKeys on and off	Left ALT-left SHIFT-NUM LOCK
Turn StickyKeys on and off	SHIFT five times
Turn ToggleKeys on and off	NUM LOCK for five seconds
Open Utility Manager	WINDOWS-U
Repeat Narrator text	CTRL-SHIFT-SPACEBAR

Table B-4 Shortcut Keys for Working with Accessibility Options

Index

E

S

INTERNATIONAL CONTACT INFORMATION

AUSTRALIA
McGraw-Hill Book Company Australia Pty. Ltd.
TEL +61-2-9900-1800
FAX +61-2-9878-8881
http://www.mcgraw-hill.com.au
books-it_sydney@mcgraw-hill.com

CANADA
McGraw-Hill Ryerson Ltd.
TEL +905-430-5000
FAX +905-430-5020
http://www.mcgraw-hill.ca

**GREECE, MIDDLE EAST, & AFRICA
(Excluding South Africa)**
McGraw-Hill Hellas
TEL +30-1-656-0990-3-4
FAX +30-1-654-5525

MEXICO (Also serving Latin America)
McGraw-Hill Interamericana Editores S.A. de C.V.
TEL +525-117-1583
FAX +525-117-1589
http://www.mcgraw-hill.com.mx
fernando_castellanos@mcgraw-hill.com

SINGAPORE (Serving Asia)
McGraw-Hill Book Company
TEL +65-863-1580
FAX +65-862-3354
http://www.mcgraw-hill.com.sg
mghasia@mcgraw-hill.com

SOUTH AFRICA
McGraw-Hill South Africa
TEL +27-11-622-7512
FAX +27-11-622-9045
robyn_swanepoel@mcgraw-hill.com

SPAIN
McGraw-Hill/Interamericana de España, S.A.U.
TEL +34-91-180-3000
FAX +34-91-372-8513
http://www.mcgraw-hill.es
professional@mcgraw-hill.es

**UNITED KINGDOM, NORTHERN,
EASTERN, & CENTRAL EUROPE**
McGraw-Hill Education Europe
TEL +44-1-628-502500
FAX +44-1-628-770224
http://www.mcgraw-hill.co.uk
computing_neurope@mcgraw-hill.com

ALL OTHER INQUIRIES Contact:
Osborne/McGraw-Hill
TEL +1-510-549-6600
FAX +1-510-883-7600
http://www.osborne.com
omg_international@mcgraw-hill.com

Designed for people. Not clocks.

People learn at their own pace. That's why our Beginner's Guides provide a systematic pedagogy. Real-world examples from seasoned trainers teach the critical skills needed to master a tool or technology.

Osborne Beginner's Guides: Essential Skills—Made Easy

Solaris 9 Administration: A Beginner's Guide
Paul A. Watters, Ph.D.
ISBN: 0-07-222317-0

UNIX System Administration: A Beginner's Guide
Steve Maxwell
ISBN: 0-07-219486-3

Dreamweaver MX: A Beginner's Guide
Ray West & Tom Muck
ISBN: 0-07-222366-9

HTML: A Beginner's Guide, Second Edition
Wendy Willard
ISBN: 0-07-222644-7

Java 2: A Beginner's Guide, Second Edition
Herbert Schildt
ISBN: 0-07-222588-2

UML: A Beginner's Guide
Jason Roff
ISBN: 0-07-222460-6

Windows XP Professional: A Beginner's Guide
Martin S. Matthews
ISBN: 0-07-222608-0

Networking: A Beginner's Guide, Third Edition
Bruce Hallberg
ISBN: 0-07-222563-7

Linux Administration: A Beginner's Guide, Third Edition
Steve Graham
ISBN: 0-07-222562-9

Red Hat Linux Administration: A Beginner's Guide
Narender Muthyala
ISBN: 0-07-222631-5

Windows .NET Server 2003: A Beginner's Guide
Martin S. Matthews
ISBN: 0-07-219309-3

9 proven learning features:

1 Modules
2 Critical Skills
3 Step-by-Step Tutorials
4 Ask the Experts
5 Progress Checks
6 Annotated Syntax
7 Mastery Checks
8 Projects
9 Network Blueprints

OSBORNE DELIVERS RESULTS!

OSBORNE
www.osborne.com